The Bonnybridge UFO Enigma
(A Modern Day Mystery)

By

Ron Halliday and Malcolm Robinson

The authors gratefully acknowledge the permission granted to reproduce the copyright material in this book. Every effort has been made to trace copyright holders and to obtain their permission for the use of copyright material. The authors apologise for any errors or omissions in the book and would be grateful if notified of any corrections that should be incorporated in future reprints or editions of this book.

Copyright © 2025 by Ron Halliday and Malcolm Robinson. All rights reserved. Without limiting the rights under copyright reserved above, no part of this publication may be reproduced, stored in, or introduced into a retrieval system, or transmitted in any form by any means (electronics, mechanical, photocopying, recording or otherwise) without the prior written permission of both the copyright owners and the publisher of this book. Names and specific locations, when necessary, have been changed to protect the identity of the individuals who are still living at the time of this publication. All stories are based on true events.

ISBN: 978-1-917778-02-2

Non fiction / Body, Mind & Spirit / Parapsychology / UFOs / Unexplained Phenomena

*Book cover design by Jason Gleaves – UFONLY
jasonufonly@outlook.com
www.facebook.com/ufonly
www.youtube.com/ufonly
www.twitter.com/@jasonufonly*

*This book is dedicated to lifelong friend and mentor,
Helen Walters, who gave so much to our subject.
Fondly remembered, sadly missed.*

CONTENTS
(Part One Malcolm Robinson)

Guest Foreword: By Jenny Randles   vii

Part One: The Bonnybridge UFO Enigma as seen by Malcolm Robinson.   P1

Part Two: The Bonnybridge UFO Enigma as seen by Ron Halliday.   P291

References: P282

Further Reading: P283

To Contact the Author: P286

OTHER BOOKS BY THE AUTHORS
MALCOLM ROBINSON

UFO Case Files of Scotland (Volumes 1 -2)

Paranormal Case Files of Great Britain (Volumes 1-2-3-4)

The Monsters of Loch Ness (The History and the Mystery)

The Dechmont Woods UFO Incident (An ordinary day, An extraordinary event)

The Sauchie Poltergeist (And other Scottish Ghostly Tales)

Please Leave Us Alone (The true and terrifying story of an Irish family and their desperate fight against the 'Hat Man' and supernatural forces)

The A70 UFO Incident (Scotland's first officially reported UFO Abduction)

The Falkland Hill UFO Incident (Scotland's most controversial UFO case)

OTHER BOOKS BY THE AUTHORS
RON HALLIDAY

Evil Scotland

UFO Scotland

Famous Scots and the Supernatural

Haunted Glasgow

Edinburgh After Dark

Alien Spirits?

UFOs The Scottish Dimension

The A – Z of Paranormal Scotland

McX Scotland's X Files

Foreword

BY JENNY RANDLES

Bonnybridge is an evocative place name I confess I never came across until known around the world in the latter years of the 20th century. The reason being the concentration of UFO encounters, some remarkable, that turned it into a 'window' area. How and why such locations exist and if they have underlying consequences is why they become fascinating. And how they endure to be puzzled over by people around the world.

The alternative perspective to the mystery is they are a consequence of the attention they receive. That when a major event happens social factors attract not just locals to look up at the sky but outsiders. In an age where the presumption of alien involvement exists, they inevitably attract outsiders to a 'hot spot' seeking the opportunity to 'see' for themselves.

So, we first must ask whether a window genuinely acts in some way like a portal to the remarkable or is an accident of observation. That if you attract more people to look then as a consequence more report what they witness. Numbers may escalate just because of the willingness to look upwards not downwards as most human beings inevitably do. The human dimension to such a location is always a factor, often media hyped with a name to fix it in the mind of readers or viewers, so the story becomes both a human one and potentially far beyond with the creation of a tourist hot spot. It has long seen the intervention of UFO researchers to investigate the most likely explanation for the events being reported.

Thankfully you are in good hands with the authors of this book. I know to respect and trust their findings and am intrigued to follow the lead to unravel this fascinating story. It is easy to think that mysteries must have mundane explanations and quite rightly that is where any good investigator starts. You should be dragged by the evidence to look further than the most likely but ponder deeper possibilities that might take you in quite unexpected directions. As a result, sometimes the ordinary is not where the trail of evidence leads and the extraordinary pushes aside your hopes of easy expectation. To be truly open minded you have to be prepared as to where the facts will lead. Because they can go in very unlikely directions.

Many years ago, a similar window area appeared in the Rossendale Valley in Lancashire focused around a quarry. I was born in the Pennine village where events involving police officers occurred. I knew the quarry well as it was directly behind where my aunty lived, and Paul and I walked our dog on visits into the quarry. The report of these events came to me as they were actually happening at 2 am. The witness, who I did not know, had my number via the radio telescope at Jodrell Bank as I was a contact point for the calls they got from the public. He described the events live. I was miles away but shared in the nature of the event as it unfolded. A one off experience. Baffling as this case was, I was unprepared for the sequel. I was visited by a security guard on the pier at Blackpool who was working there guarding the closed structure at 2 am on that same night. Suddenly a UFO just like the one witnessed during the phone call to me passed over the pier causing it to shake, before seeming to disappear into the sea. More remarkably the guard told me he passed those lonely night hours before his next patrol reading a discarded magazine. That magazine was a February 1979 issue of Titbits and on its cover was a trail for an article inside about what it called 'Britain's UFO Girl'. Which was one of the first ever interviews with me.

Much as that coincidence made me smile, another was to emerge when I became a full-time carer and with time on my hands investigated my family history. I knew that on both my parents side my family had originated in Scotland in the late 1800s heading south to work in the expanding clothing industry where the families met and married. What I did not know before was that my great grandfather actually worked in the quarry where that close encounter started. And that you could see the quarry from the house where I lived when I was born. We had even scattered my mother's ashes in view of that quarry as the house where her family lived was located right there too.

All this may be a coincidence linked to the UFO event that was undeniably real. However, what can start out as a simple story that you might presume must have an easy resolution can turn into a rather deeper mystery at the flip of a switch.

So, settle down and consider the events in and around Bonnybridge and follow the expert guidance you will get from these authors. The path to resolution will again most likely have some unexpected twists.

PART ONE

THE BONNYBRIDGE UFO ENIGMA
AS SEEN BY
MALCOLM ROBINSON

I've had many people ask me why did UFOs suddenly start appearing in the Stirlingshire skies back in 1992? I would like to make it known that contrary to popular opinion, that UFOs have been sighted in the Stirlingshire skies for more years than people would believe. Strange Phenomena Investigations (SPI) the research group that I founded back in 1979, did not start to suddenly receive UFO reports in November 1992 when official records began. I was personally involved in UFO research fully 'ten years' before the wave of UFO reports that hit the Stirlingshire skies back in 1992. There were many UFO reports made to myself from the early part of the 1980s, and I point this fact out here, simply because there are those who feel that the many UFO reports that have been generated in and around the town of Bonnybridge in Stirlingshire, are purely down to a publicity stunt pulled by Councillor Billy Buchanan and I. This is not so, and I aim to discuss this in more detail as we make our way through my part of this book. For this my own part of this book, I have drawn on some of the press stories generated by the media during the 1990's which will show you and give you a flavour of what was going on at that time. Some of the journalism was despicable as you will see. I feel that by presenting the Bonnybridge story as a yearly growing enigma, it will again allow you to understand not just the people involved, but how the media and the public reacted to these ongoing UFO sightings.

THE TOWN OF BONNYBRIDGE
(Stirlingshire, Central Scotland)

According to Wikipedia the 2001 Census stated that the population of Bonnybridge stood at 6,870 residents. In 2021, that figure had decreased down to 5,183. Before I begin with my own appraisal of the Bonnybridge phenomenon, let us take a brief journey back in time and learn a few facts about this area of Central Scotland. The river Bonny is roughly six miles in length, but longer if you include its tributaries, it eventually flows east into the River Forth. In the days of the Scottish war of Independence, the Black Douglas a fearsome warrior, passed through the village which is now known as Bonnybridge. He stopped for a drink of clear water which flowed through the village. When he had drunk some of this water, it is alleged that he said, *"This is bonny water"*, and so the river came to be known as 'Bonny Water'. A bridge was later built over the water, and the village was then named, 'Bonnybridge'. A find of an antler's axe some years ago at Woodyett near Bonnybridge golf course, is believed to belong to the Middle Stone Age, dated around 3000 B.C. This find indicates that there were people living in this area at that time, though it's suspected that they would be few in number. Another find, this time of New Stone Age pottery, turned up at Mumrills, Laurieston near Falkirk. This find showed that people had lived in this area around 2500 B.C. This whole area is steeped in history and folklore, much of which is outside the scope of this book. The Romans for instance occupied a good part of land near Falkirk, and the remains of the Antonine Wall can still be seen. The town of Bonnybridge in Stirlingshire sits four miles south of Falkirk, one of the biggest towns in Stirlingshire. UFOs in the Bonnybridge area may prove to be a fascinating subject for many people, but the history that surrounds the town, is of equal interest for the scholar of ancient Scotland.

1970S AND 1980s
BEFORE BONNYBRIDGE HIT THE NEWS
IN 1992 THERE WAS THE TOWN OF DENNY!

So, as stated above, for me, the UFO sightings above Bonnybridge and other parts of Stirlingshire, did not, as the media would inform you, start in November 1992. My UFO research clearly showed that UFO sightings went way back further than that. During the 1980s, whilst investigating the Denny UFO sightings, (A town close to Bonnybridge) I came across what's known in UFO speak as a 'repeater witness' *(someone who claims to see UFOs on a regular basis more than any other person)* This 'repeater witness was living in the town of Denny, in Stirlingshire, Central Scotland, and her name was Mrs Elsie Beveridge. A pleasant, charming woman in her late forties. I met up with Elsie at her home and conducted an audio taped Interview with her concerning her UFO sightings. The following information comes direct from that taped interview session. Firstly, I learned that this was not the first time that she had witnessed something unusual in the sky. Her first UFO observation was way back in 1971 and occurred over Glasgow. Mrs Beveridge and her daughter observed a silver domed shaped object which was stationary in the sky for a matter of minutes which then suddenly shot off at an incredible speed. At this point in her life, Mrs Beveridge had very little knowledge about UFOs and had only read little bits about them in newspapers and such. It wasn't until she moved to Denny, (a good while after staying in Glasgow) that she began to see UFOs more regularly, so regularly in fact, that she even kept a diary to log all her sightings in. Most of us would be happy if we witnessed one UFO in our lifetime, but Elsie claimed that on one occasion, she had witnessed ten in the sky at the same time! Not only that, but they appeared to be flying in some kind of formation. She was well acquainted with satellites and aircraft and was positive that what she was observing was none of those. She went on to say that what she found most peculiar were the strange quick turn manoeuvres that these objects performed, these convinced her that what she was observing was nothing man-made. Elsie's UFO sightings made the Weekly News, a Scottish newspaper. In their June 26th, 1982, issue, the headline read, 'Quiet town is UFO hot spot' and went on to inform their readers about Elsie's sightings. She was reported as saying.

"The craft I've seen have varied in size, and some have had coloured lights on them. They can move very fast or else just hover completely stationary as if they were watching or listening".

As I stated above, here were UFO sightings in the Stirlingshire area from a town near Bonnybridge '**10 years before**' the main Bonnybridge UFO sightings started. I was quoted in the Weekly News as saying.

"I really can't explain why Denny has become such a centre for UFO sightings. There are a few places throughout Britain where there seems to be more activity and a greater number of sightings. We call them, 'UFO Hot Spots', and Denny has become the latest. Although my work isn't finished, and it's too early to draw conclusions, it is very interesting indeed".

On April 30th, 1982, there was a small piece placed in the Falkirk Herald which read.

UFOs IN DENNY?

Space Invaders may be catching on in most areas, but in Denny, it's the real thing that is arousing the interest of local people. For, during the past 18 months, there have been several sightings of unidentified flying objects in the area. Now a representative of the British Unidentified Flying Object Research Association has been assigned to the area to investigate the claims. Mr Malcolm Robinson, also a member of Strange Phenomena Investigations, wants to hear from anyone in that area who has seen anything unusual in the sky. Already he has reports of yellow sphere-shaped objects and silver shapes in the sky. While he is in Denny, Mr Robinson will have the full cooperation of Cumbernauld police in his inquiries.

Of course, Scotland has had a tradition of UFO sightings way before the 1980s and 90s. In his most comprehensive book, *'The Scottish UFO Casebook'* self-published by Steve Hammond, Steve informs us that his research has uncovered the fact that a strange and fast aerial ship was seen to burn as far back as 80AD. Another aerial ship was seen from the English Humberside up to Scotland in 91AD. In 1685 a father and son plus other witnesses, observed a strange sight in the sky, which Steve believes, might have been a meteor or bolide. Steve's research features numerous UFO sightings throughout the 18th and 19th centuries up until present day. I will be referring only to the ones from the Stirlingshire area as they are relevant to this book. These will be marked with the following symbol, (*) and the name, Steve Hammond.

On the 28th of December 1978 near the town of Denny in Stirlingshire, a gentleman by the name of Ian Beveridge, witnessed a bright oval shaped object which flew over some rooftops. The colour of this object was described as orange. This report came from the Scottish 'Daily Record' newspaper, and we were further informed that Ian's mother also saw this object, which, astonishingly, she claimed almost hit an aircraft! *(* Steve Hammond).*

WENDY FORBES AND HER UFO SIGHTINGS

Wendy Forbes from Laurieston near Falkirk contacted me and informed me about some UFO sightings that she had witnessed above her hometown. Her first sighting of a UFO took place one night way back in 1968. This was, of course, well before the wave of UFO sightings in the region in the early 1990's. Wendy can't recall the exact month, but she was being driven in a car by her then boyfriend on a narrow country road near Polmont in Stirlingshire. She casually glanced out of the car window, and as she did so, she observed a large oval shaped object descending from the sky. It was coming down so low, that her initial thoughts were that it was going to crash. At this point she became hysterical and screamed for her boyfriend to turn the car back and get away from the area. This he did, and soon the car was speeding away from this incredible scene, but not before she took one final look at the object. She described the object as oval, with a rectangular band of multi coloured lights around its middle. There is no way that this was a plane she stated, and her insistence upon the matter was most compelling. As it stands, this would have to be my earliest record of UFO activity in the Bonnybridge area, and it makes me wonder if there are any other cases which proceed this one of which I don't know about?

It wasn't until the summer of 1974 that Wendy would experience her next UFO encounter, and this one, like the last, frightened her immensely. In a statement to me, she mentioned that she was at her home in Laurieston near Falkirk, when all of a sudden, the royal blue curtains in her living room turned bright luminous 'pink'. Her then husband and her five-year-old daughter all ran to the window where they saw a tremendously luminous pink oblong object which was travelling low across the sky, lower than any aircraft she stated. After a short period of time, she lost sight of it in the distance. To this day she wonders if this object was responsible for turning her royal blue curtains pink. It's certainly novel, and I don't think that I have come across anything of this nature before, light phenomena yes, but changing the colour of one's curtains! Well, that sure is different!

Her final UFO sighting occurred in the late 1970s, the date of which escapes her, but the vividness of what happened that night lives on. She was travelling in her car with her then husband heading towards the town of Bathgate in West Lothian where her husband intended to purchase another car. As they were driving past the town of Redding near Falkirk, they both became aware of a gleaming oval light which was at a high altitude in the sky. Suddenly this light stopped and remained stationary for a period of seconds. Then this strange light proceeded to come down lower and lower. It was still descending as their car approached Grangemouth (another town in the locality) As their car was travelling down a small farm road, this strange object suddenly appeared to the left hand side of their car hovering low above a field. Watching this spectacle in the back seat of the car, were Wendy's children who by now were screaming loudly. Fear had gripped the car as Wendy tried to make sense of what they all were looking at. It wasn't dark, and the sighting she informed me, was during the summer months, probably around 7 to 8pm. They decided, as most witnesses do in close proximity to UFO sightings, to quickly get away from the area, and they were no different. Soon they were speeding out of the location. After a period of around 15 minutes, the bright object sped away towards the east, heading in the direction of the town of Linlithgow.

THE 1980S
The decade that was.

The working man and woman in Scotland back in the 1980s had a tough time of it. Maggie Thatcher's Conservative Government saw fit to decimate a number of Scottish industries. Under the Conservative Government, a once proud Scottish nation saw the demise of a number of its heavy industries. With a third of all major industries lost before the end of the 1980's. Tens of thousands of once proud people lost their jobs. Scotland's famous Linwood car factory was closed, with the loss of almost 5,000 jobs. A further 4,000 workers were left on the breadline due to the demise of further car manufacturing plants at Leyland and Plessey in Bathgate. The Scottish coal industry was also hit hard, and in 1984, many Scottish miners took to strike action due to Margaret Thatcher's policies. The result was chaos with arrests of miners and violence on the picket lines. As a result of Thatcher's policies, 13 Scottish pits were closed for good. As for the music charts of the 1980s. The big stars were Madonna with six number ones during the 1980s. George Michael had eight number ones. The best and most popular selling single of the decade was "Do They Know It's Christmas?" by Band Aid, selling over 3.5 million copies. As for football. Glasgow Rangers won the Scottish Football

League 6 times whilst their city rivals, Glasgow Celtic, won just 4.

UFOs ACROSS STIRLINSHIRE IN THE 1980s

It was during March 1982 that I began to receive many UFO reports coming from around the small town of Denny which is near Bonnybridge in Central Scotland. Most of these reports, concerned strange lights that had been witnessed in the night sky and as a researcher for BUFORA (The British UFO Research Association) at that time, it was my duty to investigate these sightings, and try and ascertain exactly what was going on. Gathering witness testimonies as to what was exactly seen proved most interesting.

It was on a cold morning near the end of October 1980 that Linda Taylor (pseudonym) from the town of Denny near Bonnybridge, was leaving home to catch the minibus which would take her to work. The time was just after 06:30 in the morning, and she was looking forward to getting to work, more so to get out of the cold. As she walked along a path, her attention was drawn to what she described as a 'red vivid glow of light'. Slightly puzzled by this and getting a little alarmed, she noticed that this red light appeared to be directly above one of the houses which was further up along the road. The object itself appeared to be 'egg shaped' and at an angle where it appeared to be on end. Unfortunately for Miss Taylor, no one else was about at this particular time of the morning to share in her experience. She stood watching this object and then noticed that it had a white band of light going around its centre. Fascinated by this, she lost all track of time; indeed, she forgot that she had her work to go to as the object had captivated her interest. It was roughly ten minutes later before the next thing happened. Suddenly the object lifted straight up into the sky at a fair speed and was out of sight in a matter of minutes. Gathering her senses, Linda could find no logical explanation to explain what she saw. It was a dark morning with stars visible. One might suggest that it may have been a bright planet, perhaps even Venus. Venus as most UFOlogists know, has been taken as a fanciful UFO on many occasions. But then we have to consider that Miss Taylor states that after the object had remained stationary, it lifted straight up into the sky and was gone in seconds. This action does not suggest a planet.

UFO ABOVE PLAYING FIELD.

The Falkirk Herald of 2nd July 1981 informed its readers that six primary school children witnessed a flying saucer. This 'flying saucer' zoomed down over their heads when they were playing football in the school playing fields. This object, had a black dome and hovered above the ground during which, contained in a nearby field were some cows which took fright and stampeded. Witnesses claimed that a light beam was seen to come out of the bottom of this strange object before it was lost in some clouds. Just before it was lost in clouds, the object seemed to emit a shower of sparks. What I found most interesting about this account, was when the children went back to class, for it was there that class teacher, Jean Harris, clearly saw how shook up the children were. Sadly, the Falkirk Herald did not give the date and time of this encounter. *(* Steve Hammond)*

It was at midnight on the night of Monday the 26th of April 1982, that Mrs Alison Clarke (pseudonym) mentioned to her husband that she had seen what she had thought was a shooting star. Out of curiosity, her husband Mr John Clarke decided to have a look. Upon looking out of a fully glazed patio door, he observed what he thought was a fireball. Mr Clarke whose house is in the village of Shieldhill near Falkirk, is situated where it gives him a full and interrupted panoramic view of the Forth Valley. John continued to look at this strange object and decided to fetch a pair of binoculars (16X50) to enable him to have a better look. Through these, he observed that the object remained stationary for approximately eight minutes. It was during the last two minutes however, that there appeared to be a distinct change in the object's appearance. Mr Clarke stated.

"Over the last two minutes, there appeared to be some movement within the object, an appendage appeared to rise

from the main body without becoming detached or appearing to reduce the size of the primary object".

The appendage that Mr Clarke refers to came from the end of the oval shaped object which rose horizontally to vertically and was no larger than the primary object. Mr Clarke went on to say that the object did not appear to be solid, apart from a definite line at the bottom right hand edge, nor did the object appear patchy or transparent, rather, it appeared hazy. He estimated that the object was roughly 4 to 5 miles distant from his viewing position, which would suggest that it was roughly over the towns of Larbert and Torwood. Another surprising factor was the object's disappearance. The object seemed to reduce in size over a few seconds till it could be seen no more.

Our next case from 1982 is consistent with the types of reports that I was to receive fully ten years later. James Anderson (pseudonym) was out walking with his wife on a winter's evening in late 1982, (the witness can't recall the month). As they were walking over some scrubland near their home in Denny, they both suddenly observed a large 'glowing ball' which gave the impression that it was going to crash into a nearby dual carriageway. Racing towards where they felt it was going to crash; they found no trace of it. Both witnesses are adamant that what they observed was not a 'meteorite'. A good percentage of UFO reports coming from the Bonnybridge Region are of what I would term, 'light phenomenon'. This has also been a feature of other 'UFO Hot-Spots' and is basically part and parcel of the whole makeup of the UFO enigma.

The following year 1983, Mrs Janet Middleton from the town of Laurieston near Falkirk, Central Scotland, had her own close encounter with the unexplained. It was one evening in September 1983 that she was taking her dog Tara out for a last walk, this was because her dog was unfortunately suffering from rheumatism and had been blind for several years. It was to be put down the following day, and so this was her final walk. With a tear in her eye, Janet continued with her walk which took her beside some small hills just outside her housing estate. It was 11:30pm. She happened to glance up into the sky, and in her own words, this is what she said happened next...

"*As I was walking my dog, I happened to look up into the night sky and was astounded to see a huge 'starship' come slowly down over the hills. It had six windows, not portholes. These windows were inverted and square. There were also lights on this object which were very bright but not glaring. One light was most intense at the front of the object, and there was a yellowish light at the rear. The object itself was round on the bottom with a dome on the top. Its colour was a sort of metallic brown enamel! With little white dots ingrained within it.*".

Janet further related that as the object came over a nearby hill, she was absolutely fascinated by it, if not a little curious. However, after a short period of time, the yellowish rear lights dimmed then went out altogether which left the bright lights at the front still on. After a moment, these lights also went out, whereupon the object climbed and ascended diagonally upwards until it reached a small cluster of stars. It then, apparently, stopped in the middle of these cluster of stars before it could be seen no more. Mrs Middleton stated to me that at no time was she afraid by what she was watching; in fact, she went as far as to say that somehow, she felt very 'secure'. I also learned that this was not the first time that she had witnessed a UFO. She had witnessed some before, but never as close as this one.

The city of Stirling is 9.6 miles away from Bonnybridge, and it was near Stirling that a young girl Dorothy (11) was in her sister's bedroom. Whilst there, she saw three lights. One was red, and two were white all of which were moving in a Westward direction. Dorothy then claimed that these lights then stopped and hovered over a dairy, it was then that she saw that underneath these three lights, was a large disc. Apparently during this sighting (of which her sister saw nothing) the area became unusually quiet! *(*Steve Hammond)*.

It was either September or October 1984, the witness, Jim Wylie (Pseudonym) can't recall the exact month, when he was driving to Denny accompanied with his wife. As the road passed Pioneer Concrete on their left, they both witnessed in the sky, one single light source. It was round in configuration like a torch or spotlight they said. Jim said that if you held a five pence piece out at arm's length, then that would cover it. They continued on with their journey whilst keeping this strange light in view. Both Jim and his wife are convinced that this was not an aircraft or helicopter. On rounding a bend and looking in the direction of where this light should be, it was gone. Again, this could well be an aircraft. That said, our two witnesses would definitely bet against this.

UFO WITNESSED BY A FIRE CREW.

This next account is from the year 1989 and goes to show that UFO activity had been a feature of the Stirlingshire area for quite some time. The principal witness in this case is Robert Muir (pseudonym) whose occupation at that time was a fire fighter. Robert had been called out with 15 of his colleagues to attend a moss fire near some woods of which featured a small lake nearby. The location was Gardrum Moss, near the village of Shieldhill, again not very far from Bonnybridge. Robert cannot recall the exact month in 1989, but remembers the time as being in the early morning, around 00:30am. As they attended to the fire, a small red object was observed hovering to the left of two masts in the distance. This red light then began to come closer towards the fire engine. As the fire crew continued to gaze at the object, the object retreated somewhat and disappeared to the west. Wondering what it could be, they returned to putting out the moss fire. Someone then shouted, *"It's back"!* And they were all startled to observe the same or similar object come back into their line of vision. As it did so, it once more sped away again into the distance in seconds. By now all the fire crew personnel were wondering what on Earth those lights could be. As they pondered over the possibilities, another light, this time coloured white, was then observed coming down towards a small lake. This light then hovered above the lake at an estimated distance of around six feet and was only around 20 feet from the fire crew. Each fire crew member was nudging each other ensuring that each one of them was aware of this strange light and that it wasn't just their imagination, for this spectacle seemed totally unreal and quite out of the ordinary. Then, much to their surprise, the object 'rushed' towards them, then suddenly stopped, making a 90 degree turn and shot away at a terrific speed into the night sky. This was too much, and Robert later stated to me that at this point, each fire crew member actually felt the hair on the back of their neck stand up! But it didn't finish there! No sooner had that light disappeared, than another one, also coloured white, came into their vicinity. This object moved overhead at a fairly low height and was moving in a 'jerky movement'! It then flew directly overhead of the fire crew and moved away to the west at great speed. All these sightings occurred within a five-minute period and proved extremely confusing to the trained fire crew. Robert was under the impression that the objects he saw 'appeared' to be under intelligent control and also that 'they' were observing them.

These then are but some of the many UFO reports that I was gathering in the Falkirk, Denny, and surrounding areas during the early part of the 1980s. Admittedly, I did not receive any UFO reports from the Bonnybridge area during that time, that's not to say that there wasn't any, there might well have been, but at that point in time, any cases from that area were not channelled through to me. So, how did the Bonnybridge UFO phenomenon start? Well ten years later, I returned to this area in a quest that would see me tested to the limit with some astonishing UFO cases. But, as I was to find out, the road that lay ahead was rocky with many 'bumps of irritation' which I will refer to later. But this road also had it surprises as well, as you're about to find out.

THE 1990'S
The Decade That Was.

The 1990s began with a number of protests, as thousands of Scots rallied against the introduction of a new domestic rates system, this would infamously be known as the 'poll tax'. Thousands of Scots took to the streets to show their disgust at Margaret Thatcher's government's controversial plans, which, thankfully, would ultimately be scrapped. In 1990, Glasgow was picked as European City of Culture. In 1994 Scottish pop group, Wet Wet Wet, spent an incredible 15 weeks at the top of the UK charts with their cover of The Troggs 1960s' hit, 'Love Is All Around'. Tragedy hit a Dunblane Primary school in March 1996, where a crazed gunman killed sixteen children and a teacher. The best-selling single of the 1990s was 'Candle in the Wind' by Elton John. On September 11th, 1997, Scotland's electorate voted for the creation of a devolved Scottish parliament. Stephen Hendry aged just 21, wins the 1990 World Snooker Championship making him the youngest ever world snooker champion.

NOVEMBER 1992. THE BEGINNING.

The whole Bonnybridge situation for me started when I heard a news report (November 4th, 1992) on Central F.M. a local radio station which at that time was based in the town of Stirling, (they now have moved to Falkirk). The station was informing their listeners about a spate of UFO sightings above the town of Bonnybridge. I quickly got in touch with the presenter who had read out the piece, a Miss Jane Barrie, and explained who I was and the research that our society undertook. Jane kindly invited me into the studio to talk about the work that our society did, but not, I must state, the events in Bonnybridge, as I had yet to become involved with those. It was during my talk to the listeners of Central F.M. that I made a request for any further witnesses to get in touch with me who may have sighted what they believed to have been a UFO. I also learned at this time, that a local councillor by the name of Billy Buchanan, had been collecting all these early UFO reports from his constituents. I was given his phone number and proceeded to call him, upon doing so, I found that Billy was extremely pleased to hear from me, more so because of my capacity as a UFO researcher and someone of whom he could work side by side with on these ever-growing UFO reports. I found Billy to be a good source of information, and he explained to me that the situation was developing fast, and that many UFO reports were still being reported to him. It became clear to me at this time, that what was going on showed all the hallmarks of turning into a 'UFO Wave', which in UFO speak is a grouped series of UFO reports which centre around a particular location. It was decided by both Councillor Buchanan and I at this juncture, that the next step in our Investigations, would be to place an advert or letter in the local Falkirk Herald Newspaper, this would be to seek out any further UFO witnesses. Our letter in the Herald was published, and both Billy and I were bowled over by the amount of phone calls that we received. For my part, the calls that I personally received came from people from all walks of life, and from all segments of the community, each had a story to tell, and out of all the phone calls that I received, I only had one crank call, which it must be said, is quite surprising considering the subject matter. As the years rolled by, Councillor Billy Buchanan and I would hit the world headlines with the UFO sightings above Bonnybridge and Stirlingshire. But who is Billy Buchanan?

COUNCILLOR BILLY BUCHANAN

Billy Buchanan was born in Springburn Glasgow and moved to Bonnybridge in 1955. Billy was a former professional football player at Brentford Football Club and has also played in Hong Kong. He has also held a coaching position in Saudi Arabia. A keen sportsman, Billy has also played for some Scottish football league clubs before finally hanging up his boots. Billy is also a keen antique collector, and I remember the times when I used to visit his previous home which was situated near the canal bank in Bonnybridge. His house had to be seen to be believed, it was like a museum, and was overflowing with pictures, photographs, bric-a-brac and numerous pieces of pottery, it was simply wonderful. I remember I spent more time looking at the walls in Billy's house, than actually looking at him! Billy has also undergone hypnotic regression, and through that, he learned that he was hanged as a sheep stealer in 1692. He was also killed at the battle of Culloden and shot in the First World War. If that isn't character building, then I don't know what is! Billy is a colourful character, and I came to admire him as a person who would do a great deal for you. If you wanted something done, consider it done yesterday. As an Independent Councillor, he has fought tirelessly for his constituents to give them a quality of life that meets their requirements, and when it came to the UFO sightings over Bonnybridge where numerous constituents came to him with tales of their own UFO observations, well he didn't turn them away. He was elected to serve these people in any way shape or form, he did not tell them to go away when confronted with their UFOlogical experiences. He should be commended for this, more so for standing up and facing his responsibilities, and not shrinking and hiding away. The sad thing is, he has taken a lot of stick from fellow councillors who feel that he is making a mockery out of official council business, but the way I see it, if we had more councillors who had the guts of Billy Buchanan, then I feel that there would be many improvements in the lifestyles of the public. One should also consider that much of the money Billy made whilst working with television companies regarding Bonnybridge UFO stories, went straight to local charities. Including giving the money to local junior football clubs in order that they could buy football strips. Could the people who have knocked Billy Buchanan have done as much as him? I think not.

THE INVESTIGATION BEGINS

Now as in any Investigation, one has to always check for possible natural solutions and explanations, and it would be no different here. All lines of enquiry were undertaken to try and find a 'rational' explanation as to what the people of Bonnybridge and surrounding areas were seeing. Enquiries were put in the direction of both Glasgow and Edinburgh Airports to see if they had any aircraft in a given location at a specified time when we had a reported UFO sighting. The local Cumbernauld Airport was also contacted. Now it's fair to point out that there is heavy air traffic which over flies Bonnybridge en route to both Glasgow and Edinburgh Airports, but all the witnesses that I personally spoke to, were convinced that what 'they' had observed, was not an aircraft. They told me that they are well used to seeing aircraft in the sky, they know that they are on a flight path. Furthermore, the manoeuvres and lights on these objects, were like nothing they have ever seen before. As another line of enquiry, I also contacted Scottish Power, this was owing to the fact that one witness claimed to have seen a Scottish Power helicopter in the area checking on power lines. I phoned Scottish Power and spoke to someone there who did confirm the helicopter's presence. He went on to say that their helicopters were on power line inspection duty, and that they rarely flew at night. Most flights were undertaken during daylight hours for obvious reasons, but if they had to fly at night, then their helicopter could not be missed, as it had one bright frontal spotlight attached to the helicopter which cast a powerful light down onto the power lines of which they were inspecting. My next step was to contact the local police, this was to see if any members of the public had reported their UFO sighting there. Much to my surprise, I found out that no members of the public had reported any UFO sightings to them. Of course, one has to consider the fact, that members of the public may not wish to register a UFO sighting with their local police, through perhaps fear of not being believed, or maybe they would feel that they might be 'wasting police time'. This is common and does not just represent the UFO incidents above Bonnybridge, it happens the world over.

At 8:00pm on the 6th of December 1990, a witness claims to have seen a strange glowing round ball of light for a period of 30 minutes over the B.P. chemical plant near Grangemouth. The object/light was seen to move slowly through the clouds. *(*Steve Hammond).*

WERE AIRCRAFT THE CAUSE OF THE UFO SIGHTINGS?

As mentioned above, part of my job as an investigator, was to check out the possibility that perhaps some (if not all!) of the UFO sightings in the Stirlingshire skies might be the result of commercial aircraft or helicopters. Questions had to be asked. The following is a letter that I wrote to many airports, both in Scotland and the U.K. It read.

12th November 1992.
Dear Sir,
I write to you to ask your assistance in regard to investigation work that I am currently undertaking which concerns a spate of UFO sightings in the Bonnybridge and Denny area. This is causing quite a stir and has made much press over the past few weeks. Assistance has been offered by the police, and I now write to the airport authorities to see if

they can shed any light on the matter. My questions are as follows.

(1) Is there a flight path/corridor over the Bonnybridge area?

(2) If so, how often does air traffic traverse this area, day and night?

(3) Are there any small private airfields in this region?

(4) Are there any helicopter flights which use this air corridor, if so, which ones?

(5) I have been informed by several witnesses that there has been noticeable Military air traffic in the area, could you throw some light on this?

I do hope that you can be of some assistance to me on this matter, and I shall look forward to your reply.

Yours Sincerely,
Malcolm Robinson.

I firstly wrote off to Glasgow Airport where I received a letter from a Mr W. Gray who was the ATC Watch Manager. In part he stated.

Dear Mr Robinson,
Thank you for your letter of 12 October and the information you require is as follows.

a) Flights into and out of Glasgow frequently pass over Bonnybridge and many other areas of Stirlingshire.

b) Commercial airliners from Edinburgh and north-west Europe, eg, Denmark inbound to Glasgow and also light aircraft privately owned.

c) Helicopters do frequent Glasgow Airport and could very well transit the area to or from the East Coast.

d) Weekends in general quieter in terms of commercial traffic but given good weather busier with private flying. Cumbernauld airfield also generates its own traffic.

- (Author's note) I had asked in my letter to Glasgow Airport if they had received any reports of UFOs over the years. Here is what W. Gray Watch Manager said.

"The writer has not personally ever received a UFO report from the pilot of an aircraft, and it is many years since a member of the public has made such a report, so far as I am aware. Any unusual occurrence is logged, our function is the control of aircraft, and we have no investigative function out with ATC at Glasgow".

The following is a letter which I received from a Mr John Duck, National Air Traffic Services in London. He stated.

Dear Mr Robinson,
"Thank you for your letter of 12 November 1992 about UFO sightings in the Bonnybridge and Denny area. I shall try to answer your questions in the order you pose them".

(1) Bonnybridge is beneath the Scottish Terminal Control Area (TMA) the base of this controlled airspace is 2500 feet. All aircraft above 2500 feet are required to be under the control of an air traffic control unit. Below 2500 feet, aircraft may fly wherever they wish subject to the normal rules of the air. Within the Scottish TMA, there is the main airway carrying flights to and from Aberdeen, there will also be flights in and out of both Edinburgh and Glasgow Airports.

(2) Air traffic can, and does transit the area at all times, however, there will be only a few flights during the period midnight to 6am.

(3) Cumbernauld Airport is the nearest, there may also be any number of private landing strips on farms etc.

(4) Helicopters are most likely to be in the uncontrolled airspace below 2500 feet. Again, in this airspace over Bonnybridge they may route where they wish.

(5) Although Military activity is not in the CAA's province, there are a fair amount of Military flights in most parts of the UK outside of controlled airspace.

I hope this information is of some use.
Yours Sincerely,
John Duck
National Air Traffic Services MSU.

UFO PHOTOGRAPHED OVER THE B.P. PLANT IN GRANGEMOUTH

Just before the Bonnybridge UFOs hit the headlines in November 1992, there was a major UFO sighting in 1991 which had the added bonus of a photograph. Here is that story.

I have said many times before, that it is extremely easy to fake a photograph and claim that it represents either a ghost or a UFO. When one is researching the UFO subject, you tend to find that from time to time, someone will approach you with what they claim is a photograph of a UFO. Of course, having witness testimony backed up with a photograph of a UFO is extremely valuable, and one must look very carefully at not only the claims of the witness, but to ensure that proper analysis of their photograph is undertaken as well. Such a photograph came to my attention during the early years of my investigation into the Bonnybridge phenomena. Phil Trevis is an aspiring musician who played guitar in a local Grangemouth rock band, but on the night of November 12th, 1991 (before the Bonnybridge wave exploded) was taking photographs with a friend for a project about photography. In a written statement to the author, Philip had this to say about his sighting.

"My friend and I were taking photographs of the B.P. Chemicals Plant in Grangemouth from Polmont Reservoir, when we noticed a dim, or rather two small dim flashing lights over by the two flashing pylons at Kincardine Bridge. We watched the object which we thought was a helicopter, fly slowly over the bridge to above the brightly lit Grangemouth Stadium. We watched it hover for about 5 minutes. It was then that we noticed that the 'craft' wasn't making any noise. Normally if it were a helicopter, you would hear the rotor blades. It then turned round and faced our direction. It was roughly 2,000ft above the ground. Then it dipped and increased dramatically in speed. At the point of the photograph, (See photographic plate section)*, it was about 200 to 300 feet directly above. It was then that we heard the light pulsing 'hum' of the object. My friend and I were quite shaken at the*

time but afterwards had an overwhelming sense of excitement. Since then, I have shown only a handful of people my photograph and have also destroyed the negative. I have no reason for destroying the negative, but now obviously regret my actions."
Phil Trevis.

The actual photograph was handed over to me by a friend of the photographer at an SPI meeting held in Stirling, it was taken by a Halina 35mm, camera using Kodak 24 exposure on gold film. What one should bear in mind whilst looking at this strange photograph, is that what you are actually looking at is the underside of the object, because when this strange object was above both of the startled witnesses, Philip had to actually bend over backwards in order to take his photograph. In the photograph you can see that the middle of the object appears to be concave, various bright white lights are seen shining out from this circular object which creates a sort of halo effect in the sky around it.

So, what did our Investigations uncover? Was there a natural explanation to account for this photograph? I firstly contacted the local police to see if any members of the public had contacted their station with a similar or same sighting, no one had. I then submitted many letters (this was pre-e-mail of course) to the various Scottish Airports to see if perhaps some kind of aircraft or helicopter had been flying in this area on the night in question. Prestwick Airport at Atlantic House in Ayrshire replied in June 1995 by stating that, (A) Records for the period in question were no longer held. (B) It was improbable that a Military Aircraft flew over Grangemouth on the night in question. (C) Gas Venting often takes place at this petro-chemical plant, an occurrence which could appear alarming. Both witnesses were well aware what this 'gas venting' looked like, and this most certainly was not what they both had witnessed. Aberdeen Airport were not able to offer any explanations, as were both Edinburgh and Glasgow Airports. The Ministry of Defence in London replied that because this sighting was of no defence significance, they were unable to assist, (now where have I heard this before)! But what if anything could the B.P. plant offer in terms of information? This plant, which is extremely explosive, is a beautiful sight when lit up at night, and looking at it from a distance, one could be forgiven for thinking that they were looking at Las Vegas such is the enormity and brightness of this complex. In a letter received by the author from a Mr Bill Moore, press officer for B.P. Chemicals, Bill stated, and I quote,

"I can confirm that helicopters carry out pipeline inspection duties on behalf of B.P. Chemicals. These flights occur at fortnightly intervals and only take place during daylight hours at weekends. I should point out that the helicopters do not tend to fly over the site as they are more concerned with following the separate pipeline routes connecting Wilton and Mossmorran to Grangemouth. Micro-lights or controlled kites with cameras do not fly over the complex. I have checked our records, and there is no indication of any aircraft having flown over the Grangemouth complex on the 12th of November 1991".

Bill Moore.

In a further letter, this time from a Mr K.W. Smith, Estates & Pipelines Coordinator for B.P. Oil at the Grangemouth Plant, he stated and confirmed that B.P. Oil do not use micro-lights or any other controlled flying devices to inspect pipes, and that air space immediately above the B.P. Petrochemical complex is a *'restricted area'* to aircraft. He went on to state that according to a limited search by him, he could find no evidence of anything unusual on the night in question.

After these checks and several others, it was plain to see that nothing conventional was to blame for what both witnesses saw. Analysis on the photograph proved very little and did not help to prove the case either way, and as we know, the witness destroyed the negative for reasons which even now, he can't fully understand. In fact, he was actually going to destroy the photograph as well but was talked out of it by a friend. Having spoken to Philip on a number of occasions now, I still have no reason to doubt his honesty, and I do believe that what he and his friend saw that night, was something totally unexplainable by rational means. Sadly, Phil's friend passed away in a motor accident and so, therefore, I was unable to obtain any clarification to Phil's story. The Phil Trevis photograph is clearly unusual and is most certainly part and parcel of the Bonnybridge phenomena. The area in which he took his photograph is only several miles away from Bonnybridge itself. An unusual photograph then and one of the very few photographs that we have which shows UFO activity over Scotland.

Since I wrote the above piece and included it in my first book, *'UFO Case Files of Scotland' (Volume 1)* someone came forward who knew Phil Trevis to cast some doubt on this photograph. Of course, this is just hearsay on that individual's part, and I refrain from explaining the content of that gentleman's concern, other than to say, he said that it wasn't a UFO! Phil would tell you otherwise and sticks to his story.

1992

By now the UFO events had escalated, and needless to say, the local press had picked up on these ever-growing UFO reports. Probably the first major news story concerning the UFO sightings broke in the Scottish 'Sunday Mail', dated November 8th, 1992, it contained the typical comical headline, *"The Space Invaders Haunt Town"*. I suppose that was to be expected. Councillor Billy Buchanan was quoted in the newspaper as saying that residents were living in terror of nightly visits from strange airborne craft! (I doubt very much he said that.) What he did say though was:

"I've been swamped by calls from frightened people who've seen UFOs in the past two weeks. They are not loonies, but quite respectable folk. Too many people have sighted the UFOs for it to be dismissed lightly". Billy was also quoted as saying:

"The last thing I want to do is create hysteria. If there is another explanation for all these sightings, then I will be glad to hear it".

Whilst readers were digesting this story over their cornflakes, more research was being undertaken. I contacted the Ministry of Defence in London, asking them if they were aware of any air traffic, military or otherwise in the Bonnybridge region on specific dates that I gave them. They replied that they were not aware of any air traffic. (Whether they would own up to it or not, would of course be another matter.) Checks at the Met Office and other meteorological stations for release of weather balloons, was also undertaken, and it was ascertained that whatever these sightings were, it had nothing to do with weather balloons. Let us now take a look at some of these early UFO sightings which caused the Bonnybridge phenomenon to surface.

THE SIGHTING THAT STARTED IT ALL!

I've been asked many times what was the first UFO sighting that started the whole Bonnybridge phenomenon? One would think that because there are so many sightings, that trying to find the 'first one' so to speak, would be well nigh impossible. But we do in actual fact know. And although I accept that there are many UFO sightings before this one, this following case was the one that drove Councillor Billy Buchanan into collecting more and more reports, which eventually made him realise that something strange was going on above his town, and although not strictly Council business (!) he made it his 'own business' to find out what was going on. Here then is the case that made Billy Buchanan embark on a crusade to get to the truth.

THE JIM WALKER SIGHTING

Witness Jim Walker (pseudonym) was driving in his car from Dennyloanhead to the small town of Denny during the month of January 1992, the time was around 21:00hrs. About halfway into his journey, he approached a junction called 'Droves Loan' where he was astonished to observe a bright cluster of lights hovering above the road. His initial thoughts were that this 'must' be a helicopter, *"Mind you,"* he thought to himself, *"It certainly was flying rather low."* Soon Jim had driven directly underneath it and was gobsmacked by the beautiful array of lights which it displayed on its underside. At this point he decided to stop for a better look but was unable to do so due to the build-up of traffic behind him. He did however have an opportunity to stop his car further along the road, and upon alighting from it, observed a triangular display of lights hovering low above the road. They were, in his estimation, approximately the width of the road with the pavements combined. This display of lights was quite spectacular, and he couldn't understand why no one else was stopping their cars and getting out for a better look, for surely, they too must have seen this! Jim however did notice that passing motorists although not stopping, were twisting their necks up and looking out through their car windscreens at this 'thing'. One motorist going in the opposite direction did indeed stop his car, however, he did not get out, he only sat and looked be in bewilderment through his windscreen. After a period of time the object left the scene and Jim dived back into his car and raced off to Councillor Billy Buchanan's house in Bonnybridge. Jim is a good friend of Councillor Buchanan and upon reaching Billy's door, began hammering on the door to get Billy's attention. Billy soon opened the door and was met by his friend in an excited state who then pushed by him and proceeded to inform Billy on what he saw near Droves Loan. After listening to his tale, Billy recognised the fact that Jim was serious, and knowing him as he did, also recognised the fact that he would not lie about a thing such as this. Councillor Buchanan then knew that he would have to find out what was going on. This was to be the start of a long crusade to get to the truth and as the years rolled by that truth became harder to uncover and only served to confuse what was turning out to be a phenomenon which although no doubt was real, was proving extremely difficult to unmask. Would the small town of Bonnybridge have made the worldwide headlines it has without Councillor Billy Buchanan's involvement? Well, I will be returning to this point in a moment.

    Let us now take a look at some more UFO sightings from the Bonnybridge area, after which we will discuss the visit of

Japanese Television when they brought their cameras to Scotland. Strange lights, as we have learned, play a big part in the make up of UFO sightings, not only over Bonnybridge, but from other areas of the world as well.

This next case features an oblong shaped object which was seen by a husband and wife. It was 10:00pm on a May evening back in 1992. April Welsh (25) had just picked up her husband from his work and was travelling in her car along the Kincardine Road (just off Bellsdyke Road) towards her home in Carronshore near Falkirk. Piercing the darkness, they saw a strange looking craft which they initially thought was an airplane travelling very slowly across the sky. But it was the intense brightness of this object which made it stand out in the sky, and they knew that even an aircraft wasn't as bright as this. Deciding to stop the car for a better look, they then observed a cluster of around 18 circular lights on the underside of this unusual object. They also heard a dull 'humming noise' coming from the object. They also noticed that another motorist had also pulled into the side of the road for a better look, he too must have been bewildered by this strange spectacle. The object then headed towards a fairly large cloud then went behind it. Both April and her husband waited for around five minutes to see if this object would come out again, it did not. A little confused they returned to their car and drove home. I would point out to the reader, that this particular sighting pre-dated the November 1992 surge of reports. This incident, as well as some others, clearly shows that the reporting of UFO sightings in the Bonnybridge and Central District Region, did not specifically start in November 1992. One further point to note is that one would assume you wouldn't want to stop your journey home and step out of the car just to view an aircraft! Clearly this was something different. And different enough to stop the car and get out to have a proper look.

THE SLOGGETT INCIDENT.

The following case generated the most interest during the early part of the Bonnybridge UFO wave, perhaps due to its unusual elements! It concerns the observation of two objects by a family who were out having an evening walk. The Sloggett family, consisting of Isabelle Sloggett (Mother) aged 52, Carole Sloggett (Daughter) aged 26 and Steven Sloggett (Son) early 20s, were out walking on the back road from Hallglen to Bonnybridge on a March evening back in 1992, the time was around 7:00pm. As they were walking along this road, Steven Sloggett pointed out a circle of light in the sky to his family which they all found most peculiar. However, things were to take a more amazing turn, for no sooner had Steven pointed out this light, than it swooped down from the sky and 'landed' in a nearby Field. It then left the field and 'landed' on the road at a distance of around 60 to 70 feet behind them. Incredibly the family at this point, although slightly bemused, did not appear overly alarmed, and continued their walk back to their home in Bonnybridge. They did however periodically look over their shoulders at this strange blue basketball sized light as it rested on the road's surface. I should point out, that this road is situated in some low-lying hills at the back of Bonnybridge and is not a regular route used by road traffic. This road mainly serves farms and is indeed a back road to get to various towns and villages in the area. It wasn't until the family heard a distinct rattling sound coming from a nearby farmer's fence, that they began to become alarmed. As the Sloggett family stood staring at this fence as it vibrated. They then became aware of a 'whirring sound' followed by the sound similar to a 'door opening', then incredibly, a *"howl"!* That was it, and with that the family took off and ran for their lives. What could this intense blue light have been, surely not a spacecraft! We could speculate that it might have been some form of 'Earth-Light phenomenon' that researcher and author Paul Devereaux has written extensively about. He believes that in certain parts of the country, the movement beneath the Earth's surface, the tectonic strain exerted on the rock strata, somehow produces balls of plasma light which can be emitted upwards into the atmosphere. Any witness to this phenomenon, could be easily misled into thinking that what they were observing was a fanciful 'flying saucer'. Was this the case here? The Sloggett family were by now racing down the road, desperate to get away from whatever was making the strange noises. However, the night was set to get stranger, for as the family ran at a furious pace down the road, a blinding intense light shone out at them through a grouped range of trees. Carol Sloggett reckons that the object behind the light was shaped like a Tonka Truck. Needless to say, the family arrived home a lot sooner than they had expected!

In July of 1992, Peter Thompson (pseudonym) was on the back road to Bonnybridge at around 11:00pm, when he claimed to have seen a bluish light in the sky. He stated that he saw this strange light twice that night.

In August of 1992 at around 9:50pm, Cathy Connors (Pseudonym) from Letham near Falkirk witnessed a bright blue flash in the sky followed by a bright blue ball which she said came out of the east.

In August 1992, 22-year-old Steven Wilson from Maddiston was driving along the White Cross Road with his friend David Gillespie (21). It was around 00:30 in the morning when they both observed a peculiar object hovering above a field near a housing estate. The object was oval in shape, red in colour, and was sharply defined. They estimated that they observed this object for roughly one and a half minutes. No sound at all could be heard coming from the object.

One of the youngest witnesses that I uncovered throughout those early years of UFO sightings in the Bonnybridge area, was 12-year-old Craig Morrison. Craig had left his home in Larbert, a town close to Bonnybridge, it was either October or November 1992, he can't quite recall which month it was and was on his way to run an errand for his mother. As he was walking down the street, he suddenly heard a tremendous 'whooshing' sound come from above him in the sky. Upon looking up, he observed three red lights which were in a rectangular pattern with a curved structure below them which appeared to be hovering above some nearby rooftops. Having now stopped in his tracks in wonder at what was in front of him, he tried to take in as much detail as possible. Suddenly, the object flew off and was eventually lost to view. I have often been asked about how low these UFOs have been seen, as more often than not they are observed high in the sky. This is an easy question to answer, simply because we are not just dealing with objects that have been sighted at a high altitude, there are a number of what we call low level, close proximity UFO sightings which give the observer, 'in most instances', a great opportunity to view as much detail as they can.

As the weeks wore on, I was still receiving many phone calls from people who not only lived in Bonnybridge but lived in other outlying towns and villages as well. Some callers wanted to explain what they thought was going on, and I remember getting into some quite unusual debates with people which was stimulating if not time consuming as well. One caller, a local farmer, phoned to say (November 11th, 1992) that he had the explanation to all these UFO sightings. He felt that what people might be witnessing in the skies around the Bonnybridge area, were poachers out 'lamping'. It's a common practice which sees people going out into the fields with brightly lit lanterns in hopes of stunning foxes or rabbits which they would then shoot. He reckoned that from the UFO watcher's vantage point, their impressions would be of strange lights in the sky (or ground). This was an interesting possibility and something which our society had to consider. We never did find out if that was the case in some UFO sightings, but then again, no one is really going to come forward and admit that they were poaching now, would they? This farmer further stated that from his vantage point at his farm, he saw a lot of air traffic which he surmised was travelling into nearby Cumbernauld Airport. He had also witnessed some military aircraft in the vicinity, one of which was a large Hercules transport plane. He had also watched a Scottish Power helicopter in the area. So, it was clear to see, that this part of Stirlingshire did see a lot of air traffic traverse its skies.

In October 1992, Mr J. Mitchell (pseudonym) observed blue lights on an oval object in the sky.

UFO ABOVE ROAD
(The Patrick Forsyth Case). 27th October1992

It was around 7:00pm at night, and 37-year-old Patrick Forsyth (pseudonym) had just dropped his wife off in the town of Denny as she was going to the bingo. After dropping his wife off, Patrick then headed off towards the town of St Ninians near Stirling where he was going to get his car washed. He was driving along the A872 doing around 45 miles per hour. In the car with him, on this drive to Stirling, was his two young sons aged 11 and 6. It was a cool dark night with scattered cloud and there was a fair sprinkling of stars in the night sky. The road ahead wasn't busy, and he knew that it wouldn't be too long before he reached St Ninians. It was a road that he had travelled many times before which he knew very well. Then, on the outskirts of Dunipace at the side of the road, there was an overhanging tree. At this point, he suddenly became aware of a strange object roughly 100 yards in front of his car which he described as circular, two tiered, and had a row of green lights encircling the bottom rim of its structure. The object's upper tier appeared to be larger than the bottom tier, and it didn't appear to have any windows. It appeared to be hovering above the road's surface at a distance of between 25 to 40 feet. At this point, Patrick turned round to his two young sons sitting in the back and said, *"What the hell is that?"* followed by, *"Can you see this boys?"* Patrick went on to say that the object was completely static and noiseless, and he knew straight away that this was some kind of unidentified object, and it was like nothing that he had ever seen before. Patrick stated in an interview to Malcolm Robinson, that this object clearly was 'not' man-made.

As his car approached ever nearer, Patrick's attention was drawn to a car directly in front of him which had just entered what appeared to be an instantaneous 'fog bank' which had suddenly sprung up from nowhere. This 'fog bank' was only on Patrick's side of the road and did not cover all the road. It wasn't wispy he explained, it was like a solid fog like door. Patrick informed me that although it was a cool September evening, there were no signs of any patches of fog on the road that night. And to the side of this fog bank was this strange two tired object. Patrick then again cried out to his two young sons, *"Boys, can you see this?"* To which they excitedly replied, *"Yes dad, we see it."* Seconds later, Patrick's car entered this mysterious 'fog bank' and as it did so, he became aware of a strange 'humming sound' coming from above. He described and compared it in interview, like the sound you would hear from a washing machine on its final spin, that high pitched screeching sound. Upon coming out the other side of this strange 'misty fog bank', the strange object was nowhere to be seen. He remembers that just before his own car entered the 'fog bank', the car in front actually skidded as it entered it. Patrick can't recall seeing this other car when he went through this fog bank. This was quite surprising, as he wasn't that far away from it before they both went through this strange misty effect, and although Patrick didn't see the object again, he recalls his son shouting at him from the back seat that he could see it travelling in the direction of Grangemouth, which is a town a few miles away. In a face-to-face interview with the me Patrick was insistent that the object he saw that night, was 'not' an aircraft of any shape or design that he was aware of. Moreover, he found it extremely hard to understand where this instant fog bank had come from. When I pushed him on this matter, he said that this fog bank was sharply defined, it was not puffy but had clear cut edges like a tall oblong piece of white card. However, the most interesting point about it, was that it only went up to the white lines in the centre of the road, it did not encroach beyond them. In a sense, he said, it was like a cloudy doorway which they had entered, which stretched from the left hand side of the road to the middle of the road and was roughly 10 to 12 feet in height. He did not see this fog bank after he went through it, because when looking back, it just wasn't there anymore!

This 'instantaneous' fog bank, put me in mind of a similar case from England which happened to the Avis family on October 27th, 1994. This case was considered at the time, to be Britain's first multiple UFO abduction case. It was a late Sunday evening when the Avis family from Essex were driving along a route between Harold Hill and Aveley. Their journey was to visit relatives and was a journey that they had made many times before. However, on this occasion, things were to be different. The family, which consisted of John Avis, then aged 32, accompanied by his wife, Elaine, 28, and their three children, Kevin, 10, Karen, 11, and Stuart, aged 7, were at a point on Hacton Lane about one mile from the town of Hornchurch when as they were coming around a bend in the road, they suddenly encountered an instantaneous 'fog bank', similar to the Forsyth case. However, there are some differences. For instance, in the Avis case, the fog bank was green and covered the whole width of the road. This was a massive case researched by Andrew Collins which included the use of hypnosis where a strange abduction scenario unfolded. This case also included weird poltergeist effects at the family home. I think that this instantaneous fog bank effect is something which researchers should not ignore, for it seems to turn up in a number of UFO cases worldwide. We could speculate that this could be some kind of 'smokescreen' or dimensional effect which could render the occupants of vehicles unconscious, and that their vehicle is somehow 'looked after' in so far as it will not crash. No hypnosis was ever conducted on Patrick Forsyth in our Scottish case to see if perhaps 'something else' might have happened that night. As far as we are aware, there was no missing time either. Come what may, there is no denying that this is quite a peculiar case.

Our next sighting was made at the start of November 1992 by a father, son and daughter. They all witnessed a strange 'glowing shape' over Bonnybridge. Admittedly, this tells us little, and could be anything, but it was strange enough for the father to report it.

On Saturday the 7th of November 1992, Amy Fisher (pseudonym) from Hallglen near Falkirk, observed what she described as a red ball in the sky, which disappeared and came back into view again. Whilst not a spectacular sighting, it nonetheless fell into similar category sightings of similar objects.

Our next witness, Mary Matheson, 36, (pseudonym) got so bored looking at her strange object in the sky, that she went to bed! She states that she was looking out of her bedroom window onto woodland in Hallglen near Falkirk. It was November 8th, 1992, and the time was roughly 01:15am. She initially thought that what she was looking at was an aircraft's navigation lights. However, the more she looked, the more she realised that this was not the case, as these lights were much bigger than an aircraft's navigation lights. Not only that, but these lights also stayed in the same position in the sky. She observed these lights as blue surrounded by a white light which suddenly faded. Mary said that the light was quite intense, and that she had watched it for around five minutes. It was at this point, that she got fed up, and went to bed.

Two days later, November 10th, 1992, another strange sighting of an unusual light was observed. Witness William Owens (pseudonym) aged 43 was driving down Bellsdyke Road near Grangemouth. Here is what he reported to me in his signed UFO sighting account form:

"I was aware of a lighted object in front of me to the right, probably at a distance of one to one and a half miles over the Grangemouth Petro Chemical Refinery Complex. I was aware of the publicity in the press of Sightings in the Bonnybridge area, so I stopped my car in a lay by. I looked at the object, which was just like a light, but it seemed to be too high in comparison with other lights around Grangemouth. I thought that it was maybe a plane, but there were no flashing navigation lights."

"It was stationary for approximately one minute, then it moved to the right. Then there was a reddish light. I didn't jump to any conclusions as it was too far away to see, but I did phone Edinburgh Airport to see if there were any plane activity in that area and was told that there were none."

My initial guess as to what this might be - could have been one of those gas flares being emitted by one of the tall chimneys at the Grangemouth refinery. These flares can be seen for miles. Might part of this flame be illuminating a low-lying cloud! The disappearance of this light might have been the result of this low-lying cloud dissipating. Just a guess of course.

It was late evening on the night of Wednesday November 11th, 1992, when Bonnybridge resident James Thompson (pseudonym) observed two huge bright white lights moving slowly towards him, this was above the Greenhill area of Bonnybridge. James estimated that these lights were roughly 200 feet up in the air, but the most peculiar thing about this sighting he informed me, was the fact that the noise that he heard coming from this strange object, resembled the noise of a washing machine on its final spin! The object then proceeded to move from side to side as it hovered over a nearby field. James also noticed small red lights on top of this object and there was a distinct 'tail fin' or 'structure of sorts' at the back of the object. Suddenly there was a huge power surge of noise, and the object departed the scene at an alarming rate.

Another witness who observed one of these small coloured lights so often seen in the skies near Bonnybridge, was Bainsford resident, Harry Amble, who, on Saturday the 14th of November 1992 observed an aircraft traverse the sky, but, as he claims, this aircraft was being followed by an unusual orange light.

On the 15th of November 1992, at 6:00pm, Miss Marion Napier (pseudonym) aged 20, along with her father William Napier (pseudonym) aged 62, observed from their home in Standburn near Falkirk, an oval shaped object in the sky which displayed three red lights at the front which formed a triangle. There were also white lights at the back, two of which were flashing. After a period of 10 minutes, the object took off very fast heading towards a field on the opposite side of the road. Both witnesses then heard a distinct 'humming sound'. According to Mr Napier, the object had initially been high in the sky when they first spotted it. It wasn't until it started moving down quickly near to their position that he began to get alarmed. Like many witnesses before him, he is sure that what he and his daughter saw was not an aircraft. 11-year-old Sam Horsley (pseudonym) from Redding near Falkirk claimed to have seen a large triangle in the November sky which had red and white lights on it. I would tend to surmise that this was probably an aircraft.

A feature of my investigations that I uncovered in the Bonnybridge area, was the high level of 'light phenomenon'. Structured craft were not always reported, there were strange balls of light, some which hovered high in the sky, and some of which swooped down towards the startled observers.

THE TELEVISED BONNYBRIDGE SKYWATCH

The Bonnybridge UFO sightings were increasing, and as such were drawing more and more attention further afield. Various newspapers rung me for quotes, followed by Scottish Television's evening News programme, 'Scotland Today'. On November 16th, 1992, Scottish Television came out to Bonnybridge to film our society interviewing witnesses. That same evening, I was invited over to Glasgow to be interviewed by presenter Viv Lumsden which was transmitted live from the roof of Scottish Television Centre at Cowcaddens, and boy was it cold, no warm studios for me! Later that night, a Scottish Television Film Crew came over to Bonnybridge to film our planned sky watch. I am sure Scottish Television would dearly have loved to have been able to film a UFO that night. This would have given them the scoop of the century! Joining our sky watch on what was a bitterly cold evening was SPI's Helen Walters, my workmate Kevin Rennie, and Glasgow rock group CE IV who write and perform songs on the UFO issue. We then all headed off to some lonely moors behind the town of Bonnybridge which in point of fact was the scene of the Sloggett UFO encounter mentioned previously. And although it was a bitterly cold night, it was a beautiful sky, not a cloud to be seen. A sprinkling of stars covered a vast black velvet sky, perfect Conditions. Around 15 to 20 people started on our sky watch, all looking to the heavens in hopes of a sighting. However, the peace was soon shattered by a continual stream of cars which were all heading up into the moors, their headlights streaming in all directions casting weird beams of light into the inky blackness. We hadn't gauged for this mass interest in our sky watch, but I guess that's the power of television for you as S.T.V. had mentioned in an earlier broadcast, that there would be a sky watch being undertaken on the moors behind

Bonnybridge that night. This added interest certainly swelled our ranks. A lot of air traffic was observed during this sky watch, but I am afraid no UFOs. This was slightly disappointing, considering that we had the T.V. cameras there which surely would have captured something had it shown. Our sky watch was shown on Scottish Television the following evening and this created even more interest in the Bonnybridge enigma.

It was on the 25th of November 1992 at around 7:00pm, that Linda Buchan (pseudonym) observed from her car a large bright object low in the sky which, she states, was 'larger than the Moon'! This bright object remained stationary. As she viewed this object, she observed that at one point it shone quite brightly then dimmed until it just suddenly disappeared. The witness herself believes that this bright object may well have gone behind some cloud. I am inclined to believe that this might have been a bright star. So many astronomical objects are misconstrued by honest observers, this could be one of them. An interesting point to note however, is that the witness stated that there had been three to four lightning flashes across the sky over a period of 15 minutes (with no thunder)! Could this light phenomenon be associated with the lightning? Rather than an astronomical explanation, might it not have something to do with an atmospheric phenomenon?

Owing to the immense interest in the Bonnybridge UFO sightings, Councillor Billy Buchanan suggested that SPI should hold a public lecture in Bonnybridge to inform the local residents on what was going on. By this time even Councillor Buchanan had witnessed a UFO himself which he described as totally unlike anything that he has ever seen before. It occurred at Wester Glen above Falkirk, which is an area of land which gives one a commanding view of the Forth Estuary. He was with another couple when they became aware of strange lights in the sky. These lights appeared to be rushing around the sky doing strange manoeuvres which seemed totally unreal. Then much to their surprise, these lights appeared to land in a hollow in a nearby field then disappeared. Six years later, in 1997, Billy was to relate his personal UFO sighting to the 'Night & Day' colour supplement magazine which came out in the 'Mail On

Sunday' dated 'September 21st 1997'. Billy was quoted as saying.

"We watched it for an about an hour and I wanted to go over the fence and run across those fields like General Custer, but the woman who we were with, was getting frightened and asked to be taken home."

Billy has seen UFOs on two other occasions, one of which was an oval shape which hung in the night sky which appeared to have rods or spikes sticking out from underneath it!

1993

BONNYBRIDGE PUBLIC UFO LECTURE

A date was set, for our public meeting, January 31st, 1993, and the venue was the plush Norwood Hotel on the outskirts of Bonnybridge. Billy and I expected a reasonable turn out owing to the vast publicity that had been generated by both the local and national press, but we were struck dumb and taken aback by the huge volume of people who turned up on the night, upwards of 300 people turned up at the door, and I remember thinking would we ever fit them all in? The manager was concerned over the safety aspect in regard to a fire hazard, and as I looked again at the door, streams of people were walking in single file into the main hall of the building. Eventually we realised that we just couldn't fit any more people in, and someone was dispatched to the main door to inform the eager local people, that sadly we were full up and that we would have to close the doors. It's been estimated by others, that a good 100 people were turned away from the door that night. All this clearly showed Councillor Buchanan and I, that the local people of Bonnybridge and surrounding areas, were desperate to know what was going on. Their thirst for answers was unstoppable, and they were looking towards Councillor Buchanan and I to let them know 'what was happening'. I explained to Billy that night, that if we found answers for the Bonnybridge phenomenon, then we would solve the whole UFO mystery, but

I urged caution and stated that solving events such as these, was no easy task, that there were many people the world over trying to unravel the UFO mystery and had been doing so for years. It was plain to see that wherever this mystery lay, it was not keen to unmask itself. Ufology has been with us for many years, and I did not expect any quick cut answers which would solve the Bonnybridge mystery. I urged patience, and hoped that at the very least, something might, just might, be uncovered which would assist in the understanding of this elusive phenomenon. Incidentally, and for the record, the Norwood Hotel in Bonnybridge has since been demolished.

IS THAT A CAR IN THE SKY!

The UFO sightings were not just specifically centred around Bonnybridge, as I've shown; there were reports of strange objects coming from other outlying towns and villages. A Bannockburn family, (a town near Stirling), had a very strange experience on a cold January evening back in 1993. Mary Young (34) was indoors watching television, and her young son David aged (9) was outside playing in the snow. As it was getting late, 9:15pm, she went outside to call him in. As she approached him, David turned round to her and shouted, *"Look mum there is a car in the sky!"* Mary immediately looked up in the direction her son was pointing to and was amazed to observe bright white lights similar to car headlights, hanging low in the sky, at around 40 feet above some nearby houses. Mary immediately shouted on her boyfriend Kevin who was indoors, and upon hearing her shouts, he raced outside to see what all the commotion was about. Mary's daughter Jacqueline also came outside, and they all stared skywards wondering what the object could be. At this point, the family all went indoors to fetch a telescope that her son had been given for his Christmas, but by the time that they had found the telescope and then located the object again, the object was moving away fairly fast and away from their line of vision. In a statement to SPI Mary had this to say:

"It was oval shaped and about 40 to 60 feet long. It had a lot of red lights underneath it, and there was also a square shape of red lights of which inside that, there was a square shape of white lights. There were also two white lights at the front, and two white lights at the back. It was definitely not an aircraft. It was flying too low to have been a plane and it was making a low humming sound. It was like nothing that I have ever seen before."

In the Weekly News of 27th March 1993 Mary goes into greater detail about this sighting. She said:

"I went outside to call my nine-year-old son David in from the back garden where he was playing. I followed his gaze as he pointed to the sky and asked whether the lights he could see belonged to a car. The lights were moving low across the roof tops in a neighbouring street and there was no way that a car would be travelling at that height. At first, I thought it must be a low flying plane, but the lights were very unusual. There were massive white lights at two sides of the craft, and a square of red lights with another inner square of white lights."

"I shouted to my boyfriend Kevin to come and take a look, and all three of us dashed to David's upstairs bedroom to grab a telescope he'd been bought for Christmas. And from there we could see the machine approaching. It was travelling so fast that we couldn't keep the telescope trained on it, and the oval shaped object passed above us at about 40 feet from the ground. I have never believed in UFOs, but now I have to think again. There just was no logical explanation for what we saw."

Well, I'm pretty sure that both Mary and her boyfriend and son, would surely know if what was 40 feet above them was an aircraft or not! According to the Stirling Observer newspaper dated 10th February 1993, a number of local people from Bannockburn called the paper to report that they too had seen something strange in the sky that night.

THE CASTLECARY VIADUCT UFOS

Staying with our low-level close proximity UFO sightings, our next case not only concerns the observation of one strange object, but 'two' identical objects which were seen over the same area. This is the strange experience of the Procek family. It was the evening of the 15th of January 1993, around 8:35pm, and Ray and Cathy Procek were travelling in their car along the A80 to visit some friends in Westerwood. Just as they were approaching Castlecary Viaduct, Cathy noticed some lights in the sky and pointed them out to her husband. Both husband and wife continued to watch these strange lights until they were soon underneath them. Ray explained in his written testimony to the author, that he soon realised that the lights belonged to a large 'craft' because he could see it silhouetted against a cloud. The object was of a sharply defined triangular shape of which the nose of the craft was pointing west. The object was stationary and was roughly 300 feet above the ground, it had 3 white lights on its underside, one at the front and two at the rear, it also had several pinkish coloured lights on the rear with more white lights around them as well. It was at this point that they decided to open the large sunroof in their space cruiser car in order to obtain a better look, and, upon doing so, both Ray and Cathy continued to stare with intense amazement at this strange object. Then much to their surprise, they both noticed that only a short distance away, was yet another and similar object which was hovering low in the sky. Both objects were matt black in colour and stood out in the dark night sky due to the intense lights that both were displaying. Ray thought better of stopping the car for a closer look and decided his best course of action would be to continue on with his journey, a decision which was readily accepted by Cathy. I would rate the Procek sighting as one of the best UFO sightings that we have on file coming from the Bonnybridge area, not only because it is yet another low level close proximity UFO sighting, but more so because of the fact that not one but two similar objects were seen together and of which both witnesses are adamant were **NOT** conventional flying objects. Researchers are well aware of these flying triangles, they have been seen in many countries over the years, more so in Belgium, but the rarity is, that very seldom do you have a report which features two similar objects together! What on Earth were these two objects doing over the Castlecary Viaduct? This is not an isolated spot for UFO sightings, I have on file a number of other such reports of objects being sighted either above, or near this viaduct, for what purpose though we can only speculate and continue to monitor for similar sightings.

TOP FLIGHT UFO COVER

This was the heading from the Glasgow Evening Times dated 13th March 1993. It spoke of taking out insurance in case you were abducted by aliens in the Bonnybridge area. Here is what it said.

'Scots sky watchers are being offered protection from alien snatch squads. U.S. businessman Mike St. Lawrence is targeting the Bonnybridge Triangle with his 7 million insurance policy against being abducted by a UFO. Jokester accounting and tax advisor Mike has already sold more than 5,000 policies in the States and Britain. Now, after a rash of UFO sightings, he is targeting Scotland for the 7 million lifetime policies. He said:

"I started this UFO Abduction Insurance Company in my home town of Altamonte Springs in Florida about three years ago and it has caused a stir. I am already paying out on one successful claim from a man in New York State, in fact, I just sent off the latest instalment cheque last week. To prove the claim, all the abducted person has to do, is to get the signature of the alien who snatched him or her along with a full description of the creature. I reckon a lot of Scots could do with this policy considering the number of UFOs that have been buzzing you lately."

Needless to say, dear reader, this was all a con, but made good press, more so in the light on the ongoing UFO sightings across the Stirlingshire skies. But wait, Mike St. Lawrence was not finished. In a final quote he stated:

"Under the policy we will pay out the 7 million at 60 pence a year."

Initially I thought that this was all one big joke. There probably was never a UFO policy like this. I presumed that some bored staff member at the Glasgow Evening Times, decided on a whim, to draught up a story like this, but I was wrong. While writing this book, I decided to check the internet and see if there really was a Mike St. Lawrence and an alien insurance policy, and lo and behold, there was! From the Newsweek 90 web site, dated the 26th of July 2019, I read an article by Jason Murdock where he stated that Mike was offering alien abduction protection to any Ufologist who intended to storm the United States Air Force facility known as Area 51. Again, there was a downside. His policy would only pay out at $1 a year for 10 million years! The policy holder was informed that (and I quote):

'The alien abduction scheme says it provides $10 million compensation in the event the policyholder is beamed up. It covers medical issues (all outpatient psychiatric care), sarcasm coverage (immediate family members only) and double indemnity coverage to the sum of $20 million in the event aliens insist on conjugal visits or the extraterrestrial encounter results in offspring.'

Of course, this was all one big wind up or was it! Clearly there were some people daft enough to part with their money. Mike stated that his company had sold upwards of 6,000 policies since 1987. What I found most amusing, was the part of the policy where you had to get the signature of the visiting alien. Can you imagine asking your abductor to sign on the dotted line! Admittedly, Mike did say that his alien abduction policy was created for those who wish to give a funny gift, and as far as obtaining publicity for his company, well this one was 'out of this world'.

The UFO sightings in and around Bonnybridge, were now becoming known further afield, and numerous journalists, some of whom were phoning from other parts of the world, continued to contact our society all desperate to learn what was going on. So, it came as no surprise then, when I received a telephone call from one Junichi Yaoi a television producer from Japan. Junichi explained that he produced television documentaries on the UFO Enigma and that he had heard what was going on at Bonnybridge and was keen to bring a camera crew along to film witnesses and people who were associated with the UFO sightings. He had already spoken to Councillor Buchanan and plans were shortly made for them to travel over to Scotland as part of a 'whistle-stop' tour that they were making of some of the world's UFO 'Hot-Spots'. *"Would I be interested in assisting Nippon T.V."*, he asked. My speedy reply was, *"Most certainly"*, and plans were then drawn up for the arrival of Japanese T.V. to Scotland.

JAPANESE TELEVISION ARRIVE IN BONNYBRIDGE

If there is one thing this UFO business does, it certainly keeps you busy! On May the 26th 1993 I arrived at the Norwood Hotel in Bonnybridge to meet up with Junichi Yaoi, team leader of Nippon T.V. and discuss with him all about the Bonnybridge UFO wave. Junichi informed me that his previous documentary on UFOs attracted over 24 million viewers in his country, indeed, Junichi believes he has filmed what could well be a UFO in the skies above his native Tokyo back in December 1979. He is a firm 'believer' in the UFO phenomenon and decided that as his team were on a whistle stop tour of the world's UFO 'Hot-Spots', the chance to visit and film in Bonnybridge would be too good to miss. After a period of discussion, Junichi and I were quickly ushered onto a golf course which lay behind the Norwood Hotel. The Norwood Hotel had been the focal point of some SPI meetings, and indeed we had previously met and interviewed some local people there. The Scottish media had got wind of the Japanese arrival in Scotland, and there were a good sprinkling of journalists and T.V. crews out in force all keen to interview not only myself, but other SPI personnel who were with me on the day. These were a combination of, Glasgow rock group, CE IV, which comprised of Brian McMullan (Snr) and Brian McMullan (Jnr) along with keyboard player, Andrew Morton. Also, there that day were Billy Devlin while Billy Buchanan was in his usual jovial mood, and his happy 'banter' with the Japanese T.V. crew had them in fits of laughter, (did they really understand what he was saying!). Junichi went on to say that his crew was behind another big Scottish story, that of the Loch Ness Monster, and although they spent several days at the loch filming and interviewing witnesses, they never did catch sight of "Nessie", *"perhaps next time"* was his thoughtful words.

I had notified many of the Bonnybridge witnesses to come along to the Norwood Hotel that night to be interviewed by Nippon T.V. and I also had informed the readers of the 'Falkirk Herald' that if they had had a UFO sighting, to come along to the Norwood Hotel that night and discuss it with Junichi. The reader should accept that there is still some stigma attached to the reporting of UFO sightings, in that witnesses are sometimes reluctant to come forward and recount their stories usually through fear of ridicule. This, as I have said before, is understandable, but thankfully more and more people are now coming out with their stories and this 'fear factor' seems to be diminishing. I wondered how many people would turn up on the night to be filmed by Nippon T.V. As it turned out, around two dozen witnesses turned up, as well as numerous interested individuals, all keen to find out more. A number of filmed interviews were then conducted, after which, the Japanese T.V. crew handed out small gifts to those that they had filmed, to show their appreciation to the witnesses for taking time out to come over and participate. After the filming of witnesses, I retired to the bar for some light refreshments. Joining us at the bar was David Leslie a journalist with the News of The World (thankfully now defunct!) David's story on the Bonnybridge UFO sightings would appear four days later, which I'm afraid, considering all the information we had given him, was a 'bloody joke'! Low flying pylon indeed! Also joining us, was Veronica Johnston from Kibblesworth, Tyne and Wear who was also covering the Bonnybridge UFO sightings for her newspaper.

The evening had been a big success and showed to our Japanese friends how much activity had been occurring throughout the skies of Central Scotland. I returned home, happy to have played a part in the education of the Japanese people to what was going on in Scotland and looked forward to the following day where we had planned to do some location filming with witnesses.

Day two dawned, and I again travelled over to Bonnybridge to meet up with the Japanese TV crew, driven by Ken Sutton who was doing a grand job driving various people, here, there, and everywhere. I was also accompanied by SPI's Helen Walters. After going through all our arrangements, our first port of call was to travel over to Larbert to interview young Craig Morrison whose UFO sighting I reported earlier. Craig's parents had given him the day off school in order to be filmed by the Japanese, and I could see how pleased he was about it! After completing our interview with Craig, we continued to visit and interview further UFO witnesses. I found the Japanese to be very meticulous in their Interviewing, and also their reconstruction with some of the witnesses at the location of their sighting. Needless to say, as soon as the Japanese T.V. crew appeared on the streets with their cameras and equipment, many interested neighbours came out to have a look! Having been on the road in our two vans for over ten hours, we eventually completed our schedule of interviews. It had been a tiring day, but an extremely beneficial one. The continuous stream of jokes by Billy Buchanan had everyone in raptures and we wondered if he was not in the wrong profession! Councillor Buchanan had shown great hospitality to our Japanese visitors, for upon their arrival the previous day, they had entered the Norwood Hotel and were met by an enormous banner which featured Japanese writing on it and stitched on UFO images. Translated those words read,

"Welcome to Bonnybridge our Japanese friends."

And as a further surprise, just before Junichi and his crew retired to bed that night, Billy had booked a Scottish piper in full regalia, to play a series of Scottish tunes. This was then followed by the presentation by both Billy and I to the Japanese of a specially made cake which featured a UFO on its top surface. SPI members and friends, then all assembled to be photographed by the local press. Councillor Buchanan had proved to be an excellent host and someone who knew how to ensure that visitors from another country enjoyed their stay in Scotland. Incredibly, SPI took a bit of stick from other Scottish researchers about this cake and banner they felt that it was all a bit over the top! My thoughts on the matter were that it would be a sad day indeed when Scottish people cannot welcome and entertain overseas friends and show them some good Scottish hospitality. The visit of this Japanese T.V. crew to Scotland had really opened the floodgates of publicity on Bonnybridge, and certain newspapers were now dubbing the Town the *'UFO Capital Of The World!'* A title which I was not too happy about. Billy Buchanan and I were fast becoming some kind of celebrities. We did not seek out all this publicity as some have suggested, it was purely down to a recognisable phenomenon which was occurring in the Scottish skies. Junichi Yaoi the producer and director of this two-hour special on UFOs was quoted in the 'Stirling Observer' newspaper dated 28th May 1993 as saying:

"Bonnybridge is one of the most interesting cases I think, because it's a small area but many people here have seen UFOs."

This newspaper also stated that Councillor Billy Buchanan had been ridiculed for dealing with this UFO subject by fellow councillors. He stated that he was only acting as a 'buffer zone' between the media and local eyewitnesses, and for that, he was being ridiculed. He further stated that opposition councillors in Falkirk had already circulated caricatures of him interviewing E.T. around the council and added:

"It does hurt you a bit really, because at the end of the day I'm fighting apathy, ignorance, and a lack of vision because there are people at Falkirk District Council who have been there too long."

This sadly wouldn't be the end of Billy being slated by opposition councillors as we will see later. This incredible interest regarding these UFO sightings, were forced upon us due to the very nature of the subject which of course the public found totally fascinating. Let's be honest here, Billy and I were at the forefront of what was going on, spokespersons if you like. When all is said and done, someone has to be in a position to discuss with the media on what was going on. Information is for the people, and not for filing cabinets. I'll be returning to this theme later in this chapter. The visit of the Japanese had been a resounding success and cemented relationships which exist to this day. This was not to be the end of overseas interest in this small Scottish town, for both Billy and I were soon to be working with other foreign press and T.V. crews. The Bonnybridge UFO phenomena was not only being talked about on the streets of Bathgate but was also being discussed on the streets of Bombay and other exotic and faraway places!

As Billy was being slated in some newspapers, I decided to write to the 'Falkirk Herald' newspaper (which covers the Bonnybridge area). The title of my letter was, 'Courageous Councillor', was featured in their June 2nd edition and read:

"Sir,

I would like to commend Councillor Billy Buchanan on having the courage to take up his constituents' accounts of sightings of UFOs and assisting myself with research on such cases. Also, for showing good Scottish hospitality to the T.V. grew from Nippon T.V. who were in Bonnybridge recently to film accounts for their Worldwide Documentary. Councillor Buchanan has not shied away from his responsibility in taking up his constituents' reports. Some would have tended to ignore them and shrug their shoulders and move onto other things, not Billy".

"Be it a burst water pipe to UFO sightings, he acts in the interests of the people he has to serve but finds himself facing criticism from fellow councillors and general mickey taking. I feel that Councillor Buchanan has done a grand job, and shown that no matter what the issue, 'people come first."

Malcolm Robinson.

Prior to the Japanese film crew coming to Scotland, I had been interviewed by BBC Radio Scotland. This recording, saw me in a car with a UFO witness and his two young sons (Patrick Forsyth) where we re-enacted the events of his UFO sighting. The car's window was rolled down to get the sound of the car's tyres as it sped along the road, and the children were asked to re-enact what they shouted on that particular evening when they first spotted the UFO floating above a farmer's field. I'll tell you what dear reader, being in the car when they did this re-enactment on the same stretch of road and at the same location, well, I could almost taste the fear as the family vocally shouted out. It certainly made good Radio. At the close of day two of the Japanese TV visit, we again retired back to the bar at the Norwood Hotel where Michi Nakamura, the female producer, presented me with a cigarette lighter bearing the logo of Nippon TV for all my work and assistance to them in setting up the interviews etc. Sadly, I am still waiting to see my appearance on Japanese TV with me being dubbed in Japanese. As the promised copy of their documentary was never sent to us, or if it did, it went astray!

YOUR PRIZE IS A TRIP TO BONNYBRIDGE!

To show the reader how much the Bonnybridge UFO phenomena was growing, I received a phone call from one Carl Gant who was the managing Director of Wannabee Promotions in London. He informed me that two America film buffs, had won a prize put up by Paramount Pictures which had been held throughout cinemas and television stations throughout America, and which was based on the recently released UFO film, 'Fire In The Sky'. (This film concerns the UFO abduction of Travis Walton). Their prize was to visit some of the UFO 'Hot-Spots' around Britain in which Bonnybridge and Dechmont Woods near Livingston, was to be their only Scottish stop. John Jenkins, a fellow researcher from Penicuik and I, met up with the two prize winners, Don Johnson, (not the famous one!) and Rich Culhane both of New Jersey, and also Carl Gant who was accompanying them around the UK. We met up at the plush, and boy do I mean plush, Balmoral Hotel on Princes Street in Edinburgh. After some brief discussion, it was off to Bonnybridge to meet up with Councillor Buchanan and also some witnesses. Both prize winners also had the opportunity to take photographs around Bonnybridge where UFO sightings had occurred, and like all true Americans, were busily snapping away. Our next port of call was to travel over to Dechmont Woods, scene of the famous Robert (Bob) Taylor Incident. All five of us enjoyed the walk through the woods in glorious sunshine and I remember John Jenkins saying that you have more chance of seeing a UFO in Scotland, than you do of seeing the sun, a joke which went down well, probably because it's true! After discussing with our American visitors what went on at this specific location, it was time to head home. The day had been enjoyable for several reasons, and it had opened the eyes of our American friends to some of the UFO activity which had been occurring in Scotland.

CRITICISM OF EVENTS IN BONNYBRIDGE

It was during May 1993, that some criticism was levelled at Councillor Billy Buchanan and I in regard to these UFO sightings over Bonnybridge. In an article headed, 'Billy's Unidentified Flying Circus' featured in the Falkirk Herald a fellow Scottish UFO researcher stated, and I quote:

"I don't want to get personal, but with all respect to Billy, it was a bit of a circus, a lot of people have been upset by this. Councillor Buchanan does not appear to be encouraging serious Investigation of the hundreds of sightings, I think he is more interested in Bonnybridge getting some publicity, this makes it difficult to Investigate these sightings properly."

The researcher went on to say that most of the UFO sightings in the Bonnybridge area were likely to have natural explanations. A 'Scottish Power' helicopter was known to have been operating in the area around the time sightings which peaked last winter. I have deep respect and admiration for this fellow Scottish researcher, and of course he is entitled to his opinions. But we at SPI extensively checked with Scottish Power and they had no helicopters flying on the given dates that we supplied them with. I have said before that Billy Buchanan was elected as a councillor to serve the people of Bonnybridge, *IN ALL CAPACITY!* Was he to turn his back on his constituents just because they had come to him with tales of seeing 'Flying Saucers'? Of course not. He was elected to serve them, not ignore them. If anything, Billy Buchanan should be commended for having the courage to work closely with his constituents in the face of criticism. Billy is a colourful character, we know that, but does that make him any less a man for trying to get to the bottom of incredible incidents that were occurring above his constituency? Fair criticism is always productive, and I have always welcomed fair criticism. Since that piece in the 'Falkirk Herald' back in May 1993 that researcher has come to realise that the Bonnybridge phenomenon is indeed real, that it doesn't just belong to the town itself, but spreads out into other districts of which Billy Buchanan has no control. And as I've shown earlier, I was Investigating reports of UFO activity in this same area back in 1982, and even now, I am still receiving reports from members of the public about UFO sightings from Bonnybridge and surrounding areas. This phenomenon is not about Councillor Billy Buchanan and I 'promoting it' into extraordinary proportions, it's all about 'reality', and that 'reality' is, that there is a genuine phenomenon occurring throughout the skies of Central Scotland and to ignore what's going on would be foolish and would not be in keeping with our quest and thirst for knowledge of the understanding what is behind all these sightings. As the years rolled on, UFO sightings from this area came to the attention of other Scottish ufologists. This made them realise that this was 'not' a Billy Buchanan and Malcolm Robinson publicity drive. Independent sightings were being made, and it was clear that the sightings were not easing up.

Bannockburn Family with Japanese TV (c) Malcolm Robinson

Billy Buchanan and Malcolm Robinson 10 Downing Street 2023

Billy Buchanan. A man of the people.

Bonnybridge Sky Watch November 2nd 2014

Bonnybridge Skywatch 2014

Castlecarry Viaduct Image of what witness saw.

Denny UFO Image Patrick Forsyth Case Bonnybridge

https://youtu.be/n36KOqbwrMY

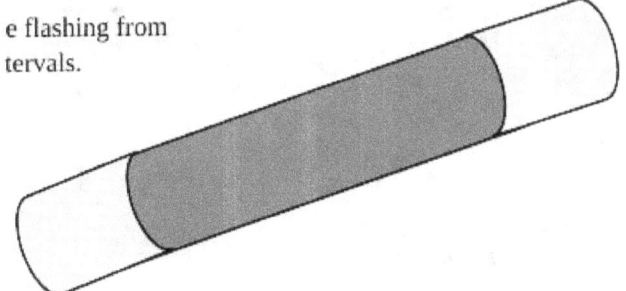

e flashing from tervals.

image of Falkirk UFO (c) Martin Alexander

Japanese TV at Bonnybridge (c) Malcolm Robinson

Our Petition to the Prime Minister 10 Downing Street.
July 2010

Patrick Forsyth and sons. (c) Malcolm Robinson

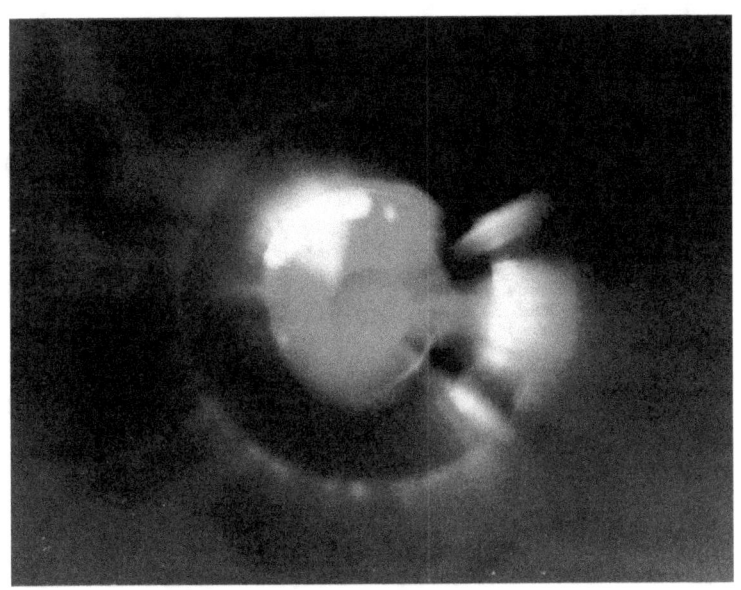

Polmont Reservoir UFO. Phil Trevis

Ray Procek Interviewed by Japanese TV (c) Malcolm Robinson

Steven Bird and Malcolm Robinson in a field near Bonnybridge

Ron Halliday and Malcolm Robinson

Strange Orb Bonnybridge Sky Watch May 2024 (c) Tress Blair

The Bonnybridge Landscape (c) Malcolm Robinson

The Slogget Family (L to R) Mother son and daughter
(c) Malcolm Robinson

The former major of Roswell with Billy Buchanan

Witness Freddy France with Japanese TV (c) Malcolm Robinson

Yonichi Yoa Japanese TV with Young Bonnybridge witness (c) Malcolm Robinson

THE OLD MAN ON THE BUS

Throughout all the seriousness of the UFO sightings over Bonnybridge, there are one or two lighter moments. I remember the time when I was travelling over to Bonnybridge by bus to interview some witnesses. It was a double decker bus I was on, and like a kid, whenever I see a double decker bus I always head for the top deck and usually the front seat if I can get it. This time however, I had to make do with the back seat as the front seats were already taken. Anyway, off I toddled to the back seat, sat down, and looked out through the window pondering about the witnesses that I was shortly to meet. Further along the route, the bus picked up some school kids who made a bee line for the top deck. Also getting on the bus at this particular spot, was an old man, who, when I saw him, put me in mind of the local town drunk (any town!). His attire and grubby demeanour gave away his stance in life, and one could easily see that he had fallen on hard times. His silver beard stood out like snow on a field and the curls in his hair were all matted and grubby. I returned my gaze to the street life outside and continued to contemplate the UFO situation in Scotland. I then became aware of the conversation being made by these school children. They were all talking about the UFO sightings over Bonnybridge. One of them turned to the old man and said, *"Hey mister, do you believe in wee green men?"* to which the old man paused, then replied with a wry grin:

"I dinnie ken aboot that hen, but wan things for sure, they better no come down and nick me fags!" (Author's note. For our overseas readers, the above translates to. *"I don't know about that young girl. But one thing is for sure, they better not come down and steal my cigarettes."*.

I was creased with laughter and thought to myself, of all the things that could happen to mankind if contact was made with aliens, this fella was only interested in them stealing his fags. This chap certainly had his priorities right!

Another peculiar sighting, again featuring a cluster of lights or indeed objects! Was reported to SPI by Colin Robertson (pseudonym) of Falkirk. It was the 12th of December 1993, and Colin had been preparing his shop for an opening on the coming Monday. As he was working in the shop, he somehow managed to blow all the lights and had to phone his son who arranged for an electrician that he knew, to come over and put everything right. Colin decided to wait outside his shop near Kings Court, and look out for the electrician, and it was while he was standing outside waiting that his attention was 'drawn' to a strange spectacle in the night sky. He saw a triangular shape of lights which he was unsure if they were individual lights or smaller grouped objects. He continued to watch, and observed them travel slowly across the sky, whereupon they suddenly stopped. After stopping for a few moments the lights/objects continued to travel in a South-Westerly direction before finally moving out of sight. 55-year-old Colin is adamant that what he saw that night was something Extraterrestrial.

1994

UFO (?) CAUGHT ON VIDEO

1994 opened in spectacular style with yet another low-level close proximity UFO sighting. The difference this time, however, was that it was captured on video! The following case was made known to me by Billy Buchanan who suggested that I get involved with it right away. It was just after 7:00pm on Wednesday the 19th of January 1994, when 27-year-old Neil Malcolm left a relative's house in Larbert, a small but busy town near Falkirk. Neil entered his Vauxhall Nova car and started to drive the short distance to his father's house, roughly about a mile away where he lived with his wife Lorraine. At this point in time both were waiting on a house becoming available, and like most young couples, had to stay with family until such times as that happened. Neil was focused on the road ahead, but suddenly something happened which was to change his perception of life dramatically. It was at this point on his journey home, that he became aware of a bright white object low in the sky which appeared to be travelling in the same direction as him on the right hand side of his car. The light looked peculiar, but he didn't think too much about it at the time. Suddenly, as Neil approached a junction at which he had to slow down, he was startled when all of a sudden, the whole interior of his car was lit up by a bright and powerful light which he was sure came from this strange object in the sky. Somewhat alarmed, he applied pressure to the accelerator and drove at breakneck speed to reach home. Upon reaching home, he raced out of the car and dashed indoors shouting at everyone to come out and see this strange object which had been following him. At first no one believed him but seeing the intense emotion that he was showing the family soon recognised that 'something was up' and that they better go out and have a look. His mother, father, brother, wife, and sister-in-law, all ran outside to see what all the fuss was about. Neil's mother Anne now takes up the story, (as related from her UFO sighting account form.)

"My son came in quite alarmed about something that he thought had followed him home. We all went out to the front door and saw a light moving slowly above the buildings across the road from our house. It was coming towards us, when all of a sudden it looked as if it revolved away behind the rooftop."

At this point as they were all gathered outside, Neil's wife Lorraine remembered that she had a video camera indoors and decided to dash inside and fetch it. Thankfully by the time she returned outdoors the object was still to be seen although was just beginning to recede from their line of vision. Lorraine managed to capture around 18 seconds of video footage of this strange object as it revolved and began to move away behind some chimney stacks. Having met and interviewed the family, I found them to be both warm and honest individuals. They were the proverbial 'down to earth' family who had managed to capture something strange on film. They were not seeking any publicity at this time, and it is only in the past few years that the family have been happy to talk about what they have seen. I took a copy of the video away for inspection at my home where

I put it through slow motion and then frame by frame advancement. On first viewing one notices a bright ball of white light, no red or green navigation lights can be seen, which travels from left to right on the T.V. screen above a building before finally being lost to view behind some chimneys. In my viewing, I found that there were three interesting points about this video. The first one was that if you looked closely, you could see what appears to be a 'small ball of light' which appears to be emitted from behind the larger parent object which then leaves the screen to the left in a 'jerky' movement. Admittedly this could be anything such is the grainy nature of the film due to it being filmed in the blackness of the night sky. The second interesting point that I found was that when Lorraine zoomed into the object the brightness disappears, and one is left looking at a 'tall vertical cylindrical object' which 'appears' to be lighted in the middle with darker shading on the top and bottom. There also 'appears' to be movement in or on the object. The third point is that just before the object is finally lost to view the object 'appears' to dip slightly, or perhaps turn, in which some kind of 'structure' appears at the rear. On the surface, this video looked extremely exciting, but I knew that I would have to conduct further tests in order to be fully happy with it. Prior to those tests, I conducted the usual lines of enquiry as we have heard from other cases. The local police stated that no members of the public had contacted them with a similar sighting that night. The nearby Cumbernauld Airport closed at 5:00pm that day. Cumbernauld Airport, incidentally, is a small airport which does not deal with large commercial airliners. Mr Paul Louden, General Manager of Air Traffic Services at Edinburgh Airport replied:

"Dear Malcolm. Thank you for your letter. The area you refer to, ie, Larbert, is underneath the Scottish Terminal Control Area. Controlled airspace starts at 250 feet. This means that below that height, light aircraft are able to fly without reference to the controlling authorities. It is therefore quite possible that some legitimate aerial activity was taking place about which 'we' would have no knowledge."

Mr W. Gray, the ATC Watch manager for Glasgow Airport stated:

"Dear Mr Robinson, I would advise you that runway 23 was in use at Glasgow Airport on the 19th of January, and, at approximately the time you mention, an inbound airliner from Aberdeen 'could' have passed over the area in question."

The witnesses have lived in this area for over 15 years and are well used to seeing aircraft regularly fly over their house, and this object, according to what they told me, did not resemble anything that they had ever seen before. It was at this point that I decided to send a copy of this video, down to the Ministry of Defence in London. Little did I know it then, but they were to keep a firm hold of it for many months before finally issuing a statement, more of which in a moment. I then took the step of sending a copy of this video to Dr T. J. Moir and Mr C. Smith of the Electrical and Electronic Engineering Department of the University of Paisley. After rigorous tests, this is what they had to say:

"We were asked by Malcolm Robinson to analyse a video of an alleged UFO near Falkirk. The video shows a light in the sky which is zoomed by the photographer to reveal what at first sight appears to be a cylindrical shaped object. The equipment used at Paisley is a sun sparc work station LX running Solaris 2 operating system. Three still images were captured using Vision Tool software and hardware. We have provisionally used the XV package to analyse the images. Preliminary Investigations are unable to resolve much detail of the images other than a blur."

PRELIMINARY CONCLUSIONS

"The object is an aircraft, (probably a private one). As the witness zooms the video camera into the object, he loses focus. This gives the appearance of a cylinder but is really the two wing lights out of focus. To confirm this, a tail light can just be seen as the object passes out of view."

For a second opinion I sent a further copy of the video over to America, to one of the world's leading video image enhancers of alleged UFO videos, Jeff Sainio. Jeff is a Staff Analyst for MUFON, (The Mutual UFO Network) which is based in Seguin in Texas. This is what he had to say:

"Two points of nocturnal light fly smoothly over a chimney. Misfocus causes the points to look larger than they are. I could find no indication of anything other than ordinary aircraft lighting."

Disappointed with this short and sweet reply, I again wrote to Jeff asking him to be more specific, and in a further letter he informed me that:

"In response to your query of the reasoning behind my conclusions that the Malcolm family video was consistent with an airplane. The lack of data left little to work with. A white nocturnal light is seen moving steadily. Zoom shows a triangular configuration, consistent with a main body light and two wing landing lights. When the image is misfocused, allowing a large enough area to discern colour, a landing white light is seen. The motion, colour, and configuration, the only apparent characteristics, appear conventional. I simply cannot think of any testing which could be useful."

Were the experts correct? Did this video only show a small aircraft? Well, the witnesses still remain adamant that what they saw and filmed that night was a UFO, and allowing for misperception, I still believe that what the Malcolm family saw that night, was indeed a UFO. But what of the Ministry of Defence? What had they to say about it? Well, when we finally received the video back, the accompanying letter from Nick Pope, stated that they could not really comment on what the object was, but it was most likely to have been a plane! These statements from various people did not deter the Malcolm family, indeed it only served to fuel their desire to get the all-important video which no one could dispute. Today the

Malcolm family have indeed achieved that aim and claim a number of unusual pieces of video footage which are indeed most interesting. Some of the Malcolm family UFO videos have been used by Television companies for use in documentaries, and it's fair to say, that out of the whole of Scotland, this family would appear to hold the most video images of what is occurring in the skies above Central Scotland. We can only hope that someday soon, a major low-level sighting will be captured on film which will make the debunkers and sceptics alike sit up and take notice of the reality of what has been going on in the skies above Bonnybridge.

UFOs ARE NO LAUGHING MATTER!

Prior to the big Falkirk UFO Conference which I will detail shortly, Columnist Graham Smith of the 'Falkirk Herald' had taken a pop at councillor Billy Buchanan in the newspaper which I felt was not deserved. I was so upset at this, that I decided to write into the 'Falkirk Herald' stating my feelings. My letter was printed, and here is what it said:

"Sir. I read with much disdain in last Thursday's Falkirk Herald the column by Graham Smith in which he poked fun at Bonnybridge Councillor, Billy Buchanan. It seems to me, that Graham appears to be uneducated as to how serious the UFO phenomenon really is. Countless millions across the globe have experienced the UFO phenomena, many of whom are high standing academic people, (I would fit Billy Buchanan in with them) I suppose however, it is not Graham's fault, because if he was aware of the immense volume of 'true' UFO reports then his column would have been somewhat different in appearance. I suppose that being different means that one is the butt of endless jokes from people who should know better."

"They laughed at man setting foot down on the Moon prior to it happening. They laughed at Marconi, they laughed at John Logie Baird. I say that sometime soon the laugh will be on Graham Smith, and I would implore his attendance at Falkirk Town Hall on Thursday June 30th when a major UFO conference will take place."

On the day of the big Falkirk UFO Conference, journalist John Smith mentioned our UFO Conference. Here is what he wrote:

'About 700 people with an interest in unidentified flying objects will watch a video at Falkirk Town Hall tonight of a strange cylindrical object hovering near a bungalow outside Larbert. No explanation of what it might be has come from the Ministry of Defence which has had the film of the incident since January. Yesterday, Neil Malcolm (28) talked about his close encounter. He said that he had been driving home from his aunt's house late in the evening when his car interior was suddenly illuminated by an intense light as he stopped at a junction on the edge of Larbert."

"I looked up and saw a cylinder-shaped thing. It was on my right-hand side all the way down the road. I got the impression that it was following me."

'Malcolm Robinson, a founder member of Strange Phenomena Investigations who has organised tonight's meeting, said the video is to be shown in a special programme on UFOs to be screened by London Weekend Television, which will also include footage of the meeting. Mr Robinson accused the MoD of dragging its heels and said that he had been pressing every few days for it to offer a possible explanation. Mr Robinson disclosed that in recent months he had had about 30 reports of unexplained, mainly disc shaped objects in the sky around Bonnybridge. Previously, from 1992 to the end of last year (1993), there had been more than 200 reports from the area, but they had tailed off for a time. Mr Robinson said that he accepted the sincerity of those making the reports.'

"I believe they are genuinely witnessing what they believe to be UFOs, but we must remember that 95% of UFO reports have natural identifiable solutions after research."

'He said that left five per cent without an explanation, making the Bonnybridge area particularly interesting because of the scale of the reports.'

UFO CONFERENCE A SELL OUT
(30th June 1994)

The UFO events in Bonnybridge and other outlying locations were gaining in momentum, and it was plain to see that the general public demanded an explanation; they wanted to know 'what was going on'. As we have learned, Billy Buchanan and I staged a successful conference in the Norwood Hotel in Bonnybridge back in 1993, but now it was time to go more public, and stage a further UFO conference the aims of which would be to explain, as best we could, all the information concerning UFO sightings in Stirlingshire that we had gained so far. It was also planned to bring along a top ufologist who would also discuss the UFO phenomenon in general, and also introduce UFO rock band, CE IV from Glasgow. Preparations were quickly underway for what would turn out to be Scotland's 'first' major UFO conference on the possibility of alien life and their visitations to planet Earth. We knew that the publicity had to be big for this one, and everyone from SPI helped to ensure that the public knew about it. The press, television, and radio were all notified and showed their interest in coming along.

The day duly arrived, Thursday the 30th of June 1994, and the venue was Falkirk Town Hall, a large commanding building which has hosted numerous other events; however, this was the first, but not the last time, it was to hold an event of this nature. Just under 800 people packed into the Town Hall with around 100 people (if not more) who were turned away at the door due to lack of any more seats. Prior to the event I recorded many interviews with numerous Scottish and English radio and newspaper reporters. I also did a piece to camera for Scottish Television (STV). They covered the event two days in a row! Most of the media were there en-masse, all anxious to learn what was going on. Fellow researcher and invited guest speaker, Philip Mantle who lived in the town of Batley in

England at that time, also saw his share of heavy media work, and no matter where you looked, one was more or less looking into the lens of a camera. T.V. crews, (some from various parts of the world!) had all turned up and were busily filming away. Actress Ghislaine Nichols was also in attendance, as was a noted Falkland war veteran. You know life is full of surprises especially in the UFO field, but it didn't come as much as a surprise when Councillor Billy Buchanan remarked that he had booked a large stretch limousine to take Philip Mantle, rock group CE IV and myself to the front door of the Falkirk Town Hall. When Councillor Buchanan told me that he had actually booked this limo I fell about laughing, *"They don't even get this in the States"* I thought to myself. And true to his word, a large 'gleaming' immaculate jet-black limo, arrived at the rear of Falkirk Town Hall.

With our eyes popping, Philip, CE IV and myself, all piled into the limo feeling a million dollars. Our driver was himself immaculately dressed, complete with black peaked hat. The plan was that he would drive ever so slowly from the rear of the Town Hall, round to the front of the Town Hall where it would look to the onlookers that we had come from some distance away. Of course, what they didn't know was that it had only been from 'around the back'! As we drove to the front of the Town Hall, we caught sight of the vast crowd that were making their way into the venue. A combination of 35mm cameras, T.V. cameras and radio microphones, all swung round to catch our arrival. The crowd then started to bend down and peer into the limo wondering who on Earth it could be. Surely this couldn't be the speakers arriving in style like this! Well, they must have got a disappointment when they saw me! We all stepped out onto the tarmac, each of us with their own thoughts on the matter. Me, well I was looking for some babies to kiss, isn't that what you do when you step out of a limo! It was pure fun however and was typical of Billy Buchanan who ensures that his guests get looked after properly, I'm sure that no one else would have gone to the lengths that Billy did over this limousine. And again, this shows how much a character he is, and someone who does not do things by half.

At 7:30pm the house lights went down, and the place was enveloped in darkness. Peels of synthesized keyboard thunder produced by Andy Morton of Glasgow rock group CE IV roared out of the large speakers at either side of the stage. This gradually decreased in volume and was replaced by the sound of crickets! A picture formed in my mind of a vast American plain of swaying wheat stalks being blown around by the wind under a starry night sky. Suddenly the sound of the crickets was instantly silenced by the sound of a large and descending UFO. The noise reached a crescendo, the curtains opened, dry ice poured out from the stage, a barrage of multi-coloured lights swung to and fro. Glasgow UFO rock band CE IV had arrived! What a way to start a conference. After two storming songs, Councillor Billy Buchanan took the stage and introduced myself where I lectured on UFO sightings throughout the years which I illustrated with slides and showed extracts from videos. Following me was Philip Mantle who spoke about some interesting English UFO cases. Phil's talk was then followed by a break in which a number of newspaper guys chased me for further quotes for the next day's newspapers. Would my tongue last the pace, I thought to myself? CE IV resumed the second half, and their special style of UFO music had the huge audience spellbound. Guitarist Brian McMullan spoke to the audience and said:

"For any of you old skywatching hippies out there, this song is for you, it's called Warminster Night."

Hippies there might have been, for this huge audience was made up from all age groups, young children, middle aged men and women, and old age pensioners, they were all out in force to hear about a subject which had captivated the Scottish press over the past 3 years. I followed on from CE IV with my second presentation which centred on Scottish Ufology, and in particular, the many UFO sightings which had been occurring in the Bonnybridge area. Sadly, due to time limitations and things over-running, I had to cut short my talk which was a great pity as I had so many cases to discuss but then again, one must try and keep to specific time schedules. Philip Mantle followed on from me and spoke about some British UFO Abduction cases. Philip is a good and accomplished speaker, and I'm sure that the audience went away with a different outlook on abductions than they had when they came in. Closing the conference was Glasgow rock group CE IV. Their stage show had been amazing with the lights and effects truly incredible. The drum work of young Brian McMullan (Jnr) had been flawless and full of intense energy. *"Good night Falkirk"* was the closing words of Brian McMullan (Snr), and was met by rapturous applause. Councillor Billy Buchanan then came onto the stage and thanked all those who had come along for making it a night to remember. All in all, Scotland's first 'major' UFO Conference had gone down a bomb and proved an education process to the people of Scotland who had been crying out for information as to what was going on. We were all pleased that it had been so successful.

TALK ABOUT BEING MIS-QUOTED!

I'd like to inform the reader on how easily it is to get misquoted in the press. As I've stated, there was a huge presence from the media there that day at the Falkirk Town Hall, all pushing for a story, and over the next few days, some silly press stories relating to this event were featured in different newspapers, all taken out of context from what I was trying to say. And although technically they were 'near' the mark, it was not quite what I meant. The Dundee Courier stated, **'Alien Ancestors, The Latest Claim',** followed by the Daily Record on the 1st of July who stated, **'Alien Life'** and the Sun in true journalistic form, **'Grandad's An Alien'.** What all these stories were referring to was my lecture at the Falkirk Town Hall when I was at one point discussing the possibility that mankind may have been seeded by 'beings' from outer space, and that we, humankind, are but an 'alien experiment', hence the reasons why we are receiving visits from the sky, not of extraterrestrial 'beings' as such, but from (possibly) our own 'forefathers'. I did say to the huge audience that this was just pure speculation on my part, but that numerous other ufologists world-wide did think that it was a possibility. The press however saw that statement differently. But to be fair, all three newspapers mentioned above, may have 'jazzed' up the story a little to make it a more exciting copy. The UFO sightings did not appear to be diminishing through 1994 indeed if people were being honest (!) they appeared to be on the increase.

One lady, a Mrs Terry Harrington from Grangemouth, visited the author with a friend to show me some photographs that she had taken which claimed to show UFOs in the sky. They were taken through her living room window and showed red light sources in the sky. Terry claimed that one object actually rushed towards her window. Her home faces onto dry wasteland. Now although the photographs were not spectacular, it was plain to see how deeply effected she was by this experience. Terry was quoted in the Falkirk Advertiser newspaper of 28th December 1994 as saying:

"I'd just come back from holiday and my camera was sitting on the table, so I just grabbed it and began taking pictures. I thought that it was going to come right through the window, and I was afraid that the flashing of the camera was attracting it towards me. If it had been an aircraft of some sort, there would have been some noise."

The newspaper went on to inform its readers that Terry had back up witnesses in the form of her friend Mary McMahon and her son Jim Gallacher. The object initially hovered from side to side and grew bigger. The most interesting thing about this sighting, however, was the fact that the larger object emitted smaller objects, which were similar to shuttle like craft, which then headed back into the larger object. Eventually, this light/object just zoomed away and was gone.

In early August 1994, a Mrs May Macleod of Falkirk observed a strange object in the sky which was flying low over Falkirk. Her sighting was featured in her local newspaper, the 'Falkirk Herald', this in turn brought forward a further six witnesses who also viewed this object.

Firstly, on the night of August the 8th 1994, 69-year-old Mary Higgins of Westquarter (near Falkirk) was sitting in her back garden with a neighbour, Kathleen Swanston (31) and her son Andrew Swanston (6), the time was around 9:00pm. Suddenly their attention was captivated by a strange silver cigar shaped object which was sharply defined and stood out well in the clear night sky. No noise could be heard coming from this object and the three puzzled witnesses stood and stared as it slowly made its way across the sky. In a telephone conversation with the author, Mary stated that this object definitely had no wings or tail fin. She further stated that she had seen the Northern Lights and Hayley's Comet, but this was nothing like either of those. Kathleen Swanston, Mary's neighbour, was quoted in the Falkirk Herald dated August 25th, 1994, as saying:

"It was a bit like the Good Year Airship that you see on T.V., only it had no lights and no windows. It was really low in the sky, but I couldn't hear and sound coming from it. I'm normally the sceptical one. If anyone had said to me that they had seen a flying saucer I'd have asked them what they had been on. But I definitely saw something, and I haven't got a clue what it was."

That same night, pensioners William Bestall (72) and his wife Mabel (68) who live in a flat on the 7th floor of a block of flats, witnessed a strange 'Catherine wheel type object' revolving in the sky. This was roughly 30 minutes after the Higgins and Swanston sighting. Initially the Bestalls' thought that this was just a bright star or planet but what changed that view was when the object which had been rotating in different directions and had its centre core lit up, shot off in a southerly direction at a speed described by William Bestall as, *"beyond calculation"!* William was quoted as saying the following in the 'Falkirk Herald' dated 18th August 1994:

"It was very clear. I saw it for about 20 minutes before it disappeared. It was going faster than any aeroplane. On a few occasions it remained static, surrounded by a brilliant glow. The outer lights would then fade, leaving a brilliant light in the middle. I didn't report it to any authorities because you always feel a bit daft."

It was only because he had started to read some UFO reports in the local newspaper that he decided to come forward with his own sighting. The article goes on to say that a number of friends of the Bestalls had also seen this mystery light, but they had kept quiet about it till now. Both William and Mabel have witnessed similar objects in the sky, and when I visited them, the view from their 7th floor balcony is absolutely breathtaking, it really is. Most of the Forth valley can be seen spread out in all directions. I felt like moving in with the Bestalls when I saw how impressive their viewing vantage point was.

On the 14th of September 1994, John Morrison (47) from Grangemouth near Falkirk, was out walking with his wife in the afternoon when they both observed a strange grey 'ring' in the sky which he states was 'not' the result of smoke or a cloud. It did not move or change shape during the ten-minute period that both of them stood and watched it for. After a couple of more minutes, both witnesses lost interest in this and decided to continue with their walk. In late September I received a telephone call from Councillor Buchanan who informed me that a 'whole street' in Falkirk had been out watching a strange object in the night sky. He gave me a contact number for a Jane Shaw and speaking with her, she told me that she and some other residents in her street, had witnessed a strange 'diamond shaped light'. Surprisingly, when I contacted the local police about this, they informed me that no one had telephoned their station with any similar reports (apart from Jane herself). Jane was quoted in the local 'Falkirk Advertiser' (the sister paper to the 'Falkirk Herald').

GIVE US MAJOR PROBE ON UFOS

This was the headline from the 'Scottish Sun' newspaper dated October 6th, 1994. It stated that Councillor Billy Buchanan had written to Prime Minister John Major at 10 Downing Street in the hope that a serious study would be carried out into the UFO sightings above Bonnybridge. He was quoted as saying:

"The local people and the village have suffered cruelly from ridicule, yet the sightings are continuing, and people have the courage to come forward."

As we shall see, both Billy and I were not quite finished with the British Government.

UFO MYSTERY IN THE FALKIRK TRIANGLE

This was the headline in the Scottish Sunday Post Newspaper which many Scots woke up to on Sunday the 30th of October 1994. The story related to seven witnesses who observed UFOs flying over the Falkirk area. On Friday the 28th of October, three cleaners at the Union Chemical Factory in Carronshore (near Falkirk) saw 5 UFOs as they headed to work. As this is quite an impressive case, I would like to quote the Sunday Post article in its entirety. Cleaner Beatrice Campbell from Carronshore stated:

"We first noticed them at 05:40am. There was one large object which had a light orange glow. The four smaller ones sparkled on and off like stars. To begin with, all were stationary. Then the large object began sending beams of light to the smaller ones. Then one of the small ones moved off towards Falkirk. At that point my flesh started crawling."

The ladies went into the factory to start their shift and told lab manager Bill Downie what they had seen. He had them draw a diagram and make a written statement of their sighting. When word of their experience spread, several more employees approached Mr Downie with similar stories. Diane Keating from Camelon, a packer at the factory, also made a written statement about what she saw. She said:

"On Wednesday evening at around 7:00pm, I was looking out of a window at home when I saw an object in the sky. It looked reddish in colour, shaped like a ball, surrounded by a heat haze. It hovered for about 10 minutes, then disappeared from view for two minutes, then came back. At first, I thought it

was a plane, but it couldn't have been as I saw a plane fly under it."

At the same time on Wednesday, factory workers Steve Leishman and Kevin Carmichael were walking to Steve's house in nearby Stenhousemuir. Mr Leishman said:

"We first saw an object which looked as if it was above the Denny Stirling area. It had a bright white colour and it moved away in the direction of Callander then came back and began to glow red orange. It was going really fast. We saw a passenger plane with its landing lights on underneath it. The object was much faster than the plane."

Central Scotland Police, RAF Pitreavie, and the Scottish Air Traffic Control Centre at Prestwick Airport, said that they hadn't received any reports of the sightings. Mark Macauley of the Royal Observatory in Edinburgh commented:

"From what you have described the sightings don't correspond to astronomical objects like meteors, planets, or communication satellites."

UFOs RETURN

This was the title of a piece making front page of the 'Falkirk Advertiser' dated Wednesday September 28th, 1994. It tells of dozens of local people who reported watching a diamond-shaped light in the sky. Councillor Billy Buchanan was quoted as saying:

"My phone was buzzing on Thursday night between 9:30pm and 11:00pm. People spoke of a bright, diamond shaped light whirling about in the sky. And some people were concerned enough to telephone the police."

The newspaper went on to say that one local woman by the name of Jane Shaw (24) of Falkirk stated that it was her boyfriend Douglas Hay (20) who spotted the strange light first. Jane stated:

"He called on me to have a look, and I couldn't believe my eyes. I've never believed in UFOs, but now I'm having to think again. There was just no logical explanation for what we saw."

Some neighbours of the couple were also reported to have rushed out and also viewed this strange spectacle.

CLASH OF THE UFOLOGISTS

It was back in October 1994 that I received a telephone call from Scottish Radio station, Radio Clyde. They asked me for information to assist them with the making of a radio show that they were planning, *"Fine, only too glad to help"* said I. Little did I know it then that the guests lined up for the show included arch UFO 'debunker' Steuart Campbell, and 'Scottish Earth Mystery Research' chairman, Ron Halliday. In a following call from Radio Clyde researcher Katie Topping, I was then informed who would be on the show, I was only being contacted to provide them with information, (being used again I thought to myself!) Anyway, fair enough, who was I to dictate to others? When I informed Glasgow rock group CE IV member Brian McMullan (Snr) about the situation and who would be on the show, he just could not believe it. Brian stated,

"Malc. You're the guy that's personally dealt with the ongoing UFO situation in Central Scotland, the man with his finger on the UFO issue, yet Radio Clyde don't want you on the show! I can't believe it." *"Brian"* I replied, *"It's no problem, these things happen, that's the way it is."* *"Over my dead body"* replied Brian, *"I'm phoning up Radio Clyde right now to complain and state the fact that if anyone should be talking about UFOs, then it should be Malcolm Robinson."*

And with that Brian completed his call to me. The following day, I received another telephone call from Radio Clyde's Katie Topping, she informed me that they had had a re-think, and that on reflection, they would like me on their show, (not a hint of what Brian McMullan had said to her). So, the clash of Scotland's three main ufologists was set for pre-recording in late October. Would Radio Clyde provide the suits of armour I thought to myself, or would it be handbags and bandages at 30 paces? I expected a most heated discussion on Scottish ufology, and boy was I looking forward to it. The day arrived and I met up with Ron Halliday and Steuart Campbell at the Radio Clyde building in Clydebank just outside of Glasgow. We were taken to a studio, sat down, and were briefed by presenter Colin Adams. Colin said:

"Look chaps, don't stand on ceremony, if you have something to say then 'say it' don't be afraid, this is a free for all. I've been informed that you all have differing opinions on the subject of UFOs which I'm sure will make for great debate, so 'go for it'".

A big smile came across my face as I looked directly at Ron and Steuart. I rubbed my hands and sat firm in my chair awaiting the bell. Before the discussion got underway, presenter Colin Adams ran an audio tape of interviews that Radio Clyde had done with people from Bonnybridge, they call it a 'Vox Pop' I believe. I also heard Councillor Billy Buchanan on tape and his presentation and style did not disappoint. With that over, the presenter turned first to Steuart Campbell and said:

"Steuart, you believe according to your new book, 'The UFO Mystery Solved', that UFOs are more myth than mystery". Steuart replied. *"The evidence does not support the claim that they are here."*

Steuart went on to demolish the idea that UFOs are alien spaceships, and that there can be no truth in alien entity reports. He continued by saying that we must accept the possibility that superior alien races (if they are such), may be well in advance of planet Earth. He continued by saying that no alien visitor could possibly reach Earth. I quickly replied that we must accept the possibility that superior alien races (if they are such!)

may well be in advance of Planet Earth with their technology, and as such, would not find it a problem to reach Planet Earth. Steuart replied that a space craft could never travel at the speed of light. *"Fine"* I said, *"But how do you know? This may well be within the bounds of reality someday, 'never say never'!* It would be so very wrong to think that our technology is superior to any alien technology. For as we know, stars and planets are being born every day, those strange visitors to the skies of our world, may be so well in advance to mankind, that we might appear to them as but small insects under a stone. Insignificant, and only worthy of a fleeting occasional acquaintance! The discussion then turned around to Bonnybridge and the huge amount of UFO sightings that had been reported there. Steuart claimed that the people of Bonnybridge were 'UFO Believers', and as such, that is why Bonnybridge has hit the headlines. I quickly responded to that outrageous statement but was cut off as the presenter brought in Ron Halliday. Ron accepted that there was indeed something unusual going on over Bonnybridge. His only gripe was to the actual number of UFO reports, which is fair enough. I've always said that there must be many 'more' witnesses who have seen something strange in the skies, but are frightened to come forward and report it, purely because the fear that they might be ridiculed.

The debate then moved on to discuss what the Governments of the world know about UFOs. Some Governments were more open about UFOs, whilst others were not. The presenter then asked me if there was one case out of all the cases that I have researched which I personally felt as being alien in nature? I replied that the A70 Abduction case had taken me off the proverbial 'sceptical fence' and placed me slap bang into the 'believers' camp. Prior to the A70 case, I was undecided as to where the answer lay in regard to solving the UFO mystery. Was it all atmospheric, hallucinations perhaps, or secret military aircraft. The A70 case had changed my perception of reality, and I now knew deep down, that the answer truly was Extraterrestrial. Steuart then broke in and said that he felt there was a natural explanation to account for the A70 case, perhaps a mirage of Saturn, although he would need to study the details of the case more closely to reach that opinion.

The conversation then swung round to the theories contained in Steuart's book, that mirages can account for a great deal of UFO sightings. Here Ron Halliday butted in and voiced his utter dismay at Steuart's way of thinking on this issue, (of which I had to agree with.) However, that said, Steuart Campbell's theories, or at least some of them, can and I am sure do, account for a small percent of UFO reports. We then moved onto discuss Gulf Breeze in America which has seen quite a large number of UFO accounts. This was in regard to a question posed by the presenter who asked, *"Why is it not the case that hundreds of people together have not sighted a UFO that they appear only to singular witnesses."* I quickly replied, *"Not so."* First of all, there was a crowd of around 40,000 people at a football match in Mexico who all looked up into the sky and observed a circular flying saucer. As for the sightings over at Gulf Breeze in Pensacola in Florida, many crowds of people have witnessed strange objects in the sky. *"The gulf Breeze sightings were started by a hoax"*, interjected Steuart, *"You know full well they were."* There has been some debate in regard to photographer and witness Ed Walters's UFO photographs. That said there have been other independent witnesses plus similar photographs to Ed's which have been taken by others which would confirm Ed's testimony. Steuart stated that he wouldn't accept Ed's testimony. The conversation then developed into, 'if there are aliens visiting us, what do they want, and would they work to the same methods that we humans would do?' The debate got quite heated at this point, and I am sure that the temperature in the room increased by a few degrees. We then moved onto the abduction issue. Steuart expressed his concern with the hypnosis which was widely used by researchers worldwide to provide some form of answer. I must admit, I too expressed these same concerns, however having said that, I still feel that hypnosis is a tool which should be used to probe the UFO mystery to see if it unlocks any secrets, but I did agree that it had its pitfalls.

Ron Halliday then expressed his dislike of Steuart Campbell's theory to explain Scotland's famous Dechmont

Woods UFO event of 1979. Steuart initially felt that what witness Bob Taylor encountered was a rare form of black ball lightning, he revised this view some years later, now thinking that what Bob experienced that fateful morning, was in point of fact, a mirage of the Planet Venus, which subsequently induced on Bob, an epileptic fit. Steuart still sticks by his revised explanation. Steuart was then asked by presenter Colin Adams if there were any cases that he couldn't explain with his theories, cases which had left him 'speechless'. Steuart replied, *"Not speechless, there are cases in which I haven't had enough information."* I then interrupted, that not only did Steuart's current book, 'The UFO Mystery Solved,' (Explicit Books 1994) disprove a lot of ufology's better cases, but his previous book to that, 'The Loch Ness Monster, The Evidence' (The Aquarian Press 1986), also dismissed "Nessie" as a living creature. I went on, *"Steuart, do you believe in anything!"* To which he replied, *"I'll admit to being a Professional sceptic!"* The presenter then asked each one of us to sum up our own feelings on the UFO mystery. What did we think? My thoughts to the listening audience, were that I for one, was glad that there are people like Steuart Campbell who made Investigators like Ron Halliday and I, sit up and take notice of alternative explanations, and as ufologists, we simply must 'keep asking questions.' Ron's closing comments were that at the moment we haven't an answer to the UFO enigma, but in his view various strange things were going on. The discussion then extended at this point into the radar detection of UFOs in which Steuart expressed his concern with radar operators not knowing their sets, and that many distortion effects can be picked up on radar, (which I too accept, but not in all cases!). At this point presenter Colin Adams said:

"Gentlemen, a fascinating subject of which we could discuss all night, but I'm afraid time has beaten us."

It had been an entertaining debate, and one that I had enjoyed taking part in. I was heavily impressed by Ron Halliday's comments, and at one part of the show, I actually patted him on the back. Although heated at times, the debate never really got anywhere. Nobody's opinions were changed, and we all went home with the same views that we had arrived with. Still, it had been a worthwhile discussion, not just for me, but for Joe Public too I expect.

STRANGE BUT TRUE?

When I first became involved in the subject of UFOs, there was very little in the way of good television coverage of this subject. I remember watching one or two documentaries, but they were too one sided, coming down heavily on all UFO sightings as having natural explanations. I used to watch the television series, Arthur C. Clarke's 'Mysterious World', and I awaited each episode with anticipation sometimes even audio recording them, (this was before the commercial use of the now common household video recorder). Indeed, I still have one or two episodes on audio tape recorded from those early days. I suppose it wasn't until the late 1980s and early 1990s, that a change in public attitude towards UFOs and the paranormal became to be noticed, more so in the T.V. coverage of such subjects. Television presenter Michael Aspel known for his Television show, 'This Is Your Life', which concerns a look back at people who are well known in the media field, be it a television star, sports star, or entertainer, was later to front a show called 'Strange But True?' This dealt with different aspects of the paranormal, from stories of ghosts to stories of amazing UFO sightings. Bonnybridge did not go unnoticed to the researchers of this show, and I received a phone call from a researcher at London 'Weekend Television' who asked me to assist them in the make up of their show, which would look into the UFO sightings over Bonnybridge. I supplied them with numerous people to talk to and locations for filming and recorded a small piece about what I felt was going on. As this was only going to be a 15-minute segment, (Strange But True? Consists of two stories which are just under 15 minutes in length), it really wasn't going to do the subject much credit, that said, what we had to do, was to impress upon the public on how serious a subject this was in Scotland, and how sincere those witnesses were that had come forward with their own sightings.

Fifteen minutes or not, we had to 'get it right.' Once complete, the show was aired over national television on the 4th of November 1994 and was immediately hailed a success by Scottish ufologists. SPI also assisted LWTV in 1997 for a follow up programme on what was happening in Central Scotland, again this was received well. We must thank the producers of shows like 'Strange But True?' for giving the ordinary man and woman in the street, an opportunity to tell it as it is. For far too long, these people have been ridiculed. The change is that people now 'know' that something strange is going on in the skies, and thanks to companies like London 'Weekend Television' and others, we can now begin to show members of the public that once you brush away the nonsensical and misidentifications, one is left looking at a very real and tangible phenomenon. Incidentally, the Bonnybridge UFO sightings were featured in the London 'Weekend Television' book, 'Strange But True?' written by Jenny Randles and Peter Hough. On page 115 can be found the title, 'The Bonnybridge UFO window' and features some cases from the Bonnybridge area, and elsewhere in Scotland. This book, I believe, was the first time in 'book form' that the Bonnybridge UFOs were mentioned. (Unless you know different!)

CALLS FOR A GOVERNMENT ENQUIRY ON THE BONNYBRIDGE UFO PHENOMENON

1994 was the year when Councillor Billy Buchanan and I decided that we simply had to get a Government body into addressing the ongoing Bonnybridge UFO situation, and although much research had been undertaken in trying to find some answers, it was plain to see that those answers were not forthcoming, and that no matter how much research was undertaken, the elusive UFOs were not going to give up their identities so easily. Of course, I had already speculated that what 'might' be occurring in the skies of Central Scotland 'could' be due to the testing of new and secret military aircraft, and if so, we, the public, had the right to know about it. Councillor Billy Buchanan decided to write a letter to the then Prime Minister of Great Britain, John Major, and explain to him about what had been going on, and that he felt that the British Government should become involved with the research into these sightings and assist the likes of SPI and others who were trying to unravel the secrets of what was happening. Billy received a reply dated 27th October 1994 from Miss K. Philpott of the Ministry of Defence. Sadly, we were again treated to the same tired old MoD statement, which stated that as these objects did not constitute a threat to the defence of the United Kingdom, then the British Government deemed it unnecessary to become involved. It goes without saying that this statement was not received too well by both Billy and I, and certain newspapers when they heard about this, cried 'cover up.' I then took it upon myself to write to the MoD with the same request, but was met with the same statement, (they must have a drawer full of them!). SPI member Christine Cameron from Falkirk wrote to John Major the following year asking that he at least consider sending some authoritative body to Scotland and look at the evidence that we had collated so far. Christine received a reply from 10 Downing Street, from a Mrs F. Khan, correspondence secretary, but essentially this was just a letter thanking her for her enquiry. We were not to be outdone, and both Billy and I continued to raise our concern with the media about the British government 'dragging its heels' over this important issue, and at every twist and turn, we ensured that the press knew our feelings about the disinterest from a Government who stated that UFOs in Scotland were of 'No defence significance.' We had low level, close proximity UFO sightings, sightings of objects above cars, above roof tops, above fields which were clearly not conventional, our checks with Airports and flying clubs proved that. Now admittedly these objects may not have interacted with those individuals who saw them, but nonetheless, they were flying in restricted airspace without permission and scaring the living daylights out of witnesses. Now if that is not a threat, then I don't know what is!

Billy and I both knew that we were hitting our heads against a brick wall as far as trying to get the Conservative Government to look into these UFO sightings. When the Labour Government swooped into power during 1997, I wrote a letter of congratulations to Tony Blair, for being elected the new Prime Minister, but also in that letter, was a request that his Government, this new Labour Government, should try and get a British Freedom of Information Act passed which would clearly help not only ufologists in their quest to get at the truth, but also other individuals in regards to other quests as well. American ufologists have had their own Freedom of Information act for a number of years now. This has clearly shown to them, that the C.I.A. the F.B.I. and the N.S.A. have all been actively involved with the UFO subject in some way shape or manner. Thankfully as the years rolled on, the British Ministry of Defence began to slowly 'drip feed' UFO files to the public, (all through their web site). Former English resident Nicholas Redfern now living in the United States, managed to prove that the British Government were indeed actively involved in the collection of UFO reports way back in the 1940s, (and indeed still are!) His book, *A Covert Agenda, (Simon & Shuster 1997),* is a wealth of information to this fact. It certainly lifts the lid on the conspiracy by the British Government to deceive its people who have a right to know about these things. I finally received a letter from 10 Downing Street, from a new 'correspondent secretary', a Mr S. Qasim who informed me that, and I quote:

"Dear Mr Robinson, The Prime Minster has asked me to thank you for your recent letter. Mr Blair hopes you will understand that, as the matter you raise is the responsibility of the Ministry of Defence, he has asked that your letter be forwarded to that Department so that they may reply to you direct on his behalf." Yours Sincerely, Mr S. Qasim.

DENNIS CANAVAN M.P.

Here we go again, back to square one. This paper chase was leading us nowhere and I should have put money on the response that I would get from the MoD. It came, and you've guessed it. It stated, *(well you know the rest don't you!).* All this did not put me off, and both Billy and my next step, was to write to elected M.P. Dennis Canavan (53) Like Billy, Dennis was elected to serve the people, would he act on such a request as UFOs? Well, we would never find out sitting doing nothing. Billy wrote to him, as did I. However, in my letter to Dennis dated 11th May 1997, I enclosed 343 British signatures, and 90 French signatures. This was to go alongside a petition that I also enclosed to Dennis which read:

PETITION

'To the Right Honourable Dennis Canavan, M.P.

The petition of a number of residents of the town of Bonnybridge in the county of Stirlingshire and elsewhere, declares that there are a number of sightings of aircraft or unexplained objects in the sky in or around the said town and elsewhere. The petitioners therefore request that the Right Honourable Dennis Canavan M.P. table formal, written Parliamentary questions as requested by Mr Malcolm Robinson of *(Address hidden)* Clackmannanshire, Scotland, and others, to make enquiries with respect to the full relevance of the Unidentified Flying Object phenomena here in the UK.

And the Petitioners remain,'
Malcolm Robinson, (etc).

Councillor Billy Buchanan received a letter back from Dennis Canavan who enclosed a letter that he (Dennis Canavan) received from The Earl Howe. Earl Howe stated in his letter to Dennis, more or less the same statements that the MoD have been saying for years. However, there was a little bit of light at the end of the tunnel, for Earl Howe stated, and I quote:

"If Councillor Buchanan has information to support his concerns that Falkirk and Bonnybridge are experiencing phenomena of defence significance, then my officials would be happy to examine this further. In the absence of such evidence, we remain satisfied that there are no phenomena in the Falkirk area which 'are' of defence concern. I hope this explains the position."
The Earl Howe.

Dennis Canavan also copied this reply and sent it to me. And although the MoD were stating that UFOs do not pose any threat, they were asking to see more evidence which would suggest that there 'might be' such a threat. Would witness testimony suffice as evidence? Witness testimony is at least listened to in a court of law, and decisions are made as to the right or wrongs of what is heard. I would say that the testimony alone would be sufficient to convince any jury. Then of course we have 'some' video evidence and 'some' photographic evidence to back the witnesses up. As yet, no one is prepared to come to Scotland and view this evidence. We can only hope that one day they will change their minds and decide to look into what we've got. That this can happen is possible, hence the continued pressure that Councillor Buchanan and I are exerting on M.P.s such as Dennis Canavan. This pressure did prove helpful, as Dennis Canavan the Labour M.P. for Falkirk West at the time, did write to the Ministry of Defence asking for an official to meet with him and his concerned constituents. The request was turned down. Whitehall stated that there was no threat to National Security. In the Daily Express newspaper of August 15th, 1995, he was quoted as saying:

"I am keeping an open mind about the issue."

Whilst the MoD stated.

"We don't have a remit to investigate or defend Britain against UFOs."

We are not alone in this quest. Prior to the MoD releasing what files, they claimed they had of UFOs over British skies, English researcher John Holman had for a number of years put pressure on the British Government in trying to get them to open up their files on UFO sightings in the UK. He has even staged demonstrations with other like-minded individuals outside the House of Lords where leaflets explaining their cause were given over to Ministers and other officials as they entered the building. This was a wonderful move on John's part to try and make cabinet Ministers wake up to the reality of what is going on. Another campaigner to get to the truth back in the 1990s was Welshman Dr Colin Ridyard. Colin, like John Holman, worked tirelessly to get an enquiry into UFO sightings in this country and also to try and get the Government to 'come clean' on what they know. Colin received a letter addressed from Lord Henley to Dennis Canavan dated the 1st of February 1995. Lord Henley was explaining to Dennis much the same as what has been stated before, ie, *'Of No Defence Significance.'* Part of Lord Henley's letter to Dennis Canavan read as follows:

"I do not believe that a meeting with Councillor Buchanan and Mr Robinson would serve any useful purpose. Should Councillor Buchanan wish to submit any further information, my officials will of course assess this in the normal way."

Colin Ridyard stated in a letter to the author, that he was appalled at the 'criminal dereliction of duty displayed by Lord Henley, even a handful of sightings is a handful that requires serious scientific study'. I couldn't agree more. Colin went on to say that he is coordinating his efforts with several of his associates from the group, Global UFO Investigation Systems, and that consequently a number of M.P.s would shortly be called upon to table Parliamentary questions. Those M.P.s were, Gareth Wardell, Alfred Morris, Sir Alan Hazelhurst, Barry Field, and Richard Aitken. Colin had prepared a document of which contained a number of questions which he hoped the various M.P.s would ask in the House of Commons, as for the Scottish UFO situation, his document read as follows:

QUESTIONS TO BE RAISED IN THE HOUSE OF COMMONS

To ask the Secretary of State for the Home Department (i) How many reports of unidentified craft have police forces dealt with in Stirlingshire on a year by year basis over the last five years, (ii) how many of these incidents were witnessed by police officers and (iii) were any of these incidents recorded (A) on camera or (B) as video footage and (iv) if recorded, are they available for public scrutiny, and if he will make a statement.

To ask the Secretary of State for Education and Employment if he will indicate (I) how much film footage of unidentified craft seen in the skies over Stirlingshire and especially Bonnybridge has been analysed at (A) Glasgow University, (B) Stirling University, (ii) how many other Universities have been involved in this type of research, (iii) what academic conclusions have been drawn, and (iv) will more funds be allocated for academic research into (A) anomalous aerial phenomena and (B) extraterrestrial phenomena, and if he will make a statement.

To ask the Secretary of State for the Home Department, (i) does his Department acknowledge that the airspace above and around Stirlingshire has been penetrated on several occasions by unidentified craft whose flight and manoeuvrability far exceed current advanced state of the art aircraft design and if he will make a statement and (ii) will he make it his policy to improve and expand the Civil Defence capability in Stirlingshire to make allowances for more detailed reporting of unidentified craft, and if he will make a statement. (iii) does his department hold any records of near misses and/or sightings of unidentified craft in the airspace above and around Stirlingshire by civilian airliners, and if he will make a statement.

To ask the Secretaries of State for Transport, Defence, and the Home Department if they will acknowledge that details of the unprecedented numbers of sightings of unidentified craft in and around Stirlingshire and especially Bonnybridge, are in the public interest and in this spirit, organise a joint televised press conference where their representatives can make public all the aspects associated with these incidents and include in this press conference such details as, (i) shapes, flight patterns, colours and sizes of the unidentified craft, (ii) where and when the craft were seen, (iii) what action their respective Departments took, (iv) the radar profiles Of the craft and, (v) all film relating to these incidents, and if they will make a joint statement.

To ask the Secretary of State for the Home Department (I) how many reports of missing persons were received by his department over the last (A) year, (B) five years, (C) ten years, (D) twenty five years, (ii) how many of these remain unsolved, (iii) how do records in and around Stirlingshire compared to the rest of the UK and if he will make a statement.

To ask the Secretary of State for Defence to explain why his Department feels it unnecessary to adopt a policy referred to in his answer of 18th December (274H) on the reporting of unidentified craft and releasing to the press details of (I) shape, flight pattern, colour and size of the craft, (ii) where and when the craft was seen, (iii) what action his Department took, and (iv) the radar profile of the craft when such details are clearly in the public interest and his Department consistently take the view that such incidents are of no defence significance, and if he will make a statement.

To ask the Secretary of State for Foreign and Commonwealth Affairs, have any foreign Governments expressed an interest in the details of sightings reported in Stirlingshire and especially Bonnybridge, and if so, will he indicate (I) which Government, (ii) for what reason, and (iii) will cooperation with such Governments be forthcoming, and if so, will he make a statement.

To ask the Prime Minister will he arrange a full scientific study of the unprecedented numbers of unidentified craft being seen in the airspace above Stirlingshire.

As yet, these vastly important questions have not been raised in the House of Commons, I can only hope, as I've said before, that these questions will be heard, and given a fair hearing, and that some progress can be made whereby the Government will open up and assist researchers not only here in Scotland, but elsewhere as well.

As I am updating the Bonnybridge UFO story, and since I wrote about some of the above in my first book, 'UFO Case Files of Scotland' (Volume 1) further official requests were made to members of Parliament. For instance, Councillor Billy Buchanan wrote to Donald Dewar MSP on the 7th of January 2000, requesting that he view our UFO files and footage. Here is Billy's letter to Donald Dewar in its entirety:

Donald Dewar
Scottish Parliament
Edinburgh.

7th January 2000

Dear Sir,

I wrote to you some months ago regarding the UFO phenomenon that has been going in now unabated since 1992 in Bonnybridge. This phenomenon has been going on for a long time and despite the media ridicule over the years, we in Bonnybridge have gained not notoriety but credibility.

I asked you as First Minister of Scotland, the man who speaks for our nation, to give me the opportunity to come to the Scottish Parliament and give MSP's a presentation with video footage, witness testimonies to show you all that this is for real, and we demand an investigation.

I appreciate how busy you are, but this is something of National Importance, and yet you have not even acknowledged receipt of my letter. I have also recently taken video footage myself that clearly shows UFOs are fact not fiction. I also have a tape, which gives credibility to the whole phenomenon. But I wanted you, at the Scottish Parliament, to listen to the evidence before I go to the media. I ask you again Mr Dewar, give me the opportunity to prove conclusively that we have a phenomenon here that requires a major investigation. This is unless you already know Mr Dewar. Hopefully the opportunity to present the case for the sake of our nation and of our people.
Yours Faithfully,
Councillor Billy Buchanan.

The above fell on deaf ears. Over the years both Billy and I have constantly hounded the British Government and the MoD to open up a Government enquiry into the UFO sightings over Stirlingshire. In May 2010, I wrote a personal letter to then Prime Minister, David Cameron asking for a Government enquiry. Here is the letter I received.

10 Downing Street
London SW1A 2AA
www.number10.gov.uk
From the Direct Communications Unit.
26th May 2010

Dear Mr Robinson,

I am writing on behalf of the Prime Minister to thank you for your letter of 14th May. Mr Cameron is most grateful for the time and trouble you have taken to get in touch. I have been asked to forward your letter to the Ministry of Defence, so that they too are aware of your views. Thank you, once again, for writing.
Yours Sincerely
Mr G. Edwards.

Well, I know that the Prime Minister is busy, but one would have thought that he would have taken the trouble to at least drop me a line himself. Yes, I know, I'm asking too much! A month later (June 2010) I received a letter from the Royal Air Force. I believe this letter is a result of my letter to the Prime Minister, which was forwarded to them. Here is what it said:

ROYAL AIR FORCE
Vicky Reeds
HEADQUARTERS AIR COMMAND
RAF Business Secretariat 8
Spitfire Block
Royal Air Force.
Our Ref: AirCmdSec/BusSec/Parl/TOC/2010

10th June 2010

Dear Mr Robinson,

Thank you for your letter of 14th May 2010 asking whether the Government will release its UFO files into the public domain. I have been asked to reply.

Since May 2008 the Ministry of Defence has had an established file release programme in place for those UFO files held by the Directorate Air Staff and Defence Intelligence Staff. As part of the programme, files are released to the National Archives (TNA) and redacted copies are made available to view on the TNA website. Those redactions made are in line with the Freedom of Information ACT 1998. It is anticipated that the release of files will be completed by the end of this year.

Those files that have already been released can be accessed at the following link:
http://www.nationalarchives.gov.uk/ufos/
I hope this information is useful.
Yours Sincerely,
Reeds.

So, there I had it, the Ministry of Defence, were releasing files. It was there in black and white. It was a start, all due no doubt, to the many UFO campaigners demanding that they follow the example of the American Defence which released many files before them. Now, this was all well and good, but Councillor Billy Buchanan and I still felt that we wanted the British Government to come to Scotland and view our files, and for them to conduct a full scale investigation of the many UFO reports coming from Bonnybridge. With this in mind, Councillor Billy Buchanan put his fingers to the keyboard and typed the following letter in July 2010 to the newly elected British Prime Minister, John Major. Here is that letter:

Prime Minister David Cameron.
Dear Prime Minister,
We as a nation are well aware of the burden of responsibility that rests on your shoulders and the decisions that have to be taken. The continuous deaths of our soldiers in

Afghanistan weighs heavy in all our minds, and to this end this should be your number one priority.

The Global financial crisis and the measures your Government have to take to try and stabilise Britain's economy shows clearly how difficult life is going to be for us all. It therefore might seem that what I am going to say is meaningless in light of these problems. I have outlined the concerns, but the issue I ask you to clarify is of national importance.

During your election campaign at a forum in Tynemouth north of Tyneside, you were open and frank during discussions on UFOs and alien life, and you were convinced that aliens have been here. You agreed that the British people had a right to know and if you became Prime Minister, you would life the veil of secrecy and give the people you represent, the truth, that is all we ask, the truth. Are you now going to honour this commitment, the people of my area, Bonnybridge, have, as I have, been ridiculed for years because of this phenomenon.

Prime Minister, I urge you to end the secrecy and let us know the truth.

Yours Faithfully,
Councillor WF Buchanan.

However, Billy was not finished with the Prime Minister. Billy asked that I should accompany him down to 10 Downing Street and hand over a petition which contained hundreds of signatures from his constituents asking for this Government enquiry into the UFO sightings across Bonnybridge and the Stirlingshire skies. Prior to that visit. Billy released a Press Statement to the media which stated as follows:

DAVID CAMERON CALLED TO ACCOUNT

Bonnybridge Councillor Billy Buchanan is once again heading for number 10 Downing Street on Monday where he will be handing in a demand letter to the Prime Minister to lift the veil of secrecy on the UFO/alien conspiracy. I have been down to London to successive Prime Ministers since 1992 to get some answers, but with no success.

The Scottish Parliament was also a major disappointment, with no action or advice except to continue contacting the MoD. But this time we have a man who promised the nation the truth if elected. Now is his chance – the people of Bonnybridge and the nation deserve it. So, let's see if Mr Cameron will deliver. Joining Billy will be Malcolm Robinson, one of the world's leading UFOlogists, and the man who led the investigation into the Bonnybridge phenomenon in the 1990's.
The truth is out there – well let's hear it.
Monday 5th July at 1:00pm at Downing Street is action time.
Councillor Billy Buchanan.

Just one final point on this matter of Governments and Official position. In June 1965, Lieutenant Colonel John Spaulding from the Office of Information, Department of the Air Force, Washington D.C. wrote a letter to the British Ministry of Defence asking them what type of enquiries they had been conducting into UFO sightings over Britain, what was their position? Well in an illuminating response from the MoD dated 24th June 1965, Lieutenant Spaulding was informed that; (and I quote in part) (A) *"We Investigate every case reported to us, and we use every assistance".* (B) *"Unlike you, we do investigate single observer sightings."* But the big shock about this letter comes when Lieutenant Spaulding is informed that.

"Our policy is to play down the subject of UFOs and to avoid attaching undue attention or publicity to it. As a result, we have never had any serious political pressure to mount a large-scale Investigation such as Project Blue Book."

Whilst as mentioned earlier, the MoD has released 'some' of their UFO files, they still have a long way to go to appease we UFO researchers. Indeed, The Ministry of Defence decided to close their so called 'UFO desk' as they felt that it served 'no defence purpose'. Furthermore, they stated that it was taking staff away from more valuable defence related activities and therefore was shut down in December 2009. That's as maybe, but one wonders if this is truly the case, and that somewhere in the corridors of Whitehall, there is an unmarked door which leads to a desk, where a clerk sits collecting UFO data from pilots, policemen and the public. We can but wonder. What I do know is that Ron Halliday and I, as well as countless others, will keep campaigning to get the British Government to listen to our claims and to hopefully work side by side with us. Are they, (The British Government) hiding something from us? Do they know something we do not? And if so, what could be so big that they have kept it hidden from us for all these years? Questions like this and indeed many others, must be answered. We the people of the United Kingdom have a right to know.

MORE UFO SIGHTINGS OVER BONNYBRIDGE

O.K. let us now return to the UFO sightings above Bonnybridge. The following case is different from the many others that I have researched from the Bonnybridge area, why? Well because in this case one of the persons involved was fast asleep in his bed and who dreamt of a UFO above his house, but guess what, whilst he was dreaming about this UFO above his house, someone else outside actually *"SAW"* a UFO above the house in which this chap was sleeping and dreaming. Strange or what? I now present the full written account which was submitted to me by the dreamer. Names have been changed to protect the witnesses' identity.

A STRANGE DREAM!

"The following account is of a dream I had on the 24th of November 1994, (Thursday morning). I remember standing outside underneath the garage door which is at the gable end of the house. I was staring upwards at what appeared to be two objects of light which were initially motionless, approximately 60 to 80 feet above the ground. The angle in which the bright light shone downwards made it hard to distinguish whether there were one or two separate objects. However, when one of the objects of light moved, I could see a concave shape with what seemed to be a rotating disc, similar to a propeller. When this object moved, it was only for a short distance, approximately 10 feet. It moved quickly in a straight line,

stopped for about five seconds, then returned to its original position. The light shining from this object was bright enough to light up the whole of our garage area, like a floodlight. Suddenly I noticed my dad standing on the path at the front of the house which leads to the garage. He too was looking upwards at the two objects. He said, 'check your watch, its six-o clock'. I looked at my watch and it was six o clock. When I looked back up towards my dad, he was walking away as if he were going into the house. I remember feeling completely relaxed and unafraid."

"I stepped forward from beneath the garage door, and as I did so, I didn't take my eyes off the objects. The object on the right hand side started to move again, but this time it made a straight line for me until it was about 3 feet away from my head. The bright light was still present, but it wasn't bright enough to cause me to look away or shield my eyes. I could see through the centre of the light which seemed to put me in a trance. It didn't make me go to sleep because I can remember as I looked into the light, that I saw what looked like a traffic cone from the peak to the base, a sort of tunnelling effect. Then the object started to move from one side of my head to the other, much like a windscreen wiper on a car. As it did so, a really relaxed feeling came over me. This feeling is really indescribable. It had a sort of calming effect, even though I didn't feel tense or stressed, and it totally relaxed my body, as if I was weightless (floating). I have had general anaesthetics in the past which you can feel relaxing your body, but this experience was really great. My head was dropped downwards at this point, I remember seeing very bright light for about 3 seconds, then the light started to fade, and I could see myself coming down onto the red chips that surrounded the garage. I didn't come to on my feet, I was lying in the 'recovery position' that First Aid people use. I could still see the light and the tunnel effect that I mentioned earlier. Then I was wakened by ringing. When I woke up, I had the feeling that I must remember what had just happened to me. At this point I heard my mum saying, "On the roof", and someone started running down the hall. I thought we must have burglars, so I jumped up and ran into my mum's bedroom. I asked what was happening and she said, "Jim had phoned to say that there was a UFO above our house", I said, "That's really weird I've just had a dream about that". I turned and ran after my dad. We both ran outside and looked up into the sky. We looked all around the house but saw nothing. When I went back into the house, I started to tell my mum about the dream, when I got to the part when my dad was saying, "Check your watch, it's six o clock", my mum said that's uncanny David, it would have been about 06:15 06:20 when Jim phoned. I looked at the clock in the bedroom, and it was 06:23!"

Well, what are we to make of that! Could we stretch the imagination and gingerly state that this 'could' have been a UFO abduction? It certainly has all the hallmarks of one. The witness, David Muir (pseudonym) aged 20 lives in Bonnybridge and to this day is puzzled by this dream/event. He did not wish to be put under hypnosis in an effort to see if there might be any hidden subconscious memories of that morning, and at the end of the day, all we are left with is an amazing story coming from the actual town of Bonnybridge and which adds (in a different sort of way) to the growing evidence that is being recorded there.

The British Government, as we have learned, seem to think that there is no defence significance in regard to these UFO sightings that are occurring over Central Scotland, well try telling that to the two startled witnesses in our next case who experienced something which 'buzzed' their car. Do you think that the following incident was of no defence significance, let's see what happened shall we? From his written account to the author, this is what witness Mark Wilson (25) had to say:

"It was Boxing Day, 26th December 1994 and the time was about 05:40am. We were on our way home from Stirling travelling on the M.9 Motorway. Jane (my girlfriend) and I noticed a large bright glowing light of which at first, we didn't take much notice of. But when we got right into Grangemouth, we noticed that this light wasn't moving, it was hovering over near Bonnybridge. We noticed as we travelled further up the

motorway, that it was moving towards us, it was as if it had a magnet on the car and it was staying at the same distance away from us but travelling along at the same speed. I took the car up to 9O MPH and this object kept pace. When we slowed down, it slowed down too. We were both very scared at this time. It was at the right-hand side of our car, and then, just like a speeding bullet, it shot over to the left-hand side of our car. A few seconds later it again shot over to the right-hand side of the car then again back to the left hand side where it remained. The object then shot straight up into the sky and was gone in seconds."
Mark Wilson.

In Mark's drawing that he supplied to the author, we can see that the object they both witnessed is shaped like a box with sloping sides and was jet black in colour. Clearly then, this was not a conventional object, no wings tail fins, or any other appendages were noted. It had come from a distance then swooped down onto the two unfortunate witnesses. Is the British Government and the Ministry of Defence seriously trying to tell us that incidents like this are not threatening to its citizens? This is not an isolated case; I have others which I'll relate throughout this book.

1994 had been a busy year for UFO investigations and dealing with the media, little did I know it then, that 1994 would be nothing compared to what lay in store during 1995. It seemed as if the whole phenomena exploded in a media frenzy of immense proportions. Sadly, it was also to see a rather unfortunate incident which received the biggest press ever, 'The unfortunate Zalus Affair', of which the full story can now be told.

1995

MORE UFOS, MORE MEDIA, THE YEAR OF ZALUS!

1995 started for one couple with more than a bang! It started with the year's first UFO sighting. It was 05:00am on the 1st of January 1995. Craig Black (20) and his girlfriend Karen Clark (16) were driving home from a friend's party, both were sober and had taken little alcohol the previous evening. During their journey home, they experienced something strange in the sky which fortunately they managed to obtain a few photographs of. Craig now takes up the story:

"On Sunday 1st January at approximately 05:00am, my girlfriend and I were travelling along the dual carriageway adjacent to Castlecary, (Scene of the Procek's double UFO sighting mentioned earlier), when my girlfriend exclaimed, "what is that"! I looked out of the car window and saw a large bright white light hovering above the trees at the other side of the field. My first thought was that it might have been a helicopter or a star very low on the horizon. I slowed the car down to around 4O MPH to get a better look. It was obviously not a star and was over the trees. What was also apparent, was that the light was not actually the whole object, but a central light. Karen scrambled for her camera and got one shot off with the flash. This was when we both got scared, for as soon as the flash went off, the object started moving. It matched the speed of the car exactly and had moved closer and was about 4OO yards away."

"The object then started moving with incredible speed towards the railway bridge we were approaching. A small tail had formed from the central light, and the object started moving up and down as though avoiding the tops of the trees. The flash on the camera had stopped working, but Karen took more photographs anyway. Also, the tail that had formed from the central light, did not follow the pattern that the object was

moving in, it stayed pointing diagonally upwards no matter which way the object moved. The object then abruptly stopped moving with the car and headed towards it. I panicked and put the foot down on the accelerator. When I turned off the dual carriageway at Banknock/Haggs, we lost sight of the object due to the fact that the slip road turns back on itself, and the countryside cannot be seen because of buildings etc. However, between Longcroft and Dennyloanhead, you can see back towards the dual carriageway, and again we could see the object. It was a lot further away and appeared to be surrounded by cloud, but it was still at a very low altitude. I then stopped in Dennyloanhead to drop Karen off at a friend's house, nobody answered, so we headed towards my house which was only a quarter of a mile away. When I reached the junction at the bottom of the street, the object was there again! This time it was maybe about 60 feet in the air and about '250 feet directly in front of us!"

"I stopped the car and couldn't believe what I saw. The clouding had gone, and I could now see the distinct outline of the object. All I could see was this impossible shape with its fixed light. There were many faint tiny red lines running around the edges of the shape, and some towards the central light. We rushed to my house and told my parents, (biggest mistake of my life!) and then went straight to my bedroom to look out of the window. It could still be seen from my window but again had moved further away and the clouds were again surrounding the shape. We left it at that and decided to get the photographs developed as soon as possible."

Craig Black.

As with all cases the usual lines of enquiry were checked to see if there were perhaps a natural explanation to account for this sighting. No agency could provide an explanation or indeed further witnesses. Only one photograph showed the bright light which the witnesses said followed their car, the rest of the photographs did not come out, (the flash if you recall wouldn't work). With the help of fellow researcher John Jenkins, we sent the one photograph that did come out to a Scottish University who enhanced its resolution from 50 times to 200 times. Sadly, this did not prove helpful, and did not make it any easier to determine what the object might be. Here we have yet another low-level close proximity UFO sighting. This object, as we recall from Craig's signed testimony, was only about 60 feet up in the air, and at a distance of around 250 feet directly in front of them. Again, we ask, should this object which did not resemble a conventional aircraft or helicopter, be classed as having no defence significance? Are the Military and those in power not interested in these types of sightings? Who's kidding who here?

The 'Scottish Sunday Express' of January 1st, 1995, featured a blazing headline which stated, **'Mystery of the UFO Capital of Britain'**. It featured the usual stories and also stated that Councillor Billy Buchanan planned to lobby local MPs as he received no reply to his communication to Prime Minister John Major. Billy was quoted as saying:

"No one can come up with a rational explanation for all these strange lights in the sky. I'm prepared to put my political credibility on the line to get answers. I got a fax from the Pentagon which confirmed that the crew of Apollo 11 had a close encounter with UFOs. The Belgian Air Force has also radar logged a number of incidents."

Science writer Steuart Campbell was quoted as saying:

"Most UFO sightings are mirages of astronomical objects or aircraft. You can generate a wave of UFO sightings if you tell people that you have seen a UFO."

The 'Falkirk Advertiser' for Wednesday January 11th, 1995, contained more UFO witnesses. Its headline was, **'Strange Encounters Continue To Mount'**, and detailed the observation by Bainsford resident, Mary Crozier (46) who witnessed a football glowing object in the early morning sky. Mrs Crozier was quoted as saying,

"I couldn't believe what I was seeing. I used to laugh at people who saw UFOs, now I believe them."

Mrs Crozier claimed that one Thursday morning at around 05:30am she got up early as both her husband and son had already left for work. When she opened the blinds of an upstairs window, she observed a light which appeared to be hovering over the Callendar estate on the outskirts of Falkirk. She initially thought that it was a bright star (as bright as the floodlights at a football stadium, she was quoted as saying). But what happened next forced her to change her opinion, for she claimed that a 'bulge' appeared in the side of the ball of light, and another smaller ball of light came out of the bulge, almost like an egg hatching. The smaller light was not as bright but had a smoky appearance. It then dropped down and hovered below the large ball to the left. According to the 'Falkirk Advertiser', another smaller light then squeezed out of the bulge in the large orb before also dropping down. Both smaller lights then joined together before moving back into the large ball of light. The sphere then zoomed off and out of view in seconds. Mary later heard that a colleague of her son had also seen a glowing light at around the same time. And on that same day, a Braes man also saw an intensely bright round object over Falkirk.

A most peculiar sighting of a large cylindrical object was sighted by Paul Jack (pseudonym) over the town of Falkirk on the 24th of January 1995. It had just gone 8:00pm, and Paul's attention was diverted towards his window where he saw unusual flashing lights. Thinking this strange, Paul got up and went towards his window then moved out onto the veranda. What he saw, he couldn't explain but knew that it resembled nothing that he had ever seen before. In a written statement to the Malcolm Robinson, Paul had this to say about his sighting:

"I stood out on the veranda and watched the lights for about twenty minutes. During the twenty minutes the lights were not moving but just hovering. Then they started to move to the left, stop for a couple of minutes, then move again to the left. It did this around 8 to 10 times. All the time the lights were flashing in a pattern. Five lights were going around in a circle

horizontally, then after the five lights went round in order there was one big long light, and then it went back to the five lights in order. These lights never stopped during the twenty minutes that I was watching them for."

Paul relates that he kept on watching this unusual spectacle until the light movement just instantaneously 'vanished' and did not reappear. Paul's 8-year-old daughter who was visiting her mother, (Paul and his wife were separated) at her house a few streets away, also saw this strange looking object from her bedroom window. Working with journalists as I do, I regularly get asked, if people only see one UFO in the sky at a time, and although the vast majority of UFO sightings over Bonnybridge and other parts of Stirlingshire comprise mostly one UFO sighting, there are one or two cases which involve observations of two or more objects seen in the sky at the same time.

ANOTHER CASTLECARY VIADUCT UFO!

Our next case features a most unusual shaped object which some might say (including myself I might add) to have been either a remotely piloted vehicle (RPV), or some form of kite or, in the truest sense of the word, 'a UFO'! And guess what! The Castlecary Viaduct pops up again as the focal point for yet another UFO sighting. We saw it in the Procek sighting when both witnesses saw two triangular objects in the sky. Then we saw it in the Craig Black sighting mentioned previously, now we have it in this case. What is so special about the Castlecary Railway Viaduct? It was 4:30 on the afternoon of the 29th of January 1995, 45-year-old David Rowston (pseudonym) was driving in his car accompanied by his mother along the M80 motorway from Stirling to Glasgow. He was travelling at around 50mph and idly chatting away about some of the day's events. Suddenly his attention was drawn towards a strange looking craft which initially he took to be some form of low flying Jet Fighter. The object was approaching the Castlecary Railway Viaduct and flew straight over it then appeared to 'slow down' and actually seemed to stop. It then turned at right angles and moved away in a different direction. By this time

David had driven underneath the Viaduct and attempted to look back, but his brief glance did not manage to spot the object again, and, as the road was fairly busy, he decided not to stop. In the drawing submitted to the author, one can see what looks like some kind of weird hang glider, a long thin oblong body with long wings at either side of the rear end of the object, and two smaller wings at the very front of the object.

What was also noticeable, was that both tips of the rear wings, curved up. There were no markings or distinguishing features about this peculiar object. No apparent canopy in which a pilot might sit, it just was a purely bizarre looking object. Flicking through some back issues of a magazine called the 'Fortean Times' (issue 85), I came across on page 49, an aircraft which although not identical to what witness David Rowston observed, was fairly close. That aircraft was the 'Predator' at that time America's newest reconnaissance UAV (Unmanned Air Vehicle). According to the article written by David Hambling, he states that the Predator is a small robotic aircraft which had been deployed in Bosnia but was grounded soon after, due to the loss of two of the five aircraft, due to technical faults.

If this was the Predator flying low over parts of Stirlingshire, what on earth was it doing there! Investigations did not uncover what this object was, and being realistic, it is hard to imagine that this object could have been the Predator operating in Scottish Airspace, (even although stranger things have happened!). A few months later, May 21st, 1995, I was astonished to see a photograph of what appeared to be the same aircraft. The Scottish 'Sunday Post' newspaper ran the story of which the headline stated, *"No it's Not Flying Upside Down"*. And showed a photograph of what they stated was a C.I.A. unmanned spy plane, a modified Gnat-750 which was pictured on a surveillance mission over the former Yugoslavia. We were told that this unmanned reconnaissance plane was in use in the Balkans from a base reportedly in Albania. Using specially developed electro-optical sensors it scans the ground and sends back vital battlefield information on troops and weapon movements. The article went on to state that the plane's makers, General Atomics Aeronautical Systems of San Diego,

California, had landed a new $30,000,000 contract to provide ten scaled up versions which would be capable of flying at 25,000 feet. Despite its clumsy looking design and 35-foot wingspan, the slow flying spy plane is virtually undetectable by radar, having been masked with Stealth type cloaking materials. The ten larger versions would carry even more technical wizardry for commercial and military use in trouble spots around the world. Again, I ask, 'was this aircraft flying low over Stirlingshire that day, and if so, why?' I knew that I had seen this shape before. It troubled me, and I began a quest to go through all my old files on UFO sightings in this country, which was no easy task I can tell you. But eventually I found what I was looking for. It's a bizarre story. Sadly, the author of this letter had not put down the date of his sighting. Worse still, the envelope which might have shown when the letter was sent, I had thrown out. However, this account which also featured a drawing by the witness, shows an object similar to what David Rowston and his mother saw near the Castlecary Viaduct.

The following incident occurred in Yorkshire England. And although not Scottish, I present it here as it is similar to the object viewed by the witness above. Every Sunday Mr Alex Mitchell (pseudonym) would set out and walk the short distance over to his mother's house in Whiston Merseyside for his dinner, and this Sunday was no different. The journey was around one and a half miles which he covered in next to no time. Upon reaching the other side of Whiston Meadows, Alex sat down on a country stile to have a cigarette before he proceeded on to his mother's. As he was sitting there enjoying his cigarette and admiring the view, he suddenly heard a peculiar noise. He looked up into the sky from where this noise was coming from and was astonished to see a peculiar little plane flying overhead at only about 50 feet above the fields. Alex could not see any wheels or engines, and there were no markings anywhere along its small bullet shaped body. It had two sets of wings, smaller flat wings on the front, and larger upturned wings at the rear (similar to our previous case). A few seconds later, a black car pulled up on a road near the stile where Alex was sitting. Alex was surprised to see two men dressed in dark suits and white shirts with black ties peering up through the windscreen at the object which was flying low in the sky. Alex was quite unprepared for what happened next, for suddenly this car with the two strange men inside, shifted into gear and drove 'through' a wheat field until the car had reached the far end of the field where it stopped. Both men then got out and gazed skywards. After a few minutes, both men got back into the car and drove off at speed. Flicking his cigarette towards the ground, Alex thought that this whole episode was most peculiar. A strange craft in the sky, followed by two peculiar looking men who drove through a farmer's field to stare at this object in the sky. *'Who were these guys'* he thought to himself. Well, a bizarre incident indeed, and as I have stated, this object looked similar to what David Rowston had seen. Could it be the same or similar object? Who knows, but one thing's for sure, these R.P.Vs (Remotely Piloted Vehicles) or U.A.V. (Unmanned Air Vehicles), if that's what this was, are extremely unusual looking devices, some of which were used during the Gulf War to fly over the Iraqi positions. If one didn't know what these really were, then they would immediately think that they had spotted a UFO, no question about it. Of course it goes without saying, that there 'must' be a percent of UFO sightings which 'are down' to sightings of R.P.Vs or U.A.V.s. But was this the case here? I don't think we'll ever really know.

The popular woman's magazine 'EVA', which actually contains quite a lot of stories about UFOs and the Supernatural, got itself involved with the ongoing UFO sightings above Bonnybridge. And in their February 1st issue of 1995, they told the story of several witnesses who had been touched by the sightings above the town and elsewhere. UFOs were the last thing on Barbara Stocks mind as she was returning home from the shops, yet she too, along with her daughter Sarah, witnessed a bright object in the sky which was flying fairly low. She described it as having many red and white lights attached to it, and in another local report, she described it like a Christmas tree in the sky. The Sloggett sighting was also covered of which I have mentioned earlier, and I was quoted in this article as saying that the fear of ridicule from people and the media, stops many more people coming forward with their UFO sightings.

ANOTHER UFO ABOVE THE B.P. GRANGEMOUTH PLANT!

I mentioned earlier about the UFO sighting and subsequent photograph which was taken by Philip Trevis over the B.P. Chemicals Plant in Grangemouth. This was not to be the only time that a UFO had been sighted over this complex. On the night of the 3rd of February 1995, James Westfield (pseudonym) aged 47, was driving his car in the direction of Grangemouth Road, when he happened to notice a small orange object which was above the B.P. plant. It appeared to be just above the burners which emit gas emissions with a large flame. Thinking this rather strange, James slowed down in order to take a better look at this thing. The object had now moved above the older part of the B.P. complex then travelled in a zig zag motion over towards Falkirk, where it was finally was lost to view. James then jumped back into his car and drove onwards to a social function that he was attending. Once he had arrived at this function, he mentioned to some of his friends about the strange object that he had seen and was delighted to hear that his friends had also seen this orange object. They saw it as they were travelling to the function in a taxi. All witnesses agree that what they saw that night was not a conventional flying machine.

"OH NO, NOT AGAIN!"

Mark Wilson and his girlfriend Jane McDonald, of whom we have mentioned earlier, did not think for one moment that they would be lucky enough to have a second UFO sighting. Their previous sighting which occurred on Boxing Day 1994 was, as we have learned, of a ball of light which came down from the sky and paced their car and went from one side of their car to the other before shooting straight up into the sky. That was frightening, but for it to happen again, was just too much. Their second sighting, which this time they had the added bonus of having friends in the car, again occurred in the early hours of the morning between 02:00am to 02:30am.

They were on their way home to Stoneyburn in West Lothian driving from Stirling on the 5th of February 1995 and were approaching Grangemouth at almost the exact same location as their 1994 Boxing Day sighting. Jane was gazing out of the window at the many stars that could be seen in the early morning sky, when all of a sudden, a large white-silvery light, shaped like a long thin box with sloping sides, swooped down from the sky, just like their last sighting, and remained above their car roof at a height estimated by them to be the same as a two story house. Suddenly a strange electrical humming sound could be heard inside the car which they presumed was coming from this object. This, needless to say, was quite disconcerting. What I found most intriguing about this case, was the fact that this object stayed with them above the rooftop of their car for just under twenty minutes, before it then illuminated into intense brightness and took on a more circular shape. It then shot over the car and Mark had a good opportunity to look up through the windscreen and have a look at its underside. He described it as completely flat and round and seemed to be a dark silver colour. There were also three coloured lights on the underside of this object. And as it banked to the left, it emitted a trail of light which was about 20 feet long. In seconds it was gone. The occupants of the car were left slightly shaken by this experience, more so the two friends of Mark and Jane's. Mark and Jane however, looked at each other and in unison said, *"Not again!"* For something to happen once to the same witnesses is a frightening and alarming event, but for it to happen twice, is beyond belief. How many more vehicles have been 'buzzed' along motorways near Falkirk and Bonnybridge that we may never hear about? Is this of defence significance? We know that civilian air pilots are not allowed to fly above motorways in this manner. Indeed, to fly above any road at such a height would incur a serious penalty and obviously involves risk to the pilot. Whoever was in control of this object, 'knew' what they were doing, for they followed the car for a good twenty minutes. One would think that even although this event occurred in the early hours of the morning, 'someone' must have seen this amazing spectacle. But if they did, they certainly did not report it to our society or to any other individuals that we know.

UFO TALKS BID BLOCKED

This was the headline from the 'Falkirk Advertiser' dated 14th February 1995. Readers were informed that both Billy Buchanan had now been refused to meet with Ministry of Defence officials at Whitehall regarding our bid to try and get the British Government to meet with us where we could show them all our evidence. The MoD in their infinite wisdom stated that there is no evidence of phenomena of defence significance and a meeting would not serve any usual purpose. Billy was quoted as being disgusted and disappointed at this, and quite right too, but he wasn't really surprised. The MoD requested that both Billy and I send them additional information and that officials would look 'closely' at them. Really! Councillor Buchanan further stated:

"There's no point in just sending down a pile of documents. It's discussions we need, and urgently."

Mary Roy (pseudonym) from Falkirk was putting her grandson to bed as he was spending the weekend with her. It was the 11th of March 1995. As she went to close the bedroom curtains, she noticed a brilliant light in the sky. Suddenly another object appeared straight ahead which appeared to have a line of coloured lights that appeared to flick forward like the lights on a Christmas tree, (not the first time UFOs have been likened to a Christmas tree in this area!). One object then moved at great speed further left and hovered over the Westerglen Transmitting Station. (The Westerglen transmitting station is a facility for longwave and mediumwave broadcasting established in 1932 at Westerglen Farm, 2 miles (3 km) southwest of Falkirk, (grid reference NS868773). The station comprises of two large pylons which stand close together and contain around four red lights which are attached to each one of them.

The other object which had been directly in front of Mary's window then moved at great speed to join the other object which was still hovering. The two objects then moved forwards and began hovering, they then returned to their earlier position above the transmitters. They maintained this position for a number of minutes, after which they began to gradually move away then suddenly, they took off at great speed into the night sky and were gone in seconds. Mary and her 8-year-old grandson, who got out of bed to see what his gran was looking at, were left feeling puzzled and slightly bemused by this amazing night-time aerial event. Investigations by SPI did not uncover what these objects were. That particular area, however, is well known for UFO sightings, and there are a number of places in which one can sky watch. The area with the pylons are away from the confines of town and street lights, so light pollution is not a problem. Farmland rises and falls around you, and as this location is fairly high up from Bonnybridge, a wide expanse of sky can be viewed. I personally have spent a great deal of time at this location on sky watches, sometimes alone, and sometimes with SPI personnel, and the area is still frequented by our society whenever we go sky watching in the Bonnybridge area.

Another double sighting of UFOs occurred near the end of March 1995. A couple were driving on the B803 towards Slamannan a town near Bonnybridge at roughly 8:45pm, when they were startled by two bright white objects which descended towards them. The objects at first glided parallel to each other about half a mile away in front of their moving car before both zooming off in different directions into the night sky. As this was quite an interesting sighting, and one of which contained not one but two UFOs in the sky at the same time, I took the step of asking the 'Falkirk Herald' if they would place my request for any further potential witnesses to this sighting to come forward, sadly no one did.

QUEST INTERNATIONAL COME TO BONNYBRIDGE

It was during March 1995 that 'Quest International', one of the UK's leading UFO research societies at the time, decided it was about time that they visited Bonnybridge and check out for themselves what was going on. In an article featured in the 'Falkirk Advertiser' dated 21st of March 1995, we learned that their team spent six nights at Bonnybridge camped out in luxury mobile homes. They took videos of the night skies and generally spent each evening gazing skywards, whether they saw anything was not noted.

Denny man Cameron Murphy (pseudonym), was, on the evening of 18th March 1995, watching television when his wife asked him to look out of the window. His gaze took him to a bright object in the sky which he initially took to be a plane. What changed that view, was when the object began to zig-zag all over the place then stop in the sky for a matter of minutes, then resume its strange zig-zagging motion again. Cameron's wife, two sons and daughter, were also witness to this strange spectacle in the sky.

SPI VISIT EDINBURGH AIRPORT

Needless to say, with all the UFO sightings that were occurring over Stirlingshire, SPI felt that we had to arrange for a visit to Edinburgh Airport and see if they could enlighten us, as to any unusual 'anomalies' that they 'might' have picked up on radar. Part of a UFO investigator's job is to get in touch with both local and national airports in regard to clarifying whether any aircraft or helicopters were in the vicinity of any given UFO sighting. This is to obviously eliminate the possibility that what was observed might just have been a commercial airliner or private jet. During the Bonnybridge wave of sightings, I was forever drafting letters, seeking answers to my questions about UFO sightings across the skies of Stirlingshire. Some airports did get back in touch with me, whilst others didn't. So, I felt the next best step was to jump into their backyard, so to speak, and pay them a visit. And so it was, that on March the 6th, 1995,

Stan Brown, Garry Wood, Helen Walters, and I turned up at Edinburgh Airport for an arranged visit where a gentleman took us up into the main control tower. Let me tell you this dear reader, it was quite a sight to see all these monitors spread out in a semi-circle across the floor, all being watched by observant individuals. Truly fascinating. I directed a number of questions to our host for the afternoon and he replied with a wealth of knowledge. He stated that Stirlingshire can see a very high amount of air traffic each day en-route to Glasgow, Cumbernauld, and Aberdeen airports. There were also a few private flying clubs dotted about the Central Region, all of which, they were in full control of. Of course, I'm pretty sure that this gentleman was waiting on one question from me as he knew what society I was from. So, in the spirit of being nice, I asked that question, which was, *"Have you ever encountered any UFOs during your time at Air Traffic Control?"* His reply was a swift, *"No"*, and that included his colleagues. He did admit that he did receive reports of UFO activity from time to time from members of the public, but they had nothing come up on their radar. Of course we had to take this gentleman at his word. Was he telling the truth? Was he guided by Ministry of Defence rules and regulations? Well, I guess we will never know. All in all, it had been a good exercise, and it was a step in the right direction between the relations of ufologists and Air Traffic Control.

I mention throughout my section of this book about how some (not all) newspapers covered the Bonnybridge UFO mystery in their own jocular style. Take Rikki Brown for instance. In his 'Look at the Unexplained' regular feature in the 'Look' section of the 'Sun' newspaper dated May 7th, 1995, he states.

"Look, one place where aliens are seen most is Bonnybridge. Now if I was an alien coming to Earth for a swatch at the place, it would be the Taj Mahal, The Sydney Opera House, Monte Carlo etc, not a wee place in Scotland. I'm not saying that Bonnybridge isn't a nice place, but you would hardly expect to find it in an alien travel agency brochure."

So, as you can see, this was the kind of press about Bonnybridge that some, not all, newspapers were writing about.

AN E.T. VISITOR CENTRE!

With all these UFO sightings occurring in his district, Councillor Billy Buchanan thought up a way in which to perhaps put more jobs into the local community, and of which, would hopefully bring more tourists to visit the area. Billy's dream was to get help to build a futuristic 'Extra-terrestrial Visitor Centre' near Bonnybridge. In the 'Falkirk Herald' of May 25th, 1995, we learn that Billy's ideas for this visitor centre, would be shaped like a glass mushroom which would be supported on a glass stem. Glass lifts would take visitors up the stem into the oval which would have three floors. Located on these three floors, would be a restaurant, a bar, sci-fi crèche, a high-tech virtual reality display featuring videos of the strange objects caught in the night sky and an observatory where tourists could scan the skies around Bonnybridge looking for UFOs. Billy hoped that this project would be funded by the Millennium Fund which is a Lottery funded cash pool for projects to mark the turn of the century. And according to this press article, he was so confident of receiving some money, that he had already asked architects to draw up some plans for the building. Billy was reported as saying,

"People can mock and say I should be talking to a doctor in a white coat, but we're living in a super technological age and people are fascinated by all this. We're talking about thousands of visitors; it will bring jobs to the area, stimulate the local economy, and put Falkirk District firmly on the map."

Billy went on to say, *"I can see a hotel complex and chalets springing up around it. All the heavy Industry is gone, we can't rely on it any longer, and tourism is one of the ways forward. Take a look at New Lanark, they started with nothing, and now they're getting two million visitors a year."*

The article finished by quoting Falkirk District Council planning official Alistair Bell who said:

> "The development would be viewed with considerable interest as it's quite unique in my experience. I'll look forward to seeing the application."

SKY WATCHING AT BONNYBRIDGE

On Friday the 16th of June 1995 SPI took members up to the moors behind Bonnybridge to conduct a sky watch. There that night were Stan Brown and his wife Jill, Billy Devlin, Graham Stuart, and David Coleman and his wife. It was a cool night with a brisk wind, but heavy cloud cover soon came in so sadly that put paid to that night's sky watch. At the end of the day, our Bonnybridge sky watches gave our members an opportunity to put themselves in the ball park, if you like, with hopes of seeing something strange, but sadly, not on that night. Another sky watch was conducted on the night of the 26th of June 1995. Attendees that night were, Graham Stuart and his friends Tommy Loftus and Tony Lafrate, followed by David Coleman and his wife, along with Jim and Craig Malcolm and two of their friends. This time, we had decided to go to a new sky watching location near Bonnybridge where thankfully we had a good clear sky. After an hour or so of just seeing the odd satellite and shooting star, we decided to move onto another location which was a good few miles away from Bonnybridge. This was the ancient four and a half thousand-year-old Pictish Burial mound known as Cairnpapple Hill. I had last visited this mound when I was an 11-year-old primary school kid on a school trip, and it had left a lasting impression on my young mind. Anyway, as we approached Cairnpapple Hill in the car, the car was enveloped in roll after roll of heavy mist. I couldn't believe the change! From a scorcher of a hot day, to hardly being able to see 15 yards in front of us. Graham and Tony decided to stay in the car, as obviously, conditions were abysmal for sky watching. However, I was desperate to see Cairnpapple Hill again after so many years. Accompanying me on the walk up to the hill, was Tommy Loftus. Soon Tommy and I were walking into Hammer Horror like conditions, with swirling mist rolling all around us. It really was an unreal feeling, and definitely made you feel that you were in the midst of an old horror movie. Needless to say, we had a job trying to stay on the path, and the torch beam was of little help as it 'bounced back' off this rolling mist.

Several minutes later, we both saw looming out of the mist, a Christmas pudding shaped hill, a hill which is steeped in ancient history. A location of which I might add, has seen its fair share of UFO activity over the years. And, as I later learned, there was a sighting of a mysterious child like figure which vanished into the night. Anyway, I could hardly see Tommy, never mind the sky, so after a short look around we headed back off to the car with the uncanny feeling that ancient eyes were following our every move as we headed off this barren landscape.

THE BIG COUNTRY T.V. SKYWATCH

During the Bonnybridge UFO wave, SPI had assisted many television and media outlets in providing information about the ongoing UFO sightings across the Stirlingshire skies. Our latest assistance during 1995, went to BBC Scotland's new leisure pursuit programme entitled, 'The Big Country' which essentially provided its viewers with 'alternative' ways of spending your Friday night instead of going to the pub, (although, mind you, there is nothing the matter with that!) So, what were SPI doing on a leisure pursuit programme I hear you ask? Well, sky watching of course. Co-presenter of the Big Country programme was Dougie Vipond, who was the ex-drummer of the popular Scottish band, Deacon Blue, who had hits such as, 'Real Gone Kid', 'Fergus Sings The Blues', 'Dignity', and a whole lot more. Dougie paid a visit with his camera crew to my home at Tullibody in Clackmannanshire. Rather than film an interview with me inside my home, they decided to film the interview with me, outside my home. Bad move! The reason being, all the school children had finished school for the day and were heading to their respective homes, some of which were in my street. Needless to say, the kids spied the camera crew and the large furry boom microphone and soon shouts of, *"Hey Mr Spaceman, any chance of a Galaxy?"* A Galaxy for my overseas readers, is a chocolate bar that you can buy here in the United Kingdom. It soon became apparent that we couldn't film the interview outside, as more and more school kids had gathered to see something in their street that they weren't likely to see again, so inside we went and continued filming there. After filming inside, we all headed off in cars to the moors behind Bonnybridge.

The idea behind the BBC Scotland show, (Filmed by Wall to Wall Television, an independent television documentary team based in Glasgow) was to inform the viewing public that sky watching was a serious activity, especially in the light of the high concentration of UFO reports coming from within Central Scotland. At one point during our filming at Bonnybridge, a large bright white light came into view, at which an excited Dougie Vipond rushed over with his camera crew asking if this was one of those Bonnybridge UFOs? I replied that it wasn't, that it was just an aircraft, or what we UFOlogists would call it, and IFO (Identified Flying Object). Admittedly, the way it had looked in the distance for a short period of time, was rather confusing, but it soon became apparent. Although the SPI team and I spent a good few hours on the moors behind Bonnybridge with the camera team, nothing strange was seen. The finished programme after editing turned out fine. I had no problems with the style or how it broached the subject matter. Also interviewed for 'The Big Country', was Garry Wood, one of the A70 UFO Abductees. Craig Malcolm who filmed a UFO near his home in Larbert near Bonnybridge, (which, incidentally, was shown on the 'Big Country') Graham Stuart, Billy Devlin, and also some UFO witnesses. Surprisingly, Councillor Billy Buchanan's interview was not used on the show which annoyed him no end, more so because it took a lot for him to get permission for the camera crew to film him at the Falkirk District Council Buildings!

OK, as this book is a social history of the Bonnybridge UFO sightings which I hope allows you, the reader, to fully understand and comprehend all what was going on over those years, there is one final tale that I should relate to you regarding that 'Big Country' televised sky watch. Are you sitting comfortably? You are! Then I shall begin. Picture the scene. Presenter Dougie Vipond was doing his piece to camera about the UFO sightings over Bonnybridge, and he kept fluffing his lines. A number of SPI members were quite close to him being filmed and we kept bursting out laughing at every mistake he was making. Yes, I know, not very professional on our part, but it was hilarious. Eventually, the producer of the show walked over to our merry little band of laughter makers and quickly told us off. At which point, after taking a telling off, we all skulked off further away from this comedic scene. Fair play to St Mirren supporter Dougie Vipond though, he went on to present further television documentaries and has made a great career for himself. Well done Dougie.

TOWN IN PANIC OVER 2,000 UFO SIGHTINGS

This was the dramatic and incorrect headline from one of the first overseas reports on the Scottish wave of UFO reports above Bonnybridge. It came from that newspaper/magazine of truth and honesty (not!) The 'National Enquirer'. Dated June 6th, 1995. The town of Bonnybridge was 'not' in panic and never was. No one actually visited us for any quotes the interviews were conducted over the phone, not that I suppose that matters a great deal! As for their 2,000 reported UFO sightings, well, I think this was probably the first time that I had read that the UFO sightings in Bonnybridge had reached a peak like that. I certainly could not vouch for it. Certainly, there was 'something' going on in the skies above Bonnybridge and elsewhere, but 2,000 sightings, no I don't think so. Both Billy Buchanan and I were featured in this article, and one may have their own views on the honesty and journalistic style of the reporting of this newspaper. The 'Enquirer' is a tabloid rag devoted to the weird and the bizarre, most of which is overly untrue, and I will leave it at that!

Back at home I was still being snowed under by many telephone calls from excited people all relating their strange experiences. When we receive phone calls of this nature, we ask the caller if they would be happy to fill out a standard UFO sighting account form. By doing this, they are assisting the research and once we receive their completed UFO forms, it gives us a better understanding of what they saw. These account forms contain a number of questions which allows the witness to tick the appropriate boxes regarding the height of the object seen, the colour and so forth. These forms suffice till we have a proper 'face to face' meeting with the witness themselves and visit the location of a sighting.

Both Councillor Billy Buchanan and I were visited by two journalists from Holland's biggest selling Newspaper, 'De Telegraaf' that year, in which a big feature was done on the UFO sightings over Bonnybridge. It appeared in the August weekend edition. Many more newspapers covered the unfolding events in Bonnybridge during 1995, too numerous to mention here. 1995 proved a big year as far as press coverage went, but the coverage would end on a more troublesome note which will become clear in a moment.

For now, let us take a look at yet another UFO sighting for 1995, and one of which occurred to 'UFO Watcher' Craig Malcolm, whose family as we have already learned, have captured a number of strange 'lights' in the sky on camcorder across the Larbert and Bonnybridge skies. It was the 14th of June, and Craig's cousin Callum had just finished paying him a visit. As Craig was walking Callum back to his car, he happened to glance up into the early morning sky, the time was just after midnight, where they both observed a strange looking flying craft. It was decided to head up in Callum's car to the area in which this object appeared to be located. They parked the car, got out, and started to watch the sky for any movement. Shortly after this, both men observed a small 'craft' which was flying about in the night sky. Craig then shouted to Callum and pointed out to him to look at a part of the sky. When he did, Callum observed a 'saucer shaped craft' which was hovering low above the ground with intense bright white lights on the upper half of its structure. This object then proceeded to hover above the ground for a short while, then appeared to direct an intense white light towards them. Suddenly this bright white light was extinguished, and they were then left looking at various multi-coloured lights which started to flash on the underside of its structure. Seconds later, the object sped out of view and was gone in seconds. Again, as in all investigations, all channels were opened up to try and reach an answer as to what both men could have seen. Sadly, nothing turned up which might have explained it, and so this case added to the growing weight of testimony that continued to be documented from the Bonnybridge area.

I have mentioned the press, and although they can 'sometimes get it right', they can mislead and use innuendo to create things which are really not there. However, I did not help this matter during the middle part of 1995 when a story was badly misrepresented by myself, and was picked up by the press, the consequences of which had reverberations which were felt around the world, and I never imagined in my wildest dreams, how big this story was to become, and how much embarrassment it caused me, but more so on the individual of whom was caught up in it all, an innocent party, and someone who had played a key role in the Bonnybridge phenomena, That person was Councillor Billy Buchanan, and that story was, 'The Zalus Affair' ! For the first time, that story can now be told the way it was.

'THE ZALUS AFFAIR'
"I GOT IT WRONG OR DID I!"

They say that it's a big man that can admit to his mistakes. I take little comfort out of that statement after an episode during 1995 that destroyed the credibility that both Billy Buchanan and I had built up in regard to what was occurring over and around the town of Bonnybridge.

For those who may not actually know what I am referring to by the 'Zalus Affair'. Well claims were made in the newspapers that Councillor Billy Buchanan was receiving visits at the Falkirk District Council Buildings by a 'man from outer space' who imparted to Billy, seemingly fantastic revelations about UFOs, why they were here and what can be found in space. It was claimed that his name was 'Zalus', and that he would be speaking at the upcoming 'Cosmic Agenda Lecture' scheduled for Monday the 9th of October 1995. This was not strictly correct, as we are now about to find out. This whole embarrassing story broke, in the Strange Phenomena Publications Journal entitled *ENIGMAS*, dated August-September 1995 (Issue 41). This is how I reported the story, in *ENIGMAS* word for word.

MR X. A REPORT BY THE EDITOR OF AN UNUSUAL VISITOR?

First of all, let me say, I just don't know what to make of it all? What am I on about? Well for those readers who also subscribe to the ever-popular Fortean Times, they will no doubt have read about Councillor Billy Buchanan and his mysterious Mr X, a 'man' who has turned up at the Falkirk District Council Buildings on more than one occasion imparting incredible revelations about mankind, why we are here, and what the UFO presence is doing here. I know, I know, heavy stuff, superb wind up, etc etc. It all started around four months ago (May 1995), when I received a phone call from Councillor Buchanan. Billy informed me that he had a 'strange visitor' come to the Council Buildings requesting to see him, and although Billy is a busy man, he made the time to see this 'man'. What followed was described to me by Billy, as something fantastic and for all the world 'unrealistic'. This 'man' went on to inform Councillor Buchanan about a Council of Nine who were overseeing this planet to ensure that we don't blow ourselves up. 'He' went on to say why mankind is here, (Billy would not disclose this to me, nor would he disclose other aspects of his talk with this 'man'). Billy informed me that at times the conversation was so technical, that the vast majority of it went over his head, he just couldn't take it in. Billy said that this 'man' was immaculately dressed, wearing a black suit, white shirt, black tie (Mmmm), and his face, well Billy informed me that he just couldn't pin down an age to it, it really was youthful, but also well aged. 'It was weird', as Billy said. But out of all the peculiarities of this 'man', it was his piercing blue eyes which held a deep fascination for Billy. Billy said that it was something about the eyes that seemed to hold all the knowledge in the world!

Needless to say, I interjected rapidly on the phone to Billy and said,

"Look, I've got to meet this 'man', this is a must. Please arrange for us all to meet for a chat", to which Billy replied, *"Malcolm, I've already asked this 'man' that. I asked for your attendance at our next meeting, and he said that he did not want to meet up with Malcolm Robinson. I'm sorry, but I did try"*. *"You'll need to try harder"*, was my quick and disappointed reply. *"Malcolm"*, Billy continued, *"This Man is wanting me to go public with all this information, what should I do"*?

I then informed Billy in no uncertain terms that he should hold back for the moment, for this could be one big wind up, and a well-executed one at that! This situation was one of three possibilities. (1) This was a wind up by a friend of one of his fellow Councillors. (2) This 'man' was a Government Agent spreading 'dis-information' to ridicule the Bonnybridge UFO situation, and/or help spread the UFO myth (!) (3) This 'man' truly was a M.I.B. (Man In Black), someone who went around visiting witnesses or people associated with UFO sightings, and either told them to refrain from going public with their UFO sightings, or left them with incredible information). And what do I Malcolm Robinson think? Well, I'll be honest with you. I've every reason to believe that it is more a wind up than anything else. Apparently, this 'man' is still visiting Councillor Buchanan. Don't get me wrong, I'm aware of all the many M.I.B. reports that we have peppered throughout the UFO phenomena, of which probably lots, if not all, were really Government agents, or if not Government agents, then private Detectives or secret police. Good God, I can hardly believe I'm writing this stuff! Is *ENIGMAS* turning out to be an E.T. American 'aliens' mag (!) I sincerely hope not.

When all's said and done, I would be failing in my duty as Editor of this humble magazine, if I didn't inform you the readers, about all the aspects of the Bonnybridge UFO saga. It would be wrong just to only inform you about the good UFO cases and not episodes like this. This issue has 'got to be addressed'. Granted I don't know a great deal about these contacts that Billy has made with this 'man', (I'm really getting kept in the dark here!). You know, I've even said to Billy, *"Look, arrange a venue with this 'man', and I'll be hiding around the corner with a long lensed 35mm camera"*. Billy replied that this would not be a good idea. By the way readers, this 'man' according to Billy, is calling himself Zalus (!) So, like I say, I would be failing in regard as an Editor of this magazine if I did not present all the facts and all that's going on in regard to the UFO situation in Central Scotland. My only concern is that I have used up good space in this magazine by writing about all this when it could have been spent on 'better things'. Ah well, we'll just have to wait and see. I will be keeping an eye on this situation, and I shall certainly let you know what develops, (if anything!).

Paranoid report by the Editor.

The above, as I say, was taken out of our society's Journal *ENIGMAS*. That was how I presented the beginnings of the 'Zalus Affair'. My article mentioned that the 'Zalus Affair' had been reported in the magazine 'ForteanTimes'. The reason why it was featured in F.T. before *ENIGMAS* was simple. The Zalus information was all set and ready to be included in our August September issue. Before it was, I had had a casual conversation with someone at the 'Fortean Times' magazine and mentioned in passing about Billy meeting this strange 'man'. Where the story really began, was when the above article printed in *ENIGMAS,* hit the streets, or rather our subscribers. A number of our subscribers were 'men from the press', journalists no less, and one of them, of whom I'll not name but worked for a local News Agency in Stirling, received his copy of *ENIGMAS,* then rang me up at home and asked if the story about Mr X, was factual. I replied that it was, that Councillor Buchanan had indeed been receiving visits at his Falkirk Office from a man who had given all this fantastic information.

With that, the reporter put the phone down and I thought that would be that little did I realise about the furore that was about to follow. At this point I would state that I honestly felt that Councillor Buchanan 'did' say that this 'man's' name was Zalus. It wasn't until a few days later when I was checking my notes of an SPI Investigation, that there before me, in black and white, was the name Zalus. I had somehow transferred the name Zalus from this case study, into the Mr X article about Billy and this strange 'man'. I was shocked, I had goofed, and boy did I have a lot of apologising to do. Before I found out my mistake however, the press had already got wind of the story, and newspapers from Bathgate to Bombay ran the story of a Scottish Councillor who was being visited by a 'spaceman'. Believe you me, when I say this story went right around the world, I mean just that. But let us take a look at some of the Scottish press reports which carried stories about the 'Zalus Affair'. Before I explain who exactly this 'man' was that was paying Councillor Buchanan all these visits.

The Daily Star of Monday July 31st, 1995, carried the heading, **'My Pal E.T. Is Set To Stun The World'**. Journalist Nick Gates told the readers about Billy meeting up with a mysterious man at the Falkirk Council Buildings. There were a number of quotes made by Billy Buchanan in this article, some of which were:

"Quite simply, what this man has to say will be the most important thing we have ever heard. He told me all about the Council of Nine, who watch over us to make sure we don't blow the planet up, and about why mankind is here, I can't really say any more than that at the moment. People may think that all this is far-fetched coming from a Falkirk Councillor, but I'm sincere, this man is set to tell us something tremendous."

Billy has always denied that he said those words to Nick Gates and all other newspapers, and in point of fact this is correct. For those statements contained in Nick's article, came via a News Agency in Stirling, and went right across the board where everyone picked them up. All statements, in all newspapers, were taken by this News Agency directly from the SPI Journal *ENIGMAS*. Nick's article did not mention the name Zalus, that came in the 'Saturday Times' (Glasgow) article on August 12th where it mentioned that he would be speaking at the Falkirk Town Hall. The Scottish 'Daily Record' then followed up the story with its own article dated August 14th. Billy was quoted in this article as saying:

"I'm afraid he might not want to go ahead with it because of the ridicule, now I'm afraid that it might be called off."

This quote was in reference to the planned upcoming 'Cosmic Agenda Lecture'. The 'Daily Mail' of the same day had Billy stating:

"I want the meeting to happen, but I'm afraid the man I've been seeing may want to pull out. I'll need to speak to him but I'm afraid he might not want to go ahead with it because of the ridicule this meeting has received. I heard one woman on the wireless saying I should be taken away by the men in white coats!"

Other Newspapers who carried the story that day, were the 'Daily Sport', with the headline, ***'Please Beam Me Up Scotty'***. The 'Daily Star' ran the headline, ***'My Alien Pal Could Miss Big Date'***. (All stating more or less the same quotes from other newspapers). But probably the worst of all the news reports that I personally saw, came from the Scottish 'Sunday Mail' dated August 13th, 1995, its heading was, ***'Our Pal Zal',*** and featured an artistic rendition of what Zalus could look like according to the stated reports! The 'Mail' then with tongue firmly in cheek, had a spot of 'name play', and gave out some comic names for famous people based on Zalus. For instance.

1. Zalex Zalmond. (Alex Salmond). Scottish Politician.
2. Zally McCoist. (Ally McCoist). Scottish Footballer.
3. Zam Fox.   (Sam Fox).   Page 3 Model.

Their final line was, Zalus buys Queens's Highland Home and renames it Zalmoral. It was obvious that this paper was taking great delight in poking fun at the whole Zalus episode. Over the course of the next few days, the media went into a frenzy over the Zalus Affair. Both Billy and my phones were virtually 'ringing off their hooks'. In actual fact, both Billy and

I had taken holidays with our own respective families to different locations, and it wasn't until we both came back, that we realised how big this story had become. Television crews were also involved, and Billy made a statement on television, to a Scottish News programme, denying whole heartily, that he had anything to do with this 'Zalus Affair'.

As I've mentioned, it was a few days before I went on holiday, that I realised that the name Zalus actually came from another SPI Investigative story that I had been compiling, and somehow it got transferred/mixed up into the Mr X article. I knew I had to come clean and apologise to Billy, if not make a public statement vindicating Billy's name. I gave Billy a call and explained that it was I who was to blame, and I would do my utmost to clear his name and prove to the world, that there was no such guy called Zalus. However, at this point it was clear that Billy 'was' still receiving visits from a strange man at the Council Buildings. At this point I didn't know his name, although it wouldn't be too long before I did so and realise that it 'wasn't' a man from space! Billy suggested that I came over to the Council Buildings and discuss this matter. A date was then set, and I travelled over to Falkirk thinking that Billy would give me a really hard time, (Boy did I deserve it!) Once there, Billy and I sat down and talked through this matter and he asked that I sign a statement to the effect that it was 'I', Malcolm Robinson, who mistakenly started off this story which was, as we know, picked up by the press. This I did, and I must admit, that I was surprised at how calm Billy was taking this. His reputation here was on the line, and I had put a very big dent in it. I also stated to Billy, that I would contact a number of Scottish Newspapers and explain to them the real story behind the 'Zalus Affair'.

One of the Newspapers I rang was the 'Scotsman', and I was interviewed at length by their reporter John Smith. In John's article dated, August 18th, 1995, I stated that it was I who got the story wrong, and that I took full responsibility for it, and all I wanted to do now, was to clear Billy Buchanan's name in all of this. After the 'Scotsman' piece, I did a number of radio interviews, again stating that it was I who had managed to get some articles mixed up for our magazine, and that the whole issue progressed from there.

But wait, I wasn't entirely to blame!

As it turned out, Billy's mysterious 'visitor' was not a man from space, but a man from Edinburgh, a chap called Geri Rogers who was going to be one of the speakers at the upcoming 'Cosmic Agenda Lecture' organised by Councillor Buchanan. He was of course, very much into UFOs, and his visits to see Councillor Buchanan were filled with talk of why aliens are here and a whole lot more. Geri also imparted information about the 'Council of Nine', (a group of Extraterrestrials who claim to be watching over planet Earth). It isn't any wonder then that Councillor Buchanan could not take all this in, and he reported to me about these visits and this 'amazing information'. On one particular phone call to me, Billy intimated that he wouldn't be surprised if this chap Geri Rogers wasn't from here! (as he succinctly put it). Sadly, the ridicule and the critics still had a field day with this story, and no matter that I had 'come clean' in the press, shouts of Zalus followed Billy around. It got so bad that Billy intended to sue the chap who instigated the very first press piece, and who put it out over the news wires.

The 'Scottish Daily Express' newspaper of Tuesday August 15th, 1995, featured a full page which was titled, 'Britain's UFO Capital' subtitled, 'The quiet village that has become a focus for alien visits'. This article contained the usual quotes from myself and featured a few UFO cases from Bonnybridge. The writer of the piece, one Richard Spalding, had evidently gone round the village speaking to locals about whether these UFO sightings were real or not. Richard paid a visit to the Bonnybridge social club where he interviewed 76-year-old, Stevie Fagin, who in true Bonnybridge wit, raised a glass of Guinness and spoke the immortal words.

"If you have enough of these, of course you'll see UFOs."

The 'Daily Star' of August 24th, 1995, had a headline which read. *Councillor's Not Top of The Pops*. It stated that Billy Buchanan had been offered £10,000 to cut a disc and that he would also be granted a spot on the popular music programme of that time, 'Top of The Pops' but only if he recorded a version of the song, 'Me and My Pal Zal'. Billy was quoted as saying.

"I've turned them down flat. I've already been subjected to enough ridicule without making a fool of myself singing."

The 'Falkirk Herald' of the 31st of August 1995 ran the headline, *'Councillor Plans Legal Action Over Alien Stories.'* And Billy was quoted that he was now seeing his lawyer over these unfounded allegations and that he was trying to restore a little bit of credibility into the proceedings. Also, in that press article, came the fact that Billy had been invited by someone who represented a record company in Luton to consider making a record, which was provisionally titled, *'My Pal Zal'*. Billy was quoted as saying,

"They were talking about a recording deal worth thousands of pounds, but how do I know that the person on the other end of the phone is genuine"? Billy added, *"If there's ever another genuine offer once this whole thing has blown over, I might do it and give the money to the community."*

On the 3rd of August 1995 a witness notified SPI that at 11:00pm that night, she happened to be looking out of her bedroom window in Falkirk, when she noticed a bright orange ball in the sky which then split into two balls, and then into three shapes. It then was seen to all come back together as one, where it suddenly got bigger and bigger, only for it to reduce in size and disappear.

THE COSMIC AGENDA CONFERENCE.
OCTOBER 9th, 1995.

Two years later, Billy was to consider that offer again, more later! For a while the press got off the Zalus story and moved onto other things: that was until the scheduled Cosmic Agenda Lecture came round, and stories once more surfaced concerning Zalus. The speakers for this second major UFO Conference to be held in the Falkirk Town Hall were Phyllis Schlemmer, an American channeler who also claimed to be in communication with 'The Council of Nine'. Indeed, she had written a book about her contacts with these 'people'. Ken McFarlane from Cheshire was also billed to speak, as was Geri Rogers from Edinburgh, who, as we have read above, was mistakenly taken for this Zalus character. The day came round, Monday the 9th of October 1995, and I went along to this Conference not really knowing what to expect. Space channelling is something which I personally have never really got into. I had read about it yes, but for me it was somewhat on the fringe of UFOlogy. The publicity for this conference stated that the conference would lend a new 'dimension' to the events surrounding the Bonnybridge UFOs. SPI members joined around 700 other people in the Falkirk Town Hall that night, which included many members of the media, press, television, and radio. Of course, it's fair to say that this large turn out by the media, was in direct response to the 'Zalus Affair'. Indeed, as I was purchasing my ticket at the box office, one lady was holding up the large queue by asking the lady inside the ticket kiosk, if an alien really was going to be here tonight. When the ticket lady stated that there was no such alien attending the conference, and that all those press stories were false, the lady about turned and said, *"Well that's it then, I won't be going in,"* and with that she stormed off. Back inside the main hall, Councillor Buchanan took the stage dressed in a black tuxedo. He then launched straight into an attack on the British Press for their mistreatment of the 'Zalus Affair' and their disrespect for the people of Bonnybridge who were trying to come to terms with their UFO sightings. Billy's outburst was met with thunderous applause, and the look on some of the press members present had to be seen to be believed. Billy then went on to state that if there was anybody in the audience tonight thinking that they were going to hear an alien speak (which he had now stated was not the case) he would personally refund their money and travelling expenses, 'no matter if they had come all the way from Australia!" Thankfully for Billy, no one took him up on his offer.

The first speaker up was 33-year-old Geri Rogers, (yes, the so-called alien!) Geri is part of a British group to support the 'Council of Nine' and to encourage greater awareness of the present crisis in human affairs. Geri and the 'Council of Nine's' main aims were to bring peace, love, and harmony back to planet Earth. Looking around this large audience, I was beginning to wonder if they (the speakers) really knew what they were letting themselves in for. Next up was the main speaker Phyllis Schlemmer, who, with her radio mike attached to her jacket lapel, paraded back and forth on the stage telling us all about her early childhood and psychic experiences. Phyllis is a writer and researcher with over 20 years' experience on UFOs and the paranormal, and she has also been the main transmitter of communication from 'The Council Of Nine.' Her book, the *'Only Planet Of Choice'*, subtitled, *'Essential Briefings From Deep Space'*, is currently a world best seller, anyway so far so good. Phyllis's early talk was quite interesting; however, she then went on a love trip which was followed by some 'New Age' sentiments of 'hugging trees' and 'love thy neighbour'. Phyllis mentioned that this was her first trip to Scotland, and she was astounded by the loving kindness shown by the Scottish people towards her, so much so, that she was considering moving here! Eventually she got round to telling us all about the 'Council of Nine'. She mentioned that the leader of the 'Council Of Nine' was a chap called Tom. She then continued by saying that mankind is slowly killing our planet and that we should all care and try and do something about it. I must admit, I was a little bit disappointed, I felt as though I didn't know much more about 'The Council of Nine' now, than I had when I had walked in the door. Sadly, Phyllis did not endear herself to the Falkirk audience when she referred to the town of Bonnybridge, as 'Bonnybrook'. Never a good move! Following Phyllis's lecture, came Ken McFarlane, who has been involved in many conferences to help raise the public's awareness in the areas of environmental issues. To me, Ken's talk was more like a Party-Political Broadcast on behalf of the Scottish National Party. Ken asked the large audience to raise their hands if they thought they had seen a UFO, at this, about half the audience raised their hands which was quite a considerable amount of people, which I suppose was not too surprising considering that the Conference was being held in a "UFO Hot Spot"! In a Sunday Post newspaper article dates 1st October 1995, Ken was quoted as saying:

"Scots are ideal soulmates for beings from outer space. Scotland by ancient tradition, is a very spiritually aware place in terms of its down to earth attitude to life and nature. The people of Bonnybridge must look for whatever message is in these happenings."

After a break, part two of the Conference began, which was a panel debate featuring all the speakers, including Councillor Billy Buchanan. They invited the large audience to ask questions. The panel took on questions like, *"What do the Governments of the world know about UFOs?" "Is there a UFO cover up?" "What's going on in Bonnybridge?"* The answers given by the panel (not by Councillor Buchanan) were answered in a 'New Age' way. These whimsical, flowery answers did not go down too well with the large audience, and I knew that it wouldn't be too long before the pot, so to speak, boiled over. It did. Suddenly a change of atmosphere was felt in the hall, outbursts from the audience started to ring out, shouts of:

"What the bloody hell has all this hugging trees, got to do with the UFO sightings in Bonnybridge?"

Followed by:

"Get off that stage woman, you don't know what you are talking about!"

One chap stood up and stated his disappointment at the tone of the meeting, saying that it wasn't doing anything for the people of Bonnybridge. Hugging trees was not the answer. Councillor Billy Buchanan broke in and calmed the situation down somewhat with a few choice words, (and sufficiently good they were too!), he said, in part:

"Look, these speakers have travelled many miles to be here tonight, especially Phyllis Schlemmer, so please give them the respect that they deserve."

At this, an appreciative round of applause went around the hall, after which the debate resumed. But by now though, people were voicing their opinions with their feet, and many people noiselessly rose to their feet and walked out. The thrusting of chairs scarping along the wooden floor as people rose to their feet and walked out drowned out the previous applause. The meeting was then brought to a close, and a vote of thanks was offered to the speakers. I'm afraid I wasn't too convinced by what I heard that night. If the 'Council of Nine' really wants to make people sit up and listen to what it has to say about environmental issues, then why don't they openly do something which will really spark peoples' interests. Something impressively 'visual'! What I would suggest is that if the 'Council of Nine' is really what it says it is, it should be able to create a visual sign in the sky. It could be over Glasgow, London, or Manchester. A large visual cross or shape in the sky on a selected date and time, or even 'show themselves' come down and speak to us direct! This would truly, once and for all, show the reality of the 'Council of Nine'. But I suppose that these 'people' 'aliens' call them what you will, work to their own agenda, and that by doing something as easy as this, well it would just be too simple. Somehow, I just don't buy it! Poor Geri Rogers, the man mistakenly thought of as Zalus, was badly misquoted in the 'Scottish Sun' newspaper where he allegedly said:

"Aliens were drawn to the Bonnybridge area as it was a 'place of freedom".

The 'Sun' stated in their laughable headline, 'Aliens Flocking to Braveheart Land' built on that comment by saying that aliens were flocking to Bonnybridge in Stirlingshire because of battles between the Scots and English! Oh, for goodness' sake! This is a prime example of newspapers hamming stories and quotes up.

It should be noted, that after Billy paid for the hire of the Falkirk Town Hall, and after paying the speakers, the remainder of the ticket sale money, went to purchase six large colour televisions that Billy then donated to six local Primary Schools within the Stirlingshire District. It should also be pointed out, that Councillor Buchanan bought Football Strips for a local Junior football club with the remainder of the ticket sale money from the June 1994 Falkirk Town Hall UFO Event. Billy was not in this to make money, as some have suggested.

SPI member Billy Devlin wrote an article about his views of the Cosmic Agenda Conference. Here is what he had to say which was featured in out November-December issue of ENIGMAS.

THE COSMIC AGENDA LECTURE
(A review by Billy Devlin)

They came in their hundreds, (around 700 the papers say, from all walks of life. Young, old, large, small, there was even a chap with large plastic pointed ears. No, not Zalus, but a member of the public who had a sense of humour, and by God, he needed it! The event had been advertised where people had been in touch with the Council of Nine (a group of extraterrestrial beings who are said to watch over the Earth to ensure that we do not do anything nasty to it) and they were supposed to divulge all, or at least some, of the information that had been given to them. It was hoped that they might shine some light on what had been going on in Bonnybridge over the last three years. In the end, the public that came were subjected to three speakers who presented three entirely different talks that amounted to a cross between an SNP rally, a Billy Graham Rally, and an open learning lecture. All of which seemed to be heralding the birth of a new nationalist religion.

Geri Rogers had obviously been to see the movie 'Braveheart' recently. Throughout his talk, he constantly told the people of Bonnybridge to speak out, support each other, and rise above apathy. There are positive benevolent entities who are willing to help them bring about a brighter future. They will find their origins in the stars. There will be a new Scotland, with a new balance of nature and a re-awakening of a nation. I felt as if I had walked into a Scottish Nationalist Party rally by mistake. Then Phylis Schlemmer took the stage. She started off by giving us a rundown of her psychic experiences when she was young. Then how she and some friends had a UFO experience. It was late 1969, early 1970 that she started to receive messages from other sources while in an unconscious state. It transpired that the messages came from the Council of Nine. Over a period of time, the information received filled four thousand pages. It was at this point I was transported to a Billy Graham rally. She started to talk about how special the place of Bonnybrook was, (That's Bonnybridge to those not in tune with the council!) How the sons of God mentioned in the Bible could have come here in the past, and the people may even be descended from them. They must be part of a group which will go forward with open minds with very proud roots and spread the word. The word love is over used in the world today. We should use kindness instead. She felt kindness throughout Bonnybridge, from its people and its buildings etc (am I really writing this!) She then went onto talk about the problems of the youth today.

By this time, the reporter sitting next to me was falling asleep. I began to wonder if I could contact my wife to ask her to tape the X Files for me (by phone of course!) Then on came Ken MacFarlane. Ah! I thought a pro here. He started to make use of the stage back drop of stars in his introduction. But then he blew up, stuttering and stammering throughout the rest of his talk. I began to look on him as a bad Patrick Moore impersonation. He talked about the psychology of UFO experiences. A hidden knowledge people have. Intuition or knowledge? The psychology of life, anger and humanism were all discussed. It was heavy stuff folks! This was not what people who turned up wanted to hear. Where 'was' the Council of Nine? Where were the explanations as to what was going on over Bonnybridge? The people wanted to learn. They wanted advice. They wanted answers. Why else would the larger majority of them stay behind in the hope that they might get answers in the question-and-answer section of the evening. Unfortunately, they were subjected to the same new religion, we love you all clap trap. No wonder some of the audience were angry. No wonder there were harsh words said. These people do not want to be patronised by individuals who only have been in Bonnybridge for a couple of hours and then retreat into their own domain, leaving it to the people of Bonnybridge to take even more ridicule for sitting through this. The people of Bonnybridge want answers, and people who are willing to work alongside them to achieve those answers.

The one good thing in my opinion that came out of this meeting, is the obvious affection which the people of Bonnybridge has for Billy Buchanan. Time and time again he asked the audience for their patience and understanding, and each time he was greeted with applause and respect. Here is a man who is listening and working with the people, and he is right in the thick of it. He has opened himself up to ridicule, but he has the people with him, he lives among them. He is standing with the people of Bonnybridge and taking the flak with them, and whether or not you believe in what he says, you have to admire and respect him for that. The people of Bonnybridge left the meeting with more questions than when they went in. Like who out there has the answer? Who out there is going to treat them with respect and listen to their stories without patronising us? There is a cry for help here.

Report by Billy Devlin.

SUE ME, SUE YOU BLUES!

The UFO sightings continued in the Bonnybridge area, and new cases were still being reported by members of the public. The 'Zalus Affair' was rarely mentioned in the press, and other than a few Zalus joke-making remarks made by some people to Councillor Buchanan, the whole thing was beginning to die down. That was until a July morning in 1997, when the phone rang. Upon answering it, (it was a journalist), I was amazed to be asked my feelings about Councillor Billy Buchanan suing me! I remember thinking that it must be someone winding me up. The journalist went on to say that Councillor Buchanan had had enough of these name calling remarks and had set the wheels in motion to sue me. I was gob smacked. Nearly two and a half years had passed since the story first started and ended. Now, here in 1997, like an old wound, it had 'opened up again'. I put the phone down to the journalist, only to pick it up again seconds later as it rang with yet another journalist. Then another, then some radio shows all wanting to do a taped interview down the phone on what I felt about being sued. By now I was in a state of shock, more so because of the deep admiration that I felt for Councillor Buchanan as a person who stood up to ridicule and fought for the right of his constituents to be heard over this UFO issue. I stated to the press and in radio broadcasts, that no matter what, if I got sued for a million pounds, Billy was still number one as far as I was concerned. Billy dropped this case against me.

BUT WAS BONNYBRIDGE A UFO HOT SPOT?

In August 1995, well known and respected UFO researcher, and author Jenny Randles, questioned in the popular Journal 'Fortean Times' issue 82, if Bonnybridge was all the result of hype and overactive imaginations! She stated that her book, *"UFOs And How To See Them"* (Anaya Publishers Ltd 1992) had sold better in Scotland that it did in England, and that Scotland was 'primed' to look for UFOs, and to expect to see more of them than it had in the past'. She then posed the question, 'Was it really a coincidence that within a few weeks Councillor Billy Buchanan was claiming to be swamped by reports from his constituents?" She also mentioned the fact that the English Town of Milton Keynes, was for a time, known as a 'window area', in other words, an area which receives a higher concentration of UFO reports than anywhere else. Nothing much happens in Milton Keynes, she was reported as saying, but one had to consider the possibility that the rise in UFO reports from Milton Keynes, may have been due to the arrival in the town of well-known and respected ufologist, Ken Phillips, sadly no longer with us. Ken, a prolific investigator, set out with intense vigour to try and find out about a number of UFO reports that had been witnessed there, and as such, attained press attention and media focus. His tenacity in tracing witnesses, (Jenny states), almost single handily 'created' the increase in case reports. I can accept that, and I can see what Jenny is implying. But was this the case in Bonnybridge? Was the ongoing UFO reports and media attention, purely down to the information that both Councillor Billy Buchanan and I were providing? I would say, yes and no! Yes, we were regularly in the newspapers, asking further witnesses to come forward with their UFO sightings, but no, I don't really think that 'we' created the Bonnybridge phenomenon, it was already there. It was a 'hot spot' back in 1982, and I have already mentioned, I uncovered a number of UFO reports from this area which in fact pre-date even 1982, so I don't think it specifically started up in November 1992, the month and year when UFO reports were first brought to the attention of the press. But Jenny does have a point. In fact, in her 'Fortean Times' article, she goes on to state that she had a conversation with the late Dr J. Allen Hynek, the father of modern UFOlogy, and she posed this question to him about 'window and hot spot areas'. Hynek was reported to have explained to Jenny, that he had observed this fact many times before, that UFO investigators, through their sheer diligence and tireless work, can probably make an area 'come alive' with UFO sightings, more than it would have done if another less educated and professional researcher was involved.

WERE BILLY BUCHANAN AND I THE CAUSE OF THE BONNYBRIDGE UFO SIGHTINGS!

I'd like to again discuss the opinions by others regarding the Bonnybridge UFO enigma having been thrust into the public domain by Councillor Billy Buchanan and myself: that there were only minimal UFO reports, and the publicity surrounding them promoted by Billy and I, made them seem 'more than' minimal. Both Billy and I were none too pleased at these accusations, and yes, it did upset me. And yes, when people saw fit to attack both Billy and I, I was quickly on the Bonnybridge defence. I mentioned above that English UFO researcher Jenny Randles (who I admire deeply and greatly) alluded to the fact that the Bonnybridge UFO events might, in part, be down to Councillor Billy Buchanan and I, hyping it all up in the media. I've stated elsewhere that Jenny also alluded to this fact in a 'Fortean Times' article. She again alluded to this in the 'London Weekend Television' book, 'Strange But True?' regarding the Bonnybridge UFO sightings. I felt that I just had to take her to task on this and wrote a review of this book where I held no punches as to what I felt was being said about this Scottish town. Jenny quickly got back in touch with me about my comments, and in part, this is what she had to say to me:

"Moving on to your review of the book, 'Strange But True?' and its glaring 'mistake' and the 'tone' adopted by its authors (Peter Hough and myself) criticising Bonnybridge. Again, with due respect, I think this was a little unfair. Firstly, let me explain that Peter and I did not have free reign to write our own views. We were not contracted by the publishers to write a book of our own choice, but as consultants to the T.V. company (LWTV) London Weekend Television. We were asked to adapt their scripts, the book had to be more than just a verbal transcript of the programmes. David Alpine as programme and book editor, had the final word on what went in, and what was left out. This was as it should have been, as the book was reflecting the T.V. series. When writing about Bonnybridge, the opinions expressed at the very end of the chapter regarding the town's use of publicity, are clearly referenced from another

researcher, namely Ron Halliday. In the book we named that researcher, as we felt his views should be attributed, as I'm sure he would have wished. However, as no interview material from him was included on the T.V. programme itself, we were asked to take out his name at proof stage. This was one instance when we argued our case over the book and lost. However, it was not unreasonable to present this man's viewpoint on the matter even so to illustrate that there were counter opinions over Bonnybridge."

At this point in Jenny's letter to me, she went on about some British ufologists having a pop at Councillor Billy Buchanan and I for presenting the Japanese film crew who came to Bonnybridge with a cake, by way of showing our Scottish hospitality to our overseas guests. She writes:

"I accept what you say about the piper and the cake. I am sure it was done out of pure Scottish hospitality, (and next time we foreigners from England come to town, I trust we will receive the same delights)! The press story which did refer to the piper, the cake, and Billy Buchanan's quip about a Japanese car factory, was, as noted in the book, surely just an innocent jest. That said, you have to see why some people might make the connection with Livingston and suggest that Bonnybridge might be seeking to enhance its status with help from UFO activity. This is all we did, repeat the comments that 'were' being made in the press and by other UFOlogists. Surely it was not unreasonable to do so. Your comments and Councillor's Buchanan's views were given as well, so it was not a one-sided presentation."

Jenny then goes on to discuss what was, or is, a UFO 'Hot Spot'. Here is what she had to say:

"Note that we do not suggest that the sightings in the first place are false, only that their promotion might owe something to opportunism, a very different thing. Equally, the two phrases that I have here emphasised, do, I trust, indicate how we subtly tend to direct the reader. We refer to the accusations as being *'cynical'* and Billy Buchanan's response to them as being, *'very fair'*. If this creates a tone which is rebuking the town, then I am at a loss to see how. For the record, I will point out my personal opinion about Bonnybridge. I do believe in the reality of *'Window Areas'*, but my problem with Bonnybridge is that there is little to indicate it has a historic track record of sightings. This is certainly what differentiates it from say the Pennines or the Brown Mountains of Texas, or the Tully region of Queensland, or La Malmot in Southern France where you can trace a window area through records dating back many decades, even centuries. Now, it may be that a track record exists for Bonnybridge, and nobody has found it or reported on it as yet. If so, that's clearly a research task for SPI. Equally, it may be that windows can spring up out of nowhere. I have an open mind on that possibility. But most theories about window areas would tend to suggest otherwise. In addition, there is no doubt from all we know about UFO activity, that only a tiny fraction of sightings ever gets reported to UFOlogists. Statistical surveys indicate this as one in ten, or even considerably less. It is therefore logical to suggest that when an area is so effectively promoted as a window, as Bonnybridge has been, indeed not just locally, but internationally, then the number of reported sightings will inevitably rocket".

"Also, locals will be encouraged to come into the open. The press and active UFOlogists offer focal points to receive sightings that witnesses might otherwise have been unaware existed. Hotlines were even set up. The opportunities for witnesses multiply beyond those normally available. All of tis is bound to increase the number of sightings flowing in by several fold. Consequently, there are important social factors at work within Bonnybridge which you cannot afford to overlook. They have also been at work in *Gulf Breeze* (another UFO Hot Spot) in my opinion with equal effectiveness. In other words, say that pre-1989, Bonnybridge generated 5 sightings per year, as did some other location that nobody thinks of as a window area. *(Let's pick Fleetwood)* (Lancashire England) *We can reasonably assume that these 5 came out of a real total of maybe 50-100 sightings or more per year. These sightings were made but mostly never reported. Fleetwood remains* unpromoted, so it continues to tick over at 5 per annum. Bonnybridge, on the other hand, becomes the focal point of attention and lots more witnesses from that 50-100 plus, are encouraged to speak out. As such, perhaps 30 to 40 sightings or even more, come in for the next year and Bonnybridge immediately appears to be a window. The process is self-fuelling, and continued attention to these reports is bound to bring more and more reports".

"None of this is to argue that Bonnybridge was nor a window area in the first place. Obviously the first sightings had to come from somewhere. This might have been an isolated flap that got the snowball rolling downhill, or it could have been a genuine manifestation of window area-ness, (if there can be such a thing!) I would not pre-judge the issue and look forward to the books and full reports that are going to come in the future. These should try to, and may indeed prove, the status of Bonnybridge. All I'm saying is that a note of caution is required. These are the views that sceptics will raise against the continued claim that Bonnybridge is the biggest window area in Britain. It may be, but do not just ignore the critics, because their views are valid parts of this complex equation. And do seek out that past historical record, for if it exists for the Bonnybridge area, then it will do more than a thousand arguments to counter the charges that this town's UFO prominence is a result of hype, not an unusual level of UFO reality."

Best wishes. Jenny Randles, Fleetwood, February 1995.

The above letter in part, initially appeared in the May-June issue of our SPI magazine ENIGMAS. In that issue, I replied to Jenny's comments and here, in part, is what I said:

"As far as Bonnybridge being a 'window area', well let's be honest, 'window areas' have to start somewhere at some time, or we wouldn't have 'window areas.' The Bonnybridge UFO 'window area' essentially opened up in November 1992 when the first reports came to our attention. However, I have on file a number of UFO reports from around the same area and also press cuttings to back this up, including a radio Scotland *interview I did about the Falkirk/Denny UFO sightings in 1982. So, this area 'did' see UFO sightings in the past. As for the UFO Hot Line being set up. This was set up by another Scottish UFOlogists, Ken Higgins, although, having said that, the SPI phone number was indeed used in a number of Scottish newspapers solely as a contact number to report any UFO sightings. There is no problem in setting up a UFO hotline, for this is only to gauge if indeed there is 'something going on'. Without it, how would we know!"*

"SPI has never at any time, said to the press that Bonnybridge 'was' the biggest UFO 'window area' in Britain. This statement was built up by the press, and for anyone who has worked with the press, well, they will know that! We did say that Bonnybridge was a 'window area', but we 'never' said that it was the biggest. There are a lot of points in Jenny's letter that I agree with, and the above points are really the only ones that I'd like to clear up. My anger was really not directed towards either Jenny or Peter, but to those other UFOlogists who, from the outset, who stated that Bonnybridge was one big publicity stunt started by Councillor Billy Buchanan and I. And before we knew it, we were being accused of 'hyping it all up."

I go onto mention in my article in ENIGMAS that Councillor Buchanan was elected to serve the people of Bonnybridge in any way, shape, or form. He could not turn his back on his constituents with these UFO sightings. He was elected to serve them, not ignore them. I also stated that not all UFO sightings came to me via Billy, there were a number of sightings that came to me independently. Yes, Billy Buchanan is a colourful character, as anyone who has met him will tell you. I have nothing but praise and respect for Billy Buchanan, and those small minded people who threw accusations at him, well, they are so misguided. There will always be a big question mark over the amount of genuine UFO sightings across Stirlingshire. Again, the press takes great delight in adding on an extra zero to any given figure. And for all those people who have sighted a UFO and come forward, how many who have also seen a UFO but 'do not' come forward, mainly through fear of ridicule, and who can blame them when you have seen what Billy and I had to put up with.

I finished my 1995 piece about the controversy about UFO 'window areas' by saying the following:

> "UFOlogists should all be sailing on the same boat, not swimming behind clutching at drag ropes. I sincerely hope that whatever happens in regard to the Bonnybridge UFOs, we will be wiser and not throwing stones at one another. At the end of the day, we are all working towards the same cause, that of providing answers. Life is never plain sailing, there will always be a difference of opinion. We at SPI do not mind criticism, so long as it is constructive. To think that we shocked and upset other UFOlogists by providing a piper to pipe in a Japanese film crew into their hotel is frankly, beyond belief. Like I say, since when did good old Scottish hospitality stop? And finally, don't forget the media's part in all this. I have worked with the newspapers for a good number of years now. They misquote you, they create innuendo, and although the reported who has worked on the story has done a good job, when he hands his story in, the editor 'may' jazz it up a bit, give it arms and legs, and do a song and dance on it. It does happen folks."

Jenny Randles was quite right to take me to task on my somewhat angry review of the 'Strange But True?' book on the Bonnybridge sightings. But that's all water under the bridge now. If it wasn't for Jenny Randles, I probably would never have got into researching UFOs. I attended many of her lectures in England, travelling by train and bus to do so. And whilst Jenny is not so much in the public domain these days, the legacy of her research and work that she has left, is there for all to see. A wonderful researcher.

Well, that wasn't quite the end of the debacle about the veracity (or not) of the Bonnybridge 'Window Area'. The editor of the popular magazine 'Magonia', John Rimmer joined the debate. Here is his letter that we published in our SPI Magazine ENIGMAS, dates August-September 1995:

"Dear Editor".

"I'd just like to chip in my twopenn'worth to the argument between yourself and Jenny Randles about her comments on the Bonnybridge so called 'window area'. I think your reply to her letter in ENIGMAS, no 40, is unfair and totally misses her main point. A great deal of nonsense has been written about 'flaps', 'window areas' and so on, but the argument boils down to simple alternatives, do these represent a real objective increase in the number of phenomena which are reported as UFOs within a particular time period, or, are the increased numbers of reports, a function of a greater propensity on the part of the individuals to report their experience publicly? This is what Jenny rightly asks, and you do not answer her".

"The Bonnybridge area appears to be blessed with a number of high-profile individuals who are effectively encouraging local people to, 'come out' as UFO witnesses. Yourself, Billy Devlin, and Councillor Billy Buchanan. Through the activities of this trio, the good citizens of Bonnybridge now know an accessible local agency which will accept their reports sympathetically. Most places do not have such a service, and people are unwilling to report their experiences to remote agencies, such as the M.o.D or BUFORA, who they do not know and are unsure how they will be treated. Thus, Bonnybridge has more UFO reports than other places. There is nothing strange about this. You have actually 'created' the 'window area' through your own hard work."

At this point in his letter to me, John Rimmer was again perplexed at our Scottish hospitality towards our Japanese guests. He said:

"I'm a bit puzzled about the piper and the cake too. The Scots are of course a notoriously hospitable and generous race, but I would not have thought, that even in Scotland, this was the usual reception afforded to a visiting Japanese T.V. camera crew. The world is, after all, snooping with them, and does suggest something rather extraordinary is going on. You are probably aware, especially those who are as old as the editors

of MAGONIA, who's collective UFOlogical memory stretches back many centuries, that over the years there have been any number of petitions circulated by hopeful UFO groups demanding that the Government, 'do something' about UFOs, or 'release the facts'. These, as is yours, were doomed to failure for the simple fact that there is nothing the Government can do, and there are 'no' relevant facts to release. Local petitions are best confined to such matters as the state of the pavements, or the timing of the last bus from Bonnybridge to Tullibody."

John Rimmer, Editor, MAGONIA, London.

All I'll say about John's letter above is. Yes, perhaps because of myself, Billy Devlin and Councillor Buchanan was on the ground so to speak in allowing people to come forward with their UFO sightings, that offered them this opportunity that other towns and cities across the United Kingdom did not. But that's not our fault. We were there to get answers. As to John's point about petitions are a waste of time. I'm sure you will find that many a petition on other matters have successfully turned the Government's hand. So not so, Mr Rimmer. If you don't try, you don't get.

The media of course has a major role to play in all this, for without them, notice of events would never have come out in the way that they had. SPI were assisting the media with stories, (with, I might add, witness permission and their co-operation). Although some did ask that we use pseudonyms as I have had to do in my part of this book). Indeed, I must point out the fact that the media assisted SPI by providing further witnesses. It was a case of. 'You scratch my back and I'll scratch yours'. This practice still goes on today throughout the world, and many UFO societies must hold their hand up and say, that this indeed is the case. And although we researchers have a duty to the witness, SPI always stressed to the witness, that their testimony, might bring forward other potential witnesses with similar tales to tell, which indeed back up their own testimony. Of course, we have a right to protect the witness from back street press journalism, but without the witness having the guts to come forward and state their case, can we ever hope to obtain the credibility that we so badly desire for our subject. I have always said that information is for the people. Researchers should never 'bury' their UFO cases in a filing cabinet, what's the point? This information, so long as it is truthful and sincere, should be made public, and SPI as a society, has worked to this principle for many a year. They say it's good to talk, well let's talk about what's going on, and not what we should be burying in filing cabinets.

THE PROSSER SIGHTING

Another low-level close proximity UFO sighting occurred to a family who lived near Bonnybridge and scared the living daylights out of them. Vera Prosser (51) was driving in her car on an October evening back in 1995. She was accompanied on this journey by her husband and daughter. They were travelling to a local garage near Falkirk to buy their lottery tickets. They had reached the Old Rechem Plant and were just chatting away about some matters of the day, when they became aware of a large light in a field. The light resembled a car's headlight on full beam. Thinking this most peculiar, they slowed down to around 10 miles per hour in order to get a better look at this strange light. Suddenly the light began to approach their car until it was directly above, whereupon it began to shine its light down through the sunroof and into the car. Heather (13) Vera's daughter was screaming at the top of her voice, *"Get out of here! get out of here!"* Vera then looked up through the sunroof and observed what she described as a thick silvery wire which was going around the bottom of this object. It was all 'twisted together' she said just like the intertwined cables on the Forth Bridge. She went on to say that the object was wider than the car and was roughly about six feet away from the car roof. What made them believe that it wasn't an aircraft or helicopter of any kind, was purely down to the fact that it was completely silent. Not a sound could be heard coming from it. Then suddenly it just took off at an incredible rate.

Upon its disappearance, Vera put her foot down on the accelerator and quickly drove home. Upon arriving home, Heather ran in tears to her best friend's house next door. Both

Vera and her husband Myles were shaken up by this experience. Vera explained in her interview with 'Night and Day' magazine the feelings that most UFO witnesses have when they have witnessed something strange in the sky, she stated:

> "At first, I was too frightened to tell anyone, people would think I was crazy. You feel so stupid, so ridiculous, but it was just so real at the time and so frightening. It's just something I wish had never happened."

Vera reported her sighting to Councillor Billy Buchanan, and it's thanks to the courage of witnesses like the Prosser Family that researchers like myself can build up a clearer picture as to what is going on.

I've worked with journalists since I began to get into this wonderful subject. Some have been great and spent a lot of time with me ensuring that everything is taken down carefully and honestly. Some journalists, and I can't really blame them all as some are told to 'spice a story up.' Journalist Alan Brown wrote about Bonnybridge in the' Sunday Times Scotland', dated October 8th, 1995. The title of this three-page article was 'Pie In The Sky' where he stated that Bonnybridge was slowly becoming home to a nut cluster of sky watchers and conspiracy theorists, a Lourdes for the trainspotters of the 21st century. He further stated that the closest that Councillor Buchanan had ever come to astral travel, was official complaints about the noise of planes from Glasgow, Edinburgh, and Cumbernauld airports. The article is rather tongue in cheek, but to give Alan his due, apart from a few mickey-takes, it's not all bad.

TELEVISION FEVER

The intensity of which these UFO sightings were captivating the attention of the public was such that more and more television crews were coming from all parts of the UK and overseas to get in on the action. A Scottish based Television Company entitled, 'Wall To Wall Scotland', who are based in Glasgow, sent representative Charlie Stuart over to Stirling to take in an SPI meeting after which he discussed his plans of a documentary concerning the A70 UFO abduction, and also the events around Bonnybridge. The series was called 'Cracking Stories' and the completed documentary on Scottish UFO events and the A70 UFO Incident, was a resounding success, and showed the Scottish public how serious this UFO business really was. 'Wall To Wall Scotland' had treated their UFO programme with respect, and it is one of my favourite programmes on the Bonnybridge UFO Phenomenon, simply because of the honesty and integrity by producer Charlie Stuart to a somewhat emotive subject. He handled it with compassion, and in a way which was not detrimental to the witnesses. Other T.V. shows that I was involved with during 1995, was BBC Scotland's 'The Big Country', (as mentioned earlier) an offbeat leisure series which was presented by Dougie Vipond, (Ex drummer of Scottish pop group Deacon Blue) and Jenni Calder. We also worked closely with Carlton Television who paid a visit to Scotland in which SPI's Billy Devlin played a big part.

THE UFOS THAT NEVER WERE!
(Shieldhill, October 1995)

All UFOlogists know that around 95% of all UFO reports have natural explanations, from Aircraft, birds, wind debris, astronomical bodies such as planets and stars and more. Any working UFOlogist knows that in the vast majority of his or her UFO case research work, nearly nine out of ten cases turns out to be I.F.Os (Identified Flying Objects). Some cases on the surface appear sensational, and some even have the added bonus of video footage to support their claims. This was the case on a SPI Investigation during October 1995 when I received a telephone call from Councillor Billy Buchanan who informed me of a couple from the village of Shieldhill near Bonnybridge who apparently had been witnessing strange lights in the sky, some of which, they had captured on video. I was further informed that a copy of that video had been sent down to 'Quest International's' Tony Dodd. I quickly got on the phone to Tony and asked him what he thought of the video. Tony replied that he was convinced that it was genuine UFO activity.

This view was also echoed by Councillor Buchanan who had also viewed the footage. At this point I hadn't seen the video footage but soon arranged a date with the witnesses to arrange a suitable date to interview them. The day arrived, and both Billy Devlin and I travelled over to Shieldhill. The village of Shieldhill is situated on top of some rolling hills, and there is quite a bit of farmland and fields situated all around the village. Also attending the witness's home was UFO abductee from the A70 Incident, Garry Wood. After exchanging some polite conversation with the family, it was time to settle down and watch what they had captured on their camcorder. But first, let me tell you from the witness own words, exactly what he claimed to have seen on the night in question. From the witness statement I take the following:

"On Saturday 21st October 1995 whilst getting up to the toilet at approximately 05:00am in the morning. I looked out of the bedroom window to see what the weather was like. To my utter astonishment, there was two flashing lights in the sky. I quickly woke my wife and shouted "Susan, quick, look at this". To which she replied, "Oh my God, what is it"? We went downstairs and opened the back door. The sky was very clear, by now the objects were far away. We stood out the back and watched them for an hour and a half. The reason we found the objects so peculiar, was because they made no sound whatsoever, and they moved very peculiar and incredibly fast. We decided to keep looking for these objects every night, and on Tuesday the 24th conditions outside were very windy, but as soon as it got dark, we started to observe these objects flying about again. We also observed, 5 intermittent blue flashes in the sky like lightning, and the sky was lighting up. There was about 10 to 15 minutes in between flashes, but on the 15th flash, the lights went out, and there was a power cut over most of Shieldhill. I could have put this down to lightning, but we were still observing these objects at the time. On the following day, Wednesday 25th of October 1995, I borrowed a video camera and set it up on a tripod stand at the back door at around 6:00pm. I started filming and filmed 40 minutes of video. The BBC pylons which can be seen at the back of our house seemed

to have some kind of significance, though what I do not know. These objects made no sound whatsoever. On the Tuesday (24th), a large triangular craft with lights underneath passed over our house making no sound at all. We phoned the M.o.D. and R.A.F. and were told that there was nothing in the area. Also, two police officers witnessed these objects. P.C. Morris McKenna, and P.C. Mitchell from Maddiston police station saw this on Sunday 29th October from our house. We were told that they did not know what these objects were, but if they came closer to our home, not to hesitate and phone them. Since these sightings, my wife and I have been contacted by other people through various sources, who have had similar, or 'worse' experiences, and who are too frightened to come forward for fear of being laughed at or ridiculed."

VIEWING THE UFO VIDEO

At this point I would ask you to remember the fact that I have been in UFOlogy for many years now, and in that time, I have seen a good number of alleged UFO videos. The majority of which, I must say, I have not been overly impressed with. So, it's not a case of me just viewing the odd video. Nearly every UFO video that I have seen, all look pretty much the same, i.e. static balls of light in a dark night sky, which I'm convinced have been bright stars or planets. Now, what you have to understand is that the people who are taking these UFO videos, are not doing it for the best of their health! They honestly believe that they are filming something strange. I have never, as yet came across anyone who has openly tried to deceive me by filming natural airborne objects and trying to pass them off as UFOs. This family appeared very honest and sincere people. Yes, admittedly, some people can appear convincing, I know that, but being in their presence, sitting down and talking to them about what they had seen, well, as I say, they convinced me.

OH DEAR!

Anyway, Billy Devlin, Garry Wood and I sat down to watch the video and is soon became apparent, that what I was viewing, was nothing but aircraft. There was one particular sequence in which flashing pulsating lights were observed, but I'll come back to that in a moment. After watching the video, we then proceeded to ask both witnesses various questions in regard to their sighting and asked them both to complete the standard UFO sighting account forms which included a UFO photographic form, all of which, they agreed to do. They did (as some UFO witnesses and prone to do) requested no publicity, which of course was adhered to. The couple then asked my thoughts as to what I saw on the video. I replied that it was too early to tell, that I would need to check with the police, the airports, the Met Office, the M.o.D. etc to rule out various things, but my honest opinion at this juncture was, that it looked like an aircraft to me. Now reader, this can always be a tricky one, you have been invited into someone's home in good faith where they are convinced that they have filmed something most peculiar. You sit there, you view the footage, and you have to be up front and honest with them and say what you believe it could be. This might not go down well of course (I've been in this position a few times so I should know) but you have to be honest with people and say it as it is.

Another aspect of their video, and one which I've seen many times on other so called UFO videos, is what we call, 'the bat like effect'. And what this is, is that when a camera tries to zoom in on a bright light source in a dark night sky, two chunks from the top and bottom of the circular white image appear to be lost, and you are looking at a 'bat like' shape. It's not a UFO, its bad focus, in the sense that the internal camera optics are trying to create the best image but due to distance and brightness, it can come up with some strange shapes, more often than not, it's this 'bat like shape'. At this point in the proceedings, I asked Danny if he could show me the area in which he had taken his camcorder footage of these strange lights. This he did, and I, Billy, Garry along with Danny's wife, all trooped out into his back garden. Now, to let you understand, Danny's back garden faces onto fields, and it has a commanding and panoramic view of the sky with no bright street lights to obscure one's vision.

REALLY!

As we all stood outside gazing into the night sky, a rumbling sound was heard coming from the sky at a distance. Upon hearing this sound, Danny immediately said:

"That's it, that's the sound I hear before I see these UFOs."

A few seconds later, a large commercial passenger airliner flew across Danny's roof (at a good height) with its navigational lights flashing on and off. Danny then shouted out:

"See, see, there it is, that's a UFO."

At this point, both Billy Devlin and I looked at each other in acute embarrassment. I then turned round and said to Danny:

"Danny, that's an aircraft."

To which he replied:

"Are you sure?"

A few minutes later Danny pointed to the horizon in which a small bright white light was flying slowly across the sky. He quickly shouted out:

"There's one, there's one."

I again stated that this was another aircraft, probably en-route to Cumbernauld airport. Dear reader, let me say, that this was as much an embarrassment to me having to tell the chap that it was an aircraft, than him telling me that it was a UFO! Danny then asked about some strange lights which he pointed out that were pulsating above a hill in the distance featuring a number of bushes and a hedgerow. I replied that I could only speculate, but looking at this as I was, it could be a car which had stopped at the side of the road (there was a road in the distance near this area) and had left its indicators on to warn other motorists that it was there as it was pitch black over at that area. I've noticed whilst visiting UFO witnesses, that than can get over excited and sometimes misconstrue ordinary mundane objects as UFOs. Now, this hill with the hedgerow and bushes, was on an incline, so it was not flat land. I could see that the witness was none too keen on my prosaic explanation, but what else could I do in that awkward situation, tell lies?

After several more minutes skywatching, mostly in an embarrassing silence, we decided to call it a night. And after some small awkward conversation, said our goodbyes. To complete the night, both Billy Devlin and I headed off to Maddiston Police Station (which also serves Shieldhill) where we hoped we could interview police constables McKenna and Mitchell. Sadly though, both men were unavailable. We had hoped to speak to them about their attendance at the witness's home. We wanted their views, their thoughts. Did they see aircraft whilst there as we had! We did however speak with a female police officer, and, after informing her why we wanted to speak to her colleagues, asked her if she knew of any UFO sightings in this area. She informed us that she was aware of this couple who had taken footage of these strange lights and that various police officers had been speaking about it at the station. She then said that she would get those police officers to call me (they never did). And this was after repeated (and boy I mean repeated) telephone calls from me to Maddiston police station, eventually I just gave up!

INVESTIGATION

My research into this couple's UFO sightings with the dates given to me, uncovered that aircraft were in the vicinity of this couple's home at the dates and times stated. This information was given to me from Edinburgh Airport. At the end of the day, whilst this case shows that more often than not, 'things aren't always what they seem' (of which this is a good example) there is no denying that other people in the Shieldhill, Maddiston and Bonnybridge area, were still seeing unusual things. I wouldn't have bothered researching the Bonnybridge wave if I really didn't believe that 'something' was going on. Cases like this though, are a learning curve. They are part of a learning process. They allow investigators to come to terms with 'people' and their perceptions. The Shieldhill UFO was a case of mistaken identity, viewed honestly, but mistakenly.

AN UNWANTED BEDROOM VISITOR?

Another intriguing case that our society were involved with during 1995, was the time when we answered a telephone call in regard to a lady who said that her four-year-old daughter had been visited in the night by a small strange 'creature'. The lady claimed that she knew her daughter well, and that she wasn't making this up and that it wasn't a bad dream or a hallucination. Something 'very real' was happening. Joining the SPI investigation that day, were Garry Wood and Stan Brown. The family lived in a block of flats in the town of Grangemouth which is around 12 miles or so away from Bonnybridge. The view from their flat gave them a commanding view of parts of the Forth Valley. The mother Amanda (pseudonym) was aged 25, and the father George (pseudonym) was aged 28, their two daughters were aged 4 and 2 respectively. Sarah being the oldest and the one who had witnessed the small 'creature'. During our Interview with the family, we ascertained that they had been observing 'strange lights' in the sky near their home for the past several weeks. Lights of which they knew, did not conform to any aircraft navigation lights. Witnessing these lights, did not really bother them much. What did bother them, however, was that for a period of several nights, their four-year-old daughter Sarah had begun screaming in her room, claiming that she was seeing 'monsters'. Amanda Initially felt that this was due to bad dreams, as most youngsters went through this period. However, it was the intensity of these screaming episodes over several nights that was to change her opinion on the matter. Indeed, on one particular night, not only did Sarah claim to have seen 'monsters', but she also said that a 'blue light' came into her room.

MORE STRANGE LIGHTS IN ROOM

Amanda, as any mother would do, started taking Sarah into her own bedroom to sleep, and for a couple of nights Sarah enjoyed a relaxed and peaceful sleep. Indeed, during this time, the parents took the steps to decorate Sarah's bedroom, perhaps a change of decor might help, they surmised. Sadly however, this did not work, and upon Sarah returning to sleep once more in her own bedroom, she began to see the 'monsters' again. One night, as the mother again entered her daughter's bedroom due to screams coming from Sarah, she happened to glance out of the bedroom window and saw at a distance, a bright white light hovering above some fields. She quickly took her daughter through to her own room and was astounded to see bright lights coming into 'her' room through the window. Amanda couldn't account for these lights and let us not forget that she lives on the top floor of a block of flats. Even car headlights, as they turned outside, she told SPI, could not have come into her bedroom like this. She has never experienced lights like this during her tenancy of this house. That morning, the mother asked her daughter to try and draw what she had seen. Being a child, and as expected, her daughter's drawing of what she had seen, wasn't too good, so Amanda tried to draw as close as she could, from her daughter's sketch. When her daughter saw this, she said, *"Mummy, you forgot the slanting eyes!"* The sketch drawn is not that different from the classic 'grey' figure seen in many UFO Incidents. One other aspect that we learned whilst interviewing the family, was that young Sarah not only saw one 'monster' in her room, but several in her room all at once!

TOUCHED BY 'MONSTERS'!

During SPI's Interview with the mother and father, I asked the question, *"Has Sarah been subjected to anything visual which might resemble these 'monsters' either through television or newspapers?"* To which the mother replied *"No".* They were quite sure that Sarah had never seen anything like this before. I then asked, *"Is it possible that Sarah has overheard you talking about the UFO sightings in Bonnybridge?"* Again, the answer was a firm *"No."* They had never spoken about the UFO sightings above Bonnybridge in front of Sarah. Indeed, for the sake of the child, they had only stayed in the family home until 9:00pm, after which they all went round to her mother's house where they stayed the night. Thankfully, nothing strange occurred at her mother's, and Sarah appeared to be sleeping fine. SPI also learned during our interview, that not only did young Sarah witness what she described as 'monsters' in her bedroom, but these 'monsters' also 'touched her' as well! Amanda informed SPI, that one of these 'monsters' had 'touched' Sarah on the shoulder. She had asked her daughter why one of these 'monsters' did this, to which young Sarah replied,

"To wake me up mum!"

Sadly, we also learned that Sarah's young sister Claire (pseudonym) aged two was now herself starting to have nightmares in which she would wake up kicking and screaming. On one occasion, Amanda noticed a large deep scratch on Claire's nose as she put her to bed one evening. Upon waking Claire up the following morning, nothing visible could be seen at all, not even a tiny scar, it was completely gone! Amanda accepts that her daughter might have scratched herself before she went to bed, but surely there would have been a slight scar in the morning, but incredibly there was none.

BLOOD ON THE NIGHTDRESS

We also learned on this investigation, that at a later date, Claire had blood seeping out of her navel which was all over her nightdress. Amanda however, believes that Claire somehow did this herself. Amanda went onto inform us that on one occasion, she herself woke up one night with the sensation of someone/thing grabbing her ankles. She looked down to the foot of the bed but couldn't see anything. This, she told us, was a very strong vivid experience. Incidentally, Amanda worked at the nearby British Petroleum (B.P.) plant in Grangemouth where Phil Trevis took his amazing photograph of a UFO as it hovered above him and his friend near the plant.

In assessing this case, one can so easily say that all these episodes were the sole result of childish imagination and bad dreams. We have all had them. Children's imaginations, especially at this young age, are quite prolific. So, one could surmise that this case has all the hallmarks of just this, 'childish imagination'. But let us also remember and consider the mother's testimony. She knows her daughter well, and she went to the embarrassing trouble to contact a society (my society, 'Strange Phenomena Investigations') all about what her daughter was experiencing. Then there are the strange lights in the sky, and also the strange lights that her mother saw come into the bedroom. The mother, as we have learned, felt someone/thing grab at her ankles, but this may have been a fugue state, which is the state between sleep and waking in which sometimes dreams can come through to the waking state for a matter of seconds and which appear real. To others, all the above information may appear to have all the hallmarks of a UFO 'Abduction', it was really hard to tell in this case, and we really didn't want to intrude too much on the family. We asked that the family keep us informed of any further developments, and if things were getting bad to call us over once more. Thankfully things quietened down, and we did not have to make any further visits to the home. However, we were left with the thoughts of, 'was this case purely the result of childish imagination'? 'Or was it something more'? Fellow UFO researcher, David M. Jacobs, PhD, has informed readers of his books that UFO abductions can also start in childhood as his research has so clearly shown. Was Claire subject to some nefarious programme initiated by 'beings' from elsewhere?

MALCOLM ROBINSON GOES TO PRISON!

Lecturing to a captive audience is one thing but lecturing to a captive audience who won't be leaving the building that you are lecturing in for at least another 30 years, is another, but then again, this wasn't to be a normal lecture far from it. This was a lecture of which I personally had a wee bit of the 'shakes' about, and that was 'before' I even got there. The venue of this lecture wasn't a town hall or ladies sewing circle; this was Shotts Prison in deepest Lanarkshire, home to some of Scotland's most hardened criminals. SPI had been invited by the Governor of Shotts Prison who himself was contacted by an inmate who had read an article about SPI and its involvement with the UFO sightings in Bonnybridge. The inmate felt that SPI should come to the prison and let the other inmates know what was going on. This inmate had taken his idea to the Governor who after listening to him, passed it, and a short while later I received a phone call from a prison officer asking me if we'd like to do it. Some might argue that SPI should not have become involved with this type of education through either a moral or political angle. Perhaps they are right, who's really to know? All I knew was that it would be a challenge, whether it was right to do it or not, I really don't know. Suffice it to say, that Billy Devlin (someone who had assisted me greatly in my SPI work) felt that we should go ahead and do it.

As it was to turn out, we were to lecture in the 'Special Unit' of Shotts Prison. This was a particular area of the prison which housed eight of the most hardened and troublesome category 'A' criminals in Scotland. The 'Special Unit' was initially introduced in Glasgow's Barlinnie Prison which housed the notorious murderer Jimmy Boyle who has since served his sentence and now lives quietly with his wife back in the community. Barlinnie's 'Special Unit' was shut down a number of years ago and was introduced into Shotts Prison a few years back. The day duly arrived, and both Billy and I nervously approached the security gatehouse of Shotts Prison. A prison official behind a large glass screen took our names, and Billy had to hand in his mobile phone. We were then ushered into a room which housed a metal detection unit, much the same as you'll find at any Airport terminal. After taking the coins and keys out of our pockets (I kept my eye on the coins; well, I didn't want anyone to steal them did I!) I walked through the unit, no beeps, I was safe. Billy and I were then ushered into the 'Special Unit' by a prison officer who was built like a brick out-house, he'd be the type of guy you wouldn't want to upset unless of course you were on the phone to him from Australia! The 'Special Unit' itself was actually quite small, smaller than I had imagined. Apart from the small cells, it housed a large gym and two craft rooms for woodwork. What amazed me was the fact that there were a number of saws hammers and chisels all lying freely about on the various workbenches. I asked one of the inmates, *"Doesn't this tempt you?"* His answer was, *"No, we don't want to spoil it for ourselves, we are not going to do anything silly in this place"*. Indeed. A large snooker table featured impressively in the centre of the room in which a couple of inmates were enjoying a game. The whole atmosphere "appeared" relaxed, but underneath it all you still very much knew that this was a secure unit, and that these were no ordinary men, they were here for a purpose, paying their debt to society for, well I guess you know what.

Both Billy and I began to sort out our slides and other pieces of items that we would both be using for our talk. By now several prison inmates had sat down as well as the prison Governor and the prison minister. Some of the prisoner's wives were also in attendance. I must admit, I was a wee bit apprehensive as I looked around at those prisoners sat before me (some of them had more tattoos than Edinburgh has seen in many a year!). Just before I started my lecture, my thoughts went back to the following day's 'Daily Mail' story which ran a short piece about both Billy and I doing this lecture. The paper had contacted Labour M.P. John McFall who was quoted as saying:

"This talk is a gross waste of public money. Rather than talking about Unidentified Flying Objects, it would seem to make more sense for prisoners to be addressed in identifiable

issues for constructive rehabilitation. Talking about flashing lights in the sky is hardly likely to set them on the right track for joining society."

John was perhaps correct, but our planned lecture was part of an incentive by the Scottish Office to rehabilitate long term prisoners, and if they (the prison), felt that a talk on UFOs would be beneficial to the prisoners then who were we to disagree with them? Also quoted in that 'Daily Mail' piece of November 1995, was local M.P. Dr John Reid. John was more open to the idea that this talk might prove beneficial, for he was quoted as saying:

"If it were a one off then it would certainly be a little bizarre to talk about Flying Saucers, but as one of the series of lectures aimed at general rehabilitation, I don't see anything wrong with it. Boredom amoungst life prisoners is a serious problem that must be tackled. Talks such as these stimulate and generate interest amoungst the prisoners and that can only be to the good."

By now I had started my talk and was well into it, so much so, that I had lost track of time and had run slap bang into Billy's allotted time of which he was to follow me with a talk on ghosts and the supernatural. I looked over to Billy and I could see that he was not pleased with me for 'stealing his time', and so I quickly wound up with the Robert Taylor case and passed the trousers round for all to see. Again, like in all other lectures that I have given, when I've showed these trousers, they are the cause of great debate, and this was still the case even here, in a controlled environment. After some questions and general chit chat with the prisoners, both Billy and I were ushered out of the 'Special Unit' and through to the security gatehouse. Normally after SPI lectures and meetings, everyone usually goes over to the nearest pub for a pint, but somehow on this occasion, I didn't think that the Governor would allow his 'Special Unit' inmates to trek over to the nearest hostelry to indulge in alcoholic beverages, so I kept quiet on that one. After getting an ear roasting from Billy

Devlin in the car going home about him not getting his chance to speak (after preparing for it all week with family and friends all wishing him well), I apologised profusely and offered to lick his boots till the next UFO landing. I got away with that one but was shocked to find that on my arrival home, that when I opened my briefcase, I found that I had mistakenly taken one of the 'Special Unit's video tapes, (I had been using extract from video tapes during my lecture). *"Oh no"*, I thought to myself, *"This is tragic; the inmates will be going spare."* The video incidentally, was 'The Wall' by Pink Floyd. I immediately phoned Shotts Prison and explained what I had done, and the exact words of the prison officer of whom I spoke to on the phone, were,

"Is that right, you know you can get the jail for that?"

I gave a half-hearted laugh and promised to return it the next day. Again, this story is to illustrate to you the reader, about the types of locations in which one finds oneself in when giving a lecture. I've often wondered where I would find myself lecturing next: an ASDA superstore, the Robert Brothers Circus! I'll tell you what; after lecturing at a top maximum-security prison, nothing would surprise me anymore.

1996

January 1996, saw another conference staged at the Falkirk Town Hall. English 'UFO Magazine' were back in town. Councillor Buchanan who staged this lecture, was quoted in the 'Scotland on Sunday' newspaper dated January 7th, 1996, as saying:

"I only want to allay the fears of the people I represent. I want to be remembered for what I did for the community, not as the urban spaceman."

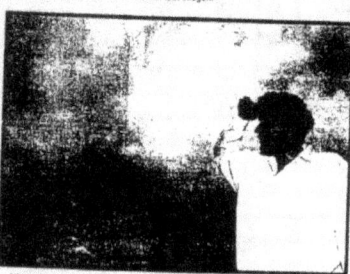

Bonnybridge featured in Dutch newspaper August 1995

Bonnybridge. The place to see UFOs

Councillor Billy Buchanan Sunday Post 1993

Crop Circles near Bonnybridge The Sun August 20th 2002

Eva magazine February 1995 Mentions Slogget Family

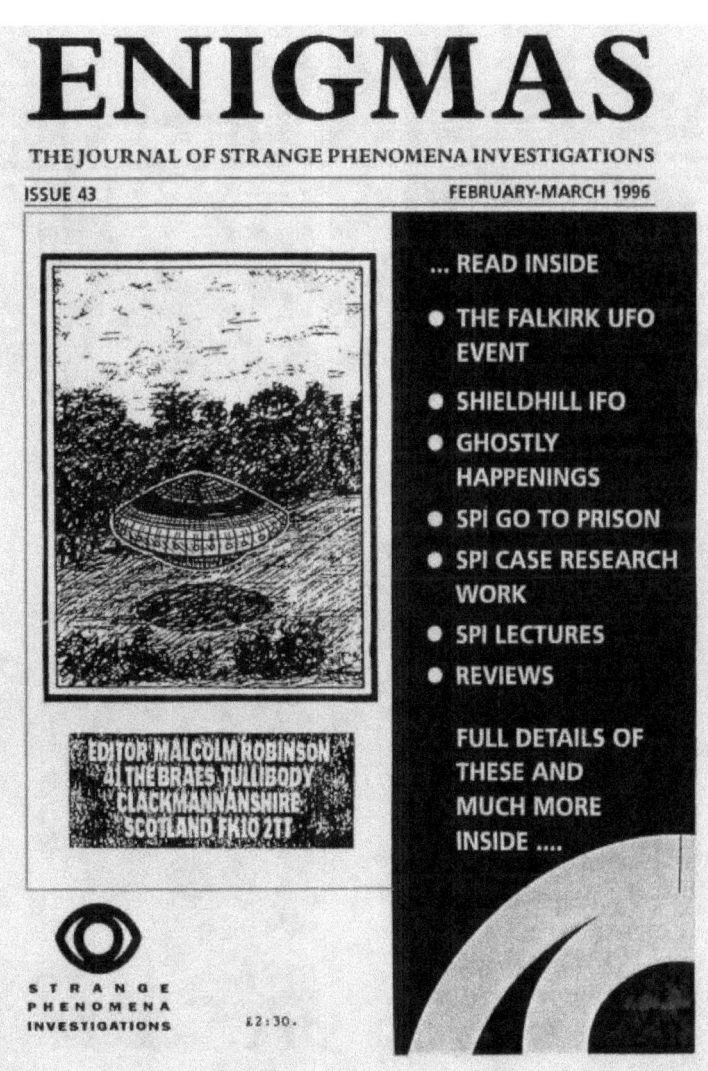

Enigmas The Journal of SPI

Now Paramount sets its sights on Bonnybridge

A world renowned American film studio is set to jet into Falkirk District to film for a programme on UFOs.

Paramount Pictures are believed to be heading for Bonnybridge in August.

The filming will be for the television show Sightings, which is shown in this country on satellite television.

It features US actor Robert Stack, who appeared in the 1960s show The Untouchables.

Filming will be carried out in the area on August 10 and 11. The news that Paramount Pictures were planning to travel to Bonnybridge came in a call from Los Angeles to Councillor Billy Buchanan.

"I'm happy to help out these companies when they want to film here, but it is frustrating when we don't get any answers as to what is happening in the skies," said Councillor Buchanan.

He also revealed that he has turned down a payment from London Weekend Television for his assistance with filming at the recent UFO night in Falkirk Town Hall.

He has asked the TV company to make a donation to a project in the Bonnybridge area instead, which the company is now considering.

Alien shapes were a feature at the recent successful UFO Night held in Falkirk. Now Councillor Buchanan (right) has been contacted by Paramount Pictures in California who are interested in filming in Bonnybridge

Falkirk Advertiser July 1994

Mystery space craft spotted over Falkirk

A PENSIONER has given his backing to claims that Falkirk District is being visited by UFOs.

Last week The Falkirk Herald reported how nurse May Macleod claimed to have seen a mysterious bright light hovering above the town's high flats.

Now retired BA case maker William Bestall believes he may have seen the same mystery object from his balcony seven floors up in the high flats.

Mr Bestall (72), of 7/6 Glenbrae Court, claims to have seen the UFO hovering in the skies above Falkirk three times since the beginning of this year. The latest sighting was at around 9.30 p.m. last Monday. "It was very clear," he said this week. "I saw it for about 20 minutes before it disappeared to the west. It was going faster than any aeroplane."

Mr Bestall made a sketch of the object which shows an object like a large Catherine wheel which he said spun backwards and forwards.

□ Brilliant glow

"On a few occasions it remained static, surrounded by a brilliant glow. The outer lights would then fade, leaving a brilliant light in the middle," he said.

Although Mr Bestall's wife Mabel (68) and a number of his friends in neighbouring Parkfoot Court have also seen the mystery light, they have kept quiet about it until now.

"I didn't report it to any authorities because you always feel a bit daft. Some of my friends ask me what I'd been drinking," said Mr Bestall.

But it was last Thursday's report in The Falkirk Herald which prompted him to break his silence. "When I read what Mrs Macleod had seen, I told my wife: 'This woman hasn't been dreaming — that sounds just like what I saw'. I've no idea what it was — It's a mystery."

The latest sighting adds to Falkirk District's reputation as a UFO hot-spot. A spate of unidentified objects above Bonnybridge last year sparked off international media interest, and an American TV show is making a programme on the subject.

William Bestall and his wife Mabel who have spotted a strange object in the skies over Falkirk. William is holding a drawing of the mystery craft.

Falkirk Herald August 18th 1994

Falkirk Herald

Glasgow Times January 1995

THE UFO MAGAZINE CONFERENCE. FALKIRK TOWN HALL JANUARY 6th, 1996

The following (in part) is a report that I wrote up for our SPI magazine ENIGMAS regarding the 'UFO Magazine Conference' which Graham and Mark Birdsall, along with Tony Dodd initiated with SPI at the Falkirk Town Hall. Here is what I said:

'Cor blimey, they don't come any better than this for the 500 plus crowd that were there. The Falkirk UFO Conference organised by 'UFO Magazine' was superb. This was UFOlogy at the sharp end. No fuzzy lights here, just pure Area 51, UFO abductions, animal mutilations, Government cover-ups. You name it, and it was being discussed here. Superb stuff. Sad to say though, that this event did not draw the 700 plus crowds of the last two UFO Conferences held at the Falkirk Town Hall, (June 1994 and October 1995). I would say that just over 500 people had turned up for this one. Of course, this could have been due to the fact that it was being held just after the New Year, and we Scots are well known for our drinking ability, may have parted with our hard earned cash on a festive 'carry out' leaving no money for the January 6th Conference! Not only that, but Falkirk football club were also at home to Glasgow Rangers which is always a big game in Falkirk. Incidentally, the final score of that match was, Falkirk 1 Glasgow Rangers 2. The Rangers goals were scored by Gordon Durie and Brian Laudrop, whilst David Hagen scored for Falkirk. Anyway, back to the conference. Perhaps the crowd numbers were down for this one due to the 'Cosmic Agenda' conference, which was held at the Falkirk Town Hall last October, where we were fed a diet of hugging trees! I'll tell you what though, for all those people who were not at this Falkirk Town Hall event, well, you missed a stormer of a conference. For ufological content, this was surely the best held event in Scotland for pure E.T. flavoured content.

Local councillor Billy Buchanan opened the proceedings, this time, not dressed in his usual tuxedo, but in a smart blue jacket. Graham Birdsall, editor of 'Quest International's' 'UFO Magazine', then took the stage and spoke about government cover ups and some major UFO sightings. He also spoke about released Government documents, most of which were heavily blacked out. He also showed on a large screen, some incredible UFO footage. Graham then went onto discuss with the audience, a number of UFO cases which I hadn't heard of before. After Graham's talk, there followed a break, in which the audience ventured out into the large foyer where a whole range of UFO items were on sale. Books, videos, magazines, models, UFO jewellery, everything bar a pickled alien. After the break, it was time for yours truly to take the stage. I thought I'd never have time to give my talk, as Graham Birdsall gave me a marvellous introduction which seemed to go on forever. Thanks Graham. Comments like yours make ufology for me, all the more worthwhile. I lectured on a number of Scottish UFO cases, and I was really getting into them, when all of a sudden, Graham Birdsall appeared from the wings of the stage and started walking towards my podium. He then placed a piece of paper down on the podium which read, *"Malcolm, 3:55pm. Sorry mate, but you have to finish at 4:00pm, Graham."* Oops, one of my main failings in any lecture that I give, and those that have seen my lectures will know this, is that I tend to run over time. I have so much to say, and very little time to say it in.

After my talk there was another break, after which Tony Dodd, a retired police officer of 25 years standing, took the stage and absolutely blew us away with his presentation. To say his talk was mind-blowing, would be an understatement. You just had to have been there to have heard this. Tony spoke about being harassed by the C.I.A. when he was over in the United States doing research work. He was also threatened with his life by them. Even his wife was threatened! Tony went on to speak about animal mutilations, sheep, cattle, deer, pigeons, and, would you believe, even mice! Each found with holes in their heads and also bodily organs were removed. This was done clinically and precisely. In some cases, these holes appeared to be cauterised by some incredible heat. Tony proceeded to show slide after slide to illustrate this point. One slide was particularly gruesome, for it allegedly showed a human mutilation. Not a pretty sight. I'm sure this photograph not only had me squirming in my seat, but the audience as well. Tony stated that these slides 'had to be shown', that the public have a right to be educated on this matter. Tony then went on to discuss about a missing Naval warship and the cover up which surrounded it. I've heard a lot of good speakers in my time, but that lecture by Tony Dodd, will take some beating.

After Tony's talk there was another break, and an opportunity for visitors to the Town Hall, who incidentally came from all over. We had people from Wales, England, Scandinavia, and even America there to talk shop and chew over what they had just heard. After this break, I took the stage along with Graham Birdsall, and Tony Dodd to take questions from the floor. Needless to say, there were a multitude of questions, and we could have been there till the following day. So, all in all then, the UFO Magazine Conference was a huge success. Purely because the public got what they wanted, and that was 'wall to wall UFOs' and not 'hugging trees'!'

Report by Malcolm Robinson.

Also, in that edition of our SPI magazine ENIGMAS, was SPI's Billy Devlin's take on how he saw that conference. Here is what he had to say:

'Well folks, I don't know about you, but my mouth is still hanging open at the thought of what was disclosed at this meeting. Not only did those present hear evidence, that, taken as a whole, should worry, and at the same time excite every man woman and child in the room, but we were also presented with some of the most gruesome sights that I have ever seen at a conference. Cattle mutilation, and my God, human mutilations. It was enough to make you lock the door and not venture out into the streets again. I certainly had one eye on the road and the other skyward as I drove home. It was a momentous occasion for Scottish UFOlogy. Never before, have so many distinguished members of the UFO fraternity agreed to speak in Scotland about a subject which more and more people up here are becoming aware of. The hall was slow to fill up at first, but I'm sure that this was due to the selection of UFO publications and memorabilia that was for sale at the front of the house.

When it did fill, it was given to Councillor Billy Buchanan the honour of opening the proceedings, and quite right to. No man has done so much for the Bonnybridge area in trying to find out what is going on. Scottish UFOlogy owes a lot to this man.

After a short introductory film showing various UFO sightings filmed around the world, Graham Birdsall was the first speaker. He delivered a mind-blowing talk about everything you want to hear and more. He spoke about the mysterious Machrihanish base, (A Royal Air Force base five miles west of Campbeltown in Argyll and Bute) which has seen its fair share of UFO sightings. Graham Birdsall told us to watch out for the massive body heading towards Earth. Hale Bopp is the comet's name, and it's so big that some folk in the know, say it has an atmosphere. Whatever it is, Graham told us to watch closely, as it may not be what it seems, (a massive UFO!) I don't know about the folk that were there, but I needed a break after that. And one came along. Exit to the bar and calm my nerves.

After the break it was Malcolm Robinson, Scotland's own, and editor of ENIGMAS. No matter how often I hear about the story of Garry Wood and Colin Wright, (the A70 UFO Incident) there is always something new that I hear which amazes me. What these two guys went through must have been the most frightening thing imaginable, and it takes great courage to come out and talk about it. Malcolm gave a very powerful description of what happened, only to be cut off in his prime before he could get into the Bonnybridge affair in any depth. There is so much happening in Scotland these days that you could fill the whole day on it alone. Maybe you'll have to talk faster next time Malcolm!

If you ever wonder what dangers an investigator puts himself up against, then go no further than listen to the tales Tony Dodd has to say. After describing in great details about an event that took place near the North Pole, concerning American, Russian, and British war ships and no less than four UFOs, well my knees nearly buckled. What the hell is going on? Tony had been receiving information from an internal source telling him what was happening. Ships closing off areas at sea. Ships going missing, and Russian ships being heard to report engaging 'craft'. As if this wasn't enough, both he and his wife were taken aside by C.I.A. agents and physically threatened. It put the job of filling in UFO sighting forms and interviewing witnesses into perspective. Here was a man willing to put his life at risk to get to the truth, and he is an ex chief inspector of police! Christ, what next!

Cattle mutilations, and if that's not bad enough, human mutilations. We are talking here about brains and spinal columns being pulled out of a body through a small hole in the head. We are talking about various parts of the body being extracted using some sort of high intense heat. No blood, no struggle. Just a carcass with its internals missing. And it's happening worldwide, to all sizes of animal. Why? And what the hell can we do to stop it? I had an incredible day at this event. I left feeling that we might be coming closer to finding out what it's all about. I felt that what we do as investigators is paying off and is worthwhile. People are beginning to look at us and are just beginning to think, that maybe there is some truth in what these guys think. Even if only half of what the speakers say is true, then there is something worth investigating out there.'

Report by Billy Devlin.

THE BUS TRIP TO BONNYBRIDGE IN THE POURING RAIN!

As someone who works with the media on a regular basis, I often get asked to participate in a whole range of different things. One such thing came up in February 1996, where I was invited to give a lecture on a bus! Yes, that's right, on a bus! This was for the 'Centre for Contemporary Arts' who were based in Glasgow. Someone from that centre had been reading all about the UFO sightings over Bonnybridge and decided that it would be a good idea to run a bus from the centre over to Bonnybridge where I, Councillor Billy Buchanan, and UFO abductee Garry Wood, would provide lectures on the ongoing UFO sightings across Stirlingshire. And so, on a wet and dreary February night, I caught the train from Stirling to Glasgow and made my way to the Centre where I made myself known to the chap who had booked me, after which, we went through some of the details about this trip to Bonnybridge. The chap then stated that he should have booked a fleet of buses, as he could have sold this trip 10 times over, such was the demand for tickets. I said, *"You missed a trick there"*, to which he replied, *"Ain't that the truth!"* After a quick drink, we boarded the bus, which was packed, every seat had been taken. I could understand that my talk wouldn't have worked on a double decker, as those upstairs would not have been able to hear me, nor watch the videos that I had brought along to play on the VHS unit on the bus.

Soon we were speeding along the wet streets of Glasgow and heading out onto the motorway. Whilst we were on the motorway, I had the misfortune to fall head over heels into the stairwell of this large single decker. Let me paint you the picture. Here was I, booked in the official capacity to provide a lecture on the UFO sightings over Stirlingshire. All was going well. I was standing right at the front of the bus next to the driver, when all of a sudden, the bus screeched to a halt, and yours truly went head over heels. I'd like to say, 'arse over tit', but I better not! Suddenly I found myself upside down in the footwell of this bus. My misfortune was greeted with rapturous laughter from all quarters of the bus. I sprung up, as if nothing had happened, dusted myself down, and carried on from where I left. What had happened was a car had screeched to a halt right in front of the bus. This car never allowed himself any distance between his car and the bus. Thankfully our driver was prepared for this. This, dear reader, could have ended so very differently. Anyway, we parked up outside Falkirk Town Hall where we were due to meet up with Councillor Billy Buchanan, sadly Billy didn't appear, so it was onwards to the farmland behind Bonnybridge where part of this trip was to allow passengers of the bus, an opportunity to do a sky watch. That was the plan anyway, but hardly anyone left the bus, due to the incessant downpour of rain. Yes, good old Scotland, doesn't let you down. Admittedly, it was February after all. There were a few hardy souls who left the bus armed with their binoculars trained on the sky. But within seconds, puddles of water formed in the rim of their binoculars, and they soon thought better of this. So, back on the bus, back to listening to me rabbit on about the UFO sightings, after which UFO abductee Garry Wood gave a passionate speech about what had happened to him and his friend Colin on the A70 road. After Garry had given his harrowing account, it was onwards back to the 'Centre for Contemporary Arts' in Glasgow. It had been an interesting night, and unbeknown to me, there was two newspaper reporters on the bus that night, one from the 'Scotsman' newspaper, and the other from the 'Herald'. Here is what Barry Didcock of the Scotsman newspaper had to say in his piece published on Monday, 26th February 1996:

A Return Bus Ticket To The West Lothian Triangle

'The little green men failed to show, as did the flying saucers, but the testimonies of the other people on the Bonnybridge UFO tour almost had Barry Didcock convinced of their existence'.

He stood entranced as the white disc floated first away from, then towards him, eventually coming to rest on the flat surface. It throbbed with a weird luminosity. Tapering away beneath it, was a strange inky black body. The terrain under his feet was red and dimpled. Around him the ait crackled with the noise of something that sounded almost like music, rhythmic, yet peculiarly tuneless. *"£1:55 please"*, no UFOs yet, he thought handing over the money, but this Guiness tastes good. Could do without the M. People tape though. Time, 6:58pm. Place. The bar of the Centre for Contemporary Arts in Glasgow. Mission. To take the CCA's much vaunted UFO tour of Bonnybridge, which forms part of its ongoing season of events dedicated to the mysteries of the universe. Yeah, yeah, it's easy to joke, but flippancy has its own defence. Doubt and derision are easy bedfellows, and scepticism is just an open mind approaching a problem which contradicts its experience. And standing in that bar mulling over the prospect of a face-to-face encounter with the little green men on a dreich night in the back of beyond, yours truly is Mr Doubtful, Mr Derisory, and Mr Sceptical all rolled into one. The tour itself takes the form of a bus trip to Bonnybridge, the heart of the so called, West Lothian Triangle, an area of Central Scotland which has seen a huge number of reported UFO sightings over the last few years, 2,000 extraterrestrial glimpses at the last count. The tour has been sold out for weeks. Indeed, various tabloid newspapers have even seen fit to mark the event, *(UFO watchers descend on Bonnybridge tonight)*. These 'UFO Watchers', when we board the bus, seem an unremarkable lot. In place of the troupe of oddly attired conspiracy theorists and eccentrics I had expected. I find a largely young crowd of normal looking people. 'First preconception blown'. Our guide for the evening is Malcolm Robinson who founded Strange Phenomena Investigations (SPI in 1979 and is also the chief investigator in Scotland for the British UFO research Association (BUFORA). A sincere and personable man, he takes the microphone and nails his colours to the post as we crawl through Glasgow's late rush hour traffic.

> *"There is no denying that there is something unusual being glimpsed in the skies of the world."*

Uh-oh, Twilight Zone speak already. As if he has read my mind, Robinson then launches into a spiel about the need for sceptics to examine the facts before dismissing the UFO theories out of hand. He has grown accustomed to the way the media mocks his obsession, but is perfectly happy to share his views, nevertheless.

> *"The main reason that I work with the media, is to get the message across",*

'He counters quite reasonably'.

Garry Wood, our other guest speaker for the evening, is not so forthcoming. His tale of abduction by aliens of himself and his friend Colin Wright is also well documented, though he is bitter about the way the media have treated it. Robinson outlines the story, but it is Wood's own account which is genuinely chilling.

"It terrifies me even thinking about it" he says. *"My sense of reality and about what normal life is all about has changed now."*

Whether you buy the whole story or not, meeting Wood, and hearing that sort of testimony makes you realise that 'something' happened to him that night. And now, far from coming over all evangelical about it, he just wants some answers. Second preconception blown. Next stop is Falkirk where the bus is to pick up Councillor Billy Buchanan, a controversial figure who has championed the West Lothian Triangle theory. Unfortunately, he fails to show. *"Must have been abducted"* quips Robinson through an interminably long council subcommittee meeting seems a more likely answer. So, at last the bus moves onto Bonnybridge itself and drives right through. Finally stopping to allow us to allow us to get off for a spot of skywatching at a place to which Robinson has recently taken a German film crew in the hope they could catch a UFO on film. They didn't, just as we see nothing more unusual than a few passing cars whose occupants stare in curiosity at the bedraggled punters enjoying a cigarette in the rain. The place has a haunting atmosphere, however, and as talk turns to the subject in hand, one man confides that he himself has seen a UFO ten years ago hovering over Glasgow. Like Wood, he is slightly embarrassed by the whole affair and simply wants an answer. He refuses to give his name. However, James, a musician, is more open. He too has seen UFOs and admits to being a firm believer, but he says it is Garry Wood's embarrassment which convinces him of the veracity of the tale. James' band, the Painkillers have a single out soon, it's called UFO.

A dreich night, visibility zero, nothing for it but to head back to Glasgow. On the way, Robinson plays a series of video tapes, consisting largely of news reports. We see him on top of Scottish Television Headquarters with Viv Lumsden, in the field with binoculars, and chairing an SPI meeting. The mood on the bus is quiet. People chat in low voices or watch the video clips as the city approaches. And me? Well after three hours on the move, I am right back where I started, in the bar of the CCA sinking a pint of the dark stuff and chatting about UFOs. I didn't see one, but talking to those that have and those who believe, well it makes it all seem that little bit less ridiculous. Three hours and already Messrs Doubtful, Derisory and sceptical, are looking a lot less sure of themselves.

Report by Barry Didcock.

And there you have it dear reader, once a journalist has the opportunity to speak to UFO witnesses and learn more about what it is that we are all so fascinated by, then it isn't any wonder that he or she may start to come off that proverbial sceptical fence.

BILLY BUCHANAN ALMOST QUIT OFFICE!

I heard that Councillor Billy Buchanan was planning to retire as the councillor of Bonnybridge. According to the 'Falkirk Herald' of March 1996. Journalist Tom Hunter stated that Councillor Buchanan was to tender his resignation in a few days' time, he quoted Councillor Buchanan as saying:

"I have ongoing commitments that I don't want to leave unfinished. Once they are complete, I will tender my resignation. I will make a full statement nearer the time, but I have sweated blood and tears for Bonnybridge, now there's no blood left, just tears. I will also be leaving this area to try and make a fresh start. This will please many people for different reasons. It's a heartbreaking decision for me."

Tom Hunter goes on to state in his article that Billy burst onto the political scene in 1992 when he won a landslide victory in the Antonine Ward on Falkirk District Council. He then took the Bonnybridge seat on Central Regional Council in 1994 with yet another emphatic victory. (Incidentally, I remember that about the time of the re-elections, Billy had said to me that he was concerned that he might lose his seat due to his involvement with the UFO sightings over Bonnybridge. I told him not to worry, he would walk it and walk it he did). In 1996

Billy won a seat on the new Falkirk Council. According to Tom's article, one senior Councillor stated, *"We've heard all this before. I think he'll tell everyone he's going, then bow to public demand to stay on."* Billy was also criticised for his absence from District Council meetings, and a spokeswoman was quoted as saying that Councillor Buchanan had attended only one meeting since last August. Billy, like I, had been under pressure for different reasons, but I knew deep down that Billy had the courage to stand up and be counted. I knew that he would fight back and regain the confidence and credibility that he was so used to showing to all and sundry. I was right, for a few weeks later it became clear that Billy was to stay, and thankfully he did not tender his resignation, and continued to fight the cause of not only the UFO sightings above his constituency, but to ensure that the under privileged received benefits and help as they so rightly deserved more so as we come into the 21st century. Billy is certainly a character, and no one can fault him for what he has done for the Bonnybridge community.

In the early hours of the 7th of January 1996, a family who lived in the town of Grangemouth near Bonnybridge, had a very unsettling experience. A mother, daughter, son, and a nephew, had been observing what looked like a star in the sky. At first it was moving east, then changed direction and appeared to be pulsating. This report featured in Steve Hammond's book, 'The Scottish UFO Casebook', then states that the mother, who had been trying to get some sleep, had the distinct impression that her daughter was being taken from her bed. Also at this juncture, the family dog appeared to get restless. The family then shared a pair of binoculars, and through these, they were amazed to see three lights shoot out from the top of the object, and two lights shoot out from the bottom of it. The lights then retracted into the object, and the object appeared to be coming in their direction approaching their house. As it did so, all family members noticed a now distinct V shape. The object (or whatever it was) then changed direction again and headed towards an aircraft at which point a dark grey mist appeared and the object vanished! *(*Steve Hammond).*

POLICE SPY CAMERA CATCHES UFO?

According to the 'Falkirk Herald' dated April 25th, 1996, a strange bright light was captured on police T.V. cameras. The story goes that a Hallglen woman telephoned the police to report that she was observing a strange light above her home. Superintendent Jim Forbes from the Falkirk police was quoted as saying:

"We received a phone call from a resident in Hallglen who was concerned about a bright light in the area. Our officers responded but found nothing. However, a couple of hours later our CCTV operators turned their cameras towards Hallglen and there was a light on the screen. We're quite sure there will be a simple explanation for it."

Catherine Penman (40) was quoted in the Falkirk Herald as saying:

"My husband Scott was out in the shed and when he came in, he said that he thought he had seen a UFO. At first, I didn't believe him, but the more I looked, the more that I thought he could be right. It was a really bright light which was down low. At first, I thought it was a star, but it was 10 times bigger than a star and was really close to the house. I watched it for two hours, and then it moved. I contacted the police because I thought it was so unusual. Th because of the length of time that it hovered in the air. There is no way that it could have been a helicopter or a plane. It's quite freaky when you see something like that."

For me, this may well have been a planet, probably Venus. However, I wasn't there, I can only speculate. But many people have mistaken this bright astronomical object as being a UFO, more so, when you consider that these witnesses watched this light in the air for two hours!

Another astounding UFO sighting from this year, was witnessed by a family from Stenhousemuir near Bonnybridge.

The 'Falkirk Herald' of August 1st, 1996, tells us that Audrey Batchelor (20) along with her boyfriend Jim Donnelly and mother Claire was puzzled by what they all saw at the end of July, hovering over fields in the direction of Denny. Audrey now takes up the story:

> "Jim and I were getting ready to go to Glasgow last Thursday night. I was sitting in the car with my son Dale when I looked up at the sky and saw this ting hovering. I peeped the horn, and Jim came out and saw it as well. That's when he shouted for my mum."

Jim was quoted as saying:

> "It was really big and had different coloured lights all around it. It definitely wasn't a helicopter. I've never seen anything like it. We tried to walk towards it, but it was gone in a split second. I don't know anything that could move that quickly. It just disappeared."

It was early evening on the 25th of July 1996 when four members of a Stenhousemuir family witnessed a brightly coloured object which was hovering over some fields. This object appeared to be surrounded by flashing lights and was heading in the direction of Denny. A short while later the object quickly disappeared. *(* Steve Hammond)*

COUPLE'S ENCOUNTER WITH A SPACESHIP

This was the title from the 'Falkirk Herald' dated August 8th, 1996, which outlines the strange UFO sighting by Laurieston couple (Laurieston is a town near Bonnybridge) John Norval (45) and Wendy Forbes (43). Admittedly this particular sighting was not in the Bonnybridge region but was witnessed when the couple were on a camping holiday near the town of Callander in early August. They claimed that it was around 01:55 and they were returning to their camp site when they were both astonished to see a weird object hanging in the air over Loch Lubnaig. John was quoted as saying:

"It was just like a traditional flying saucer. Like a child's top, but flatter and covered in bright flashing lights. I don't drink, and I don't take drugs. It definitely wasn't a helicopter, for that's the only thing that could hover like that. It didn't move for ages, then all of a sudden it turned sharply to the left, travelling about half a mile in the blink of an eye. It then shot up into the cloud, then came back down again on the same flight path, then it hovered again. This time however, it went off to the hills on the right. Then it shot away and disappeared. I've been high as a kite since I saw this. I used to be a sceptic, but I'm a believer now. There is no doubt in my mind what I saw."

John's partner Wendy told the 'Falkirk Herald' that this object was also seen by an English couple who were also staying at the camp site. Both John and Wendy watched this spinning object through binoculars for around 20 minutes. She went on to say that this was not the first UFO that she had witnessed, she saw something 20 years ago which she couldn't explain. So here were a couple from Laurieston near Bonnybridge, on a camping holiday and witnessing a UFO. It was clear that UFOs were not just hovering over this Stirlingshire town. The following month, October 1996, saw what all Scottish UFOlogists regarded as the best ever video footage of a UFO to have been taken in Scotland.

CSETI VISIT SCOTLAND

Of course, the growing number of UFO reports that were coming from Central Scotland, did not go unnoticed by overseas ufologists, and on October the 1st 1996, a small group of people from the American research society CSETI, (Center for the Study of Extraterrestrial Intelligence) left their base in Baltimore USA and travelled over to Scotland. Heading this group was well known and respected ufologist, Dr Steven Greer M.D. Steven had been notified about the UFO sightings that were occurring in Bonnybridge by crop circle researcher Colin Andrews and decided that it would be a good place to visit. The aims of CSETI are to visit and document all areas of high UFO incidents, and to try and build up a picture from the world's 'Hot Spots' and present this information to the public. Having arrived in Scotland, they then met up with Craig Malcolm of whom as we have learned earlier, has taken a number of interesting pieces of video footage which claim to show UFOs. Craig took the party to a location near Bonnybridge where they began scouring the skies from the car. A few minutes later, Shari Adamiak, Research Director of CSETI, felt a distinct sensation of a light pressure in his chest. Apparently, Dr Greer also experienced this. They then observed coming out of an unusual crescent shaped cloud, a silver disc. In his internet statement about their trip, Shari Adamiak states that although this was a brief view of a UFO, it nonetheless was an important event, in the sense that Dr. Greer had also felt the presence of the object several seconds before it's appearance, and both he and another member of the group, also experienced a presence immediately prior to seeing it. That night the group travelled to Cairnpapple Hill where they set up camp. However, our good old Scottish weather decided to rear up once more and the night was beset with howling winds and the threat of a storm. They left the site, but before doing so, observed some strange distant lights in the sky which performed unusual manoeuvres. Leaving Cairnpapple, which incidentally is an extremely exposed area, they headed off for another site which wouldn't be so exposed where they remained for a good part of the night, but nothing unusual was observed.

The following day saw the CSETI team break up into different groups. Some of the group left to explore Stirling and Loch Lomond, whilst the other remaining members remained at their base, a farm near Bonnybridge. It was there that they met up with some witnesses who informed them about some UFO sightings that they had seen. One witness explained that he had observed a disc shaped object which had shone a light down onto the nearby Drumbowie Reservoir. Owing to this man's testimony, the group later that night, decided to do a sky watch in that area, but nothing unusual was sighted. However, on their way back to the farmhouse at around 02:22am, Shari observed a blue, white ball of light which was slowly flashing on a ridge directly to their left, at a distance of around a quarter of a mile. Knowing that there were not any radio masts at that location which contained lights, they decided to stop the car for a better look. Upon doing so, the three members of CSETI observed a large triangular 'craft' which either had transformed from this light or came from it. Continuing to gaze at this unusual spectacle, they noticed that this object had a red flashing light at one point of its structure, and a blue flashing light at another. In the centre, were two very large white lights. Shari states that the entire craft appeared light in colour, and at arm's length, it would be roughly one and a half inches across. The group had their car windows down, and the sunroof was open, and a few minutes later, this large silent 'craft' flew over the top of the ridge heading towards a radio tower mast which contains three red lights. It then dipped down below the ridge and headed in the direction of 'Take Me Down Lookout'. Sadly, the rest of the CSETI team who had been following in another car behind, somehow managed to miss this important sighting. Both cars however, sped off in the direction of 'Take Me Down Lookout', and once there, were fortunate to observe some flashes of white light along a distant ridge. From there the group then headed off to the Carron Valley Reservoir where several other unusual flashes were noted in the night sky. The group then left this area at around 03:30am and headed back to base. The following day was CSETI'S last in Scotland, and the evening was spent at the Malcolm Family's restaurant near Larbert where a group of around 15 to 20 people heard Dr Greer speak about CSETI'S 'Project Starlight' whose aims are to obtain the 'best available evidence' for a briefing package which would be submitted to the public showing how serious the UFO phenomenon really was. While CSETI was at the home of the Malcolm family, it gave Craig Malcolm an opportunity to show several of their UFO videos which they had taken in the area.

Now, that night saw the loan of what was described by some Scottish UFOlogists, as probably the best piece of UFO video footage taken near Bonnybridge. The footage showed an object which appeared above a house. This was given over to CSETI and caused a rumpus with other Scottish UFOlogists who said that this important video should have stayed in Scotland, at least until investigations had been conducted and a proper evaluation of the video had been undertaken. However, as it later turned out, in a letter from CSETI member Neil Cunningham to Malcolm Robinson, Neil stated, that in actual fact, after close inspection of the video with specialised equipment, the video was not deemed good enough for their 'Best Available Evidence Video Project' which they now aimed to present to the U.S. Congress. The video, he went on to say, basically just showed a triangular formation of lights, and compared with the 'Flying Triangle' videos from Belgium and Russia, was not of a high enough standard. As of writing, I am unsure what happened to that video, if we ever got it back. If you the reader know different, then let me know at the address at the end of this book. We'd like to take a proper look at it ourselves.

According to Shari Adamiak, the CSETI visit to Scotland had been a great success and had cemented relationships between themselves and the people of Bonnybridge. They applauded the people of Bonnybridge for understanding what CSETI is attempting to do for the world. CSETI are still going strong today with Steven Greer at the helm. The next day the group left for Iceland, and more skywatching and Investigations.

THE BEST UFO VIDEO FOOTAGE FROM BONNYBRIDGE?

As stated earlier, 1996 was to prove a major year for UFOs captured on video. However, Tuesday October 15th, was to prove a major day in the annals of Scottish UFOlogy, and a day that won't be forgotten in a hurry. For that was the day in which an amazing piece of video footage was shot which most certainly "IS". The best documented visual footage of a UFO ever seen in Scotland. The story goes that Barry McDonald (27), and his eight months pregnant girlfriend Jane Adamson, were travelling in Barry's car towards the town of Camelon near Falkirk. The time was roughly 6:40pm when Jane happened to notice a bright and unusual object in the sky. With all the commotion concerning UFOs in the area which they were very much aware of, they ensured that they did not lose track of the object and decided to stop the car for a better look. Jane by this time was screaming to Barry that it was a UFO, to which Barry replied, *"Don't be stupid, it can't be a UFO."* They reckon that they stood and watched it for around 20 minutes during which time the object which initially was white and stationary, changed to a more saucer shape and became orange in appearance. Remembering that he had a video camera in the boot of his car, Barry dived round and quickly opened the boot and took out the camera where he managed to secure around 30 seconds or so of footage of the object before it vanished from the sky. Barry described it as just as a light being switched off. This case was researched by co-author Ron Halliday who stated in the local and National press, that 'this' was the best video footage that he had seen taken of a UFO in this area. I would have to say, that after viewing the Barry McDonald video, I have to agree, that this "IS" the best footage that I've seen. A view which is shared by other SPI members. According to Ron's research, no aircraft were in the sky during the time this UFO was in the air. An amazing video then, and consistent with what the people of Bonnybridge and surrounding areas have been seeing.

UF GOT THE GREATEST EVER FILM OF A FLYING SAUCER

(Yes, this was how it was spelled out!) This was the sensational title by the 'Scottish Sun' newspaper dated 14th October 1996 and was given over to another piece of UFO footage which my fellow co-author Ron Halliday was involved in. It was taken by Margaret Ross (63) Margaret had taken 23 minutes of footage of what she described as a UFO hovering over her home at six am in the morning on September 27th. After 15 minutes, this hovering object started to change shape and morphed into a half-moon shape with four diagonal bars of high intensity brightness. Margaret was quoted as saying:

"It began rotating and returned to its original shape, then it sped away eastwards in the direction of Linlithgow. It didn't frighten me. I was just fascinated by the changing shape."

What was most interesting about this sighting was that Margaret's sighting was also backed up by her daughter Alexis (42) and her family from their home, two miles away. Alexis was quoted as saying:

"I saw it changing shape. It was awesome. My husband and also my two children saw it too."

Ron Halliday who viewed Margaret's footage, was again of the opinion that this indeed was another special piece of UFO footage. As for me, well, I have never seen this piece of footage so I can't comment on it. But if it impressed Ron Halliday, then that's good enough for me.

Kevin Schofield a staff reporter of the 'Falkirk Herald' was still keeping abreast of all what was going on in the skies above Bonnybridge and was covering every story that featured UFO sightings. However, he was to become involved with a story which was puzzling, but of which most probably held a natural explanation. During the morning of November, the 6th 1996, Patricia Cook was out walking her dogs in a forest near Tamfourhill and came across two strange 'nests'. They were about five feet wide with one built around a puddle and the other one built around a stone. There were approximately 100 small pieces of wood which made up these 'nests' and they looked quite out of place. In Kevin's article in the 'Falkirk Herald' dated Thursday November 14th, 1996, Patricia Cook gives this statement:

"I was walking the dogs when the two objects caught my eye down in a ditch, they looked like two large baskets. I'd never seen anything like it, they were so perfect. The whole thing is just so strange."

Kevin contacted local primary schools to see if perhaps they had been undertaking a project in the woods, but as it turned out they hadn't. The local police were also quoted as saying that they would like to get to the bottom of the mystery. It is generally accepted by Scottish researchers, that these strange 'nests' were the result of some high school prank, but whether they were meant to be taken in the overall UFO context, is up for speculation.

MORE VIDEO EVIDENCE OF UFOS

On the 27th of November 1996, Maddiston man Andrew McLeish (33) was out walking near the Muiravonside country park. He is a keen bird fancier and was watching some rooks as they nested in some trees. By now it was getting dark, and the time was somewhere in-between 4:30pm and 6:00pm. Suddenly his attention was drawn to a bright and stationary light which was just above the horizon. As he was at a position which was quite high up, he was at a great vantage point to see much of the landscape spread out before him. He had with him his video camera as he had been filming some wildlife some moments before. Now however, the video camera was trained on this bright white light, and as he focused upon it, he wondered if it could just possibly be, one of those so called 'Flying Saucers' that he had read about in his local newspaper. The object continued to shine bright in the dark sky and did not appear to be moving at all. Suddenly, a second independent object, very similar to the first, started to approach the first light from right to left as you would look at it on a T.V. screen. Now here was something strange he thought to himself, this appears as if it's on a direct collision course with the first object, and he wondered if he was about to capture what could be an air crash. As the second object continued to get closer and closer, the first main object began to move slowly away from it. Then this second object returned to the left of the screen and disappears from view, whilst the initial object can still be seen receding from view. Andrew is sure as he can be that what he saw that night was not the result of aircraft or helicopters. He informed me that he would have heard their sound as it was a very still and calm night. Having interviewed Andrew, I then saw the tape which showed these strange lights, and I would have to admit, that for the first time in a long while, this video had me stumped!

As a researcher, I have been sent many UFO videos, the vast majority of which were clearly just ordinary mundane lights in the sky, from aircraft to helicopters, and from stars to planets. It is amazing what people actually believe are UFOs! This one was different, and was clearly above all others, (apart from the Barry McDonald UFO video of which I did not research). I conducted all the normal investigative procedures and found that there were no aircraft in the sky in that area at that time, that night. All other investigative channels turned up negative in regard to providing an explanation. I had the opportunity the following year, to show this video on a live BBC Nationwide Breakfast Television programme which gave the public a chance to view this and make up their own minds. And although, admittedly, we are just dealing here with two bright light sources in the sky, the characteristics of these lights do not 'appear' to conform to ordinary aircraft.

At this point in time, although we now have a number of very interesting UFO videos taken of objects in the Bonnybridge area, none of them are clear cut 'nuts and bolts' machines, we only have footage of lights, mostly white lights as in Andrew's case. However, in the Barry McDonald UFO video, one can clearly see a combination of coloured lights on the object that he captured on tape, and its quick disappearance would clearly indicate that it was not a 'man-made' object.

1996 ended more quietly than it had begun. My own newfound enthusiasm for the subject, was again at an all time high, and I looked forward to the challenge of 1997.

1997

TOPPS FARM, A PLACE TO SEE UFOS?

There is one location which would appear to be doing a roaring trade as far as entertaining human guests who visit Bonnybridge, and that is Topps Farm near Denny and

Bonnybridge. In the 'Falkirk Herald' of January 23rd, 1997, we learned that Jennifer Steel and her husband Alistair who bought the farm back in 1994, have entertained many UFO hunters from around the world. It was in 1994 that Jennifer was contacted by a party of UFO enthusiasts who asked if she could put them up, in order that they could take in the sights around Bonnybridge and do a bit of sky watching. Initially Jennifer thought that it was a 'wind up' but soon found out that they were sincere. The party had travelled all the way over from Texas, and their trip was organised by 'Beyond All Travel', a firm which specialises in putting on holidays to places in which there has been a high concentration of UFO sightings. 'Beyond All Travel' provide an information package on the internet which notifies people to many of the UFO sightings from around the world. Apparently, they have around 15,000 UFO enthusiasts. The visit of CSETI, (Centre for Scientific Extra-terrestrial Intelligence) mentioned earlier, had their base at Topps Farm. Jennifer, who is also the Chairwoman of the Falkirk Tourist Association, was quoted as saying in the 'Falkirk Herald'.

"The Loch Ness Monster is used as a tourist attraction, so why should we laugh about something which could attract tourists to the area?"

Why indeed! I'm glad that Topps Farm is providing a service such as this, for as I mentioned earlier, UFO fans from around the world need a base from which to operate from, and the lovely hospitality that one receives at Topps Farm, ensures that they get it. *(Malcolm's Note. Sadly, since I initially wrote the above piece a few years ago, the farm no longer caters for visitors and is now just a family home)*

It was the 31st of January 1997 and Stuart Small (20) was driving his girlfriend back to her house in Maddiston, which is a small town near Falkirk. Also, in the car that night, was Stuart's mother Elizabeth. They had left Hallglen near Falkirk, and were approaching St Catherine's, when Elizabeth who was idly gazing out of the window, spotted a strange looking object in the sky. She alerted her son to this object and asked that he stop the car, which he did. Whereupon they all got out and had a good look at the object. Stuart stated that the object, which was now stationary in the sky, resembled a double decker bus with all its lights on. Laura Mitchell, Stuart's girlfriend, stated that the object looked like a baking bowl in the sky with a mass of lights all around it. The object (which looks like an upside-down bowler hat in all the witnesses' drawings) hung motionless in the sky for around 30 seconds, after which it took off at great speed and left the area. Another interesting point to be noted with this case, which may or may not have a bearing, is the fact that the town of Maddiston, had a power cut shortly after this sighting, which also blacked out Brockville, the Falkirk Football stadium. Coincidence!

GERMAN TELEVISION (PRO 7)

It was during February 1997 that our society worked with yet another foreign Television Station. This time they came from Germany and the television station was called 'Pro 7'. As usual, I provided them with witnesses to talk to (only those who had agreed to being interviewed) and locations in which to film. Pro 7 also filmed one of our SPI meetings which was held in Stirling and travelled around Scotland visiting and interviewing people who had seen UFOs. It was good fun working with German Television. However, my own particular interview, which was filmed on the slopes of the Ochil Hills, was done in extremely rainy conditions. There was I trying to look calm and composed and discussing those perplexing UFO sightings in the Central Region, whilst all the time I was being continually drenched by rain. Sadly, the German film crew had a hard time of it with the Falkirk District Council. The crew had hoped to Interview Councillor Buchanan at the Council Buildings but were unfortunately refused admission by Falkirk Council Chief Executive, Walter Weir who turned them away. Walter was quoted in the Scottish Sun Newspaper of February 14th, 1997, as saying:

> "I did not deem it appropriate for Falkirk Council to be linked to a story on UFOs."

Quite a shame really, because all they wanted to do was to film Councillor Buchanan, but it was plain to see that there was still some 'ill feeling' and a sense of disdain by other council members at what Councillor Buchanan was getting himself into. I'm pleased to say that the interview went ahead, but it was filmed elsewhere. The documentary went out on German Television a few weeks later, and now many people from all over Germany now know all about these perplexing UFO sightings in Scotland.

THE QUEST INTERNATIONAL CONFERENCE 1997

March 1997 saw the arrival once more, of 'Quest International' who were in Scotland to put on another Conference at the Falkirk Town Hall. This time I was not billed as a speaker. On the agenda this time, was Graham Birdsall, Tony Dodd, American researcher John Carpenter, and a speaker from South America who was talking about the intriguing Chupacabras case, which was the capture of an alleged 'alien creature'. There were around 300 people gathered at the town hall, which although is a good sized number, fell short of the 1992/93/94 UFO lectures. This particular conference was a wealth of information which proved of immense value for all those that did attend. Leading ufologist Graham Birdsall, sadly no longer with us, was quoted in the Dundee Courier as saying:

"It's an area that has one of the highest concentrations of UFO sightings in the world. But why that's the case, is the million-dollar question. Investigations into the sightings are continuing, and we are hopeful we can find some sort of answer at the conference to account for what is happening here."

STAR WARS RAGE OVER UFO TALKS

I should point out that prior to 'Quest International' coming to Scotland to stage another one of their conferences at the Falkirk Town Hall, there was, shall we say, a bit of a, 'to do'.

And by that, I mean, some Scottish UFOlogists were not too happy about the English coming north and getting involved with our UFO witnesses. They felt that the English should stick to their own country and their own UFO sightings and leave the Scottish UFO reports to the Scots. And whilst some might say that this is a bit childish, we could put it like this. Would a Scottish ice cream van going down south to an English town and selling their wares there be welcomed with open arms! Probably not. I am all for sharing and assisting other UFO societies, but some Scots were a bit peeved by our land and our witnesses, being 'got at' by English researchers. Oh, it all sounds so childish now, and whilst writing this piece I can say that. But at the time! In the Scottish 'Sunday Mail' of 2nd March 1997, Scottish UFOlogist and musician Brian McMullan (who does not suffer fools gladly) when speaking about the cost price that 'Quest International' were asking people to pay to get into their conference. Was quoted as saying:

"We usually charge £2:00 entrance fee. They're charging £7.50 which is a rip off, and you can be sure it will be £10:00 next year. Quest steal a lot of stuff for their magazine and talks, instead of really investigating cases for themselves. There will be someone there from SPI to make sure they don't start quoting our cases and passing them off as their own."

The 'Sunday Mail' goes on to tell their readers that this squabble, as they called it, all started when the Leeds group seized on a Scottish case where a Fife woman claimed to have come face to face with an alien. *(Author's note. We believe this to be one of the witnesses from the Falkland Hill UFO Incident)* Brian said that the Leeds group did not investigate this sighting properly. However, the 'Mail' tracked down former police officer and 'Quest International' investigator Tony Dodd who stated:

"We did investigate it, but that's because we got to it first. What we are doing, is no detriment to them. I don't think that there are any hard feelings."

At the end of the day, it was all a bit of a storm in a teacup. I have a lot of respect for that group (no longer operating) and sadly some years later, we lost two stalwarts of that Leeds group in Graham Birdsall and Tony Dodd who passed away. A big loss to British UFOlogy. I present this moment in time regarding this fall out, as it was all part and parcel of the whole Bonnybridge story. It would be remiss of me to leave the above out. This as I say, was a moment in time, and needs to be told.

BAIRNS ARE OUT OF THIS WORLD!

It was in May 1997, that Scottish football club Falkirk, (nicknamed 'The Bairns') reached the final of the Scottish Cup. Their opponents were Kilmarnock F.C. The town of Falkirk and surrounding areas went into a 'Cup Final Frenzy', and the demand for tickets was high. At this time, the comet Hale Bopp was in the sky and many people felt that this was a good omen that Falkirk F.C. would win the cup. Football Fanzine Editor John McNeill had this to say:

"In 1957 there was a comet in the sky when Falkirk beat Kilmarnock to lift the Scottish Cup. Forty years later we are back in a cup final with yet another comet in the sky."

Billy Buchanan, in typical Billy Buchanan style, was quoted in one of the Scottish newspapers as saying, *"When we win the Scottish Cup, we'll be over the moon!"* Billy was shown in the newspaper as wearing an alien mask with a Falkirk football scarf tied round his neck. Incidentally, in keeping with omens and traditions, the Falkirk players' bus was to leave the town of Bonnybridge to go to the cup final in Glasgow, just as it had done back in 1957. Sadly, all these omens and prophecies went out of the window, as Falkirk lost their match to Kilmarnock by one goal to nil, maybe it was the wrong comet!

The 'Daily Star' of July 31st, 1997, ran the headline, *'May The Farce Be With You'*, and went on to talk about Star Wars ready to erupt over the 'Zalus Affair'. Incredibly, as in some cosmic freak joke of coincidence, the date of July 31st, 1997, was the same month, in the same newspaper, from the same reporter (Nick Gates) from where the Zalus story first appeared, [July 31st, 1995]. Sadly, the July 31st, 1997, piece featured a mock up photograph which showed Councillor Billy Buchanan as someone from the recently re-released 'Star Wars' movie, I was depicted as Luke Skywalker which saw me pointing a gun at Billy's head. Both of our faces were superimposed onto these 'Star Wars' characters. This I felt was inciting the issue even more, and it certainly didn't help matters. The 'Daily Mail' of July 31st, 1997, carried much the same news details about this story as did the 'Daily Star'. Thankfully both newspapers quoted me factually when I said that I had got it wrong, and that I was man enough to put my hands up and say so. And there the matter rested. Billy did not sue me, and he and I still remain friends today and work together in the spirit of corporation with the understanding that the 'UFO Issue' is bigger than both of us, and that being together on this important UFO issue, is vastly important. The press had had their day on this event, and like all things, tomorrow is another day, bringing more news stories and more things to report. For me though, it was unfortunate, and showed how easily it was to mix up things which can lead to them being mis-represented in incredible ways. No one could have envisaged how 'big' this story would become, and although it put a dent in what Billy and I were trying to achieve at the time, much water has flowed under the bridge. New UFO cases have emerged: the UFOs just won't go away, there is still so much more to be done.

Since the Bonnybridge UFO wave began, many people from all parts of the world have visited this small town just to see for themselves what it's like and get a feel for the place. They want to try and understand what it is about this small Scottish town that has apparently proved so fascinating to 'visitors' from 'elsewhere'. There is nothing of any significance, either in, or around the town of Bonnybridge. History tells us that there were Bronze Age settlements in the area, and of course the Romans had settlements in the area as well. Other than local industry and business, there is nothing overly significant in the Bonnybridge area. This is why Councillor Buchanan felt it necessary to try and provide a 'visitor Centre' in which people who have travelled many miles to get to the town, would at least have a place to visit and something to see.

MORE T.V. AND RADIO COVERAGE

1997 saw a number of UFO cases being reported to our society, most of which were really nothing spectacular, just lights in the sky, a lot of which were astronomical objects, stars, and planets. But it was clear the UFO sightings in the Bonnybridge area, were either becoming less frequent, or people were just fed up reporting them. I placed another letter in the local 'Falkirk Herald' newspaper asking members of the public to contact me if they had had a UFO sighting, I did not receive one single reply, an incredible turnaround from November 1992 when I was simply flooded by phone calls. In June 1997, the Michael Aspel show, 'Strange But True?' were back in town to record yet another programme about the UFO sightings in and around Bonnybridge. The outrageous Scottish comedian Scottie McClue whose talk radio programme had been taken off the air due to complaints (which is a shame for it was wonderfully funny!) mentioned the visit of the Aspel show, then made fun of the Bonnybridge UFO sightings. In his 'Sun' newspaper column of June 20th, 1997, Scottie McClue stated, *"Extra-terrestrials exist, how else do you explain Andrew Lloyd Weber's coupon?"* (Coupon is a Scottish word for face). Scottie went on to say in his own style of special wit and wisdom:

"I'm all for learning. They could teach us about distant galaxies, and we could teach them how to make chips" *"And what if they are bad aliens, they might want to eat us? Not all of us though, just the fat folk."*

Scottie McClue is a colourful character, and his wit and good old Scottish banter, will sadly be missed from Scottish Radio. The 'Strange But True?' show went out on nationwide television during October 1997 and proved, just as the last time, to be a huge success. It was during late August and early

September, that many newspapers carried the story about the GRIP Ltd Insurance firm that specialised in protecting you with cover should you ever be abducted by aliens! It would cost the person who took out the insurance, about £100 a year and also covered you in case you got pregnant by aliens! Boss Simon Burgess stated in the Scottish daily Record of September 12th, 1997, that:

"There are plenty of people out there who want to believe in all sorts of strange stuff and want protected."

Oh yeah! He went on to say that he was happy to admit that his company was parting the 'feeble minded' from their money, but that he didn't see anything wrong with it! The insurance firm stated that most of their 100 U.K. customers came from the Scottish village of Bonnybridge, a figure I would most certainly dispute. This obviously was one big con, and many people recognised this firm for what they were. But I still find it incredible that anyone would wish to be parted with a sum of money like £100 just to feel safe. But then again, there are a lot of strange people about! Since the National Lottery began in 1996, there have been a number of lucky winners, but as the lottery progressed, a pattern began to emerge which was quite noticeable, in that a high number of lottery winners lived in a certain region, and that region was where all the UFO sightings had been occurring in Scotland. That area was soon to be dubbed by the press, as the 'Golden Circle'.

This circle took in an area of around 15 miles, and covered the towns of Linlithgow, Falkirk, and Alloa. Indeed, there are two lottery winners who stay not far from where I live, Bob and Anne Westland who won just over 3 million pounds. However, although there have been a number of lottery winners who live in this area, nobody from the town of Bonnybridge has (as yet!) won. I have been asked by numerous journalists and members of the public if there is 'anything in this'! i.e. that this might have something to do with UFOs and aliens? My reply is straight to the point, *"no"*. This is all but pure chance and provided the press an opportunity to capitalise on a potential story due to the locality of where all the winners came from.

One is obviously going to have more winners from the heavily populated Central Belt of Scotland, than they are from the more isolated parts of Scotland. Incidentally, I haven't even won ten ponds yet on the lottery! Another interesting point about Bonnybridge is the fact that the area has twice the number of twins than anywhere else, double the National average! Why this should be, no one really knows.

THE BONNYBRIDGE UFO THEME PARK

As stated throughout this book, Councillor Billy Buchanan is a colourful character and someone who will walk miles to do something for you. He has always been someone who wants to do his best for his town and will go to the ends of the world to do so. Of course, Billy has taken some flak over the years about associating himself with the UFO enigma in Bonnybridge, but that was only because there 'WAS A GENUINE' phenomenon occurring there. Some have stated that Billy's next venture, to try and get a UFO Theme Park built in Bonnybridge, was just 'pie in the sky' and another stunt for publicity for himself and Bonnybridge. Not so, say I. Nothing could be further from the truth. Billy's idea for a UFO Theme Park was a great idea, something that would boost local economy and put Bonnybridge on the tourist map. What's wrong with that! Look at 'Elvis Presley Boulevard' in Memphis. There you will find a whole range of things to do with Elvis, from Graceland Tours to souvenir shops. Then there is Loch Ness in the Scottish Highlands, you can't move for model Nessie's in the local shops. All this is revenue based and allows people to soak up the atmosphere and have a great time. So, Billy's idea about a UFO Theme Park was something that I feel was warranted. On the front page of the 'Falkirk Advertiser' dated Wednesday October 15th, 1997, the headline read, *'UFO Theme Park Hope'*. It informed its readers that interest was mounting in developing a theme park, complete with encounter centre, restaurants, and UFO education centre. Councillor Buchanan was quoted as saying:

"I have been publicly ridiculed, and the people of Bonnybridge have been ridiculed, but they still have come forward with what they have seen. Now we are getting credibility, and interest has been generated all over the world. It is only right that Bonnybridge should benefit from jobs and investment that such a project would bring."

The piece went onto say that Billy was shortly heading off to Roswell New Mexico and that he had put in an application to the National Lottery Fund and was speaking to a consortium of businessmen who had expressed an interest in the project. Billy went on:

"Bonnybridge was a hive of heavy industries, now it is an unemployment black spot. I am not promising anyone anything, but I want to do the best for the people I represent. If bringing them a theme park will create jobs and attract investment, that is good for the area."

Sadly, gutter press journalism reared its ugly head again, and in the 'Scottish Sun' newspaper dated October 16th, 1997, columnist Rikki Brown had a pop at Billy, and would you believe the people of Bonnybridge. In part he said:

"Since the Bonnybridge aliens, if they exist, haven't made contact by now after thousands of sightings, it may just be that Bonnybridge lies in the path between their intergalactic pub and their intergalactic kebab shop. It's just drunk aliens passing through. There's probably a very rational explanation for the sightings, such as everyone in Bonnybridge is nuts."

Now, I don't know about you dear reader, but I feel this is defamatory. And whilst I understand that some journalists (thankfully not them all) like to poke fun at people and situations, this constant attack on Billy and the people of Bonnybridge was getting tiresome.

MUSIC FOR THE STARS!

During 1997, Councillor Billy Buchanan (46) had been busy, not all of it council business. During his free time, he cut a record at a studio in Bonnybridge entitled, *'The Lights of Bonnybridge'*. The song was written by John McIntyre and Alex Murchison. The Scottish 'Sunday Mail', in their own inimitable style, stated in their article on October 26th, 1997, and I quote:

'The controversial Falkirk Councillor has cut a record which he hopes will rocket him up the pop charts. It's all about the weird and wonderful sightings that have turned the Stirlingshire village of Bonnybridge into the UK's UFO capital. Billy believes the catchy tune will strike a chord with music fans and he hopes the words will make the Ministry of Defence see the light, and agree to a Government enquiry into the strange phenomena.'

Billy was quoted as saying that he has had an enquiry from Japan about marketing the disc. As of this book going to press, we are unaware if this Japanese company have secured this deal. That said, Billy did send me a disc of him singing this song at a night club in Bonnybridge, and it's actually quite a nice wee tune!

MORE UFO SIGHTINGS

The following press report comes from the 'Falkirk Herald'. Unfortunately, I didn't put the date down for this one. It tells of more people who came forward with their UFO sightings. Norman Robb (23) and his friend Dan Dobbie, (17) were on their way to Brockville (the home of Falkirk Football club at that time). Norman was driving down Ochiltree Terrace when his attention was drawn to a huge object overhead. He stated to the 'Herald':

"It had red and blue lights and one bright horizontal beam. I collected Dan from his house, and we watched this thing for a good five minutes. I've taken a lot of abuse since I admitted seeing it. But I definitely saw something. It wasn't a helicopter or an aeroplane."

Norman's friend Dan had this to say to the Herald:

"It was a disc shape, hovering, then moving fast and slow."

The 'Falkirk Herald' also informed its readers about three Grangemouth nurses, Rhona Bye, (26) Mary Gardiner (51) and Irene Barclay (42) who also saw something strange in the sky which appeared over the former Falkirk Ice rink. Mary Gardiner had this to say:

"It had yellow, green and orange flashing lights. It was weird."

Fellow nurse Rhona Bye had this to say:

"It was spherical but had spokes sticking out of the sides. It was quite low down and still."

This was backed up and fellow nurse Irene Barclay who stated:

"It certainly didn't look like a plane."

I was quoted in the 'Herald' as saying that these sightings probably had a natural explanation. And whilst I wasn't there, my feelings that these sightings might have been a helicopter. Having said that, the witnesses did not report any sound with their sighting.

STILL DREAMING OF A UFO VISITOR CENTRE

In a newspaper article in the Scottish 'Sunday Post' dated November 16th, 1997, Billy was again putting forward his dream that a UFO visitor centre should be built near Bonnybridge. Billy stated:

"I've already had significant interest from potential investors and a local developer has identified a possible sight. What we need now is something on paper."

The article went on to state that Billy was contacted by Sarner International Ltd who specialise in visitor attractions and theme parks such as 'Viking Land' in Norway, and 'Volcano Land' in Singapore. Another interested party was U.S. based Catalyst Entertainment who actually built a UFO attraction in China which drew in 5,000 people an hour! Billy went on to say in this fairly large article that:

"We need a place for people to go. I've had visitors from America, Australia, and Yugoslavia turning up at my door."

In a sense this is true. Even I have had numerous calls from people from various parts of England and overseas, who have told me that they are coming to visit Bonnybridge and ask me 'where is the best place to go'! So clearly there is a market for this type of thing, and I for one, do hope that this fanciful project will one day see the light of day. (As of writing, July 2023, this visitor centre was still on the drawing board, and for the moment, it looks like that's where it is going to stay. Great shame really).

1998

We read about the UFO which was photographed by Phil Trevis near the B.P. Oil Refinery at Grangemouth earlier. Well on the 2nd of February 1998, another strange object was witnessed close to this oil refinery by a number of witnesses. They said that they observed a 'light beam' coming down from this strange craft which was in full view for several minutes. Initial thoughts that this must be a helicopter or some kind of aircraft. These thoughts, however, were soon dispelled as three military aircraft approached this strange object. As soon as the military aircraft got close to the object, they suddenly veered off, and as they did so, this object too shot away from the area at great speed. It is noted that the Ministry of Defence claimed that there were no records of any low flying training (!) *(* Steve Hammond)*

BRIAN McPHEE

1998 was also the year in which resident Brian McPhee from the Raploch area of Stirling was filming a number of strange objects in the Stirlingshire skies. This came to the attention of Britain's 'UFO Magazine'. English researcher Chris Martin decided to make the 900-mile round trip from his home to visit Brian where they sat down and discussed Brian's numerous UFO sightings. One of the filmed images that Brian showed Chris, is what appeared to be a black triangular shaped object which flew over Stirling Castle. It was whilst in Scotland, that Chris Martin had his own UFO sighting. From Chris's article entitled, 'The Scotland F.T' written up for the UFO Casebook web site, he states:

"After dropping off Brian McPhee, we headed back down the M9 motorway toward Edinburgh. As we were approaching the outskirts of Edinburgh, I noticed to my right what I thought to be an aircraft coming into land and made a passing comment about low-flying aeroplanes. Within the space of a few seconds, the "aircraft" banked sharply to the left and was almost immediately directly over the Motorway which was when both Neil Cunningham and I could clearly see three huge red saucer-shaped lights flashing on and off randomly lining the top side of the craft. We could now also clearly discern the outline of a typical deltoid Flying Triangle UFO."

"I grabbed the video camera and shouted at Neil to pull over immediately, however it crucially took several seconds for us to come to a halt on the hard shoulder by which time the FT was heading away from us toward a wooded area to our left. I eventually locked on to the object through the viewfinder and shot maybe 10-15 seconds of video. Within 3-4 minutes, the FT had disappeared out of sight and both Neil and I was left reeling from this encounter. Neil was particularly stunned

because he realised that had he stopped the car maybe 30-40 seconds earlier, we would have had in our possession probably the most clearly defined videotape of the elusive Flying Triangle UFO ever captured. But then, there is always next time."

English researcher Russell Callaghan who reported for the now defunct 'UFO Magazine' at the time and who had viewed one of Brian's UFO videos, was quoted as saying in the Scottish 'Daily Record':

"Some of the manoeuvres and detail on the 15-minute tape were quite stunning and closely resembled the kind of activity recorded in the skies over Mexico."

What Russell was referring here to, was a multitude or white orb like spheres which had been witnessed by thousands of people in the skies above Mexico. *(*Steve Hammond)*

UFO ROAD SHOW!

During April 1998, Councillor Billy Buchanan, a man of many ideas, came up with a new one, and that was to take a travelling 'UFO Road Show' out into the Primary and Secondary schools of the Central Region (more so Bonnybridge and Stirlingshire). Councillor Buchanan kindly asked me if I would like to get involved, a request that I quickly jumped at. However, events were soon to transpire which would put a spanner in the works of our best laid plans. But more of that in a moment. But first, why a 'UFO Road Show'? Well, I am of the honest opinion that life is an education. All of us are learning every day about things around us (and also above!). The success of the T.V. show the 'X-Files', and other such UFOlogical shows, have gone a long way in quenching the thirst of many young and enquiring minds, who are now looking at the subject of UFOs with open eyes. Both Councillor Buchanan and I, truly felt at this time (still do) that by bringing this information into the classroom, then that would go a long way to help educate those young and enquiring minds.

I gave a talk to a classroom of school children at Abercromby Primary School in the town of Tullibody in Central Scotland back on the 14th of November 1994, and not only did it go down a treat, the class teacher, a Miss Nichol, told me that that was the best-behaved class that she had ever seen. They were transfixed with my talk on the UFO sightings over Bonnybridge.

I know that when I was younger, I would have loved someone come to my school and talk to me about UFOs. Sadly, Billy and my intended 'UFO Road Show' never got off the ground. It was shot down in flames by education authorities who stated that we would not be allowed to lecture in any schools regarding our work into the UFO sightings over Bonnybridge. This made the newspapers, and I was contacted by the 'Scottish Daily Express' who asked me for my comments on this decision. My reply was that I thought that the education authorities were very 'narrow minded' in their attitude, and that they should realise that the children of today are crying out for information of this nature. Depriving children of a lecture in regard to a subject which I'm sure they would find fascinating just because it's not strictly school curriculum, was in my view, ridiculous: end of quote

Now I fully understand the possibility that 'some' children might have been frightened by what both Billy and I had to say. That said, we would have taken out any 'unsavoury' aspects in case it gave them nightmares. We would just have stuck to UFO sightings, and not so called 'alien abductions'. That would have been going too far. It was not our intention to put nasty images in a child's head which might disturb him, it was purely and only about making the kids think 'out of the box'. Children are not stupid. They see lots of programmes on television about UFOs these days, all both Billy and I were intending, is to bring that information into the classroom. Anyway, as stated, it fell by the wayside. But never say never!

1999

During January 1999 the town of Bonnybridge in Stirlingshire was again featured in the Scottish newspapers.

This time it concerned, would you believe, a UFO landing spot! Apparently, a Glasgow academic by the name of Yan Tung Li, came up with an idea of trying to get someone to build a landing beacon to help extraterrestrial visitors/UFOs, to land in Bonnybridge. Yan Li, from Strathclyde University, believed that a huge luminous flashing tower could have benefits for the town. He reckoned that tourists would flood to the town to view the beacon, and that ETs might decide to come down in their flying saucers. Mr Li's primary intention was to promote interest in science, though, as he put it, 'Science Fiction'! Needless to say, that venture never got off the ground.

THE NAUGHTIES
The beginning of Covid
2000

Some of the major events during the so-called noughties were the attacks on the World Trade Center in New York on the 11th of September 2001 where 2,996 people were killed; 230,000 people died in the Indian Ocean tsunami on 26 December 2004; pop icon Michael Jackson died on the 25th of June 2009. That font of information Wikipedia was launched on 15 January 2001, and on the 30th of March 2002, Britain saw the death of Queen Elizabeth, the Queen Mother, who died aged 101. And let us not forget that dreadful virus, 'Covid' which reared its ugly head initially in China in 2019, and surfaced here in the British Isles from January 2020, with various lockdowns and restrictions.

DO WE HAVE ANY UFO ABDUCTIONS IN BONNYBRIDGE?

People often ask if there have been any UFO abductions and instances where alien 'beings' have been seen in association with these UFO reports from Bonnybridge and Stirlingshire. Well, there are few and far between, certainly nothing that this author has researched in the area. In his book, 'The Scottish

UFO Casebook', author Steve Hammond informs his readers of a strange case of a humanoid being seen in Falkirk! The details he gives are sketchy, but what we do learn is that a chap called Scott Garvie was walking back home from work on the 10th of August 2000, (the time is not given) when he suddenly became drowsy. Then, no doubt to his surprise, he found himself not where he was a moment ago, but somewhere which was both light and dark at the same time. It was here, where he encountered a strange looking 'being'. He describes it as short, with sunken green eyes, no mouth, with a sandy coloured skin texture. One peculiar observation that he noticed, was a hole which he saw which was between the neck and head of this 'being' above the spine. After this observation, he recalls nothing more. Yes, I too, would love to know more about this incident. If you are reading this book Scott, do get in touch.

(* Steve Hammond)

BONNYBRIDGE AND ROSWELL (Twin Towns?)

As we have learned, Councillor Billy Buchanan is quite a character, and one of the more interesting if not challenging things that he undertook, was to try and twin the American UFO town of Roswell in New Mexico with the Stirlingshire UFO town of Bonnybridge. In 2001 Billy visited the mayor of Roswell, a gentleman by the name of Mr. Bill B. Owen, where they met up to discuss this interesting proposition. One Scottish newspaper had Billy saying:

"Roswell has a population of just 50,000, but it is a draw for thousands of tourists interested in the UFO phenomenon. That pumps millions into the local economy. However, we want to emphasise both places have more to offer than UFOs, and we hope to take along people with tourism and business links to promote more general commercial tie-ups."

The newspaper than had a quote from the mayor of Roswell who stated.
"We welcome the twinning idea."

At the time of writing (December 2023) this has still not come to fruition.

Late July 2002 saw SPI members gather at the Royal Hotel on Bonnybridge High Street where I, along with fellow Scottish UFO researcher Brian Allan, gave presentations on the UFO sightings over Bonnybridge. Upon completion, a crowd of around 30 people took off in a convoy of cars to the moors behind Bonnybridge for a sky watch. Sadly, it was an inclement night, and cloud cover hindered what we hoped would be a good clear sky. Nonetheless, it provided a good opportunity for like minded souls, to gather together and participate in something which we all felt was beneficial. The 'Falkirk Herald' newspaper covered this sky watch in their August 1st edition.

CROP CIRCLES APPEAR NEAR BONNYBRIDGE!

Much has been made of the thousands of crop circles that have appeared all over the world, the majority of which can usually be found in the fields of southern England, notably Hampshire and Wiltshire. Opinion is divided as to what causes them. Some say aliens, some say weather phenomenon, and others say they are all hoaxed. I know for sure, that the vast majority of crop circles are hoaxed, and I know a number of people who cleverly make them. It's not as difficult as you might think folk. Anyway, I'm digressing. Two crop circles were found in a field near Bonnybridge in August 2002. The Scottish Sun newspaper dated August 20th, shows a photograph of Councillor Buchanan standing in front of them. Billy was quoted as saying that they were clearly visible from the brow of a nearby hill and that they were generating a lot of interest. And finished with:

> *"We've had numerous UFO sightings, but this is a new one on me."*

In the 'Falkirk Herald', Billy was quoted as saying to reporters Alan Muir and Marjoribanks, that he was 99.9%

certain that these crop circles were hoaxed but that they had caused an awful lot of interest. He went on to say:

"Hundreds of people have come out to look at the site which is very near the Falkirk Wheel, and that can't be a bad thing. It's another facet of the Bonnybridge phenomenon."

The 'Herald' went on to say that a Mr Taylor who owned Carmuirs Farm on whose land the crop circles appeared, said that he was more than happy for people to come out and see these crop circles, but they should also respect the countryside code. These crop circles could be seen from the A883 road between Falkirk and Bonnybridge.

August 2002 was another big year for media interest in the Bonnybridge UFO enigma. NTV Russia and TV Asahi from Japan had visited the village and interviewed locals. NTV Russia is the biggest independent broadcasting company in Russia with around 100 million viewers. Director and Chief correspondent Audrey Cherkasov stated to the 'Falkirk Herald' that they were there for the story of the Bonnybridge UFOs and that no wise man can think we're alone in the universe. She further stated that as yet though, they hadn't seen any UFOs above Bonnybridge. Councillor Buchanan was quoted in the 'Herald' as saying that he was glad to help out all these TV crews and that the interest would be good for the people of Bonnybridge and Falkirk District. He went on to say that he hoped that all this latest publicity would help to galvanise efforts to secure a UFO centre for the town. He stated:

"There are thousands of people coming now. We need a heritage and UFO centre where we can collate all the UFO information and celebrate the tremendous history of Bonnybridge. Everybody wants to know about Bonnybridge, we've got to cash in on that. We're on a winner here."

In 2002 Bonnybridge was voted the world's top 'UFO Hot Spot'. In second place jointly were countries Italy, France, and Canada. Councillor Buchanan was quoted in the world's press about the twining of the two towns, he stated:

"It will be a great day for Bonnybridge and put it firmly on the map. There are a lot of disbelievers, but they cannot find explanations for all the sightings". "Roswell has a population of just 50,000 but it is a draw for thousands of tourists interested in the UFO Phenomena that pumps millions into the local economy." "However, we want to emphasise that both places have more to offer than UFOs, and we hope to take along people with tourism and business links to promote more general commercial tie-ups". Roswell Mayor Bill Owen said, "We welcome the twinning idea it would be an interesting possibility that would benefit both communities."

THE SECOND BRITISH NATIONAL UFO SKYWATCH

One thing that I enjoy doing is providing an opportunity for people to get involved in our sky watches, and on July 27th, 2002, I organised Britain's second National UFO sky watch. The first National sky watch that I arranged, was held in Rendlesham Forest in Suffolk England. A number of sky watchers met up at the Royal in Bonnybridge High Street whereafter we all headed off in cars to the moors behind the town of Bonnybridge. Sadly, on this occasion, nothing unusual was spotted.

According to 'The Scottish UFO Casebook', written by Steve Hammond, he mentions a very brief incident where an object was seen to land on the Bonnybridge gold course in late March 2004. Sadly, there is no further information about this incident. In March 2022, I appeared on the SKY History programme, 'UFO Conspiracies', hosted by Craig Charles and Sarah Crudass. Watching that programme that night, was Sean Buckley. He quickly got in touch with me to inform me of his own UFO sighting in the Stirlingshire area, which was also observed by his friend. Here is what he had to say to me.

"Hi there Malcolm",

"I'm messaging you as I saw you on Craig Charles UFO program and in relation to the sightings In the Ochil Hills. I

moved to Stirling in 2007, I met my then partner and settled down in Alva. One evening in I believe it was 2008 or 2009, I was dropping friends off at Stirling train station as they were traveling to Australia. My partner was a long serving employee of Stirling University gardens and grounds. Kevin and I were driving back from Stirling over the hill near the Wallace monument. As we drove round the corner with the monument on our right-hand side, we both suddenly and immediately noticed, an extremely large object hovering in the sky but not very high from the top of the hill. This was at the back of the University, near the duck pond area. I suppose it's the Sheriffmuir area. The object was large and wide, and appeared rounded but rectangular in shape, it could well have been a disk. Kevin told me to pull over the car straight away, which I did. We were parked on the left-hand side of the road where there was an opening. I couldn't believe what I was seeing, and neither could Kevin, who has also lived at the foot of the hills his whole life. (I'm from Orkney) The UFO was emitting what I can only describe as a green glow. We both opened the car door and got out. The object appeared to move upward with thrust and stop again. At this point I was terrified, I get shivers thinking about it now, and if I think about it too much, I actually get emotional. It was overwhelming. I can only describe it as like seeing or experiencing a ghost. Kevin was shocked, and said it made no sense what he was seeing. At first, I thought it could have been lights being shone up into mist, or people on the hill with torches. It then moved at a 45° kind of angle rapidly and stopped again. I had begun to shake at this point with both excitement and fear. Kevin then said we have go up on the hill, I don't think you could have paid me a million pounds to go up that hill that evening! We watched for perhaps two minutes and did try to take photos on our older phones, but it was just black. Phone cameras weren't up to much in the dark back then. Before we did get back in the car, Kev encouraged me to drive along the main road round and to go up the small side road up to Sheriffmuir. I agreed. We managed to peel our eyes off the UFO, which I genuinely felt was watching us, or certainly making its presence felt. As I was driving, my hands were shaking so much, and my mind was racing."

"I carried on driving to Alva. Kevin was unhappy with me, but a horde of people or even an army would not have made me go up there. I've always believed and been open minded, more so when we saw that UFO in such good detail which was not very far away from us either I would genuinely love to hear if anyone else saw or experienced anything on that evening. I've looked at online forum's and posted on them a few times to see if anyone responded, but no luck. As soon as we got home that evening, I was straight on the computer, looking how we could report what we saw. Stuff come up about the Ministry of Defence etc but we really didn't want to go down that route. At that time there didn't seem to be anywhere to report it, other than a Facebook status and telling people by word of mouth. Kevin and I haven't really spoken in recent years. I believe that he is still at Stirling University, he also told his colleges at the University what we saw, however, he wasn't taken seriously. I keep an eye out for local reporting's on that area for other UFO sightings. I'm not entirely sure, but I just genuinely feel like there is some kind of energy or something really odd going on around that area. I believe last year a man from Bridge of Allen reported an encounter in the same area. I re messaged my friends in Stirling at the time to remind them of what Kevin and I experienced. I'm not really sure why I'm reaching out to you, but as you are an enthusiast, I feel like the story won't fall on deaf ears. It's certainly been one of my most memorable moments of my time living down south."

Best wishes Sean Buckley.

Malcolm's Comments: Unfortunately, I was living in England during 2008/2009 and never knew about this sighting. Something that big simply 'must' have been seen by others. This might be one that I have to trawl through the newspapers and other UFO files and see if I can find anything. Could this have been a large advertising dirigible!

BONNYBRIDGE UFO SKY WATCH.
1st November 2014

Over the weekend of 31st October to the 2nd of November 2014, the city of Stirling in Central Scotland featured its very first 'Scottish Paranormal Festival' where a combination of ghosts, ghouls, vampires and more brought the paranormal to this historic town. The event, sponsored by film maker, Peter Broughan, also featured various lectures and workshops for believers and sceptics alike. I was also a speaker at this prestigious event, and I also organised a sky watch at the UFO Hot Spot town of Bonnybridge in Stirlingshire. Fellow UFO and Paranormal researcher Dave Hodrien who runs the Birmingham UFO group, also assisted in this venture, and together we had a merry band of sky watchers all keen to see if we could pick up something strange across the Stirlingshire skies. Our merry band of sky watchers all assembled outside the Albert Halls in Stirling where the main festival events were being held, after which, we arrived to meet other sky watchers in Bonnybridge. A number of journalists attended our sky watch, all keen to perhaps witness what others had been seeing in this small part of Scotland. Unfortunately, the UFOs didn't show, but it had been a great exercise in informing those people who were attending a sky watch for the first time, to learn about what you can normally see in the sky, as opposed to what normally you wouldn't expect!

According to the 'Falkirk Herald', dated 28th June 2016, a UFO was sighted over the town of Airth in Stirlingshire. Here is what they reported:

'A motorist reported seeing a UFO today that was 'big, black and cigar-shaped' and disappeared from sight at great speed. James Kennedy, from Kilsyth, was driving from Kincardine today at around 11am when he noticed the object in the skies above the village of Airth. "It was a huge thing, black

and cigar shaped. At first, I thought it was a jet. I stopped the car and got out and thing just disappeared." There have been no further reports of the object'.

So, short and sweet, but it showed that the 'Falkirk Herald' were still happy to publish UFO reports in their paper.

THE SCOTTISH UFO AND PARANORMAL CONFERENCE 2017

The Falkirk Herald newspaper of 2nd July 2017 published an article regarding our annual Scottish UFO and Paranormal Conference. Here is how they reported it to their readers.

'From UFO sightings, ghostly going-ons and encounters with demons, a day packed with paranormal activity arrives in Falkirk. The annual Scottish UFO and Paranormal Conference will take place at Falkirk Town Hall on Saturday, July 8, 2017, taking a look at a variety of weird and wonderful topics.

Organised by Malcolm Robinson, founder of Strange Phenomena Investigations, *(Author's Note: Not strictly true, the event is also organised by Alyson Dunlop Shanes and Ron Halliday)* the conference will explore mystery sightings and events across the UK and from further afield. Malcolm, who has written five books on the paranormal, said:

"I set up SPI back in 1979 and I was very sceptical then. But it's like anything in life; once you get your hands dirty and you spend the night in a haunted house or two, you start to think, maybe it's all true. "I've had my hair pulled, I've been kicked, slapped... by nothing. "I've seen a chest of drawers rise up into the middle of a room, move to the other side then slowly settle down again. "I just wish sceptics would look at these things with an open mind and weigh up the evidence. The vast majority of UFO stories have natural explanations. It's only a very small percentage that cannot, at this point, be explained."

Malcolm will speak on UFO 'Hot Spots' from around the world', discussing those closer to home including Bonnybridge and Dyfed, West Wales. Following on from these locations, he will then take a look at hot spots such as The Nullabor Plains in Australia, Area 51 in the Nevada Desert, The Mysterious N. Triangle in Russia, the infamous Skinwalker Ranch near Utah and sightings over Mexico and Norway. Also tackling all things extraterrestrial, paranormal researcher Andrew Hennessey presents his findings of the small ex-coal-mining town of Gorebridge, near Edinburgh, which has been the scene of extraordinary UFO activity at least over the last 20 years. Author Ron Halliday will examine the extent to which the supernatural influenced the lives of the famous and through them influenced world events, while investigator Innes Smith will be looking at how we assess evidence and examines some problems facing the investigator, detailing some well-known and little known cases and inviting all of us to find our own threshold for 'boggling' at the evidence. Also on the bill are mystic Alyson Dunlop who will explore the world of angelic beings, while author Tricia Robertson will discuss the survival of human consciousness after physical death, and spiritualist medium Gary Gray will aim to lift the veil between this material world and the spirit realm. Malcolm added:

"My goal in life is to continue researching cases pertaining to the strange world of UFOs and the paranormal and hopefully provide some form of answer to account for what at present eludes us. At the end of the day, it's just to let people make up their own minds and they don't have to believe a word of it."

FAR EAST FILM CREW ENJOY THEIR UFO DAY IN BONNYBRIDGE

This was the headline that appeared in the 'Falkirk Herald' dated 4th September 2017. The article went onto state, and I quote:

'A documentary film crew from Tokyo got a first-hand experience of the Bonnybridge UFO phenomenon last weekend. The Japanese visitors were in the country to capture images for a film they are making on mysterious occurrences in Scotland

and Bonnybridge fame as a centre for intergalactic visitation had apparently spread to the Far East because it was top of their list of places to see.

Councillor Billy Buchanan, a well-known supporter of the Bonnybridge UFO connection, was the Tokyo team's guide throughout the weekend, showing them local sites before hosting a sky watch as night fell'. Councillor Buchanan said:

"We took them to the back of Bonnybridge by Greenhill and quite a number of people turned up to take part including famous UFO expert Brian Allan, who gave a talk on the night. It went well and the film crew got a lot of footage for their documentary. The film crew couldn't believe we have nothing in the village to capitalise on its UFO reputation."

Bonnybridge is said to be the UFO capital of the world with over 300 reported sightings.

UFO Sighting and Video taken near Bonnybridge Stirlingshire

A gentleman by the name of Jack Conner got in touch with me to relate his own UFO sighting, where he managed to capture some footage on his camera. Jack now takes up the story:

"Hi Malcolm,

On July 18th, 2018, just before 8.30pm, I was inside my house while my 7-year-old son was outside playing in the garden with his friend. It was a warm summer's night with a very clear, bright, and blue sky. My son suddenly called me outside because there was an unusual object which he could not identify flying over our house. I went outside, and the three of us (me, my son, and his friend) watched a circular metallic object come from approximately the vicinity of the Bonnybridge area behind our house, fly over the roof of our house, and then gently arc across the fields and country of the Forth Valley heading in the general direction towards the Grangemouth oil refinery approximately. 6 miles away. We can see this refinery in the distance across the flat Forth Valley from where we live."

"The object was clearly metallic but had no visible means of propulsion. It was not an airplane or a helicopter. It travelled silently above our heads making no noise. It seemed to be intelligently controlled. It was not drifting like a balloon. The only other explanation besides UFO that could occur to any of us, was a drone, but it did not have the visible propeller blades of a drone. My son had previously played with a toy drone outside our house, but this was not anything like he had played with, and besides, it was higher up than a toy, though clearly visible to the naked eye given the good light conditions that summer evening. I pulled my iPhone out and took some shots and a couple of videos."

"The iPhone camera does not quite capture the view of the object which we got with the naked eye where it seemed 'closer' to us, however shots have been captured by the phone camera of the circular metallic object (elliptical and seeming slightly tilted on its axis) that flew over our house and then across the surrounding countryside heading towards Grangemouth. The best is probably the first (of two) videos when the object was flying directly over the house and was closer, before it headed out across the flat country of the Forth Valley. I continued to watch the object as it receded into the distance and away from my vision, flying silently over the Forth Valley, and I continued to take some iPhone snaps. These show the surrounding flat countryside next to our house, across where it flew. I only have one other significant thing to report as I watched the object recede from my view. That was, there was a burning smell in the air, almost like burning rubber or as if the hot air was charged. (However, as it was the summertime, there could have been another explanation, for instance, a neighbour's BBQ, though it didn't smell like a BBQ) For the last couple of years, I've joked with my son that we witnessed a UFO, but other than telling my family and a few friends, I've not publicised this more widely. However, it would be interesting for you to investigate whether anybody else in the area saw the unusual object we did that evening; or perhaps could come up with a rational explanation *for what it was. Was somebody flying some kind of circular metallic drone that evening? Viewed at the time by the naked eye, the object was much more distinct and seemed 'closer' to us than the camera was able to capture but the phone camera has been able to capture something."*

"The above is a full account for you (with photos, videos) though I am happy to discuss any details with you further if there is any more I can add. For the moment, at least, I would prefer to stay anonymous so I would be grateful if for the moment at least you treated this account as confidential. Thanks for your time and attention to this and feel free to get back to me should you wish to discuss or advise further."

Best wishes. Jack Conner. (pseudonym)

SPI endeavoured to come up with an explanation to account for this one, but sadly all lines of enquiry drew a blank.

Sandra Lincoln UFO Sighting
Cowie Stirlingshire, Central Scotland

Here is another witness who saw something strange in the Stirlingshire skies. Here is what she said to me in an e-mail:

"Hi there.

"I saw the piece in the Falkirk Herald about the strange light in the sky above Grangemouth. Not sure if this is helpful, but last January (2019) I saw a large white light in the sky above Cowie Caberboard * It was there every night and sometimes early morning. It didn't move, it just sat there for ages, then disappeared like a candle going out. I posted on Facebook about it where some others had seen it too. After a few weeks I saw it again, but it moved and flew right above myself and my partner. It was noiseless and looked like a large boat in the sky. It flew right over us in Throsk, (Author's note. A town in Stirlingshire) *and headed towards Stirling Castle and disappeared. I have never seen it since. The one night I didn't have my phone!"*

Sandra Lincoln (pseudonym)

* Sandra mentions in her e-mail to me the company called Cowie Caberboard. The correct name for this company is Norbord UK Ltd, which is an international producer of wood-based panels. Sadly, again, we never got any further forward with this sighting.

George Henderson UFO Sighting
Near Grangemouth, Central Scotland

It all started with witness George Henderson (32) from Grangemouth, a small town in Central Scotland near the UFO 'Hot Spot' of Bonnybridge. He e-mailed me to tell me about a strange bright white light that he had seen in the sky over several evenings. The object was spotted near the B.P. Petro-Chemical Refinery Plant at Grangemouth. George described the light as being intensely bright and would sit in the same area of sky between the hours of 8:00pm and 9:30pm. There was no sound to this object and there were no other lights associated with it. George was aware of the flight paths of aircraft in this vicinity, as they flew towards Glasgow and Edinburgh airports, so as far as he could be sure, this wasn't an aircraft. He also ruled out a helicopter, a 'Chinese lantern', and a drone and also a bright star or a planet. On the 12th of October 2020, George took some video footage of this strange light, and also some still photographs. Of course, it's easy to say that due to the time spent in the same location, that it must have been a bright star or planet, that would be the easiest explanation, right! Well, it certainly had all the hallmarks of being a bright planet, but George was insistent that it wasn't, and that eventually the bright object would disappear. And so, I did what I normally would do with any given sighting. I pulled out all the stops to try and find an answer. I sent e-mails to Police Scotland to see if any members of the public had called their station with similar sightings, I sent e-mails to Edinburgh and Glasgow Airport, and also NATS, (The National Air Traffic Services) I also e-mailed George's local newspaper, The 'Falkirk Herald' asking them to let me know if any readers might have observed the same object. Well, the response was both good and bad. Glasgow Airport stated:

"Hi Malcolm, Grangemouth is not within our controlled airspace, this would need directed to Edinburgh as it's within their Class D Airspace. Hope this helps."

This was followed by a response from National Air Traffic Services who said:

"Dear Mr. Robinson
Case 933328

"Thank you for your enquiry received on 15 October 2020 regarding a possible UFO sighting near the B.P. Refinery plant at Grangemouth, Stirlingshire, Central Scotland. NATS does not coordinate or investigate sightings of UFOs, which should be reported to the police. We are therefore unable to provide any further information about this."
Regards Wendy. Community Relations Team.

So, no luck there. I never heard back from either Police Scotland or Edinburgh Airport. However, James Trimble, staff writer at the 'Falkirk Herald' contacted me to say that they were running a piece in the 'Herald' and fingers crossed, I might get some response. I'll say! No sooner had the piece been featured in the 'Herald' and the Glasgow 'Evening Times', than a number of UFO reports came flooding in. The title of the 'Falkirk Herald's' piece was, 'Footage of 'UFO' captured in night skies over Scottish town' subtitled, *'A man believes he has video footage and photographs of a craft from another world'*. Typical back street journalism, whilst the crux of James's article was fine and stuck to the facts, the subtitle, stating that a man believes that he has footage and photographs of a craft from another world, was downright insulting and incorrect. George has never said that. No wonder UFO witnesses are frightened to come forward with their UFO sightings!

Linda Able UFO Sighting.
Between the towns of Plean and Bannockburn

Linda Able saw the UFO on the same date as George Henderson mentioned above. This is what Linda had to say

"Hi Malcolm,

"It was seen in the early hours of the morning. (12th October 2020) It was northeast in the sky from the A9 between Plean and Bannockburn, so more of the Alloa/Kincardine direction. It wasn't moving and it didn't seem to be twinkling like a star would, which made me think it was a planet, but I'm not sure. It was a lot brighter and bigger than the other stars in the sky as you can see in the photograph with the clouds. There are stars to the left of the bright object. My colleague thought it was strange, which is why we took photographs, and when I read the article in the Falkirk Herald, I thought I would get in touch. If you could keep me anonymous if discussing this with anyone else that would be great thank you."
Thanks, Linda Able. (pseudonym)

Malcolm's Comments:
Again, after extensive research, we could not uncover what it was that Linda saw.

Jerry Quaker. UFO Sighting.
Polmont, Stirlingshire, Central Scotland

Our next witness also saw the story about the Grangemouth UFO in the Falkirk Herald newspaper. Here is what he said to me in an e-mail:

"Dear Sir,

I was interested in the UFO story on page 15 of last week's issue of the Falkirk Herald. I live near Falkirk, and many months ago I observed that circular white object from my upstairs bedroom window. I saw that bright light on at least two different occasions. It was there at the same time on the occasions that I saw it. I usually go to bed between 10.30 and 11.00 pm. Looking from my bedroom window, it appeared to be in the direction of Polmont, or much further to the right of Grangemouth from my angle of observation. I thought it might be a helicopter with a search light, but I opened the window and didn't hear any sound. On the first occasion I observed it, the speed at which it suddenly disappeared away to my right, well it couldn't have been a plane or helicopter. On the second occasion, I observed it for about 25 minutes but then I went to bed, so I have no idea how much longer it remained there. I have no idea what that bright light was, but it was rather unusual. Lights can be deceptive at night".

"*It didn't occur to me the bright light that I saw many months ago may indeed be a UFO. It was very bright and about the size of a small football. It was like a search light. As I said in my previous email, the thing that caught my attention was the speed of departure. In my estimation I don't think a plane, or a helicopter could generate that speed from a standstill so rapidly and disappear so quickly. I wish you every success with your projects.*"

Kind regards Jerry Quaker. (Pseudonym)

FOOTAGE OF A UFO CAPTURED IN NIGHT SKIES OVER GRANGEMOUTH

This was the headline featured in the 'Falkirk Herald' newspaper dated, 14th October 2020. Written up by James Trimble it stated, and I quote:

A Grangemouth resident believes he has video footage and photographs of a craft from another world. The sighting, which happened on the evening of Monday, October 12, 2020, near petrochemical giant Ineos, is now being investigated by professional UFO hunter Malcolm Robinson. Mr Robinson, the founder of Strange Phenomena Investigations (SPI), said:

"The witness, who wishes to remain anonymous, has, over the past few weeks, observed a circular white object in the sky near the refinery plant on consecutive nights beginning at 8:00pm and concluding at around 9.30pm. The witness a respectable gentleman with a responsible job, is convinced what he saw was not an aircraft, helicopter, or drone. Indeed, he managed to take photographs and a piece of video footage."

Mr Robinson, who has assisted Provost Billy Buchanan with research during the wave of UFO sightings in Bonnybridge the 1990s, is looking for anyone else who has witnessed strange objects in the night skies above Grangemouth.

On the 28th of October 2020, I received an e-mail from Jack Queen (pseudonym) He stated, and I quote:

"Dear Sir,
I was interested in the UFO story in page 15 of last week's issue of the Falkirk Herald. I live in Falkirk, and many months ago I observed that circular white object from my upstairs bedroom window. I saw that bright light on at least two different occasions. It was there at the same time on the occasions that I saw it. I usually go to bed between 10.30 and 11.00 pm. Looking from my bedroom window, it appeared to be in the direction of Polmont or much further to the right of Grangemouth from my angle of observation. I thought it might be a helicopter with a search light, but I opened the window and didn't hear any sound. On the first occasion I observed it for about 15 minutes. The speed with which it suddenly disappeared away to my right couldn't have been a plane or helicopter. The second occasion I observed it for about 25 minutes, but then I went to bed, so I have no idea how much longer it remained there. I have no idea what that bright light was, but it was rather unusual. Lights can be deceptive at night. It didn't occur to me the bright light that I saw many months ago may indeed be a UFO. It was very bright and about the size

of a small football. It was like a search light. *The thing that took my attention was the speed of departure. In my estimation I don't think a plane, or a helicopter could generate that speed from a standstill so rapidly and disappear so quickly. I wish you every success with your projects."*
Kind Regards. Jack Queen.

WORLD UFO DAY 2021

The 'Falkirk Herald' of 2nd July 2021 featured a piece written by staff writer Kirsty Paterson who informed the readers that the town of Bonnybridge was to take part in the annual, 'World UFO Day'. Here is how they reported it:

Falkirk Provost welcomes UFOlogists to Bonnybridge.

The Provost of Falkirk is celebrating World UFO Day by welcoming some of the UK's leading UFOlogists to his Bonnybridge ward. Friday is World UFO Day and Provost Billy Buchanan is delighted that his village will once again be the centre of attention among those who firmly believe the truth is still out there. And it seems there are plenty of people who share that point of view. A recent survey of 2000 people found that on average 24% of Brits believe they have seen a UFO at least once in their lifetime. The survey, conducted by Buzz Bingo, found that 25 per cent of people in Glasgow claim to have had an alien experience. Provost Buchanan was unphased that Bonnybridge didn't feature among the places where having seen aliens was almost commonplace. Nevertheless, the town has for many years been known as one of the UK's top places to see UFOs in the heart of the area known as the Falkirk Triangle. As a long-standing councillor for the area, Billy is passionate about its history and remains open-minded about what might be in the skies above. He said:

"A lot of people say it's a lot of rubbish and we've had a lot of ridicule for it, but these people are really interesting to speak to and I am delighted they are coming to support the area."

Among the visitors is Malcom Robinson, founder of 'Strange Phenomena Investigations', who recently made a programme about the phenomenon. The location of the Sky watch will be kept under wraps to avoid disturbance.

Bonnybridge Community Centre, Sky Watch.
3rd July 2021

Well, our sky watch was not kept under wraps as such. It was well mentioned on social media. Here is what I wrote about the sky watch on my Facebook page:

Well, I'm pleased to say that SPI's part in the World UFO Day Sky Watch went off well. Over 20 people turned up to participate in the event, and, after initially meeting up in the car park adjacent to the Bonnybridge Community Centre, we all headed up in a convoy of cars to the designated meeting place that Provost Billy Buchanan had arranged for us all to meet. Billy had provided some plastic chairs for people to sit on and also provided a box full of crisps and cans of iron bru and bottles of water for those who liked to nibble whilst watching the skies. Not only that, but Billy was also on hand with his trusty midge spray to ensure that those wee pesky blighters didn't annoy those assembled too much.

The location was perfect, and one had a commanding view downwards looking over the countryside. A rolling mist could be seen lying over parts of the ground which eventually dissipated as the night wore on. When we arrived, the sky was 95% clear, but eventually cloud cover came over later. It was around 11:10pm when I assembled all the sky watchers together to brief them on what to expect of the night. I also spoke about some of the UFO sightings in Bonnybridge, and how it all started for me. I then turned it over to Provost Billy Buchanan who informed everyone about his role in the Bonnybridge UFO sightings and how this small Scottish town was at one point, dubbed the 'UFO Capital of the World'. Billy is a wonderful speaker, and at times had the assembled crowd in giggles with his patter. SPI's psychic Ian Shanes also spoke about what his views were on these so-called alien entities and how mankind should interact with them. All good stuff and very thoughtful. I then asked other people to bring forward their own stories all whilst our eyes were scanning the skies. By now the cloud cover had covered most of the sky, but the good thing was, it didn't rain. Well, a few tiny specks for about a minute, but after that none at all. Indeed, it was quite cool, and not cold at all, so much so, that I was out there without a jacket!

I then mentioned to those assembled about Arthur Shuttlewood, a former newspaper correspondent at the 'Warminster Journal' in Warminster (the English equivalent to Bonnybridge). Arthur used to shine a torch up into the night sky and was surprised to receive strange lights coming back at him. So, needless to say, when in Rome and all that! we just had to do the same. There were a few attendees who had brought with them, some very powerful lasers, and boy, were they powerful! Within seconds the Stirlingshire sky was awash with dancing green lasers lights, one of which produced a stunning square box of circular lights. Someone piped up and said that people miles away would be surprised to see this and would no doubt think that the UFOs were back in Bonnybridge. So, if we have reports in next week's 'Falkirk Herald' newspaper you know what caused it. Sadly, our desired attempt to draw forth any possible UFOs didn't work. But in the crowd was a lady well known to me, she asked me to call her Wooshwa.

Now please understand that there are many people who deal with the subject of UFOs in their own way. This lady claims to be from another planet and is here on planet Earth to help people come to terms with the visitors. I spoke to the assembled crowd saying that Wooshwa would attempt to bring forth her space friends by what she called her calling. However, her calling in point of fact, comprised of her singing in a strange language towards the sky. Yes, it looked kind of strange, but that's the thing folks, we were here on a sky watch, and I was prepared to allow anyone to show their wares 'so to speak'. Wooshwa followed that by talking out in a strange language, again hoping to entice her sky friends to appear. Although none of us assembled could see anything, Wooshwa did say that they were near, and that there was a strong presence, a heavy presence around. I've no problems with people doing their own thing. We are well aware that Steven Greer and his friends also try something similar to try contact UFOs. At this point we then tried another attempt to bring forth UFOs. Wooshwa had everyone join in a circle and lock arms, where we all sent out loving and positive thoughts, again hoping that we could bring forth these Bonnybridge UFOs. All but one saw nothing. One chap said he saw a bright white light move from one part of the sky to another very quickly. That could of course have been anything, but then again!

The sky watch was being filmed for a documentary on Scottish UFOs, and prior to arriving at the sky watch area, the lady who was doing the filming, had us all filling out disclosure forms, I'll keep you all posted as to what transpires with the intended documentary. It was great to have one of my daughters at the sky watch, Karen, along with her boyfriend Garry. My other half Carole was also in attendance. Provost Billy Buchanan then made a statement to the crowd about taking me and some others to Roswell New Mexico where he hoped to get Bonnybridge twinned with Roswell. Billy has already been to Roswell and met the mayor of the town, and I believe discussions are still ongoing. Billy then presented me with a large bag regarding the twinning of both towns.

At the end of the day, it had been a great night. Yes, some might see the singing to the stars part a bit off the wall, but at the end of the day I was happy to try it. Yes, some might say that it wasn't scientific, but advances in science come in many ways! It was great to meet old and new faces, some of whom it took me a while to register, as I hadn't seen them for many years. My humble apologies for my failing memory (lol) So we never saw any UFOs, but it had been a great night, where like-minded people came together to share and enjoy their passion that is UFOlogy.

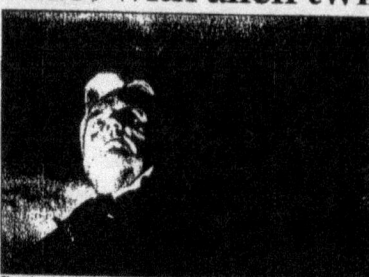

Press cutting Sept 2005

Scottish Newspaper

UFO WATCH

Major plea for probe into the twilight zone

PRIME Minister John Major has been asked to launch a top level probe into weird sightings above a tiny Scots village.

For the people of Bonnybridge claim they have become a laughing stock for reporting a series of UFO sightings.

Over the past two years, villagers' reports of strange sights have sparked off a flood of interest from paranormal investigators.

Channel 4 spent days in the area filming a documentary with eyewitness accounts. And a Paramount Pictures crew is due in from Hollywood to make a programme for the world-wide networked series Sightings fronted by TV's Elliot Ness — actor Robert Stack.

But in a letter to Mr Major, local Councillor Billy Buchanan says: "More than 600 people have come forward and the area has been visited by media and Ufologists from all over the world.

BILLY BUCHANAN: Letter to Major asking for an inquiry.

"The local people and the village have suffered cruelly from ridicule — yet the sightings are continuing

"In light of the high interest of sightings, I ask you, as Prime Minister, to order a top level inquiry."

Mr Buchanan added: " The people of Bonnybridge are sick and tired of being branded a bunch of cranks."

Scottish Newspaper asking for a Government enquiry

Scottish Sun August 2015

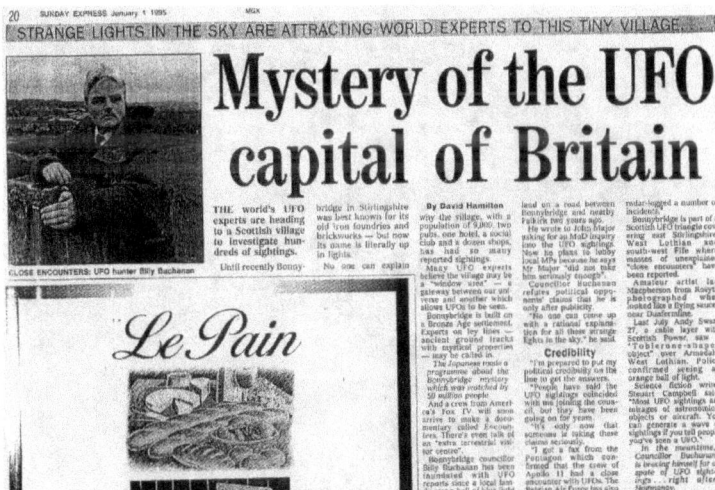

Sunday Express Jan 1st 1995

The Sun 14th October 1996

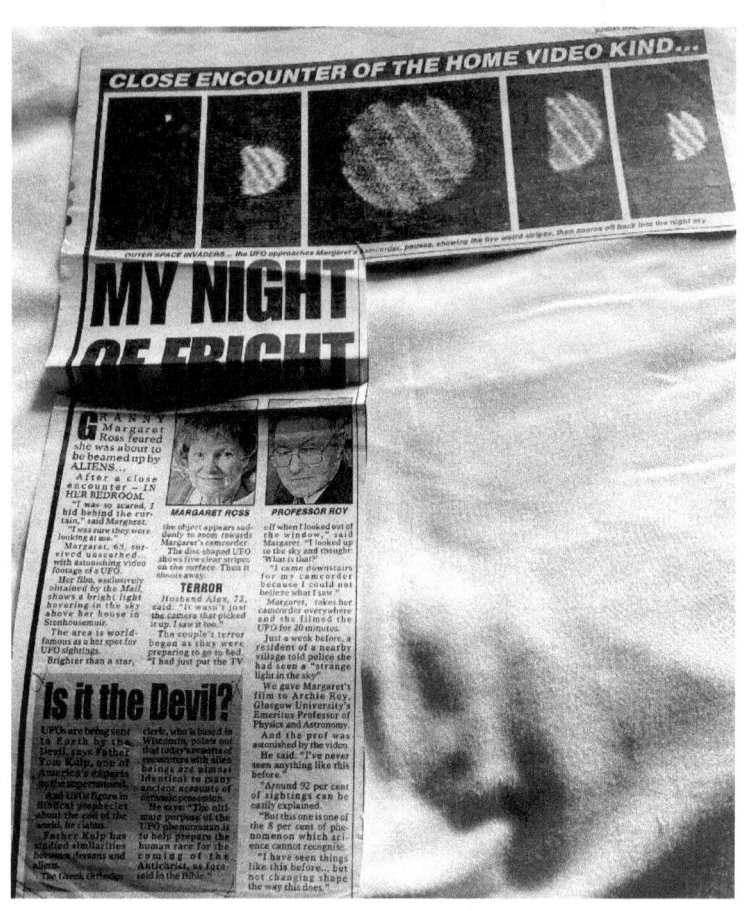

Sunday Mail May 5th 1996

The Guardian Newspaper

The Japanese come to Bonnybridge 1993. Scotsman newspaper 27th May 1993

UFO Event A Sell out 1994. Falkirk Advertiser

CAPTAIN KIRK INTERESTED IN THE BONNYBRIDGE UFOS?

Back in March 2022 I travelled over to Bonnybridge library where I was interviewed by the hit American T.V. show, the' UnXplained' which is hosted by William Shatner, better known as Captain James T. Kirk of the 'Starship Enterprise,' although I should point out, that he wasn't there in person, just a film crew from the states. Before my filming, the 'UnXplained' interviewed Marius Kettmann who they had flown over from Germany. Councillor Billy Buchanan was also featured on this programme (Episode 332). Again, this goes to show that the media were still very much interested in what was happening over Central Scotland back in the 1990s. Here is how Jill Buchanan mentioned this T.V. show in the 'Falkirk Herald' published 30th June 2022.

"UFO hot spot: Bonnybridge back in the spotlight in TV show The UnXplained"

The UFO sightings in Bonnybridge back in the 1990s continue to interest people from around the world. This week an American television crew visited to interview people about how the small village became the UFO capital of the world. At one stage there were 300 alleged sightings of unexplained flying objects in a year and saw Bonnybridge become Scotland's answer to Roswell.

Three decades later and the interest is still there. In May a BBC Radio Scotland show was broadcast to mark the 30th anniversary of Bonnybridge's first ever UFO sighting. Now it is to feature in the popular American TV series The UnXplained which is hosted by William Shatner, better known as Captain James T. Kirk from the Star Trek Series. One of those who was interviewed was Malcolm Robinson, founder of Strange Phenomena Investigations. He said:

"The recording was held at the Bonnybridge Library, and I supplied the film crew with UFO photographs, witness statements and drawings/illustrations of the many peculiar UFO events seen in the Stirlingshire skies over the years. I also spoke about some of Scotland's other major UFO sightings the famous A70 UFO incident, and the Dechmont Woods UFO incident. The UnXplained show is designed to inform the viewers about the facts behind the world's most fascinating, strange and inexplicable mysteries."

Former provost, Councillor Billy Buchanan, was also filmed regarding his part in the Bonnybridge UFO sightings. The programme will be broadcast on the Sky History channel and also the Blaze channel. Malcolm added:

"I must admit, I thoroughly enjoyed my interview, and I look forward to seeing it later this year. "Later this year, I will also be seen appearing on the Channel 5 three-part programme on the history of the Loch Ness Monster which I filmed a few months ago at the Foyers Bay Lodge Hotel on the shores of Loch Ness."

30th ANNIVERSARY OF THE BONNYBRIDGE UFOS

I think it was in April 2022 that I received a telephone call from a chap at BBC Radio Scotland who said that he would like to interview me regarding the 30th anniversary of the Bonnybridge UFO sightings. I must admit when he said the 30th anniversary I was quite taken aback. Was it really 30 years ago since the very first sighting? It clearly must be. The show was to be called, 'Close Encounters of the Bonnybridge Kind'. The programme was being produced by Gus Beattie and would introduce two local lads, Kris Cummins, and David O Gray. Their quest was to interview various people who had dealings with the UFO sightings over Stirlingshire, from witnesses to researchers. Both Kris and David grew up in Bonnybridge. And so it was that both Kris and David along with another researcher, paid me a visit at my home in Sauchie where we sat outside where I shared by thoughts and feelings on what I had learned during my investigations on the Bonnybridge UFO Enigma. Also on this radio show, were Billy Buchanan, Craig Malcolm, Bill Whiteford, Malcolm Cowie, Michelle Gray, Jack Rolland, and Roswell resident Jack Batson.

SLAMANNAN UFO

One aspect of UFO sightings, which admittedly is not a big factor of the Bonnybridge UFO Phenomenon, is of UFOs being chased across the Scottish skies. These cases are few are far between, but that there are such cases, should, at the very least, make one consider that something unusual is going on. Take for instance our next case which occurred on the evening of August 4th, 2022. Two elderly pensioners were at home in the town of Slamannan enjoying a relaxing evening, when due to darkness prevailing, 72-year-old Eleanor Morris stood up to draw the blinds shut in the back bedroom. As she did so, she was astonished to witness what she described as a rugby ball shape on its side with five extremely bright lights dotted around its underside. The object was moving fairly fast and was going in and out of the clouds. She rushed into the front room to tell her husband but by the time she did so, and they both looked out of the living room window it was disappearing into the distance. It was at this point that Eleanor's husband Walter recalled another strange aerial sight that he himself had witnessed four years previously (2018). He stated that he and his wife had come back from walking their family dog and he was outside his home brushing the dog down, when he happened to look up to his left and was amazed to see a bright orangey red ball going through the clouds. As his wife came to the back door, two jets came flying extremely fast over his roof top. In the UFO report form submitted to the author, he said that the jets were only about 20 feet above his house. I can't accept that, as no aircraft are allowed to fly that low, more so over residential housing, but that is what he stated in his report form. Anyway, these jets raced after this orangey red ball and were soon out of sight. One may speculate as to what this orangey red ball was. Whatever it was, it proved interesting enough for two jets to race after it. Again, another interesting aerial spectacle in the Stirlingshire skies.

TIC TAC SHAPED UFO SPOTTED!

On Friday 12th August 2022, Mason Anderson was sitting outside his home. The time was roughly between 1:15pm and 1:20pm, Mason's wife had just arrived home from work and joined Mason sitting outside. Looking skywards, they saw that there were no clouds in the sky, and it was sunny and clear blue sky as far as the eye could see. Whilst scanning the sky, Mason said to his wife about the number of planes which had been climbing out of Edinburgh airport all morning. Then, not long after Mason's wife had sat down, another plane flew overhead. As Mason looked up at the plane, his eye was drawn to something flashing higher and behind. He pointed it out to his wife who also saw what could only be described as stationary random flashing lights. Mason stated that was no object seen to the naked eye, so he assumed that it was quite high. His assumption was based by the passing high-altitude planes which crisscrossed above the town whereby you only see the contrails from the engines but no discernible plane shape.

Being curious, Mason decided to fetch his binoculars, and manged to focus on the area where the 'lights' were. During this time the 'lights' did not move and appeared to be stationary. Through the binoculars, he could clearly make out, a cigar shape object which although stationary, appeared to be moving on the spot with the object rotating anti-clockwise and at an angle at one point. It constantly varied its direction while staying stationary. Most surprising, was the 'halo' or what would better be described as 'light see-through clouds' forming a perfect circle, which was thicker and denser at the outer edge of the circle at one end of the object. The object in the centre was a medium grey in colour, with what would best be described, as a different lighter material at each end where the lights were observed. Furthermore, lights would appear to be flashing from both ends of this object at random intervals. *(See illustration in the photographic section)*

The object was observed for approximately 30 minutes in the same point in the sky which would be above Falkirk Centre, before it moved relatively quickly towards the Forth Road Bridge and Leith, Edinburgh heading towards Fife. Mason also stated to the authorities that no sound could be heard from the object even though high-flying commercial planes (34000 feet +) can still be heard.

Incidentally, I decided to send a FOIA (Freedom of Information Act form) to Police Scotland regarding this sighting as I did feel this was something significant. They responded on the 2nd of September 2022, which in part stated:

"I refer to your recent request for information which has been handled in accordance with the Freedom of Information (Scotland) Act 2022. A search of our systems has been carried out for the relevant date, time, and location; however, no incidents of relevance were found."

I TOO SAW WHAT MASON SAW!

I received an e-mail from Morris Sinclair (pseudonym) dated 16th August 2022. Morris came forward when he had read about Mason Anderson's UFO account in the 'Falkirk Herald'. He stated:

"Hey Sir,
I am a pilot that was flying this day. On the early hours of Saturday morning there were two confirmed reports of an unidentifiable object over the Glasgow Falkirk region. I however wasn't able to see as I was travelling south, but air traffic had a lengthily conversation about it. I thought I would let you know.
Thanks." Morris Sinclair.

Another reader of the 'Falkirk Herald' who had read the account of Mason Anderson featured above, was Johnny Nairn (pseudonym) he e-mailed me in August 2022 to say the following:

"Hi,
A colleague at work spotted the article in the Falkirk Herald and was gobsmacked, because I had told her pretty much the same account that was featured in the Falkirk Herald article, that I too had seen the same craft! It was first seen by my son around 1.30pm moving in a North-South trajectory from the Fife region towards the Borders. It was at a high altitude and looked like a tic-tac but a silver/grey colour. My son messaged me to tell me, much to my initial disbelief. I mocked my son by text, then 20 mins later, a 'craft' appeared twice to me roughly over Slamannan/Binniehill area but was viewed by me from Roughrigg, Longriggend. It could've been further east, possibly towards Edinburgh airport. On its second appearance in this same area, I dispelled my initial dismissal of what I'd seen. When first seen, I resolutely told myself, "No- it's just an optical illusion". Some illusion! It moved with the defined jumps, akin to a laser pen doing a cross-like manoeuvre. It was moving towards the Slamannan direction, before moving in literally a second or so, to directly over Longriggend Village as viewed from nearby Roughrigg, where I live. The craft then performed a succession of unbelievable manoeuvres akin to a dance before suddenly shooting off skyward and out of view in a spiralling motion."

"The craft was an ovoid tic-tac approximately the length of a fighter jet, perhaps 50-60 ft long. Perhaps 12 to 15 feet height. On closer view (still considerable altitude) it appeared 'cloaked', its camouflage, such that it was, was difficult to distinguish from background/skyscape when moving at speed. The slightly unnerving aspect for me, was its seeming awareness of me! It seemed to be wilfully attracting my attention. It's hard to explain without sounding like a crackpot, but it seemed like it knew where I was looking, and was moving deliberately, making cross shapes and with the intent that I observe it? I didn't expect my son's sighting to be confirmed by my own, and the timing is so exact to the report, that one has to assume the same craft. I've had two other craft sightings, years back now, very brief, and at distance, but unquestionable (to my senses at least). This was on another level entirely. I felt

enormously privileged and was left with a deep, almost spiritual feeling of having achieved some kind of 'contact' of a vague sort. I do firmly believe in existence of both man-made and alien UAP's, and other races/species infinitely more advanced, evolved and developed than our own. I am a professional man, over 35 years' service in care (NHS) and you'll have to trust me when I say, that I have no underlying psychosis or a reputation for confabulation! I'd pass any polygraph. I know what I saw. Moreover, I know what I felt. It's unsettling. You tend to ask yourself 'why me'? Are they only seen when they want to be? It was all very theatrical, almost a performance! My comment at work was "I sound nuts, but I don't believe for one minute that dozens of people across the area didn't also witness that craft on Friday". Then the phone rang, "You're not going to believe me". To which I said, "Oh yes I do"! Hopefully I'm just one of those dozens. Disclosure draws ever nearer."

Regards, Johnny.

GO SCOTLAND AND THE BONNYBRIDGE UFO SKYWATCH

Back in August 2022, I was asked by tour company, 'Go Scotland', if I would like to give a lecture on the UFO sightings above Bonnybridge and also provide an opportunity for American tourists who had booked through 'Go Scotland' to take part in a sky watch. This I readily agreed to. The day duly arrived, which, as it would turn out, was a very sad day, as it was the funeral of Her Majesty Queen Elizabeth the second (19th September 2022). I took myself along to the Bonnybridge Golf Club where, after a hearty meal, I gave a lecture to around 15 or so people who had come to Scotland from all over the United States. After my lecture, I took all those far travelled tourists, onto the golf course where we all scanned the skies in hopes of seeing something strange, but as usual, nothing. All in all though, it had been an interesting night and the American tourists all climbed on board their tour bus and headed off into the night, with, I hope, a semblance of what this part of Scotland had to offer. Strange days indeed.

LARGE TRIANGLE UFO SPOTTED NEAR BAINSFORD, FALKIRK

On the evening of Thursday, the 22nd of October 2022, around 7:45pm, Lyn Selby was walking home from work and was enjoying the view of Jupiter, when suddenly she noticed a red flash. She was then stunned to observe a large triangle shape in the sky full of lights, some pulsing red and white. She knew straight away that this was unusual, and she started to freeze with the sight of it. After a further few seconds, she relaxed and watched as this object passed between her house and a neighbour's house at a distance in the sky. Lyn quickly went round to her back garden where she watched this unusual sight move away in a straight line and eventually disappearing behind a large old birch tree. Like most witnesses, she was sure that this was not an aircraft or helicopter, more so as the triangular shape was made up of lights on each side.

In February 2023, Bonnybridge councillor Billy Buchanan took part in yet another documentary on the UFO sightings over Bonnybridge. The short documentary was entitled, *'The Bonnybridge Files. The Town With The Most UFO Sightings In The World'*. This You Tube video received over 61,000 hits in less than two weeks!

THE SPI BONNYBRIDGE SKY WATCH
(September 6th, 2023)

Well, I am pleased to report that our Bonnybridge UFO Sky Watch on the 6th of September 2023 proved a great success. The day started off with a visit to my home in Sauchie Clackmannanshire by 'Talk T.V.' who interviewed me about the UFO sightings above and around the small Scottish town of Bonnybridge in Stirlingshire Scotland. Once the interview was completed, it was time to head off to the town of Bonnybridge itself where our planned sky watch was due to take place. The first part of the journey along the motorway was fine, but then we missed a turning and overshot the exit for Bonnybridge. Thankfully a few minutes later, we saw another sign for Bonnybridge, but this secondary route more or less took us around the British Isles before we finally arrived in Bonnybridge 15 minutes late to join the crowd of sky watchers who were assembled at the meeting point in Bonnybridge High Street. My apologies folks. This was quite embarrassing for me because I had previously told people to be at the meeting point for 9:00pm, and here was I, the organiser turning up late. Ah well, at least I wasn't driving (lol).

THE SKY WATCH

Upon arriving fashionably late, I spoke to around 25 to 30 people assembled in the car park on what to expect on the sky watch. Fiona Buchanan, the wife of Bonnybridge Councillor Billy Buchanan, then stated to the sky watchers where we would be heading for and asked us all to ensure that our cars stayed in convoy for the 10 minute journey which would take us up beyond High Bonnybridge to where the sky watch would take place. The area for the sky watch was on farmland owned by Councillor Buchanan's brother. Soon the 15 plus cars were all pulling out of the car park outside the Scot Mid shop on Bonnybridge High Street. Upon arriving at the sky watch location, we were met by the ever friendly and jovial Billy Buchanan who directed the cars up onto the grass verge. Upon alighting the cars, we then made our way to the sky watch location which was just off the road. The night sky was showing a mymarid of stars all spread out across the vast dark sky. In all my 45 years of sky watching, this was the best and most perfect sky watching conditions. There was not one single cloud in the sky. An orange crescent Moon could be seen down low on the horizon as it slowly made its way up and across the heavens, this capped off a truly magnificent scene, unequalled in any sky watch I've ever attended. Earlier in the day, Councillor Buchanan, and his brother, had erected a gazebo at the site, of which inside was a table loaded with bottles of water, crisps, and chocolate for our merry band of sky watchers.

It was great to see some fellow UFOlogists and friends at the sky watch. Attending on the night was the drummer from CE IV rock group Brian McMullan (Jnr) along with his friend. Also attending were 'SPI's' Billy Devlin and fellow Scottish UFO researcher and author, Ron Halliday. 'SPI's' psychics Steven Bird and Ian Shanes were also in attendance, as were film makers Kelly Young and Kevin who are making a documentary on the famous Dechmont Woods UFO Incident, which they tell me should be completed and ready for viewing in November this year. I have already filmed my part in this and look forward to its release. Ex BBC Producer Natalie Humphreys and Spanish film maker, Inma de Reyes were also in attendance. I am working with them both along with Councillor Buchanan, for a Netflix movie on the Bonnybridge enigma, but more on this at a later date. One chap had travelled all the way from Kilmarnock in Ayrshire to be with us, now that's dedication for you.

SPEECHES

Once we had all assembled at the sky watch site. I gave a short speech (yes, I can do short speeches, a rarity I admit, but they do come out once in a while lol) where I spoke about why we hold these sky watches and further stated that if anyone had had their own UFO experience, to get it off the their chest and speak to Talk T.V. who had travelled up from London to film this event. This was their opportunity to tell the world what they saw. I'm pleased to report, that a good few people took up my offer, and during the course of the sky watch, were seen talking to the camera crew. After my short speech, I invited Councillor Buchanan to say a few words about his involvement with the Bonnybridge UFO enigma. Billy did not disappoint and spoke clearly and concisely about how he became involved in these events. After Billy, I invited fellow Scottish UFO researcher Ron Halliday to say a few words about some of the sightings which had taken place around the Bonnybridge area.

HARMONY!

Following Ron, we had some questions, and Mark Anderson asked Billy about the time when he had seemingly met an alien, a woman by the name of 'Harmony', who, along with UFO Contactee Phyllis Schlemmer (Yes, here of the Council of Nine fame!) came to Scotland back in the 1990s to give a lecture (along with others) at the Falkirk Town Hall. The story is too long to go into here, suffice it to say that she was 'human looking' but had deep dark black eyes. Billy thought that there was something unusual about her, and it was whilst they were having dinner, that the long-sleeved top that 'Harmony' wore, rode up over her hands (which had been covered) and showed a scaly wrist and forearm. Needless to say, Billy was taken aback at this, and truly believes that 'she'(!) was not from this world! After this bombshell, Billy then asked those assembled if there was anyone here tonight that believed that they had seen or encountered an alien. Three people came forward to give their own accounts of this. First up was SPI psychic, Steven Bird, followed by Ian Shanes, and then by a young lady called Katherine Swinn. I can't say too much about what they had to say, as this was being filmed for television. But I dare say we will be hearing a lot more from the intriguing Katheine Swinn.

LOOKING SKYWARDS

After these astonishing revelations, it was time to crane our necks skywards and look at this incredible night sky. It's hard to put it into words of how beautiful the night sky was. All I can attribute it to, is to liken it to a massive dark piece of cloth of which someone had sprinkled lots of glitter over. Simply stunning. And what with no town or city light pollution, well it just gave one the perfect conditions. So, did we see anything unusual I hear you ask? Well, some people saw what initially looked like a satellite cross the sky, but it did so erratically and quickly disappeared. If this was a satellite, it should have been seen for longer than the 10 seconds or so that it was viewed for. Other than that, sadly nothing more was reported (unless someone is keeping quiet!) Being early September, the night was surprisingly cool, but it was those pesky Scottish midges that took great pleasure in feasting upon us poor sky watchers. I knew they were Scottish midges, as it was their wee tartan waistcoats that gave them away.

A SURPRISING REVELATION!

This sky watch also provided an opportunity for like-minded souls to share their own UFO stories and I could hear a good few being spoken about. Which brings me to my shock of the evening. Now most of you know that I wrote a book about the Dechmont Woods UFO encounter, where forestry worker Robert Taylor encountered a large domed shaped object in woods near Livingston Central Scotland. Well, a gentleman approached me and introduced himself as a councillor from Bathgate, and what he had to tell me just blew me away. He stated that when he was a young boy in 1979, he and a friend and gone up to Dechmont Woods the day or so after Robert's UFO encounter. Upon entering the clearing in the woods where the incident occurred, they were met by three military soldiers wearing (as he can recall) green tunics and a cap on their heads. They were asked what they were doing there, whereupon they stated they were there to see where the UFO came down. Well, they were quickly and abruptly chased out of the area and told not to come back. As they were young, and these men were adults, they quickly heeded the advice and took to their heels. This gentleman is going to send me a full report about this later, and I should be in a better position to fill in the gaps and tell you more. The thing that shook me about this, is simply that I have never ever heard about the military being involved in the Dechmont Woods UFO case. I have been asked this question many times over the years about any military presence in the woods, and I always said there was none. And here we had a man who related this incredible tale at our sky watch, which (depending on how you see it) opens up a whole new can of worms. So, this is one that I will chase up.

GREAT SUCCESS

So, all in all, the SPI sky watch was a great success. The people who had travelled far and wide to be there, not only heard about some of the UFO sightings in the area, but also heard about Councillor Buchanan and I, and our tireless efforts to get the British Government involved in what's been going on, (all to no avail I should add). We finished the sky watch at 12 midnight to allow people to head home, most of whom had work in the morning. As stated, Talk TV were there to film the sky watch and their filming of the event eventually came out on You Tube, which for me, was covered fairly. It should be noted, that on the Talk TV footage of the Bonnybridge sky watch, former MoD spokesperson Nick Pope, who now lives in the United States, gave an apology to Councillor Billy Buchanan. This came about because over the years, Councillor Buchanan has demanded that Nick Pope give the people of Bonnybridge an apology as Nick has always said that there was nothing of significance occurring in the skies above Bonnybridge. Nick now accepts that this was not the case, and that there had been some unusual sightings of what's been termed, UFOs, in the Bonnybridge skies. So, better late than never! My heartfelt thanks to all who attended our sky watch, and I do hope that you gained something from it, even if it was just a sore neck!

10 DOWNING STREET VISIT 7th OCTOBER 2023

For those that know me, know that I have always been a UFO activist, and by that, I mean, I don't just read books about UFOs, I actively get my hands dirty, and that comprises organising sky watches at Scottish UFO 'hot spots'. I also stage local UFO meetings and assist with UFO conferences. All this is fine, but that's only to educate people about the UFO presence. There is one thing that means so much to me, and that is taking the UFO message a stage further, a lot further!

Over the years, Bonnybridge Councillor Billy Buchanan and I have campaigned to the British Government that they should actively look into the UFO subject. Both Billy and I have been down to 10 Downing Street in London to hand in demand letters and petitions to various Prime Ministers asking that they take a long hard look at the evidence that we have gathered in Scotland. We have told them that we will gladly turn over all our UFO files in return for a proper investigation. The people of Great Britain elected these Prime Ministers, and therefore they should sit up and take note when we ask them to do something.

I have been a UFO and Paranormal researcher for over 45 years, and in this time, I have collected a vast amount of data which has shown to me, that the subject of UFOs (Unidentified Flying Objects) is most certainly real. I accept that the vast majority of UFO reports can easily be identified as having natural explanations, but not them all! For many years, the subject of UFOs has been laughed at by not only members of the public, but through various media outlets as well. But now the screw has turned.

The United States of America openly declare that they have a UFO presence!

Over the past few years, The Pentagon in America, has finally and openly declared to the American public, that yes, UFOs are 'real' and that they have been studying them for years. The declassification by the U.S. Department of Defence of footage shot by Navy pilots despatched from the 'USS Nimitz', the 'USS Theodore Roosevelt', and the 'USS Princeton', cleared showed aerial objects whose flight characteristics far outclassed anything that current aircraft can achieve. America have also had this year (2023) Congressional hearings devoted to the UFO subject, in which staff from the American armed forces took part, each of whom openly declared to their own UFO observations. And let us not forget, that even the prestigious Space Agency NASA, even held their own panel looking into UFO sightings this year. The point here is this: the United States of America have come clean and openly declared that they have a UFO situation in their skies of which they are actively trying to understand.

It is now time for the British Government to do the same.

Both Bonnybridge Councillor Billy Buchanan and I decided that if ever there was a time to capitalise on what America had undertaken, it was now. Now was the time to strike while the iron was hot. And so, on the 7th of October 2023, Councillor Buchanan, and I, once more travelled from Scotland to England with a heightened purpose. And that purpose was to demand that the British Government do likewise and open up their own files from both the Ministry of Defence (MoD) and the armed forces. The UFO situation is not just an American phenomenon, it is a global one. And both Billy Buchanan and I were in London to demand that our elected Prime Minister Rishi Sunak be honest and upfront and show the British people, that like America, Britain too, has been touched by the UFO presence. Rishi Sunak was elected to serve the people, by the people and not shrink from away from any questions put forward to him.

As mentioned above, both Councillor Buchanan and I had already visited 10 Downing Street in the past, where 'demand letters' were presented to various Prime Ministers, namely, John Major, Tony Blair, Gordon Brown, and David Cameron, all of which fell on deaf ears. But now things were different. Now America was coming clean. Both Billy and I were demanding honesty and transparency. We hoped that Prime Minister Rishi Sunak would have the guts to implement a full Government enquiry into the UFO situation in Great Britain, for not to do so, would not be in keeping with his election promise to serve the people of this country with openness and clarity.

The Ministry of Defence, 10 Downing Street, and Westminster.

So, on a glorious hot October day in 2023, I met up with Councillor Buchanan and our film crew who were there to record our visit for an upcoming documentary on UFO sightings across Scotland. After being miked up, we were ready to make our way over to 10 Downing Street at an agreed time of 2:00pm. At about four minutes to 2:00pm, a tremendous noise of people shouting, horns blaring, flags being waved and smoke canisters being waved about, met our view. Police sirens were wailing from various police cars and motor cycles as they tried to keep order. This large crowd then congregated outside 10 Downing Street, at the exact same time as Councillor Billy Buchanan and I had planned our own event, that of handing a demand letter to Prime Minister Richie Sunak. Needless to say, that plan was scrapped, but just for the time being. So, we had to resort to plan B, which was to walk the short distance to the Ministry of Defence Building to hand in a further letter. Well, would you believe it, it was shut! After ringing a door bell a number of times, we were met by silence. The lights were on, but nobody was home! There was a line of police vans parked on the street outside the MoD building with police officers inside, all gazing out at both Billy and I and our film crew as we did a few pieces to camera. Thankfully they stayed in their vehicles and did not come out and ask questions. As Councillor Buchanan was staying in London longer than I, he said he would go back to the MoD Building on the Monday and hand the letter in then. (This he did.)

So, with filming completed, it was time to head back to Downing Street where thankfully the noise and the crowd had abated. Billy and I approached the police presence at the gates of Downing Street and explained why we were there, and that was to hand in this 'demand letter' to the Prime Minister, or at the very least, ask one of the serving police officers to take it off our hands and deliver it himself. They refused to take the letter. A police officer stated that they were not allowed to take any letters from members of the public, that any letters would need to go through other channels. We explained that the last time we were there (2010) a police officer gladly accepted and delivered our letter to the then Prime Minister, David Cameron. But this was not to be the case now. Things had changed. It was at this point that Councillor Buchanan took out from his case, a laminated copy of our 'demand letter' to the Prime Minster and read it out to the large crowd of tourists that had gathered outside Downing Street. As Billy was reading out the letter, this large crowd of people were busily snapping photographs and video on their mobile phones. Well, at least those people knew why we were there!

"You Can't Film Here"!

Our next and final port of call was Westminster, the seat of British politics where a further two letters that Billy had drafted were going to be handed over to two Scottish MPs. Billy was requesting in the letters, that they ask for a Government enquiry into the UFO sightings across the British Isles. The letters stressed the fact that the United States of America were leading the way with UFO disclosure, and that Great Britain should do the same. Well again things did not turn out the way we planned. There was a police presence outside Westminster and after explaining why we were there, we were told in no uncertain terms, that they too, couldn't accept any letters. Not only that, one particular jobs worth guy, started pushing our film crew about saying that we had no permission to film there. Our Spanish film crew, Joao, and Nelisa told him to politely 'jog on', and that this was public land, and that they had every right to film there. Astonishingly, the guy backed down and scurried off with his tail between his legs. At this point, a famous face approached Councillor Buchanan and said, *"Oh hello, Billy, I've not seen you for a while."* Now, I was looking at this woman and saying to myself, *"I know that face, but who is it!"* I initially thought that it was a famous actress. Billy explained to her about why we were at Westminster, whereupon I too joined the conversation about UFOs over British skies. It was at this point that she noticed that I was wearing a small Ukrainian badge on the lapel of my jacket displaying its nation's colours of yellow and blue. She then pointed to her silk scarf around her neck which was also yellow and blue, and said that she too, supported Ukraine, and with a swift change of tact, she told me (politely) that I should be more concerned for the poor Ukrainian people with the flying objects above their heads (bombs) that I should be with UFOs! Well, that was me told! So, who was this famous face I hear you ask? Well, it was a former Tory M.P. and junior Health Minister, Edwina Curie. (Remember the egg carry on!) She was also in the popular T.V. show, 'I'm a celebrity, get me out of here'. So, we chatted to her for a short while then bade her farewell. Our film crew had drawn a large attendance whilst chatting to her, and again many members of the public were happily snapping away on their phones.

So, all in all, whilst we didn't manage to get our 'demand letters' out to those we wanted to on the day, those letters will go out recorded delivery. But that's by the by folks. The issue here was to get the British public aware of the UFO issue here in the U.K. I'm pleased to say that Billy's and my visit to London made a number of British newspapers who covered our visit, so, that in itself was a result.

Flogging A Dead Horse!

Some might say we were basically flogging a dead horse, that the powers that be will never admit to a UFO presence. The evidence is overwhelming. Yes, there are many misidentifications of normal mundane objects. Yes, there are fake videos and photographs, but once you whittle all that nonsense away, you are left looking at some astonishing UFO cases. We could ask ourselves, 'WHY'? Why is America now coming clean with UFO disclosure? We've had the Congressional Hearings. We've had NASA doing their own investigations into these sightings with a panel of scientists and one former astronaut, and we've had the Pentagon releasing the astonishing footage of fast-moving objects filmed by Navy pilots. Now either they truly are coming clean or, it's some form of 'false flag'. In other words, what we are seeing in our skies is our own technology, and they are happy for the ground-based observer to believe that what they are observing are fanciful flying saucers!

But could there be something even more sinister behind all this? What if some Governments of the world are actively working alongside an alien presence, and they are slowly drip feeding the public about the UFO presence as something big is about to happen! Speculation on my part for sure, but it hangs on in there as a possibility, a very loose one I'll admit, but a possibility, nonetheless.

Look, you and I know that something is afoot. Bonnybridge Councillor Billy Buchanan and I went to London to shake the tree, to see what might fall out. I honestly can't see Billy and I going back down to London to do the same thing again. NOW was the time to do this. America was coming clean (well to a degree!) we just had to shake the Downing Street tree. If ever there was a time to put pressure on the British Government on

UFOs, it was now. Let's see what, if anything, happens. But I sure won't hold my breath.

Before I close, I just want to say that while we probably won't be back down to Downing Street again, Billy and I plan to visit the Scottish Parliament in due course and ask those same pertinent questions. You never get anything in life if you just sit on your backside. Action, and plenty of it, is the order of the day.

A NEW BONNYBRIDGE SKY WATCH SITE!

Since I came back to Scotland in 2021, I have ensured that my society, SPI have continued to hold UFO sky watches at various locations throughout Central Scotland. I was keen to hold another sky watch at Bonnybridge but sadly on this occasion Councillor Billy Buchanan couldn't attend and so therefore we didn't have access to his brother in law's field as we did on a previous occasion. In this regard, I, along with SPI's psychic medium Steven Bird jumped into Steven's car, and we headed off to Bonnybridge to scout out areas for an upcoming sky watch which we were going to hold on the 18th of May 2024.

As we travelled along the winding roads above Bonnybridge it soon became apparent that it wasn't looking good for a new sky watch area! Yes, there are loads of fields, but the small road that leads through them, does not allow for any reasonable parking for upwards of six cars. After driving around the Bonnybridge area for a good 45 minutes or so, Steven was spiritually guided into a camping and caravan park, where once driving along the long entrance road, I decided that I would ask the proprietor if we could use his land for a few hours for a UFO sky watch. I knew that I was taking a chance with this as he may laugh me out of town. Goodness knows what his reaction would be to this request! Anyway, as we approached a barrier which led into the caravan site, Steven called out to me, *"Have you seen this, look over there."* I followed his pointed arm, and my eyes fell on a sign saying, 'UFO Landing Site'. What the devil was going on here?

Just then, a chap driving a four wheeled buggy with his dog on the back, roared up to us out of nowhere. Here we go I said, he will chase me off his land when I ask him that I want to bring a group of people to stand in his field and look at the stars. Well.............How wrong was I? This chap proceeded to tell us that he was right into UFOs, and that a UFO landed on his property a few years ago. Furthermore, he has had lots of visitors from all over the U.K. coming to his caravan park to look for UFOs. He went on to say that he would love to have us on his property, not only that, should we ever wish to hold meetings or lectures, we could use his cabin which is on site. He ushered both Steven and I into his cabin where we both saw the benefits of holding meetings here. The walls were furnished by his paintings where he further stated that this cabin is also used for music and social events. Amazing.

The gentleman, (Ian Hogg) told Steven and I where this UFO came down onto his property back in 2011. After some more conversation both Steven and I visited the site which has a commanding 360 degree uninterrupted view of the sky. Perfect for sky watching. Ian Hogg bowled me over with his discussion on dimensions and greys. This chap was far from being the indifferent farmer that I expected to meet. If ever you wanted someone who shared the same interest as you, and who owns fields and property and would allow you to use them for a sky watch, then you could do no better than have this chap in your camp. What a man, what a find! Steven Bird told me as we drove away from the property, that spirit had put this in place for us. I certainly wouldn't disagree with him. Unbelievable. What a find. What follows, is a report I compiled of that particular sky watch.

BONNYBRIDGE SKY WATCH.
SATURDAY 18TH MAY 2024.

Around 15 plus like-minded souls met up outside the Bonnybridge post office on the evening of Saturday 18th of May to take part in our SPI sky watch. Our sky watches are set up to inform not just our SPI members, but the general public as well in regard to what one can expect to see in the sky and what 'not' to expect. In other words, strange aerial objects flitting around the sky. And as we were in a so called 'UFO Hot Spot', we had high hopes that perhaps we would see something which many others have witnessed in the skies above Bonnybridge over the years.

After a brief chat, it was time to head off in convoy to our new sky watch site, that of the Wheel Camp and Caravan Park which sits just a few miles away from Bonnybridge. Once all the cars had parked up, I then invited our merry band of sky watchers into the Ceilidh House, a wooden building set up on the camp site specifically for those campers and caravaners who have travelled from all over the U.K. to chill out. We had the full use of the Ceilidh House for our sky watch base, and after we all had assembled inside, I gave a short talk about what to expect at a sky watch. Also attending our sky watch, were a few, mums and dads with their children who were staying over at the camp site, who were sent to us by the camp site owner, Ian Hogg. When I asked if anyone had any questions, one wee boy who was staying over with his parents at the caravan site, spoke up and told us about the ghost in his house that kept knocking over chairs. Nice one son.

After that brief chat inside, I then assembled all the sky watchers outside, where we then walked up and over a pile of solid, (but in part, a crumbly shale like mound of earth which ran for a good 50 or so yards) to a track that led to the sky watch site. There were a few falls over this earthen hurdle, but thankfully no one was hurt. The owner of the camp site told me that he aims to clear all this earthen mound away so that a clear, and uninterrupted walk can be made to the site.

After a beautiful warm sunny day all over Scotland, our night time sky was obliterated with a hazy misty cloud. There was not one single patch of clear sky to be seen. This for me, was the worst sky watching conditions that I have faced anywhere in the British Isles. Thankfully it wasn't cold, although the temperature did drop a few hours later. Also, the horse and buggy ride which the camp site owner had promised us didn't happen. In a telephone call to me from the owner earlier in the day, he said that as he had had quite a tiring day, he would have to forgo this. Once we all had walked up to the sky watch site, and had placed our fold down chairs, I then proceeded to inform those assembled about some of the Bonnybridge UFO story. The sightings, the media, and the British Government's role in what was going on. After which some people broke off into little groups to do their own thing.

With us on this night, was Tress Blair (Wooshwa) who is in contact with 'beings' not of this Earth. Tress, and I'm sure won't mind me for saying this, is a controversial character who claims to bring forward her 'light beings' and their energies, so I asked her if she would like to try an experiment where we could try and see if this could happen on the night. Before we tried this experiment, SPI's medium Steven Bird opened up with a protective prayer which ensured that no harm would come to the group.

Around 14 of us, formed a circle and raised our hands skywards where Tress then spoke out into the night air, asking that her 'light being friends' come forward. She then proceeded to speak out in a strange language, followed by her singing in this strange language. A language which she states is from her home planet of Sucruma. Yes, all this does sound bizarre, but who are we, to judge others? Who are we, who chase ghosts and UFOs, to decry anyone else about what they do? I think that it's a disgrace when people attack other people simply because they are different. It will never happen on my watch. Whilst Tress could see small beings standing around us, we couldn't. That said, there were a few people who did pick up strange 'energies' that surrounded our circle. One lady in our group could not close her open outstretched hands. (She did eventually, but it took a while.) In a photograph that I took as I stepped away from the group, you can see a thin light coming down from the sky to our group. Also, if you squeeze up on the photograph, you will see two small orbs in the sky. Again, some may say that all this is 'airy fairy', but again I say who are they to judge!

SPI's Steven Bird also felt bizarre energies a few hundred yards away from our main sky watch location. Whilst the sky didn't clear on the night, this was still a successful night, for it provided a great opportunity for people to get to know one another, share stories, and build lasting friendships. I particularly enjoyed watching a bizarre ring bell door cam footage shown to me by Margaret Tollan of a strange light next to her house. This small light got larger, then shot away to the left and was gone from sight. And whilst I suggested a few possible explanations that could account for this strange footage, even I was floored by this, and my feeble attempts to explain away this footage didn't even sit right with me!

The following are people who turned up on the night. Steven Bird, Mark Anderson, Paul John Grey, Gavin Dow, Mark Wilson, Mike Porter, Ian Abbott, Margaret Tollan, Emma Pear, Tress Blair, Andrew Hyde, Anna Bell, Stuart Bell, Stevie Bell, Elisha Bell, Gordon Stuart, Angela McDade, Janette Gillespie, Marie Adens, and a few others whose names I didn't get. There were at least another seven people, those mums and dads with their kids who came up to the sky watch site. So, whilst the sky wasn't great on the night, a good time was still had by all.

ANOTHER BONNYBRIDGE UFO SKY WATCH.
29th JULY 2024

In June 2024, I was contacted by a Russian 'You Tube' Blogger who said that they were coming up to Scotland from London where they are based, to film the Edinburgh Fringe Festival, The Kelpies, the Falkirk Wheel and also film at Loch Ness. They also had heard about the UFO sightings across Scotland and wanted to film those who had witnessed these UFOs, and that my name, Malcolm Robinson, seemed to come up in every search that they did on the internet. I arranged with the You Tube Bloggers that they could film two sky watches, our planned one near the A70 where both Garry Wood and his friend Colin Wright encountered a black shiny two-tiered disc hovering above the road and another sky watch at Bonnybridge. Anyone who knows me, knows that I fully support Ukraine, and I abhor the illegal occupation of Ukraine by Russian Military forces. Owing to this fact, I asked the Russian crew if any of his team, supported President Putin and his Government. They replied that they did not, and such, I decided to work with him. They filmed myself and members of SPI on the evening of the 27th of July 2024 near the scene of the A70 encounter. Two days later, I once more met up with Russian crew where he filmed an interview with me at home after which we headed off to the 'Wheel Camping and Caravan Park' near Bonnybridge for another sky watch. Prior to heading up to the camp site, they filmed an interview with me talking about the Bonnybridge UFO sightings as we walked up Bonnybridge High Street. From there we went for a pint in the Cornhill Inn where the guys did a vox pop with some of the locals. Bad move! Some of the locals said that the Bonnybridge UFO sightings were a load of nonsense. To say I was embarrassed would be an understatement. Clearly, they spoke to the wrong people! Anyway, as this was a hastily arranged sky watch, we only had 8 people there, the smallest amount of people that I've ever had at a sky watch. What with having a big sky watch two days ago, and with people having to get up for work tomorrow, a kind of knew that they wouldn't be many people there. As for the sky watch itself, we all trekked up to the sky watch site where the Russian chaps filmed some more interviews with me and a few who were there. So, we were only there for around 30 minutes when the Russian chaps said that they had enough footage and would make their way back to their hotel in Glasgow, but, if I didn't have a lift, they would take me back to Sauchie. So, long story short, I who organised this sky watch, had to do a runner and get this lift back to Sauchie. This was the second time today that I was embarrassed. I mean not only was that the shortest sky watch I've ever organised and been on (around 30 minutes) but to leave people just because unless I took this lift I wouldn't get home was embarrassing, (I don't drive). The other sky watchers lived too far away to offer me a lift. So, not the night I had envisioned, (those dam midges didn't help!) but nonetheless, we got a lot of filming done. But oh, how I hope that they don't use that pub footage. Only in Scotland eh!

SUMMING UP

SO WHY BONNYBRIDGE, WHAT'S SO SPECIAL?
(Is there a so called 'Falkirk Triangle'?

So, for me, Malcolm Robinson, how do I try and sum up the Bonnybridge mystery with all that has gone on? Well, it's well neigh impossible! So much has transpired from November 1992, the official year from when the sightings began. Suffice it to say, that the cases presented here, are illustrative of what has been going on, and they are part and parcel of the whole Bonnybridge UFO mystery. Of course, the million-dollar question that is regularly asked is, *"Why Bonnybridge?"* What is so special about this place that attracts these 'Flying Saucers' and strange aerial lights. This is a question that I have asked myself many times, and there is no clear definitive answer. I usually reply to this question by stating that Bonnybridge is what's known, in UFO speak, as a 'Hot Spot' or a 'Window Area'. This is an area which receives a higher concentration of UFO reports than anywhere else. Bonnybridge does not stand alone as being a UFO 'Hot Spot'. There are other locations spread out throughout the world which also has received the same captivating interest as Bonnybridge. Gulf Breeze in Florida for one, followed by Mexico City and Belgium. Of course, this doesn't answer our question, we are still left scratching our heads looking for answers. I remember Billy Buchanan being asked this question by a journalist, and in Billy's own illuminating style, he responded by saying,

"Well, why Bethlehem."

Billy was stating that baby Jesus could have been born anywhere in the world, it just so happened that it was Bethlehem. So, this same analogy applied to Bonnybridge, i.e., that it *'Just Was'!* In an article in the 'Scotsman' newspaper dated 15th September 1994, staff writer Brian Pendreigh asked Billy the same question, *'Why Bonnybridge?'* Billy replied:

"Why should there be so many sightings in Bonnybridge? We've got a Bronze Age settlement across the road here. I don't know if it's an attraction or whatever, but a lot of sightings have been taking place in places of historical interest."

The small town of Bonnybridge was catapulted to more or less the same status as the English town of Warminster, of whom back 1965 also received many UFO reports. Warminster was known the world over by many UFOlogists, as the place to visit during the 1960's. I mentioned that 1997 saw a decline in UFO reports but was amazed to read in the newspapers that according to some, the UFO sightings in Bonnybridge were rising to 2,000 reports, then 3,000 reports, which I find totally unacceptable and unfounded. I have always said that the true number of UFO reports that I personally would accept as being genuine, are in the region of around 300 sightings. To say that there are 3,000 UFO reports from Bonnybridge, is sheer nonsense and I would dearly love to have a look at those supposed 3,000 cases. Let us not forget dear reader, that newspapers tend to exaggerate, I'll say no more!

JUST SAYING

I've never been happy with the media stating that there is a Falkirk Triangle. An area where there are a significant number of UFO sightings than anywhere else. It makes for a great newspaper heading, but not one that I am happy about. Indeed, I've done a number of interviews with the media over the past few years, and they always go on about this Falkirk Triangle. They are stunned when I say that there is no such thing: it's media hype. What I tell these media hacks is that yes, there are a number of interesting UFO sightings across the central belt of Scotland, but there is no bloody triangle. Indeed, the guys at the 'UnXplained' T.V. show who filmed me were none too pleased when I said there is no triangle, just an area across the central belt of Scotland that has seen an increase of UFO sightings. Needless to say, my comments on the triangle were cut away from the show. So, no Falkirk Triangle. The Central Belt of

Scotland yes. Indeed, some media outlets have different variations of where this so-called triangle is situated, (their newspaper sketches are all different!) Anyway, please note from this old UFOlogist that the media are trying to bring the realm of the Bermuda Triangle into a Scottish UFO triangle.

WERE THE MILITARY BEHIND THESE UFO SIGHTINGS?

As I have already explained, one must try and find a rational explanation to account for any given UFO sighting. I had already ruled out normal air traffic due to my inquiries with Air Traffic Control at numerous Scottish Airports. It was now time to check on the military aspect, to see if perhaps they were behind these mysterious events. Could the Ministry of Defence shed any light on what was going on? It was now time to find out. The following are extracts from a letter dated the 13th of April 1993 which I received from Nick Pope, who was at that time, Secretariat, (Air Staff) 2a Room 8245 at the Ministry of Defence in Whitehall London. This is what he had to say:

"I am aware from other UFO researchers that there has been a wave of UFO sightings centred on the town of Bonnybridge, but the Ministry of Defence has received no reports from this area. But I am aware of the media speculation about Aurora."

The reason Nick had mentioned the Aurora aircraft, was because I had also asked the MoD if they could tell me if it might be the newly designed Aurora spy plane that might be behind some of these sightings. Nick Pope continued:

"As you know, the position of the U.S. authorities is that no such aircraft exists. With regard to Military activity that might explain sightings, I am unable to suggest anything other than the fact that Bonnybridge is in an area which does see some Military jet activity from time to time. R.P.V's, (Remotely piloted vehicles)*, would certainly not be operated anywhere*

near Bonnybridge, and would be flown only in ranges. I hope this is helpful and I wish you luck with your research."
Nicholas Pope

Of course, some might say that the British MoD would not discuss with anyone that they did have their own new and exotic flying machines in any area of Great Britain, especially if they wanted it to be kept a secret, but it would have been wrong of me had I not contacted the MoD to inquire of this issue. Of course, many people can be misled into thinking that what they were watching in the sky was a fanciful 'Flying Saucer', which later turns out to be just a bright star or planet. The Patrick Forsyth case mentioned earlier, clearly showed that we are dealing not only with high altitude UFO phenomena, but a low-level close proximity one as well. Even though our society was still being inundated with UFO reports, all the usual checks were maintained. The contacts with airports, the contacts with police and other agencies, were all kept going, I guess I must have been a thorn in the side of official bodies during those early UFO years! Indeed, in late 2023, I submitted a Freedom of Information request (FOIA) to Police Scotland asking them to answer some pertinent questions that I had on the UFO sightings in Scotland. Here is their reply dated, 22nd December 2023.

Freedom of Information Response
Our Reference: FOI 23-3105

Your recent request for information is replicated below, together with our response.

1) How many UFO sightings were reported to Police Scotland during the 1990s?

2) How many UFO sightings were reported to Police Scotland from the year 2000 till 2023?

3) What is the procedure at Police Scotland when receiving a UFO report, what do you do?

4) Does Police Scotland have an overall statement to make regarding the UFO sightings over the town of Bonnybridge and Central Scotland?

5) Does Police Scotland refer any UFO sightings to any Scottish Airport for further information?

6) Does any Scottish Airports inform Police Scotland about any given UFO sighting?

In response to these questions, I regret to inform you that I am unable to provide you with the information you have requested, as it would prove too costly to do so within the context of the fee regulations. As you may be aware the current cost threshold is £600, and I estimate that it would cost well in excess of this amount to process your request.

As such, and in terms of Section 16(4) of the Freedom of Information (Scotland) Act 2002 where Section 12(1) of the Act (Excessive Cost of Compliance) has been applied, this represents a refusal notice for the information sought. By way of explanation, the only way to provide an accurate response to your request would be to manually examine each and every incident report for the time period requested to establish whether any reference of paranormal activity/UFO is mentioned.

There is no specific classification on our incident recording system, STORM, which refers to paranormal activity/ UFO sightings and therefore given the volume of reports that would require to be read this is an exercise which would far exceed the cost limit set out in the Fees Regulations. Regarding your request for whether Police Scotland have a procedure when receiving a UFO sighting report, I can advise you that this information that there is no procedure which specifically relates to these circumstances. As such, in terms of Section 17 of the Freedom of Information (Scotland) Act 2002, this represents a notice that the information you seek is not held by Police Scotland. If you require any further assistance, please contact us quoting the reference above. You can request a review of this response within the next 40 working days by email or by letter

(Information Management - FOI, Police Scotland, Clyde Gateway, 2 French Street, Dalmarnock, G40 4EH). Requests must include the reason for your dissatisfaction. If you remain dissatisfied following our review response, you can appeal to the Office of the Scottish Information Commissioner (OSIC) within 6 months - online, by email or by letter (OSIC, Kinburn Castle, Doubledykes Road, St Andrews, KY16 9DS). Following an OSIC appeal, you can appeal to the Court of Session on a point of law only. This response will be added to our Disclosure Log in seven days' time. Every effort has been taken to ensure our response is as accessible as possible. If you require this response to be provided in an alternative format, please let us know.

So, not much joy there, unless I was happy to cough up £600 for the privilege. There is no denying that Bonnybridge has indeed been propelled to cult status. A town in which will be forever known as the 'place to see UFOs'. I do accept that at times the whole issue surrounding Bonnybridge was a bit of a circus. Was it simply because Councillor Buchanan and I 'were' high profile in the area which attracted the press? Or was it because there truly was a genuine phenomenon occurring there in the first place? Make up your own mind! My own part in the proceedings regarding the Bonnybridge UFO sightings, is that I conducted my Investigations honestly and above board. We put on conferences and distributed information about what was going on to many people (as did other Scottish researchers). At the end of the day, I do honestly feel that there was, and no doubt still is, a phenomenon occurring in the skies above Bonnybridge and Stirlingshire that clearly merits our attention. Councillor Buchanan and I have tried very hard to get the British Government involved hoping that they might set up their own Investigation and assist our society in getting to the bottom of what is going on. Councillor Buchanan is still looking for answers, but I'm afraid he may never find them. For if we had an answer to account for 'why Bonnybridge', then we would obviously have answers for 'why Gulf Breeze', 'why Mexico' etc. Billy Buchanan, as we have learned, has had an extremely hard time over the Bonnybridge UFO sightings, which I feel is totally unjustified. He had the guts to represent his constituents in this matter, and deal with their concerns, how many other Falkirk District Councillors would have done that? Not many I bet you.

As I have alluded to earlier, a vast majority of the individuals who telephoned my house with their UFO sightings, did not return the UFO sighting account forms that I sent them to complete. This is indeed unfortunate, for their testimony may have gone a long way in hopefully solving these UFO sightings. However, one can only work with what they have got. I'll never know for sure, how many other UFO witnesses there are across Stirlingshire who also observed these UFOs but who failed to get in touch with me. Indeed, might there even be what's been termed, 'UFO Abductions' somewhere either in Bonnybridge, or Stirlingshire as a whole? Again, unless someone comes forward, we will never know. Of course, this book primarily concerns itself with the UFO sightings above Bonnybridge and Stirlingshire, this area was the focal point for a vast amount of UFO sightings. Now, that's not to say that UFO sightings were occurring elsewhere throughout Scotland, they were. Other big cases during the 1990s was of course the A70 UFO Incident which concerned the abduction of two men on a lonely stretch of road between Edinburgh and Tarbrax. Then we had the Craigluscar UFO photograph of 1994, plus other UFO sightings across Scotland. So, although there were indeed other cases spread out throughout Scotland, the Central Belt was the prime focus for these sightings. Why could this be? Obviously, the Central Belt of Scotland is highly populated, more so than Northern Scotland, so in that regard the likelihood of more reports per populace will indeed increase.

I would like to point out to the reader, that the Duke of Edinburgh was a regular subscriber to 'Flying Saucer Review', a journal based on worldwide UFO sightings. The Duke initially developed an interest in UFOs from his uncle Lord Mountbatten, who, history tells us, wrote an official report about a UFO that was reported to have landed at his Broadlands Estate in Romsey, Hampshire England back in 1955. It should also be noted that Philip's former assistant, Sir Peter Horsley, a former senior Royal Air Force Commander who died in 2001, was instrumental in providing Prince Philip lots of information about UFO sightings throughout the U.K. In Peter Horsley's autobiography, *'Sounds from another room'*, he states that Philip also asked Sir Peter to bring in people who had witnessed UFOs and aliens to Buckingham Palace for private discussions. In one particular visit to Buckingham Palace, Sir Peter brought the captain of a BOAC flight which was en-route to Canada who had witnessed a UFO, to meet up with Philip and bring along his official report of his sighting. A good friend of mine, John Hanson, informed me that Philip has read a number of his 'Haunted Skies' books, which details UFO sightings across the British Isles. Sadly, Prince Philip passed away on the 9th of April 2021 aged 99. And let us not forget, that WW2 Air Chief Marshall Sir Hugh Dowding who orchestrated the 'Battle of Britain', was a great believer in Flying Saucers'. The reason I mention all this, is just to highlight to the reader, that it's not just the ordinary man and woman in the street which has had a fascination with UFOs, Royalty have had their eyes to the skies over the years as well.

The UFO sceptics may say that all UFO sightings are a combination of ordinary mundane objects viewed honestly but mistakenly. Some may even say that all the UFO sightings are our own black budget technology: super stealth aircraft for instance. It goes without saying, that there are indeed some weird looking drones and new technological aircraft being flown and designed across the world. But what if there truly are, 'craft' from other worlds being sighted in our skies. What would be the implications of an E.T. presence on Earth's religions? What would an open disclosure of alien craft do to the various churches of the world? Probably more alarming, would be the use of alien technology falling into 'one' country's hands. Would that one single country then control the world? Would an alien civilisation take over planet Earth, would we be the slaves? These are questions which any sensible man should be asking themselves. The 'what if' scenario. What if one day all this becomes reality, will mankind be prepared? Will we an action plan? Or will our ignorance of the UFO enigma be our downfall? This, 'what if' scenario could also relate to the world's economy and also the impact on mental health. Would traditional industries start falling by the wayside? Would we be dealing with friendly aliens, or aliens with a deceitful covert agenda? Would their very presence on Earth give us a new pandemic with viruses that we can't control? Will the introduction of an alien race be beneficial to human society? Will they help mankind move further to the stars? Or will an alien race decimate the human race. Decimate our society. Decimate our culture, and decimate what we as the human race, have built up since the Earth was formed? If mankind is not prepared to seriously look at the UFO enigma, then that may be our biggest downfall. *'Be prepared or be prepared to fail'*.

Both Ron Halliday and I, would love to hear from anyone who has witnessed UFO sightings not just across the Stirlingshire skies, but Scotland as a whole. Please see our contact details at the close of this book. At the end of the day, I'm afraid that we are no further forward in answering the many questions that surround the Bonnybridge mystery, more's the pity. But investigations continue, and we can only hope that someday, something might transpire which will give us that much needed breakthrough.

WHAT OTHER UFOLOGISTS THINK ABOUT THE BONNYBRIDGE UFO SIGHTINGS

Both Ron Halliday and I decided to give the reader a look at what some other UFO researchers thought about the Bonnybridge UFO sightings. Here is what a few of them said.

BRIAN ALLAN

In some ways the 1947 sighting of nine objects moving rapidly above Mt Ranier, in Washington State by private pilot Kenneth Arnold, which is now used to define the start of modern Ufology can be compared with a 1992 encounter near the village of Bonnybridge in Central Scotland. What local businessman James Walker saw when driving on a quiet road between Falkirk and Bonnybridge, caused him to stop his car. Just ahead of him, hovering above the road, was a glowing star-shaped object. As Walker gazed through his windscreen fascinated by the glowing object, he felt a shudder of fear course through his body. Then, abruptly, the object shot off at tremendous speed and disappeared. At this point, understandably alarmed, the businessman left the area as quickly as he could, so it's probably fair to say that the Bonnybridge enigma began at the same time, because this encounter was a precursor of literally thousands of similar sightings of lights in the sky, landed craft and also alleged encounters with whatever was on board the craft. There was even an account of an alien abduction.

This ongoing wave of sightings produced the not unreasonable question, *"Why Bonnybridge?"* which in turn generated the rather glib and unhelpful answer, *"Why not Bonnybridge"?* However, this just will not do, because there has to be a very good reason why this otherwise rather unremarkable location became an internationally recognised 'UFO hotspot'. Of course, it is more than likely that many of the sightings were mundane and due to misidentified aircraft, weather conditions or even satellites, (even the old chestnut of marsh gas gets a mention), but a hard core of the sightings cannot just be explained away so easily; so, what is it about this particular location in the Central Scotland that seems to attract UFOs? There have been several reasons given, some more likely than others. It has been suggested that Bonnybridge (and the surrounding area) just happens to be located at one end of a 'portal', a 'stargate' if you like that connects two points in space/time, and these 'craft', (if that is what they are) use it to cross unimaginable distances in the blink of an eye. Where they go and what they do after that is anyone's guess. Perhaps the geology of Bonnybridge is geomagnetic in nature, because it is known that various locations here on Earth where UFO sightings, along with a variety of other anomalous events occur, are also locations of powerful geomagnetic anomalies. Skinwalker Ranch is a good example of this.

Other opinions suggest that these craft might well originate right here on Earth as part of an ultra-secret black-budget military project, well maybe, because these are ongoing and the public knows nothing about them, but if so, then why test them in such a relatively densely populated area? This raises another question: if the UK government did know would it tell the public? The answer to that is no, they would not, because the UK authorities are notoriously secretive about information of this kind. This is the reason that so many misdemeanours, especially of those in the upper echelons of UK society, are hidden away from public scrutiny until long after their deaths, and even then, the authorities are reluctant to release the information. This is true of events that occurred during the First World War and even now are still classified: the same kind of perverse logic allows any knowledge concerning the existence of extraterrestrial spacecraft (and of course their occupants) to be concealed from the general public. Perhaps we will not know for sure until the evidence is so overwhelming that it just cannot be hidden any longer. As far as the Bonnybridge enigma is concerned, one has to ask if it's still happening? The answer is that it's likely that it is and the only reason that it is no longer reported it that people have simply stopped looking.

(Author's Note) Brian Allan is a well know author and lecturer on all things weird and wonderful. Brian was also the editor of 'Phenomena Magazine'.

THE BONNYBRIDGE UFO FLAP. PHILIP MANTLE

What we call a UFO 'flap' usually refers to a concentrated series of UFO sightings lasting for days, months or even longer and usually restricted to a particular geographical area or region. This is not always the case as for example there was a huge wave of sightings across the USA in 1973. The flap we are looking at hear is the one associated with Bonnybridge in Scotland during the 1990's.

We are fortunate to have the authors of this book involved in the research and investigation into the Bonnybridge flap actually as it was happening. I saw firsthand the interest in these events when I took part as a speaker at a conference along with Malcolm Robinson in the 1990's. The venue was packed with members of the public simply wanting to know what the hell was going on.

Before we get carried away, I must emphasise that as a UFO researcher and investigator I know that most UFO sightings reported to either me, the authors or anyone else for that matter have a logical explanation. Other sightings simply do not have enough data to draw any conclusion which leaves us with a very small amount of sightings that remain unidentified. The percentage of unidentified sighting is usually put at around 5% but in my humble opinion it is much less than that and well under 1%. Therefore, very few reported sightings remain unidentified after investigation. However, having said that even the sightings that can be easily identified remain part of the equation when it comes to a flap.

Therefore, it is safe to say that the vast majority of the sightings reported during the Bonnybridge flap were of conventional everyday objects. The most usual culprits are of course aircraft and astronomical objects. But what causes sensible, ordinary everyday members of the public to see a conventional object in the sky and report it as something out of the ordinary. This happens all the time but why does it escalate during a flap to hundreds of people and not just Mr Smith out walking his dog. There may be many reasons why hundreds of people report sightings during a flap. To kick it off there may have been a sighting that featured in the local news media. This may cause members of the public to look skyward for the first time. This may be followed up with interviews of the witnesses and local UFO investigators which in turns obtains more media coverage and the snowball starts to grow as it steadily rolls downhill. There could be a popular culture influence as well. Was there a movie or TV series that featured UFOs. In the 1990's for example we had the massive TV series 'The X Files' and the movie 'FIRE IN THE SKY' telling the story of Travis Walton's alien abduction. These were no doubt also featured in the news media. Sometimes, as in the Bonnybridge flap, there is someone who is local and becomes a kind of torch bearer for the flap, in this case this may have been Councillor Billy Buchanan. Again, such an important figure obtains more media coverage and on we go. More media coverage, more people look skyward, more reports are received. Eventually of course the snowball comes to a halt and flap dissipates and then disappears.

I'll give you an example how an educated, honest businessman can view something conventional and turn into something out of the ordinary. Back in the 1980's I had a phone call from a gentleman who only lived a few miles from me in West Yorkshire. He told me of his sighting of a dome-shaped UFO giving off coloured lights that he had witnessed from his back garden about 1.00 am. I was busy at the time, so I sent his standard UFO report form which he duly completed. On the form was a great drawing of the dome-shaped object along of course with all of the sighting details. I phoned him up and thanked him, only for him to say he had seen it again in the same place. I asked him if he saw it again to phone me no matter what time it was. Sure enough, a few days later he phoned me around 1.00 am and this time I jumped in my car and made my way to his home. We walked into his back garden, and he pointed to this amazing sight in the sky. It was of course the planet Venus, and I politely informed him of this. As I walked back through his living room, I noticed on the coffee table a UFO book. This chap had read his first ever UFO book, walked out into his back garden and looked to the sky and bingo there was this massive UFO in the sky, or so he thought. It wasn't a UFO but the planet Venus which I had suspected all along. Now, amplify this with all of the parameters above and you could end up with a flap.

There will of course be those that disagree with me here and that's fine, but this is what I have learnt during my 40+ years as an active UFO investigator and researcher.

(Author's Note) Philip Mantle is a long-standing UFO researcher and author from the UK. He was formerly the Director of Investigations for the British UFO Research Association and was the MUFON Representative for England. He is the founder of Flying Disk Press and publisher of this book.

JOHN HANSON

I'm a retired police officer who has spent nearly 30 years researching reports of UFO activity which in the main (as opposed to an ill-informed public perception that 90% can be explained away rationally) The evidence of literally thousands of witnesses from all walks of life which includes senior RAF officers, shows that the events that took place in Bonnybridge, is identical in its similarities of observed behaviour and physical characteristics to other high peaks of UFO activity which took place in 1947, 1967, 1977, and 1990/1996. These are in general not misidentifications or explainable phenomena. What they are and where they come from is still unexplainable. The very fact that the Government has gone to such great lengths to suppress sightings by classifying them for many years corroborates in all probability they haven't a clue themselves! Sadly, the courage of our citizens in coming forward to merely tell what they saw often ends in ridicule.

(Author's Note) John Hanson is a retired CID Officer in the West Midlands Police and first became interested in the UFO subject in January 1995, after colleagues sighted a UFO hovering over some trees. This was the trigger for his curiosity; prior to that the very mention of UFOs and 'flying saucers' was impossible for him to accept as having any reality in the modern world. The publication of ten Volumes of Haunted Skies which painstakingly catalogue thousands of reports of UFO's/Close Encounter experiences by the public from 1940 onwards, is a project that John and his former partner Dawn Holloway had been working on for many years. John is now working on many book projects alongside colleague Shirley Ann Edwards. Their objective is to educate the public and therefore have published the books at their own expense. (NB): Info taken from John's web site. http://www.hauntedskies.co.uk/

BILLY DEVLIN

The UFO events that occurred in the now famous 'Bonnybridge Triangle' was my first involvement with anything involving supposed 'unidentified' flying objects. I had always been interested in the subject and it did not take me long to contact Malcolm Robinson and the group he ran by the name of Strange Phenomena Investigations after reading about them in a local newspaper. Malcolm was deeply involved in the investigations along with the charismatic councillor Billy Buchanan. My first meeting was at a large gathering at the Norwood Hotel in Bonnybridge. Billy had become the central conduit in the whole Bonnybridge affair. It was his life's mission, alongside Malcolm, to help gather as much information as they could to find answers and to put pressure on the Scottish and British Governments to set up an investigation into what was actually going on around Bonnybridge.

The first case I remember was listening to the reports from a family known locally as 'The Sloggetts' who had a terrifying experience while walking towards the town of Bonnybridge on a clear March evening. They observed a large circular light in front of them. The object proceeded to land in a field opposite them. Suddenly a door opened giving off a high-pitched howling sound that terrified the hell out of them all. They ran home, locked the door and racked their brains to try and find an explanation for what they had just experienced. Around that time there were many tales of lights in the sky, objects landing with strange figures approaching people only to disappear as quickly as they appeared. The list of occurrences grew with more and more people gaining enough confidence to come forward and talk about their own personal experiences.

The UFO 'explosion' that occurred in the area and the experiences of the people initially encouraged some to do their own investigations into what they themselves had experienced. People wanted answers and not being satisfied with what they had been given by the authorities decided to set about creating their own groups to find the answers themselves. They would be contacted by local people who had a similar experience, and they would try to help each other to understand. Strange Phenomena Investigations became the central source for many of these people. We would meet up with them and like-minded people to form groups and friendships and many joint collaborations occurred. I remember one such family that had many experiences of seeing strange lights and strange objects in the sky. They became so involved in the subject that they built their very own viewing platform in the back of their garden. It was a high construction akin to the outlook mast on a ship and it swayed precariously in the wind, but it did not stop them climbing up and spending many a cold night with camera in hand hoping to catch something. They did film a few strange events that warranted further investigation but as I explain in many sightings we have been shown 'Why would a UFO need red and blue flashing landing lights.'! Then there was John. One dark evening he was driving on the back roads over the Bathgate hills on his way home from work when all of a sudden, a 'Silver Man' appeared running alongside his van. Obviously shocked in disbelief he put his foot to the floor to 'get the hell out of there' but the silver man remained at his side until all of a sudden it disappeared as quickly as it had appeared. What was it? Who was it? We will never know but to this day John is convinced he saw something. He was a very intelligent, very private guy who had many paranormal experiences. He was reluctant to go public. He set up his own group where like-minded people gathered to investigate other similar sightings. You can understand why he was reluctant to go public. Many people were, and still are, ridiculed and humiliated when they came forward with their experiences. Many move on from what has happened and try to forget or live with what had happened. Others would go the other way and wanted as much publicity as they could in the hope that they could gain some financial reward or fame from what they were willing to sell and tell to the press. Unfortunately, the minute you go public to the press with any UFO or paranormal occurrence you lose control, and all sorts of lies and tentacles grow and multiply. All of a sudden, plausible, credible incidents are blown up and become an object of fun and ridicule. I have always admired the courage of the people who came forward and still come forward within the Bonnybridge area. There was a lot of publicity generated for the area. Some would say later the media frenzy was pumped up deliberately by the local councillor to obtain funding and attention for a much-deprived area. I must admit there were times when I was sitting taking down notes or listening to evidence while visiting claims of UFO visitations and wondering why I was actually there. On more than one occasion I would be standing outside a house or location being told by the claimant that there was a large UFO hovering directly above, feet away from their roof or head. I was standing in the exact spot and saw nothing. Some so called 'tuned in' people would claim this was because I was not 'dimensionally tuned in' to accept what was above me. A bit like the emperor's new clothes syndrome. I must be an inferior kind of human being if I cannot see it! I am sure within this new publication by Malcolm and Ron you will read accounts of strange encounters that will make you doubt what you read but the one thing to remember is that in the vast majority of Bonnybridge cases what you read is an account of an event that the recipient believes happened to them. When you sit face to face with these people, as they recount what happened, you can see in their eyes, face, or actions, that something happened to them or appear to them that is unexplainable. It had affected them and in some changed their lives forever. Who are we to question or doubt them. Yes, we may come up with some possible plausible theory that we think is correct, but you then have to explain to them what they saw. Some accept it and others become angry or even violent when you explain the UFO they thought they saw was in fact a satellite or planet. There are no experts. We can only do our research and investigations and hope in the end we come up with a plausible answer. There is an analogy in the UFO fraternity that states that of all the hundreds or thousands of sightings that have been reported, if even just one percent are true, then just that one percent should cause us all to ask the question as to why someone has not been honest enough to tell us that we are not alone, and that we do indeed get visits from time to time by beings from other worlds. This same analogy can be applied to the sightings within the

Bonnybridge triangle. Even if one percent of sightings that the people reported were true, then the area around Bonnybridge should be an area that should always be held in high regard within the UFO world, Indeed the world!

(Author's Note) Billy Devlin has had a lifelong interest in all things weird and wonderful. And played a big part in SPI Investigations during the 1990's. Billy is still a researcher with SPI, and we thank him for his continued support.

IN CLOSING

Well, I hope you have enjoyed reading my part of the Bonnybridge UFO story. Bonnybridge and those weird aerial sightings have played a big part in my life, and it sure has been an interesting journey. I now turn you over to my colleague and fellow researcher Ron Halliday. Ron will now take you on his own personal journey regarding the UFO sightings over Bonnybridge.

(Malcolm Robinson January 2025)

MALCOLM'S REFERENCES

Wikipedia
ENIGMAS Magazine.
www.falkirkherald.co.uk/news/ufo-sighting-in-skies-above-falkirk-1226075
https://www.falkirkherald.co.uk/news/event-to-shed-light-on-the-unexplained-1105143
https://www.falkirkherald.co.uk/news/people/world-ufo-day-falkirk-provost-welomes-ufologists-to-bonnybridge-3293860
www.ufocasebook.com
www.stevehammond.org
https://www.newsweek.com/florida-alien-abduction-insurance-area-51-raid-mike-st-lawrence-saint-lawrence-agency-1451238
https://www.falkirkherald.co.uk/news/people/footage-of-ufo-captured-in-night-skies-over-grangemouth-3003450
https://www.falkirkherald.co.uk/news/far-east-film-crew-enjoy-their-ufo-day-in-bonnybridge-1084727

FURTHER READING

The following books whilst not exhaustive on the study of UFO's, are a good place to start. Most of these books can be found on Amazon.

Above Top Secret. Tim Good. Publisher: William Morrow; Reprint edition (20 Sept. 1989) ISBN-13: 978-0688092023

Abducted. Anne Andrew, Jean Ritchie. Paperback: 320 pages. Publisher: Headline Book Publishing; New edition (3 Jun. 1999) ISBN-13: 978-0747259138

A Passage Through Eternity. Philip Kinsella. Paperback: 280 pages. Publisher: Independently published (2 Feb. 2018) ISBN-13: 978-1977067289

Electric UFOs. Albert Budden, Blandford Books, 1998. ISBN: 07-137-268-57

Haunted Skies. (Various volumes cataloguing UFO sightings throughout the U.K. from 1939 through to present day. By John Hanson & Dawn Holloway. E-mail them at info@hauntedskies.co.uk

Livingston Enigma (Dechmont Law). A Tectonic Approach, John Dykslag (Self Published) 2007.

LightQuest. Andrew Collins. Paperback: 416 pages. Publisher: Eagle Wing Books, Inc. (2012) ISBN-13: 978-0940829497

McX. (Scottish X Files). Ron Halliday. B&W Publishing, Edinburgh, ISBN: 1-873631-77-4

Of NO Defence Significance? John M Jenkins. The Pen-Y-Coe Press (1997) ISBN. 0-9531984-0-5.

Pascagoula-The Closest Encounter. Calvin Parker. (Flying Disc Press) ISBN: 9781-9829-95843.

Sky Crash. Jenny Randles, Brenda Butler, Dot Street. Paperback: 400 pages. Publisher: Harper Collins Publishers Ltd; New edition (22 May 1986) ISBN-13: 978-0586066782

The UFO Handbook. Alan Hendry. Publisher: Doubleday; First Edition (1 Aug. 1979) ISBN-13: 978-0385143486

The Truth Agenda. Andy Thomas. Paperback: 386 pages. Publisher: Vital Signs Publishing; Revised edition (1 Jun. 2011) ISBN-13: 978-0955060816

The UFO Mystery Solved. Steuart Campbell. Explicit Books Edinburgh ISBN: 0-9521512-0-0

The Dechmont Law UFO. Phil Fenton. Newstar Publishing 2012.

The Dechmont Woods UFO Incident. Malcolm Robinson. (Feb 2019) ISBN: 978-0-244-15911-5

The Falkland Hill UFO Incident. Malcolm Robinson. (October 2022) ISBN: 9798-3516-822-04

The A70 UFO Incident. Malcolm Robinson. (February 2022) ASIN: BO9RG7RXR1

The Benhar Encounter. Gilbert Nelson (Pseudonym!) Dorma Publications, 65 Constable Road, Northants, England, NN18 ORT.

The UFOLOGY Umbrella. Jason Gleaves. Flying Disc Press. ISBN: 9781-793-055-002.

UFO Encounters. Jason Gleaves. Flying Disc Press. (2022) ISBN: 9798-4043-74971.

UFO Case Files of Scotland (Volume 1) Malcolm Robinson Publish Nation. ISBN: 978-1-907126-02-04

UFO Case Files of Scotland (Volume 2) Malcolm Robinson Publish Nation. ISBN: 978-0-244-95154-2

UFO Scotland. Ron Halliday, B&W Publishing Edinburgh, 1998. ISBN: 1-873631-839

UFO Study. Jenny Randles. Hardcover: 208 pages. Publisher: Robert Hale Ltd; First Edition (11 May 1981) ISBN-13: 978-0709188643

UFO Landings. (Philip Mantle) Flying Disc Press. (2020) ISBN: 9798-654-537-966

Without Consent. Philip Mantle. Publisher: Fortune Books Ltd (2002) ASIN: B00I63L8YU

You Can't Tell The People. Georgina Bruni. Paperback: 496 pages. Publisher: Sidgwick & Jackson; Main Market edition (9 Nov. 2001) ISBN-13: 978-0330390217

Zones of Strangeness. Peter A McCue. Paperback: 560 pages. Publisher: Author House UK (28 Feb. 2012) ISBN-10: 9781456778422

TO CONTACT MALCOLM ROBINSON

Research group Strange Phenomena Investigations (SPI) are always interested to hear from anyone who believe that they may have had a UFO or paranormal experience or indeed may have a photograph or piece of film footage which may appear to show something paranormal. If so, please contact Malcolm Robinson at the address below. (all submissions will be treated in confidence)

Malcolm Robinson.
You can e-mail the author direct at malckyspi@yahoo.com
Facebook: www.facebook.com/malcolm.robinson2

"We make our world significant by the courage of our questions and the depth of our answers".
Carl Sagan American astronomer, cosmologist, astrophysicist, astrobiologist, author.

ABOUT THE AUTHOR
MALCOLM ROBINSON

Malcolm been interested in the strange world of UFOs and the paranormal for as long as he can remember, and in 1979 he formed his own research society, entitled, Strange Phenomena Investigations, (SPI). The aims of SPI are to collect, research, and publish, accounts relating to most aspects of strange phenomena, and to purposely endevour to try and come up with some answers to account for what at present eludes us. SPI are the oldest UFO and Paranormal research group still operating in Scotland.

MALCOLM'S TELEVISION WORK

Scottish Television News (STV) – Independent Television Network (ITN) – BBC Reporting Scotland – Channel 5 – Sightings (U.S. T.V. Show) – Japanese Television – German Television – Mexican Television – Australian Television – Dutch Television – Italian Television – Strange But True? (With Michael Aspel) – Grampian Television – GMTV (with Eammon Holmes and Lorraine Kelly - The Disney Channel – Loose Lips (with Melinda Messenger and Richard Arnold. - SKY Discovery Channel – SKY History Channel – ITV This Morning (with Philip Schofield and Amanda Holden) – SKY News with Kay Burley. The Unexplained with William Shatner. Ancient Aliens, and many more.

DOCUMENTARY MOVIES
(That feature Malcolm Robinson)

The Pentagon UFO Files (2022) Space Force, The Dawn of Galactic Warfare (2022) Aliens at Loch Ness (2022) The Dechmont Woods Case (2023) Loch Ness, They Created A Monster (2023) The Loch Ness Monster, 'Hunting The Truth' (2023) UFO Government Files Declassified (2023)

RADIO

BBC Radio Scotland. - Radio Clyde – Talk FM – BBC Northsound – BBC Radio 4 – Central FM – The Howard Hughes show – Coast to Coast with Art Bell and George Noory – The Whitley Streiber Show. And many others, both here in the U.K. and overseas.

ARTICLES

Articles by Malcolm have appeared in many of the world's UFO and Paranormal magazines. Malcolm has assisted many of the U. K's National and Regional newspapers in connection with stories concerning ghosts, poltergeists, and UFOs.

INFO

Malcolm was the very first Scottish UFO researcher to speak in the following countries, United States of America, (Laughlin Nevada). France (Strasbourg) Holland (Utrecht) Ireland (Carrick on Shannon & Galway) Malcolm is also one of the few people on this planet to have gone down into the depths of Loch Ness in a submarine. He is also an international author and lecturer and is the assistant editor of the Outer Limits Magazine. Malcolm is the first Scotsman to give a lecture on UFOs and the Paranormal on a cruise ship, when he presented two lectures to holiday makers on board the Marella Discovery on an East Coast cruise of the USA and Canada, October 2023.

AWARDS

2017. UFO & Paranormal researcher of the year. Given at the Paraforce Conference in Witham, Essex, England.
2019: 40 Years Continuous operations of SPI. Given at the Outer Limits Conference in Hull, Yorkshire, England.
2021. The Tartan Skull Award. Presented at the Scottish UFO & Paranormal Conference (over Skype)

***

(My book is dedicated to all those UFO witnesses who have had the courage to come forward and tell their story)

Part Two

Ron Halliday

CONTENTS

Part Two:
The Bonnybridge UFO Enigma as seen by Ron Halliday.   P291

Chapter One:
The Bonnybridge UFO flap unmasked. The Background.   P293

Chapter Two:
A mystery that intrigued the world.   P296

Chapter Three:
Claims and counter claims.   P313

Chapter Four:
In full swing, the impact of video evidence.   P325

Chapter Five:
Can we explain the Bonnybridge Phenomenon?   P335

Chapter Six:
Strange stories and controversies cloud the central UFO issue.   P352

Chapter Seven:
Bonnybridge in isolation. The Falkirk Triangle Controversy.   P368

Chapter Eight: How can we account for events in Bonnybridge? Where do UFOs come from?   P380

Appendix: P414

To Contact Ron Halliday: email: ronhalliday168@sky.com

THE BONNYBRIDGE UFO FLAP UNMASKED!

CHAPTER ONE
THE BACKGROUND

In the 1990s the village of Bonnybridge in central Scotland appeared out of obscurity to become the focus of media attention. What was the reason for its abrupt emergence into the limelight? It was over the unlikely subject of Unidentified Flying Objects. In a short space of time the village earned a reputation as the world's premier UFO hot spot. How this came about is a strange story of claims and counterclaims. A fascinating tale of how a modern myth developed in less than a few years. In the following chapters I aim to map out the extraordinary route by which the sleepy village of Bonnybridge gained its celebrity status as a key location for UFO encounters. And to explain how this remarkable transition from a pleasant but nondescript place to international fame came about. Were there in fact up to 8,000 reported sightings of Unidentified Flying Objects as one researcher claimed? Or was it on the other hand 'all got up by the media' as some suggested? I hope to mark out the process by which Bonnybridge became a byword across the globe for the UFO phenomenon.

My investigation will focus on the period 1990 to 1996 but covering events in the years before and after to give a complete picture of what occurred including the various personalities involved. It was during this period (90-96) that the village's reputation became enmeshed in public consciousness. Of course, Bonnybridge's fame lives on, continuously being recycled in TV programmes, internet discussions and podcasts. But its reputation did not emerge from a void. Many streams fed in to create the river and I aim to explain just how these circumstances came about and assess the extent to which we can believe in Bonnybridge as a genuinely remarkable UFO hotspot.

So, what and where is Bonnybridge? It is a village of around 6,000 people located in the middle of Scotland's central lowland belt roughly halfway between Edinburgh and Glasgow. It is situated near the Bonny, a tributary of the Carron River, hence Bonnybridge. Some commentators have referred to it as 'isolated', but that is far from being accurate. It is only few miles from Grangemouth which has housed one of the biggest petroleum works in Europe. Furthermore, it edges on to the town of Falkirk with a population of around 34,000. In fact, the Falkirk Council area boasts a population of over 160,000 and Bonnybridge is situated within though on the outskirts of this region. The village does, however, occupy an elevated position overlooking Falkirk town which gives it a clear view of our otherwise light polluted skies and there are several areas around the village which are regarded as excellent skywatching spots for UFO enthusiasts. Like many areas of Scotland, it has seen a decline in heavy industry and fresh avenues of employment are always an issue for consideration by the area council.

I must admit to a personal interest in the district. I was the Scottish National Party parliamentary candidate for the Falkirk East constituency in the 1987 and 1992 elections. Many of the areas mentioned in connection with the events in Bonnybridge I visited while canvassing for votes guided by my respective election agents Robert Spears and Craig Evans. Owing to my involvement in the politics of the area I became aware that there was a considerable amount of local pride in each particular location with people feeling a close connection to their particular community. The 'Falkirk Herald' which was and still is the main local newspaper claimed a readership of 100,000 in the early 1990s and gave a round up each week of events in each community in the area it covered. One's heart goes out to the journalist with responsibility for compiling it! The communities covered in the Falkirk Herald's weekly roundup gives a good indication of the areas which feature in the Bonnybridge story. These were as follows:

Laurieston:Brightons:Reddingmuirhead:Muiravonside:Reddi -ng and Westquarter:Camelon: Bannock and Haggs: Shieldhill: KIncardine: Larbert and Stenhousemuir:Bonnybridge: Dennyloanhead: Airth: Denny and Dunipace: Grangemouth:

Maddiston: Grahamston: Standburn: Plean: Polmont: Slammanan, and Limerig:California: Carron and Carronshore, and Avonbridge.

As can be seen from the list above the 'Falkirk Herald covered a diverse and extensive circulation area. And it can be said accurately that Bonnybridge did not stand in isolation as it was situated only a few miles distant from most of the communities mentioned. Falkirk District is in fact a loosely connected area of small towns and villages with the focus on Falkirk hence 'Falkirk District Council'. It's interesting to note that the bulk of UFO sightings reported and included as part of the Bonnybridge phenomenon occurred in the areas above. Unfortunately, Bonnybridge was not included in the Falkirk East parliamentary constituency when I stood for parliament which might have made the experience even more interesting!

CHAPTER TWO

A MYSTERY THAT INTRIGUED THE WORLD

An aspect of events in Bonnybridge that fascinated me and still does is why and how this small village came to capture world-wide interest. And it happened so quickly. You only have to look at UFO incidents in other areas the USA, for example, or Australia or even Brazil to realise that important encounters were taking place which should have outmatched Bonnybridge in terms of media interest. But it was this comparatively obscure, sleepy village which captured the imagination from one end of the globe to the other. How on earth did this come about?

It all began quietly with no indication of the tsunami to follow. I'd been investigating UFO reports for several years and had many contacts in the media, so I first became aware of the Bonnybridge UFO phenomenon through being rung up by the press to comment on particular incidents. Initially, I wasn't sure what to make of it as there seemed no obvious reason why Bonnybridge should emerge as a focus of UFO activity. However, given that multiple encounters were being reported it suggested that 'something' out of the ordinary was going on, but what? Furthermore, I learned that experienced investigator Malcolm Robinson was involved in looking into events so I knew that whatever was happening must be of significance.

The startling aspect was that not only were there eye-witness reports, but video evidence too and a lot of it. It suggested that what was occurring was more than simply misidentification of everyday objects though as is always the case with UFO reports misidentification would certainly explain a high proportion of sightings. Even so there were a large number that couldn't be simply dismissed. In his book 'Open Skies, Closed Minds' author Nick Pope claimed there had been 8,000 sightings which was certainly staggering if correct. In retrospect evidence suggests that the number of reports were well below that figure, but undeniably there were a significant number of sightings which couldn't be simply dismissed under the heading 'misidentification'. The local councillor and key figure in the developing story, William - usually Billy – Buchanan, was quoted as stating that reported sightings had reached two thousand a more reasonable but a still phenomenal number. It's likely that both figures were too high, but in Buchanan's case he could speak with some authority as a person who was directly involved in events unlike Nick Pope. Nick certainly didn't investigate events at Bonnybridge directly so where Pope obtained the figure of 8,000 sightings remains a mystery, but it may well be that Pope relied on another source. However, the fact that he chose to mention it in his book published in 1998 demonstrates the extent to which Bonnybridge had captured the attention of the Ufology community.

The investigators get involved.

All that, however, was still to come and in 1992 events were still in their early stages. Fellow ufologist Malcolm Robinson has described in various documents how he first became aware of UFO activity at Bonnybridge - on the 4th of November 1992 -when he heard councillor Billy Buchanan speaking on Central FM, a local radio station. Buchanan described local residents approaching him with reports of UFO encounters. Malcolm got in touch with Buchanan and the rest as they say is history.

My route into the Bonnybridge phenomena was, as I indicated less dramatic or direct. I missed the Central FM broadcast, so I first became aware of events when journalists rang me to ask for my comments on what was happening in Bonnybridge. I was somewhat sceptical at first because the sheer volume of incidents claimed struck me as extraordinarily high given the level of reported UFO cases in Scotland generally up to that point. So why had this village suddenly become a 'hotspot'. But as witnesses began to contact me, I soon realised that 'something strange' was taking place on, around and in close proximity to Bonnybridge. Eventually I became heavily involved in the Bonnybridge saga, quoted in various newspaper articles and appearing on radio and television including GMTV, 'Totally Dr WHO' and the car quiz, 'Test Drive' in which I was interviewed by the TV personality 'Grado' among other programmes.

A Developing Story - at top speed!

The reports and media interest seemed to increase by the day. I did raise questions about the impact of media comments on events at Bonnybridge. I felt it was becoming a bit of a feeding frenzy with any sighting of an apparently odd object in the sky being turned into something unexplained. This, attitude, I considered, could be clouding the issue and with the resulting exaggerated reporting meant that significant UFO sightings could be missed. I feel that wild estimates of the number of reported incidents justified concerns I expressed at the time. But even so there was no doubt that the number of sightings coming in were extraordinarily high and proof that something inexplicable was happening in the skies over Bonnybridge. And media interest was not surprising given the evidence that was emerging on an almost daily basis. On top of that certain events had a particular impact in developing the apparent Bonnybridge enigma.

The Norwood Hotel meeting, Bonnybridge

As reported by the 'Sunday Post' headline of 31st December 1993, 'Ufologists and psychological investigators will attempt to explain the mystery of the many UFO reports.' It was also claimed that that some of the witnesses to the sightings would undergo hypnosis. The aim of this procedure, apparently, would be to uncover subconscious memories of being abducted by alien beings and taken aboard a UFO. The meeting had been organised by Councillor Buchanan in the hope that some clarity would emerge to explain all the strange sightings being reported by locals in Bonnybridge One of those invited to attend and, hopefully, shed some light on events was UFO expert Malcolm Robinson. An amazing 200 people - or maybe 400 according to an article written by Billy Buchanan in 1997- turned up undeniable proof that whatever was happening in the skies had sparked the interest of a significant number of the public. Malcolm Robinson later told me he was taken aback by the size of the turnout!

The reference in the article to 'hypnotic regression' certainly aroused a bit of controversy. The problems associated with hypnotic regression are well known and generate quite strong differences of opinion. The well-known organisation the British UFO Research Association banned the use of it because of the uncertainty of its results. I'm not aware though that any such action was taken to hypnotise witnesses in any of the Bonnybridge UFO cases. Hypnosis undertaken with the A70 UFO encounter witnesses Gary Wood and Colin Wright did result in spectacular accounts of alien abduction, but doubts over its validity remain and its use in this case was criticised by some ufologists. However, at the very least it did confirm that something 'out of this world' had happened to Colin and Gary. It's worth noting too that the police in both the UK and the USA have had witnesses to crimes put under hypnosis so its use can't be automatically ruled out as a possible tool.

There's a curious footnote to the Norwood hotel. In October 1993 the Falkirk Herald reported a disagreement between local councillors over the demolition of the hotel which, according to a letter to the 'Falkirk Herald from councillor Buchanan appeared to be the proverbial 'storm in a teacup' and seemed to arise from a misunderstanding. It's a pity that a venue so closely connected with putting Bonnybridge on the UFO chart had to go.

Japanese Film Crew September 1993

The arrival of a Japanese film crew was a certain indicator that Bonnybridge was arriving on the world UFO map. A report in the 'Stirling Observer' of 25th September 1993 stated that Malcolm Robinson believed that Bonnybridge was one of the world's 'windows' into another dimension. It also reported that the film crew had come to the area with the intention of interviewing local eyewitnesses to UFO sightings. To welcome the visitors councillor Buchanan had prepared a cake shaped like a UFO. A fitting tribute one might think!

Bonnybridge became such big news that even the 'upmarket' press took an interest. The 'Guardian', a normally somewhat strait-laced publication, printed a lengthy article on 31st October 1995 which despite the time of year - Halloween - adopted a more or less serious evaluation of the phenomenon.

And, almost as surprising as Japanese interest, a meeting held in Falkirk Town Hall to discuss Bonnybridge UFOs was reported as far away as the 'Shropshire Star' (9th October 1995) which commented on the huge crowd expected - 500 - and the international experts on UFOs who would address the gathering. Councillor Billy Buchanan was reported as saying that he hoped the meeting might offer some explanations as to what had been going on over Bonnybridge. The significance of this key event in the Bonnybridge story is discussed later in the book.

Various events stirred up further interest. A 'sky watch' was arranged with ensuing media interest and was broadcast on television. As is often the case with organised Sky watches nothing of interest was seen or captured on camera. UFOs, unfortunately, don't appear to order! But the media coverage led to many more UFO sightings, and I was one of the ufologists who questioned whether it was now possible to separate genuine, unexplained sightings from the obvious mis-sightings that planets and plane lights, for example, generate. Even other Ufologists took note. In her book 'UFOs and How to See Them', author Jenny Randles pointed out that Scotland was a focal point for UFO activity. And then in the 'The Paranormal Year 1993', Randles noted that 'in... the Bonnybridge area...witnesses were getting quite concerned about the level of lights-in-the-sky reports' adding, 'A councillor in the Bonnybridge area actually called in Ufologists to help calm down the population and both Malcolm Robinson and Ron Halliday responded. Indeed, Halliday set up a hotline for callers to report events and obtain solace and this was very busy in the lead-up to Christmas'.

'Strange But True'

Even more publicity followed as the 'Falkirk Herald' of 3rd November 1994 reported. Under the headline, 'Bonnybridge

Mystery Featured in New Book' the paper detailed the launch of the book 'Strange But True' which had been published to coincide with the television series of the same name. The Bonnybridge UFO phenomenon featured in both the book and the TV show. In fact, the Bonnybridge enigma had been given a whole chapter to itself and included interviews with local witnesses and various experts on the UFO subject. Both the book and television show attempted a balance by including the views of those who doubted the 'alien visitation' explanation and took a more down-to-earth view of events. Nevertheless, the inclusion of Bonnybridge emphasised that by 1994 it had certainly embedded itself in public and media consciousness.

Arguably the television programme 'Strange But True'? caused even more of a stir as the programme regularly pulled in a large audience. The 'Falkirk Herald' splashed it under the headline 'Bonnybridge tunes in to television show on space aliens.' The account ran, 'Bonnybridge is to be featured on a nationwide television programme next week because of the number of UFO sightings in the village. ITV's "Strange But True"? hosted by Michael Aspel has interviewed some of the people in Bonnybridge who have reported "close encounters" with what is believed to be alien spaceships. The programme to be screened on Friday November 4 at 8.30pm will examine the evidence from local people and experts. Bonnybridge hit the headlines last year [sic!] after a series of sightings of objects in the sky'.

In both the book and television well-rehearsed explanations from both sides of the argument were trotted out and some fresh views expressed. So was Bonnybridge, for example, the site of a "window" to another dimension or parallel universe? Or alternatively do astronomical "mirages" cause witnesses to believe they are viewing UFOS when in reality they are encountering no more than an atmospheric or similar disturbance. It was also suggested that once an area becomes known for UFOs the sightings snowball, more cautious observers become encouraged to report events they otherwise would have kept to themselves no matter how apparently insignificant. It all feeds into the supposed phenomenon and enhance the 'hotspots' reputation as in the case of Bonnybridge. As to the origins of

Bonnybridge's fame the programme reported the by now often repeated claim that it all sparked off after a local man reported a sighting to Councillor Billy Buchanan. Buchanan had then via the local press appealed for other witnesses to come forward and received 150 calls in three days with sightings, of course, continuing to the present (that is 1994). No other insights were offered which was in my view a lost opportunity which confused the true origins of the Bonnybridge 'hotspot' for decades. It's interesting to note that the 'Falkirk Herald' in its 'Strange but True' report commented on the fact that recent UFO sightings had been located more towards Falkirk than Bonnybridge. A perceptive observation which was usually missed at the time and has been since.

BBC Radio Show, 1996

In 1996 Bonnybridge became the venue for a radio show dedicated to the UFO phenomenon with local people being encouraged to take part. BBC Radio Scotland were planning to record a one hour "Speaking Out" show in Bonnybridge Community Centre. It was an evening event being held on a Tuesday between 7-8pm. The show aimed to focus on the topics of aliens, UFOs and to seek an explanation as to why Bonnybridge was supposedly a centre of paranormal activity. The show was hosted by Ruth Wishart a well-known journalist and TV personality of the time. It was quite a catch that a writer better known for more serious topics had agreed to chair the event. The BBC press release indicated that a panel of UFO experts would be there to put forward their own explanations as to what was happening in Bonnybridge and answer questions from the public. The recording went ahead, and the programme aired on Boxing Day, 26th December. I was invited to attend and was present for the event. There was a decent turnout though not as many as might have been expected given the publicity the village had received and well below the famous Norwood Hotel event. What was striking, however, was when Ruth asked for comments from anyone living in Bonnybridge she was taken aback by the lack of attendance by locals from the famous village. The audience consisted almost wholly of people other than Bonnybridge residents. That was curious given the hype associated with the village, but did emphasis the fact which should have been obvious that the bulk of UFO sightings came from the general Falkirk district rather than the village of Bonnybridge itself.

UFO Complex

By 1995 Bonnybridge was so well established in the public imagination as a UFO hot spot that constructing a permanent installation to celebrate its fame was under consideration. On the 25th of May 1995 the Falkirk Herald under the headline, 'UFO Complex Bid is out of this world' announced that plans were under consideration to cement Bonnybridge's reputation for UFO sightings. The project envisaged a visitor centre which would be shaped in the form of a giant mushroom made of glass built under the flight path of the alleged UFOs visiting the village. Councillor Buchanan who had done so much to establish the village's word-wide reputation was closely involved in the proposal and made the reasonable point that if it attracted tourists to the area that would be a definite plus for the Falkirk district. Finance, of course, was a critical issue, but the hope was that the Millenium fund the Lottery funded cash pool for projects to mark the turn of the century would provide the money for this out-of-the-world project. It was claimed that architects were in the process of preparing plans and that the 'centre for alien studies' would consist of a giant glass oval on top of a glass stem. Glass lifts would carry visitors up the glass stem to the oval shaped structure on the top. This building would be made up of three floors with a restaurant, bar, 'sci-fi creche', a virtual reality display and an observatory where tourists would be able to sky watch for UFOs.

On the face of it, it seemed a bit pie-in-the sky but Buchanan made the point that people were interested in high-tech visitor centres and that a project as the one envisaged would have a knock-on effect in bringing hotel jobs to the area as well as publicising it. Given the decline of heavy industry, it seemed a not unreasonable proposal. Other projects which might have been viewed as fanciful had experienced great success and the case of 'New Lanark' - Robert Owen's factory now a major visitor attraction in Lanarkshire was given as an example. Fantasy? It was certainly ambitious and it's possible to pick holes in the project. How likely was it that visitors would see a UFO? Highly problematic it has to be admitted. But in the sense that the idea would attract people to the area it's hard to see any objection to the plan. And given the decline of heavy industry as Buchanan commented then tourism is one way of plugging the employment gap. But would the amount of cash involved be worth the potential return? We'll never know because in the end the project didn't get off the drawing board. However, given the vast sums spent on, for example, the white elephant of the Millenium Dome in London then arguably Buchanan's project deserved no less a serious consideration.

And the potential for 'UFO tourism' was not simply in the imagination it was, in actual fact, already happening. The 'Falkirk Herald' pointed this out under the heading 'The Intergalactic lady'. The article concerned 'Topps Farm' near the town of Denny which according to its owners' husband and wife combo Jennifer and Alister Steel had become a mecca for UFO hunters, particularly those from the USA. According to the Steels they had had over 40 skywatchers staying at the farm all of whom were aware of Bonnybridge's reputation as a world hot spot for observing UFOS. It was further proof that the village had gained a global reputation on the UFO map. And this was not fantasy or an exaggerated story because I was intimately involved with one of these visits. It was organised by 'Beyond Travel' which specialised in trips to places of supernatural or 'otherworldly' spots. Joyce Murphy was the person I liaised with, and I took UFO witnesses and others interested in the subject to a meeting with Joyce and company at Topps Farm. 'Beyond Travel' in fact took tourists to sites across the world. I acted as guide when we visited Loch Morar, site of the aquatic monster Morag. On this occasion I went with the US visitors to mysterious Cairnpapple seen as both a UFO spot and a place linked to ghostly sightings. I remember wandering around in the dark chatting about a whole series of strange events linked to the site. A fascinating night infused with typical American enthusiasm.

As Jennifer Steel reported the reputation Bonnybridge had earned attracted such as the 'Center for Scientific Extra-Terrestrial Intelligence' described as the world's elite band of UFO hunters. According to Jennifer they were "entranced" by the area. Jennifer explained that a favourite sky watch site was 'Tak-ma-doon' hill which gave UFO hunters an excellent view across the Falkirk area and beyond. The UFO buffs had an explanation for what has happening in the area: that the alien visitors were watching over us to make sure we didn't damage the environment. Like Billy Buchanan, Jennifer Steel emphasised the benefits to the area in attracting UFO tourists. She made the point that the Loch Ness monster was used as an enticement to people to visit Loch Ness and the UFO phenomenon was no worse than that as an encouragement to people to visit the district

It's interesting to note that by the end of 1993 the 'Falkirk Herald', after initially being less enthused, was giving Bonnybridge the attention it deserved. In the year end roundup journalist Kevin Schofield included the arrival of the Japanese film crew with their claim that Bonnybridge could be the world's top UFO site. The report repeated the claim that 200 people had witnessed UFOs though this was well below numbers that had been touted in the national media. However, despite the hype, it's fair to say that scepticism over the village's claims was widespread. In his 'Round and About' column in the 'Falkirk Herald' Robert Paul raised several telling points. In the first place it seemed reasonable to ask that if aliens are travelling to the area why do they disappear as quickly as they appear? Fair comment you would have to say. It is true that sightings of UFOs don't generally last any great length of time though it is reasonable to point out that in the case of the Bonnybridge phenomenon several UFOs had been captured on video which at least gave an opportunity to examine the evidence rather than relying solely on witness reports.

Robert Paul also raised the issue of the vast distances that alien spacecraft would have to travel to arrive here. This is a perfectly reasonable point, and Paul specifically mentioned the star Proxima Centauri - the nearest to our planet at 4.22 light years distant - making the point that travelling at a speed of say

35,000 miles per hour it would take a spaceship 80 years to cover the 25,000 billion miles to arrive here! However, we can't second guess by what process beings from the vastness of the universe might be able to develop a system to jump huge distances in a comparatively short time. Nor can we be sure that we are dealing with objects from way 'out there'. We could be seeing by some strange means into a future or even a past era on earth. Any explanation is possible and though the practicalities as we view them from today's perspective appear to suggest travel from other planets is not possible, we can never be sure just what advanced technology might achieve. We could be launching if not in our lifetime, the UFOs of the future.

Councillor William Buchanan
Bonnybridge & Larbert Ward
Scotland,
William.buchanan@falkirk.gov.uk

Prime Minister David Cameron

Dear Prime Minister,

DEMAND NOTICE

We as a nation are all well aware of the burden of responsibility that rests on your shoulders and the decisions that have to be taken. The continuous deaths of our soldiers in Afghanistan weighs heavy in all our minds and to end this should be your number one priority.

The global financial crisis and the measures your government have to take to try and stabilise Britain's economy shows clearly how difficult life is going to be for us all. It therefore might seem that what I am going to say is meaningless in light of these problems. I have outlined the concerns but the issue I ask you to clarify is of national importance.

During your election campaign at a forum in Tynemouth north of Tyneside you were open and frank during discussions on UFO's and alien life and your were convinced that aliens have been here. You agreed that the British people had a right to know and if you became Prime Minister you would lift the veil of secrecy and give the people you represent, the truth, that is all we ask, the truth. Are you now going to honour this commitment, the people of my area, Bonnybridge, have, as I have, been ridiculed for years because of this phenomenon.

Prime Minister, I urge you to end the secrecy and let us know the truth.

Yours faithfully

COUNCILLOR WF BUCHANAN

Billy Buchannan Letter to former Prime Minister David Cameron

UFO'S
FACT OR FICTION?

PRESENTATION AND DEBATE

ON
Thursday
30th JUNE 1994
AT 7.30pm
IN FALKIRK TOWN HALL

SPECIAL GUESTS:

Malcolm Robinson (Investigator Lecturer)
Philip Mantle (Investigator Lecturer and Author who will be promoting his <u>NEW</u> book "Without Consent")

PLUS THE SENSATIONAL SOUNDS OF C.E.IV

Hosted by Councillor Billy Buchanan

There is a bar available
Tickets £4 Concessions £2 (Availability Limited)

Falkirk Town Hall poster for UFO Night 1994

Falkirk Council

Donald Dewar MSP
Scottish Parliament
Edinburgh

7th January 2000

Dear Sir,

I wrote to you some months ago regarding the UFO Phenomenon that has been going on unabated since 1992 in Bonnybridge. This phenomenon has been going on for a long time and despite the media ridicule over the years we in Bonnybridge have gained not notoriety but credibility.

I asked you as First Minister of Scotland – The man who speaks for our nation to give me the opportunity to come to the Scottish Parliament and give MSP's a presentation with video footage, witness testimonies to show you all that this is for real and we demand an investigation.

I appreciate how busy you are but this is something of national importance and yet you have not even acknowledged receipt of my letter. I have also recently taken video footage myself that clearly shows UFO's are fact not fiction. I also have a tape, which gives credibility to the whole phenomenon, but I wanted you, at the Scottish Parliament, to listen to the evidence before I go to the media. I ask you again Mr Dewar, give me the opportunity to prove conclusively that we have a phenomenon here that requires a major investigation. That is unless you already know Mr Dewar. Hopefully the opportunity to present the case for the sake of our nation and of our people.

Yours Faithfully,

[signature]

CLLR. BUCHANAN

Letter to Donald Dewar from Billy Buchanan

10 DOWNING STREET
LONDON SW1A 2AA
www.number10.gov.uk

From the Direct Communications Unit

26 May 2010

Mr Malcolm Robinson

Dear Mr Robinson

I am writing on behalf of the Prime Minister to thank you for your letter of 14 May.

Mr Cameron is most grateful for the time and trouble you have taken to get in touch.

I have been asked to forward your letter to the Ministry of Defence, so that they too are aware of your views.

Thank you, once again, for writing.

Yours sincerely

G Edwards

MR G EDWARDS

Malcolm Robinson letter to David Cameron

CAA House
45–59 Kingsway
(main entrance Kemble Street)
London WC2B 6TE

Mr M Robinson

8PP4/15

Telephone: 071-379 7311
Telex: 883092

25 November 1992

Dear Mr Robinson,

Thank you for your letter of 12 November 1992 about UFO sightings in the Bonnybridge and Denny area.
I shall try to answer your questions in the order you pose them.

(1) Bonnybridge is beneath the Scottish Terminal Control Area(TMA), the base of this controlled airspace is 2500 feet. All aircraft above 2500 feet are required to be under the control of an air traffic control unit. Below 2500 feet aircraft may fly wherever they wish subject to the normal rules of the air.
Within the Scottish TMA there is the main airway carrying flights to and from Aberdeen, there will also be flights in and out of both Edinburgh and Glasgow Airports.

(2) Air traffic can, and does transit the area at all times, however there will be only a few flights during the period midnight to 6am.

(3) Cumbernauld Airport is the nearest, there may also be any number of private landing strips on farms etc.

(4) Helicopters are most likely to be in the uncontrolled airspace below 2500 feet, again in this airspace over Bonnybridge they may route where they wish.

(5) Although military activity is not in the CAA's province there are a fair amount of military flights in most parts of the UK outside of controlled airspace.

I hope this information is of some use.

Yours sincerely

John Duck
National Air Traffic Service MSU

NATS letter November 1992

UFOs
FACT OR FICTION?
SPECIAL UFO EVENING

In Falkirk Town Hall   On Thursday 30th June 1994
Doors Open at 7 for 7-30pm

With Philip Mantel and Malcolm Robinson

Ticket £4   (£2 Concessions) with Giant Video Screen and Bar

UFOs Fact or Fiction ticket for Falkirk UFO night 1994

CHAPTER THREE
CLAIMS AND COUNTER CLAIMS

For a period, things did get heated between the investigators involved and at one point Councillor Buchanan wrote an irate letter to me finishing with the phrase 'Get Lost'. That I must emphasise was in the distant past! What had led to sharp differences of opinion? In December 1993 a newspaper headline appeared referring to Billy Buchanan's 'Flying Circus' - an eye catching phrase - and as I was quoted in the article it appeared as if this comment had come from me. But it hadn't. In fact, I had made the comment that with all the media stories popping up in connection with Bonnybridge we had to be careful that it didn't simply become a circus of news making it harder to separate genuine UFO reports from wild claims. In the same article I was reported as saying that most of the Bonnybridge sightings were likely to have natural explanations, for example a 'Scottish Power' helicopter which had been operating in the area around the time that sightings had peaked the previous years. I added 'that it left some which merited serious investigation which was hard to do in the atmosphere of excitement which had been whipped up'. I didn't think my view was unreasonable in the circumstances, but not everyone agreed. To clarify the whirlpool of claims circulating around Bonnybridge I wrote to councillor Buchanan to suggest that a committee be set up to include various interested parties to review the UFO reports in an amicable manner. However, due no doubt to the 'flying circus comments' he had taken I guess a jaundiced view of me so wrote ending with the line, 'I have only one thing to say to you. Get lost'. That was me told! So, unfortunately, nothing came of my proposal, but perhaps in the circumstances it was understandable. I did, as an alternative, suggest a public debate involving those directly involved in researching the Bonnybridge phenomenon and other experienced investigators, but nothing came of this either. Meantime while these differences of opinion were being aired the intensity of interest in Bonnybridge was phenomenal. At one point, according to the 'Glasgow Herald' of 4th March 1996, Buchanan had talked of resigning from the council due to the stress of dealing with the situation in Bonnybridge. Certainly, there was huge interest in developments there and, of course, with it scepticism and criticism not an easy position for a councillor to find himself caught in the middle of.

One central issue which brought out differences of opinion arose from the number of reported UFO sightings. Nick Pope in his book, 'Open Skies, closed minds' had mentioned a figure of 8,000, but this came late on in the history of the Bonnybridge UFO phenomenon. It certainly wasn't an accurate figure. But given the numbers thrown about by the media it's hardly surprising that extravagant estimates were being suggested. Indeed, was it possible to come to a conclusion over how many reports or alleged sightings were actually coming in? On a rough judgement I would consider it in the low hundreds, but still a significant figure for a compact geographical area, limited population base and the short time scale involved. In an attempt to clarify just how many sightings we were talking about I interviewed fellow ufologist Malcolm Robinson who had been closely involved in events at Bonnybridge. The text of this interview was published in the winter/spring 1996/7 issue of 'Phenomenal News'. This was the publication of the group 'Scottish Earth Mysteries Research' which I had set up and chaired. The interview ranged widely over topics of interest to the UFO community but of course dealt with Bonnybridge as a key issue. The relevant part is given below:

Halliday: "Speaking of Bonnybridge, Malcolm, could you clear up something that's always intrigued me. Were there 200 UFO sightings, 2,000 UFO sightings or 8,000 UFO sightings as Nick Pope's claimed"?

Robinson: "I'm very glad you asked that question, very glad. I'm sick and tired of quotes of 2,000 - that's the latest number of sightings from Bonnybridge. It gets quoted right, left and centre in all the newspapers, and I can assure the readers of your publication that it is total nonsense. The UFO reports stemming from Bonnybridge were nowhere near the 2,000 quoted in the press. I feel that perhaps the press has added an extra zero, if you like, on some of these sightings. My own research that I've personally done indicates to me UFO reports in the region of say between 300 and 350 UFOs. It's a figure I'm comfortable with. It's a figure I feel representative of what's happening in Bonnybridge".

Halliday: "Ok, but to be fair to the press, Billy [councillor Billy Buchanan] did claim much higher figures".

Robinson: "It was [name deleted in original] who stated that strange figure. He got me on the phone and said, 'Mr. Robinson, how many things would you say happened in Bonnybridge over the past few years? By this time there would have been around 150, it was back in 1994. And he says, 'Oh, no, I've heard there've been about a thousand or up to two thousand sightings. Wouldn't you agree? I said, 'No, I wouldn't agree.' And he continually stressed the figure of 2,000 sightings. And then the chap turned round and said, for every one person who reports a sighting from around Bonnybridge or surrounding areas surely there must be 2 or 3 people who also saw something and didn't come forward. Hence, multiplication of the figures would extend them?' So, I said, 'Yeah, that's possible, but it's only speculation. We must deal in hard facts.' So, to basically sum up that, the true figures stemming from Bonnybridge, Denny, Slamannan, Falkirk and certain parts of Central Scotland fall between 250 and 300 reports".

(Thanks to Viv Alexander, editor of 'Phenomenal News' who transcribed the tape.)

So that was clear enough from Malcolm Robinson, 200-300 reports rather than 2,000 or more. However, looking back on this interview from a 25 plus years' perspective I'd agree that the journalist who interviewed Robinson had a fair point. It's absolutely true that all the UFO sightings made by the public do not come to the attention of investigators. In fact, I've had individuals come to me decades after the event to report an incident that he or she witnessed. However, I'd have to agree with Malcolm Robinson in that we can only deal with figures that we are definitely aware of. Anything else, as Robinson said, is just speculation. If we have 200 reports, we can't simply double it on the basis that another 200 sightings weren't reported. Yes, I'm sure some UFO reports didn't come our way, but the number involved is pure guesswork.

I wasn't alone when it came to querying the way events were developing over Bonnybridge. One ufologist active during this period wrote to me making the following comments,' I have been greatly bewildered and amused at the recent goings on [in the UFO world] in particular with the BONNYBRIDGE FIASCO [bold in the original] which has become quite comical and has caused more credibility and damage to the subject of Ufology than any other situation I can remember.' He continued, 'it is strange how easily learned individuals can be misled and fooled. A few lights in the sky and all of a sudden everyone jumps on the UFO bandwagon. A simple report of green lights by one individual could have been mistaken for a meteor shower, a plane, a helicopter, car headlights reflected etc, but no, everyone joins the craze-fuelled media, and a simple green light becomes overnight everything ranging from a Gondola with Christmas lights, a banana shaped spaceship, a cigar with wings and what happens next? Public meetings, UFO cakes to welcome aliens and all sorts of announcements that we have a resident alien Mr./Mrs. Zal-us in our midst. (Nice to see them using our alphabet for their surnames). It was around this time I asked myself 'Do I really want to associate myself with this nonsense and the emphatic answer - NO!' [communication to the author].

Another researcher also active at the time referred to what was taking place as the 'Bonnybridge fiasco' [letter to the author]. Opinion was certainly divided! In 1997 I wrote an article for a new magazine titled, appropriately, 'The New Ufologist' which unfortunately lasted only for a few issues. In it I discussed the Bonnybridge phenomenon mainly querying the number of claimed sightings, drawing attention to the fact that while Bonnybridge had earned the title of' 'UFO capital of the world' sightings were actually coming in from a wider area than just the village itself, but agreeing that the volume of reports was way above what have been expected for the population base.

In response to my piece fellow Ufologist Malcolm Robinson gave a lengthy account covering his view of the Bonnybridge situation and dealing with the issues raised in my article. Robinson noted that, 'Yes, perhaps Bonnybridge was "not" the main focus for these UFO reports [and] That in reality these events did stretch over a wide region of Stirlingshire in Central Scotland.' Robinson continued, 'The key player of course was local councillor Billy Buchanan, the press as Ron rightly says picked up on this and used his "stature' in the community as a figurehead for these incredible events. 'Robinson added, 'History will show that the next key player to become involved was myself [that is Malcolm Robinson] who assisted Billy in the collection of these ever-growing UFO reports. Now don't kid yourself readers, there was a phenomenon occurring here, that will never be in dispute. Accusations were levelled at both Billy and I of, dare I say it, "creating" this whole wave of reports, (try telling that to the independent witnesses!!) Readers nothing could be further from the truth. I researched Bonnybridge (and other nearby towns) with [*will* in the original but assume that was just a typo!] diligence and a desire to get to the truth. I followed the normal channels of Investigations, i.e. Airports, Police, Ministry of Defence, Met Offices, etc etc... I agree with Ron that the tabloid press had a field day with Bonnybridge, and they helped along and built up this incredible story. But to their credit the press did bring forward other witnesses, so we can at least thank them for that.' In conclusion Robinson noted, 'What angers me most is the silly press figures of UFO sightings in and around Bonnybridge, from around 2,000 reports it's now, I believe, went [sic] up to 8,000 reports. What nonsense don't believe a word of it. My own research has shown to me, that the true figures of bona fide UFO reports which I cannot shift, lies between 300 to 350 reports, and you can take that to the bank!'

I believe that the above article represents Malcolm Robinson's view of Bonnybridge up to the present. There were some individuals who suggested that Malcolm and I were in a dogfight over Bonnybridge. This was far from being the case. I had and have, great respect from Robinson's diligence in investigating UFO reports. In fact, he's probably the most determined Ufologist around in attempting to get to the truth of any sighting that is reported to him. There were areas of agreement and disagreement between us, however. We both accepted that the number of UFO reports in the area were at a higher than expected level given the population base. Furthermore, significant video and photographic evidence had been produced to support eyewitness reports. I would agree without hesitation that 'something' out of the ordinary was going on. But where I would have an issue is in the number of reports that Robinson claimed at the time, that is the figure of 300 to 350 even though this was well below numbers being bandied about and appeared a more realistic estimate.

How many UFO reports?

As I mentioned, earlier, in 'The Scottish UFO Casebook' (published 2022) author Steve Hammond compiled UFO reports from across Scotland for the 1990s which also, of course, covers the Bonnybridge 'hotspot years'. Hammond gives a total of 177 Scottish sightings for this period (the 1990s). The list was gathered from various sources, but a significant base consisted of reports printed in the press and so any press coverage of Bonnybridge sightings should have been included.

In 'UFO Case Files of Scotland' published in 2009 and authored by Malcolm Robinson 37 cases from the Bonnybridge area are referred to. When I set up the 'UFO Hotline' I was certainly inundated with calls, so many that it was impossible to follow them all up without an army of helpers, so I can confirm that Bonnybridge was a 'phenomenon' but I would be talking of dozens of reports rather than hundreds. And certainly not thousands. But this for me adds to the intriguing nature of the Bonnybridge UFO epidemic. Just what was going on? A real mystery.

Finally, to dispel any suggestion that Malcolm Robinson and I were at loggerheads I'll reveal correspondence between us. After the tragic Dunblane shooting of 1996 Malcolm decided to retire from UFO activity. He circulated a letter saying, *'I write to inform you that as from the date stated above [16th March 1996] I shall no longer be having any involvement with the subject known as UFOs, ghosts, poltergeists and associated paranormal phenomena... My main reason for this decision is in the light of the recent Dunblane tragedy.'* I, of course, was taken aback by Malcolm's decision writing to him, 'I was stunned by what you had to say. I know probably more than most how much SPI has meant to you...We have had our differences, but I have no wish to see SPI come to an end or you to stop your involvement with the paranormal.' For some months thereafter Malcolm Robinson forwarded to me letters he had received detailing UFO reports to follow up. I would also note that Billy Buchanan and I resolved our differences, and he invited me to take part in a TV broadcast outside Bonnybridge which I was delighted to be involved in with him. It was harmony restored. Furthermore, as one of the organisers of the 'Scottish UFO and Paranormal Conference' I was delighted that Billy Buchanan agreed to be the conference host for several events and also gave a talk on Bonnybridge on one occasion.

However, as the basis for the fame of Bonnybridge is based on the claimed number of UFO reports I thinks it's essential to look at the cases reviewed by writers who have covered events in the area. Principal, of course, is Malcolm Robinson who covered Bonnybridge in his 2009 book, 'UFO Case Files of Scotland', as I have previously mentioned. For ease of summarising, I have listed these later in the book and in the text have focused on the conclusions drawn from them. In total, Malcolm lists 47 cases. Nine of these predate the 1990s so we are left with 38 cases for the crucial period 1990 to 1996 an average of under 6 cases per year. Broken down by year: 1990 (1 report): 1992 (7 reports): 1993 (3 reports): 1994 (8 reports): 1995 (14 reports): 1996 (3 reports) and two cases undated.

For comparison, I examined the data gathered by author Steve Hammond in 'The Scottish UFO Casebook' in connection with Bonnybridge in the 1990s. It should be noted that Hammond does not necessarily give the name of the individual or individuals linked to the sighting he records, but he does, importantly, give the source. From this compilation we come to a surprising conclusion. [Please note that once again for ease of summarising I have listed the cases involved towards the end of the book]. If we take the evidence for the core area and dates Hammond has given, he provides a total of ten cases. A reader who knew nothing of the 'Bonnybridge Phenomenon' might wonder how it became such a world hot spot on such a limited number of sightings. But Hammond has focused on, as I have indicated, cases from the core area, that is places closest to Bonnybridge which partially explains why the number of sightings he lists does not look particularly remarkable. Furthermore, some cases did not necessarily appear in the press or in published books so might not have been included.

There is one final important source. In his book, 'Zones of Strangeness: An examination of Paranormal and UFO Hot Spots', writer Peter A. McCue devotes a chapter (and references elsewhere) to 'The Bonnybridge UFO Phenomena' (pp281-302). Once again, I have listed the cases he mentions later on in the text and will deal here with my conclusion. McCue refers to twenty-four cases in connection with the Bonnybridge phenomenon. Of the cases covered seventeen occurred in the core period of the 1990s. McCue, of course, isn't attempting a comprehensive survey of Bonnybridge UFOs and his chapter on the subject is only one in a lengthy book which covers a variety of phenomena. He gives an excellent summary of the overall events with a clear assessment of the UFO cases he examines. However, McCue's reasoned account suggests that the thousands of Bonnybridge sightings claimed by some is well short of the mark.

In my own book, 'UFO Scotland', which covers the history of the UFO phenomenon from 1947 onwards I gave Bonnybridge a significant amount of coverage both in individual witness reports and in a discussion of the path by which the village had become a world 'hot spot'. I reviewed eleven cases in total which were the ones I judged were of the most significance. I could, of course, have included several more, but as it was a book which covered the whole of Scotland and the complete period between 1947 to 1997 Bonnybridge was allocated a reasonable amount of space which included a fairly extensive discussion of Bonnybridge's ascent to 'stardom'.

I hope readers won't feel that I've laboured the point. I believe it is justified to deal with it in depth as the reputation of Bonnybridge as a UFO hotspot rests on the claimed spectacular number of sightings of potential alien craft. Nick Pope published the massive figure of 8,000 UFOs reported. Councillor Billy Buchanan - the individual at the centre of events - gave various estimates from 2,000 upwards. Malcolm Robinson eventually came to a more realistic, I suggest, figure of 250 to 300 cases. However, in his coverage of the Bonnybridge events in his 2009 publication 'UFO Case of Scotland', Robinson covers only a small proportion of this number, that is around 12 percent if we base this on the upper number of three hundred UFO reports he suggests.

However, claims of even several hundred sightings are pure speculation and we can only make an assessment based on known, that is recorded sightings. But Robinson is surely correct in indicating that the number of sightings was well over the thirty-eight he describes. I can testify via the phone calls that came in through the 'hot line' that there were, at least, several dozen more which it was nigh on impossible with the resources available to follow up. The cases listed in the later section, therefore, are those in which the report was investigated and details corroborated. This, in my view, is the appropriate way to proceed though some cases may have unfortunately not made it to the published literature or grabbed media attention. Thirty-eight documented cases in a period of seven years suggests a fair degree of UFO activity, but is it enough to justify the term 'Bonnybridge Phenomenon'? Was, in fact, the phenomenon the volume of UFO reports or the level of interest generated in Bonnybridge? A large number of UFO reports were in anyone's book at a low level, that is vaguely defined or at a distance. The typical UFO sighting of a strange light in the sky constituted the vast majority of sightings. The best video evidence in particular the Barry McDonald video hit the media in 1996 well after Bonnybridge gained its reputation as a world hotspot. Why Bonnybridge? It mystifies me too. Furthermore, as a survey of the above sightings demonstrates the vast majority of sightings came from areas admittedly close to but outside the village of Bonnybridge itself. But it is Bonnybridge which will forever be associated with the UFO flap. You can only come back to the association of Councillor Billy Buchanan to Bonnybridge which made the village the focus of media attention.

Councillor Billy Buchanan inquiry: An attempt to get to the core of the mystery

By October 1994 events had reached such a pitch that councillor Billy Buchanan supported by investigator Malcolm Robinson had asked Prime Minister of the time John Major to launch a 'top level probe' into the Bonnybridge sightings. Buchanan also asked Dennis Canavan the Member of Parliament for Falkirk West to raise the issue of Bonnybridge UFOS in the House of Commons. It was said that Bonnybridge residents had become a 'laughing stock' for reporting so many UFO sightings. Billy Buchanan was quoted as saying that the people of Bonnybridge were 'sick and tired of being branded a bunch of cranks' pointing out that UFO reports were continuing to come in. It was for this reason - looking for an answer to the phenomenon - that Buchanan petitioned John Major to 'order a top level inquiry'.

The attempt to involve the government wasn't 'out of the box'. In fact, in the United States various 'projects' had been set up to investigate the UFO phenomenon. The arrival of the modern UFO phenomenon is generally dated to 24 June 1947 when Kenneth Arnold flying his plane over the Cascade Mountains in USA's Idaho state spotted nine strange objects flying at speed. He didn't, incidentally, describe them as 'flying saucers' it was a term coined by the media. But for whatever reason, Arnold's sighting caused a sensation, and the UFO phenomenon was put firmly on the map. But was it all fantasy? The United States Airforce didn't seem to think so as by September 1947 they had set up 'Project Sign' which explicitly stated that, 'It is the opinion that ...the phenomenon reported is something real and not visionary or fictitious'. That seems clear enough. The Airforce was planning to investigate a phenomenon that was based in reality and not the product of witnesses' collective imagination. Not everyone in the military was happy with the establishment of 'Project Sign' and were openly sceptical of the reality of UFOs. As a result 'Project Sign' morphed into 'Project Grudge' in February 1949. This adopted a more sceptical approach to the subject but was still taking an interest in reported sightings and what they might be. The project lasted only a few months being ended in December of the same year on the basis that UFOs did not represent a threat to the USA as they could be explained by witnesses' misinterpretation of natural phenomena. That was the official line.

However, in March 1952 interest resurfaced with the initiation of the more famous 'Project Blue Book'. It has been described by some Ufologists as a 'cover-up job'. That is an attempt to discredit UFOs as a genuine phenomenon. Whatever the real reason it suggests that there was a continuing official interest in UFOs in the USA, particularly among the military, interest which has carried through to the present with congressional hearings into the subject and testimony from officials supporting the reality of the phenomenon. And no less a person than President Jimmy Carter wanted answers. In 1976 when he was a candidate for the presidency he stated, 'If I become president, I'll make every piece of information this country has about UFOs available to the public and scientists. I am convinced that UFOs exist. I have seen them'. The fact that he never managed to put these words into practice speaks volumes on the limits of presidential power and the influence of the military among other more shadowy organisations.

The USA was not alone in its interest in UFOs. In February 1959 the Royal Canadian Air Force set up a procedure in co-operation with the US Airforce to share information on UFO sightings. Maybe the public are unaware of the close links between the USA military and Britain. Information is shared on a daily basis so it's more than likely UFO reports coming in over British controlled airspace were passed to the USA. And the same could be true of those European countries linked in the North Atlantic Treaty Organisation - NATO. Information on incursions into NATO airspace are routinely shared.

The evidence suggests that the Western powers are and have been interested in the UFO phenomenon since day one. The UK's Ministry of Defence denied for decades they took

UFO sightings seriously before finally owning up to recording them and then releasing those reports that had been gathered. So, the attempt by Buchanan and Robinson to press the government to investigate events in Bonnybridge could have born fruit. You would think that given what was happening a committee of inquiry could have at least shed some light on the matter. However, it has been claimed that governments including our own are well aware of the facts behind the UFO phenomenon but simply don't want to share information with the general public secrecy being second nature to the ruling elites. According to retired major David Grusch in his testimony before the US Congress the US government has been aware of 'non-human' activity since 1930s. Evidence, of course, denied by the Pentagon. It's interesting to note that as far back as 18th January 1979 the House of Lords debated the subject of UFOs. At 7.07pm on that day the Earl of Clancarty opened the discussion by drawing attention to what he claimed was an increase across the world of sightings and landings of UFOs and, as a result, the need for international government cooperation. According to Lord Rankeillour, 'France leads the way in UFO research. It has followed up sightings with police teams, scientists, and scholars and since 1950, the *Deuxieme Bureau* of the army.' Did the UK ever embark on a similar investigation? We will probably never be told. It took decades for the Ministry of Defence to admit they were recording UFO sightings and have never admitted to any more detailed interest on the basis that there's no evidence that UFOs pose a threat to national security. You wonder how they can be so sure. Do they know something we don't?

CHAPTER FOUR
IN FULL SWING - THE IMPACT OF VIDEO EVIDENCE

The Margaret Ross Video

In his book 'UFO Landings UK' (2022) Philip Mantle makes the point that UFO researchers in general come to recognise that, as he did, you 'quickly learned that the vast majority of UFO sightings had a conventional explanation. Stars, planets, aircraft, birds and balloons...'. But Mantle then goes on to point out that some incidents can be designated as ones of 'High Strangeness' and gives as an example UFOs that have landed. In the case of Bonnybridge I would suggest that incidents of 'high strangeness' are the large volume of video footage that was taken.

By 1996 I'd been following events at Bonnybridge for several years. However, I had not organised a large-scale sky watch in the area. The opportunity arose to coordinate with interested groups across Scotland and to carry out an extensive joint survey of the skies for any possible UFO incursions. As various newspapers reported, for example, the 'Edinburgh Evening News', and 'Dundee Courier' the 'Scottish Earth Mysteries Research' organisation (of which I was chairman at the time) were arranging various sky watches to take place on the weekend of 16 August 1996. As the papers noted the 'largest vigil will be held at Bonnybridge' which as the Dundee Courier noted 'has already been dubbed the UFO capital of Europe' with 'thousands of unexplained sightings in recent years'. So even by 1996, four years after the initial reports hit the media, the Bonnybridge phenomenon had certainly not run out of steam. In fact, events were to reignite and propel the village into another burst of intense public interest.

On the 14th of October 1996 the 'Sun' newspaper headline reported, ' UF [sic] Got The Greatest Ever film of a flying saucer'. The account told of the experience of 63-year-old Margaret Ross who lived in Stenhousemuir a couple of miles north of Bonnybridge. On her camcorder she had captured a series of pulsating lights hovering in the skies near her house. She had first spotted the object on 27th September and managed to video the UFO. As she watched the mystery object changed to a half-moon shape. An image taken from the video shows a series of bars across the moon image, at a diagonal, glowing intensely. After rotating and changing shape, it shot towards the nearby town of Linlithgow, so moving in an eastwards direction. In an odd coincidence, Margaret's family who lived a couple of miles distant, alerted by Margaret, also witnessed the UFO and confirmed that the object changed shape as Margaret had described.

On one of my visits to Margaret's house I did see one of the objects that she had videoed though it was difficult to make out exactly what it was. Nevertheless, it was proof for me that Margaret had captured on film an object which definitely appeared out of the ordinary. The UFO could not be instantly dismissed and was certainly a sighting that required some investigation. However, it has to be accepted that camcorders can distort objects, particularly at night with a limited light source and when that object is at a distance. So video footage requires expert assessment to make sure that we are not viewing an obviously identifiable object which the camera has distorted in some way. Margaret's sightings sparked wide interest. Various news outlets covered it including the 'Dundee Courier' and 'Daily Mail' with comments from several UFO 'experts'. Reportedly, I said, 'it is one of the best footage I have seen from anywhere in the world. Such a length of footage is very unusual.' Ken Higgins, chairman of 'Scottish Research Into UFOS' who I worked with on various cases was also reportedly impressed by the video footage. The footage was passed to the late Archie Roy, a former Professor of Physics at Glasgow University and a recognised authority on the supernatural who commented, 'Around 92% of sightings can be easily explained, but this is one of the 8% which science cannot recognise.' Coming from a well-known physicist this was significant backing for the Ross video. So, it seemed that Margaret Ross had filmed a genuine UFO and this had a significant impact on how the public viewed the Bonnybridge phenomenon. It was not simply a figment of the collective imagine, but an event worthy of investigation. Margaret's video evidence in addition aroused the interest of both the BBC and STV and I took part in recordings at Margaret's house which were broadcast on Scotland's main tv news bulletins. One aspect which I found curious was the slightly different versions of the Ross video story that appeared in the press. The 'Sunday Mail' of 5th May 1996 featured Margaret's experience with still photos taken from her video which revealed a round object of various colours and five stripes across it. It quoted Margaret as having been sure that 'aliens' had been watching her and she had hidden behind her bedroom curtains as a result. However, on the occasions I spoke to Margaret, while in her house or on the phone, she at no point expressed any fears about the UFO sightings she'd filmed and, on the contrary, confirmed that she had been more excited than anything else about her experience. Her husband, Alex, according to the article, confirmed that he too had seen the object. They'd spotted it with the 'naked eye' as it was so prominent, and it was this initial sighting that led to Margaret's determination to video the UFO. Meanwhile, as described in the 'Daily Mail' of 14th October 1996 the video showed a pulsating bright object in a clear sky south of Margaret's house. According to this account the UFO stood still for fifteen minutes then transformed into a half-moon shape crossed by four diagonal bars which exhibited a brightness of high intensity. The UFO disappeared after 40 minutes. Margaret told the paper that she had risen at 6am and having looked out of her window saw what she described as a giant snowball sitting in the sky. As she watched, according to the report, the edges of the 'snowball' became pointed, but the object didn't move though it started to pulsate. After several minutes it changed to a half circle shape and four diagonal stripes appeared. Margaret was reported as saying that she was convinced it wasn't a star, or a plane or a helicopter.

Meanwhile, the 'Dundee Courier' also of 14th October 1996 carried a similar account though it referred to Mrs. Ross of Falkirk (rather than Stenhousemuir or Larbert). It reported that she had captured startling pictures on her camcorder from her bedroom window, but said this was at daybreak rather than at a specific time. It also mentioned a pulsating object in a clear sky to the south of her home. It further confirmed that the 'snowball' was far bigger than, and brighter than a star and had remained stationary for fifteen minutes. I don't want to labour the point and it's possible that information was passed to the papers from a single source, but I've included these reports because they chimed with the account Margaret gave me when I interviewed her face to face. She didn't deviate from the story she gave to me and to the various reporters who spoke to her or in her account she gave on television. There was no doubt that Margaret genuinely believed that she had captured on film something quite extraordinary. As any UFO investigator should be I was, of course, cautious. It's a well-known fact among researchers into the phenomenon that a very high proportion of UFO sightings are misidentifications of everyday objects. I once drove for a couple of hours to see a video of an alleged UFO to realise within seconds that what had been filmed was simply the planet Venus. Ouch! I've heard similar tales from other investigators. So, footage has to undergo proper examination and evaluation. I absolutely respected the opinion of Professor Archie Roy, but for my own sake I requested expert analysis from audio-visual consultant, John Morrison. John's assessment of the footage is given in full below.

John Morrison Reviews of Margaret Ross videos

The details below are direct quotes from John's evaluation of the Margaret Ross video:

'A bright object is certainly being filmed which may be in the sky although it could be a spotlight from a high building in the distance. A range of different colours are visible through, white, green, red and a cyan [greenish-blue] type colour'.

'Object appears stationary and does not appear to perform any aerodynamic manoeuvres'.

'The object does not appear to rotate about its axis or bank left or right to any noticeable degree'.

'The object does not appear to have conventional flashing strobes as seen on all commercial/military aircraft, also no lit windows are seen which could be used to identify an airliner'.

'The object is in my opinion too far from the camera to make any further analysis worthwhile, but that is not to say the object is of no interest'.

'The photographs which were published in the local/national press show a de-focused image of the light source and cannot be taken as the actual shape of the object/light which was filmed. De-focused images continue to be published by various magazines/newspapers under the premise of being the UFOs' actual shape.'

Of course, Margaret Ross produced more than one section of video footage though this might not have been clear from reports in the press. Below is John's second by second analysis of more UFOs Margaret captured on her camcorder. This review referred to one filmed on 26th September 1996 at 6am which lasted for 21 minutes and 59 seconds (figures on the left give the video timings):

0:00:00 Start of footage. 'Object appears to be moving out of shot, to the right'.

0:03:10 New sequence. 'Object in middle of screen and apparently closer to camera and possibly twice as near as in last sequence or [a] possible use of [the] zoom'.

0:03:41 'A violet glow appears below the object. The glow seems to alter in intensity. Coloured red and white jets/exhaust seem to be visible exiting the underside of the object. A red flash is sometimes observed coming from the sides of the object. The flash only lasts for approximately 1/25th of a second, also the time interval is not constant as an aircraft strobe light would be'.

0:09:27 'The object appears to be in focus up to this point. Object then appears to change into triangle type shape & then vanishes very quickly'.

0:10:07 New sequence begins.

0:11:04 (audio) 'Dog barking in background'.

0:12:06 'Object emits a red flash of light. 6 frames after the red flash a jet of greenish/white exhaust or light is ejected from the underside of the object'.

0:12:28 'Camera de-focuses to reveal a half-moon type shape. Lots of moving about of the camera before the start of the next sequence'.

0:13:58 Start of new sequence.

0:14:40 'Object becomes triangle shape again. Red and green flashes are visible beneath the object'.

0:15:27 'Object is de-focused again'.

0:20:06 'Break in sequence/new sequence. Now image and background are brighter, possibly due to this sequence being filmed when the sky was brighter or possibly due to the gain control being used on the video camera'.

0:21:50 End of footage.

John's conclusion was, 'This video footage is almost exactly the same as that shot on the 27th of April 1996, also by Margaret Ross. The only difference being the triangle shape and the clarity of the defocused portion of the footage. Again, it was a de-focused image that was printed in the newspapers/magazines. A little research by these publishers could have told them it was a de-focused image and not the true shape of the unidentified object. This video is more interesting than the last due to the triangle image which appears, but it is still too far away to make any sort of judgement on what it actually is, but once again I do not believe it is a conventional aircraft as no standard aircraft strobes are visible and no standard aircraft lighting patterns are visible. Several colours and bursts of colours are indeed visible, as are the coloured 'jets' beneath the objects. Colours visible are white, red, blue and a white with a slight red tinge. There is certainly some object there, but due to its distance, it is impossible to determine exactly what it is.

Report prepared by John Morrison on 12th February 1997[.]'

[My thanks to John Morrison for permission to quote all of the above]

John produced excellent reports which I believe is an important reminder to UFO investigators of the difficulty of assessing video evidence particularly when taken at night. But if it was a UFO or alien craft, what was it doing in this area?

Crop Circle: A Possible Connection

The Margaret Ross sighting raised several issues. One that didn't come up at the time and only struck me later was an incident that had occurred a few years earlier. Margaret had mentioned that the UFO had headed in the direction of the nearby town of Linlithgow. In July 1992 I investigated a crop circle which appeared in a barley field on Bonnyton farm beside Linlithgow Loch. According to the 'Lothian Courier' farmer Michael Clark, a long-time resident, commented, 'We get it in that field every year'. However, there has been some suggestion that the appearance of crop circles is related to the UFO phenomenon and even that it marks the spot where a spacecraft shaped object has either landed or hovered. I'm not arguing for that explanation as there have been many suggestions as to what causes the appearance of crop circles. I simply mention UFOs as a possible link, but it could of course be a simple coincidence.

Barry McDonald Video: the evidence piles up

A little more than a week after Margaret Ross's sightings hit the headlines the media were reporting even more dramatic footage. And this time taken in broad daylight by twenty-seven-year-old Barry McDonald of Hallglen, an area a few miles to the east of Bonnybridge. Barry accompanied by Jane Adamson were driving towards the Camelon district of Falkirk when according to Barry he,' suddenly saw a bright light in the sky ahead.' The UFO seemed to be hovering in the area between Falkirk and Grangemouth. Video and still footage of the object revealed a distinct saucer shape. The UFO then turned orange in colour - perhaps building up speed to move - then turned white again and disappeared. It either did this by travelling at a fantastic speed or alternatively by some kind of masking process which hid it from human view. In theory, therefore, the object could have been there for some time and only inadvertently or by design revealed itself. There were some who voiced the view that given the large number of UFO sightings in the area there might have been a 'mother ship' in the vicinity.

In other words, a large craft circulating the Earth from which smaller UFOs were emerging to explore. So, it could have been the 'mother ship' that had appeared on the McDonald footage. One odd thing was that Scottish Air Traffic Control at Prestwick reported that they had received no reports of unusual activity. But what does 'unusual' mean in this context. Had they been expecting this? Were they aware of similar activity in the area? Had advanced alien technology simply prevented the UFO registering on our less sophisticated instruments? All of these were potential solutions to the mystery.

Barry's video of the UFO lasted no more than thirty seconds. Nowhere near long enough to come to a definite conclusion, but bright and clear enough to confirm that some indefinable presence had been caught on camera. The media certainly thought so. Sky news gathered Barry and me into a van which then rushed us both to their then Edinburgh studio before any other news organisation could get hold of us! Barry's footage was then broadcast to millions world-wide allowing a vast audience to bear witness to the amazing encounters that were being captured on film at the Bonnybridge hot spot. One issue that requires clarification in relation to the McDonald video is the timing of the incident. In 'UFO Scotland' (published in 1998) I gave it as 6.40pm. The same time was given in the 'Falkirk Herald' newspaper. However, on October 15 when the UFO was filmed sunset would have taken place at 6.15pm, but the still taken from the video appears to show an object filmed in good daylight. I cannot at the time of writing locate the original notes of my interview with Barry. And I now wonder if by a slip of the timing 16.40 (i.e. 4.40pm) became 6.40pm. The timing of 4.40pm would make more sense given the amount of daylight that appeared in the published photo.

My re-assessment of this is possibly confirmed by Barry's comments in the 'Sun' newspaper that, 'It was still daylight...'. Furthermore, as stated above, although the actual tape is no more than 30 seconds long Barry reported that they 'watched it for twenty minutes' before he remembered that he had his camcorder in the boot of the car and captured the UFO on film. Barry commented that though he had watched the video nearly one hundred times he was baffled as to what it was. Tellingly, he said that before this event he had considered UFOs as a load of nonsense. It often takes an actual experience to convince a person of the reality of the phenomenon.

I was reported as saying that Scottish Earth Mysterious Research, the organisation I chaired, would carry out a 'deeper analysis of the tape' and that I had ruled out the usual explanations such as 'weather balloons, stars, aircraft and helicopters'. So, it may reasonably be asked, 'where is the deeper analysis'? Unfortunately, it never happened. Although I had of course viewed the tape I was not able to get hold of a copy for further investigation and the video, it has to be said, had become quite a prized item and appeared on various TV programmes. So, unfortunately, at the time of writing I've no idea where it ended up! So, two pieces of video footage undoubtedly intriguing, but unfortunately not definitive shots of an alien craft achieved a major blitz of publicity because of the association with the village of Bonnybridge. The village by now almost had a touch of magic about it so anything out of the ordinary connected to it seemed to be guaranteed media interest. But in terms of UFO sightings there was more, much more.

Craig Malcolm interviewed by the 'Scotsman' newspaper reported that over the previous fifteen years he had compiled eighteen hours of video footage which he believed proved that something hard to explain was taking place in the Falkirk area. Craig did allow me to view some of the film which certainly did capture several odd UFOs in the area, sightings which were hard to explain away as natural objects. Craig was reported as saying that he had his first UFO sighting in 1991 which he described as a disc shaped object, but since then had seen UFOs in a variety of shapes including tubes, cigar-like, spheres, and even ones shaped like triangles. These sightings reflect my own experience of investigating the phenomenon, including Bonnybridge, that there's no single UFO design. There's a rich mixture of UFO types. Craig Malcolm indicated that his footage had been sent to the 'Search for Extraterrestrial Intelligence' (SETI) in the USA which, he said, had confirmed that as high a level as 90% of the objects captured were genuine UFOs. This is an extraordinarily high number so worth noting when evaluating the Bonnybridge phenomenon. The standard belief among UFO investigators is that possibly as many as 95% of UFO sightings are misidentifications of natural objects. Perhaps this figure needs to be seriously reconsidered.

CHAPTER FIVE
CAN WE EXPLAIN THE
BONNYBRIDGE PHENOMENON?

So where did the Bonnybridge phenomenon come from? Can we believe that it sprung apparently out of nowhere? Did its roots lie a lot earlier than is believed? And can we isolate it from the Scottish UFO scene as a whole?

It has to be admitted that it is difficult to determine exactly where the UFO Barry McDonald filmed was hovering. There were some claims it could be over Grangemouth rather than Falkirk. This is interesting because in the previous year 1995 there had occurred a well-documented UFO sighting. Often UFO sightings involve one witness, but in this instance seven people claimed to have spotted several unidentified flying objects. These objects were first spotted at 5.40 am when a group of cleaners including Beatrice Campbell heading to work at the Union Chemical Factory at Carronshore observed a large object with an orange glow accompanied by four smaller ones which were sparkling on and off. In a startling follow up the larger UFO sent beams of light to the smaller objects. Could this have been a form of communication?

Another witness Diane Keating from Camelon, described seeing from the window in her home at 7pm a ball shaped object with a reddish colour which appeared to be surrounded by a heat haze. This UFO appeared to be hovering, disappeared for a few minutes then reappeared. The witness was convinced that it was not a plane as she saw one fly under the mystery object. So it must have been a considerable height above the ground. Two factory workers walking towards the nearby village of Stenhousemuir also witnessed an odd object. This time the UFO was described as having a bright white colour and travelling at speed in the direction of Callendar Park a local recreation area. It then returned and started to glow an orange colour. According to the witnesses it was travelling very fast much faster than an airplane. In fact, it's impossible to describe even a majority of UFO reports that came in, but those described below can give a flavour of the events that were occurring.

A double page spread in the 'Daily Record' of 26th April 1995 (the headline: 'Beam me up Bonnybridge') carried a report about 73-year-old William Bestall who lived in a high rise flat in Falkirk. Mr Bestall claimed that he had observed a very bright light over the town of Cumbernauld which is situated about 21 miles away by road though nearer as the crow flies. As the light moved closer Mr Bestall realised that there were in fact two separate lights. Both objects stopped and hovered close to the flat before moving away. The incident had a significant impact on Mr Bestall who commented that he was a sceptic before this encounter. It should be noted that there is an airport in Cumbernauld but on this occasion it's hard to use this as an explanation as the lights seen came so close to the high-rise flats. The same article also carried a report of two boys who said they had taken a photo of a UFO over Grangemouth. The incident occurred when a bright light burst through the cloudy sky terrifying the lads who dropped to the ground but managed to snap a photo of a UFO. According to the 'Daily Record' 'the photo...has baffled the world's experts.' I have never viewed the photo but given that the snap was taken in 1992 years before the advent of mobile phones with camera capability I'm unclear as to how the photo could have been taken unless the boys had a video camera which doesn't appear to be the case. As far as I'm aware no more was heard of this particular photo although given it was taken at night it might in any event be hard to identify the object that had been captured.

On 10th November 1992 a male witness reported seeing a blueish white light in the sky. It was, he said, very bright then disappeared behind a cloud. In one of those curiosities the witness reported that a colleague had seen a light the night before but thought the chap had made up the story for the papers! A warning to UFO investigators to take a cautious approach to alleged sightings of unidentified objects! Another sighting in November 1992, which was subsequently reported in the 'Stirling Observer', involved Bonnybridge farmer William Denholm who managed to film a strange light hovering in the sky. The footage was going to be analysed, but it's unclear whether anything that couldn't be explained as other than a natural object was discovered. Whether it did or not the incident fed into the melting pot all of which helped to produce the 'Bonnybridge Phenomenon'.

On 24th October 1996 Catherine Penman of Hallglen witnessed an unexplained light above her home. The object was first spotted by her husband, Scott, who came out of the garden shed to report to his wife that he believed a UFO was hovering in the sky. According to Catherine the light was very bright, low down, several times brighter than a star and very close to the house. She watched the UFO for two hours and when it moved, she contacted the police to report the sighting as she was convinced that it couldn't be either a plane or helicopter because of the length of time it had been sitting there. When the police initially responded to Catherine's call they couldn't see the object. However, a few hours later the light was spotted by their close-circuit cameras when they zoomed in on the Hallglen area. This, allegedly, sparked a UFO alert as even the police were, apparently, baffled by the object their cameras had captured and were carefully examining the footage. More sightings of unidentified objects emerged. In August a family in Stenhousemuir were astonished to see a 'brightly coloured object' hovering in the sky towards the town of Denny. In early October a postal worker watched a 'mystery object' which was also hanging in the sky near Denny. Could it have been the same UFO on a return trip? Then on November 11th, 1992, a witness reported seeing two prominent white lights moving slowly in his direction from the Greenhill area in Bonnybridge. As he watched the progress of the UFOs he heard a humming noise. The mystery object which had a small light on its top rocked from side to side then disappeared.

Two months earlier on 20th September 1992 Steven Wilson was driving from Whitecross to Maddison, a village located close to Bonnybridge, when he and a friend who was with him observed in a field beside a housing estate a hovering object. It struck them as odd and out of place. They described the UFO as oval in shape and coloured red. The object made no noise that they were aware of even when it suddenly shot upwards and disappeared all within a matter of seconds.

Then more video footage made an appearance. This was taken by a witness living in Falkirk on Thursday 27th November 1996. According to the account given he left his house around 4pm then walked to Muiravonside Country Park. It was from this location that he filmed two strange objects. The witness watched a plane fly over and noted that you could clearly hear its engines and see the strobe lights. Not long after the plane had passed, however, a more mysterious object appeared. It was round in shape and was hovering over the hills at Torphichen, in the direction of the town of Bathgate in West Lothian. The object doubled in size and gave off a brilliant whiteness. It changed its shape from round to oval. A second object appeared higher up about a quarter mile southwest of the first object which then descended till it was level with the first object. Both objects were of similar brightness. The first object slowly moved away and vanished as if a light switch had been turned off. Meanwhile the second object continued hovering, but then it became increasingly bright till it shone a brilliant white. At the same time, it changed shape then moved away to the southwest and vanished in a split second. You immediately think that the answer could be 'aeroplane lights' which might seem an obvious explanation, but these were apparently ruled out as no known flights were in the vicinity at that time. But to go back to the beginning. There are various accounts of how the Bonnybridge phenomenon got underway. But certainly, it appears to centre round the person of councillor Billy Buchanan. It could be that the sighting by Jim Walker may, in fact, have been the first report that came to the attention of Councillor Buchanan. However, the most frequently cited incident, the one that sparked it all off was that involving Mr George Wilson, a local carpenter by trade. It was Wilson who knocking at Buchanan's door one evening told him that he had seen a UFO hovering over a nearby road and observed it for as long as ten minutes before it shot off. Buchanan got in touch with the local press looking for any other eye-witnesses and so George Wilson's encounter appeared in the 'Falkirk Herald'. The report appears to have been a significant trigger in sparking wide interest in Bonnybridge as a potential UFO 'hot spot'. Oddly, the' Falkirk Herald' showed less interest in Bonnybridge

UFO reports than the tabloids in the early stages and the paper's first mention of any sightings did not appear until the 12th of November 1992 edition. It appeared under the headline: 'Close encounters: witnesses tell of seeing unidentified flying objects'. This article referred to the encounter experienced by a mother and her daughter. The two had observed a strange object hovering over bleak moorland as they headed to their home in Kincardine, a small village on the banks of the Forth estuary but on the north side rather than the southern area where Bonnybridge lies. Mrs. Barbara Stocks accompanied by her thirteen-year-old daughter had observed an odd shaped object low down in the sky. It was described as a large red and white triangle with dotted lights. Mrs. Stocks compared it as similar to the gable end of a house with Christmas illuminations. A word of caution may apply as the area is close to the flight path of planes landing at Edinburgh airport, but on the other hand familiarity with planes in the area would allow witnesses to identify an object which appeared as out-of-the-ordinary.

But clearly the report was only one among many. To take another incident, Mr. Allan Cassie, a forty-year-old bricklayer along with his 14-year-old twins Leona and Allan (Junior) had caught sight of a strange glowing shape over Bonnybridge. His wife Bridie was of the view that it didn't appear to be either a plane or helicopter. Allan, senior, had first noticed the object because it wasn't moving. In other words, it appeared to be the classic hovering UFO experienced by so many witnesses to the phenomenon. Meanwhile another witness, a businessman who declined to be identified, described his encounter. It had happened around 10pm at night when he had been driving on the high road linking Falkirk and Bonnybridge and spotted a very bright light in the sky. The light didn't seem to be moving, but as he drove nearer it shone ever more brightly. By now he realised it was a cluster of lights but with no obvious shape. When the witness was only a few hundred yards from the object he stopped the car and got out to get a better look, but the object moved off in a different direction. It did occur to the witness that it might be a helicopter, but he reported no noise except a low hum.

One aspect of the developing Bonnybridge phenomenon that

surprised me was that it took the local press up to November 1992 to report the famous encounter of the Slogget family which had occurred as far back as March 1992. This incident earned almost mythical status as the origin of the whole Bonnybridge UFO legend even though it wasn't the event that triggered councillor Billy Buchanan's involvement. The Sloggett incident took place at around 7pm as several members of the family mother, brother and sister were out for a walk along country roads between Hallglen and Bonnybridge. Carole Sloggett reported that 'something' seemed to land on the moors and as they approached the spot a blue light filled the road. They heard a door open, what sounded like chains being rattled and a howling sound. She described a vehicle like a Tonka toy emerging from the wood and a giant flash of light. She got the impression they were being photographed. It was clearly a frightening experience though exactly what had happened seems mystifying. Had a spacecraft landed? Was the family being snapped? Why would aliens want to photo them? Was it simply a coincidence of straightforward incidents that somehow combined to create what appeared to be an otherworldly experience? It might be apart from the appearance of the blue light which has convinced me that something supernatural had in fact taken place. I think that it's interesting that while Buchanan was later lambasted for generating 'UFO Bonnybridge' he was not mentioned in this early article which is further evidence that the events were underway before he became significantly involved and adds credence to his explanation that he only acted in response to witnesses approaching him with their sightings.

    By December 1992 the 'Falkirk Herald' had wholeheartedly taken up the UFO theme perhaps spurred on by the interest being displayed by the national press and by television. The paper observed that reports were coming in not only from Bonnybridge but from other areas including Denny and Falkirk. And this spread of sightings across the Falkirk district was certainly a continuing theme. Norman Robb and Dan Dobbie on their way to Brockville the home of Falkirk football club (nicknamed 'The Bairns') spotted as they drove down Ochiltree Avenue a huge object described as having red and blue lights and a horizontal beam of exceptional brightness. Norman and Dan watched the UFO for five minutes and were convinced it wasn't a plane or helicopter. Then three nurses on their way to work also experienced a strange sighting. Mary Gardiner an auxiliary nurse described the object as emitting yellow, green and orange flashes. Rhona Bye made the fascinating observation that the UFO was spherical in shape but had spokes protruding from the sides. This is astonishing because it's a reminder of the object encountered by Bob Taylor in his famous 1979 encounter at Dechmont Law. Taylor described seeing what appeared like a second world war mine emerging from the hovering UFO he came across. I'm not aware of a similar object encountered nearby which makes the nurse's observation all the more interesting.

Subsequently, reports of UFOs flooded in. Near Christmas time Mark Wilson reported a cigar shaped UFO which followed his car even though he attempted to shake it off. The object seemed determined to follow Mark appearing no matter which way he drove till eventually it shot off. A disturbing though curious experience. What was the intention of the UFO in apparently pursuing Mark? Was it planning an abduction? But no abductions or attempted abductions were reported in this immediate area. Or was it no more than an interest in human activity? One more puzzle which at the moment we simply can't answer. In 1993 Ray and Cathy Procek on their way to Cumbernauld to visit friends caught sight of an object which Cathy, a school dinner lady at the time, described as 'an elliptical shape with bright lights around the edge'. As they drove under a viaduct, they opened the roof of their 'Space Cruiser' car and to their amazement spotted two identical craft both hovering silently and appearing triangular in shape. These and other eyewitness encounters helped to build a picture that Bonnybridge was a special place for UFO sightings. It boosted credibility in the existence of unidentified flying objects - whatever they might be - so that ever more witnesses were willing to come forward and report what they had seen no matter how extraordinary it appeared on the surface. And so the sightings continued to roll in.

In January 1995 a Bainsford hairdresser Mary Crozier

reported a strange, shaped UFO from the window of her home at Carronside Street at around 5am on a Thursday morning. Mary claimed she spotted an object which shone as brightly as floodlights on a football pitch. As she watched a bulge appeared on the side of the UFO and then a smokey ball of light emerged followed by another ball as if the UFO had been hatching these objects. The lights then merged and shortly after the sphere shot off. On the evening of 9th October 1996 two witnesses, brothers, watched a UFO carry out an amazing series of manoeuvres from their bedroom window in Falkirk. The men were looking towards the Westerglen TV mast located in Shieldhill when they became aware of a white light that appeared above the tree line. In an echo of the Mary Crozier sighting the light then split into three and each light moved off in a different direction, one to the east, one to the north and the other west. The light to the east stopped moving, hovered, and began to glow and pulsate. After a short period of time this light returned to its original spot and the other two lights also moved back to their original position. Curiously, the lights repeated these actions for several minutes then simply faded away. Was what followed simply coincidence? A helicopter appeared shining its searchlight and flew over the area where the UFOs had been active eventually disappearing from sight. It's hard to believe the arrival of the helicopter was pure coincidence. It's possible the UFOs had interfered with television transmission or whatever other secret communications the mast was being used for so the military were sent out to investigate.

As to the UFOs themselves, it's often been reported by witnesses that the object they see splits up which suggests that perhaps we are dealing with one main craft and that from that larger craft smaller ones are released. It's true that witnesses don't necessarily describe the objects as being of different sizes, but it is of course difficult to compare the bulk of objects particularly at a distance. It's interesting to note that following the Barry McDonald video there were suggestions that we could be dealing with a 'mother' ship out of which other UFOs were emerging. The appearance of strange balls of light was the most frequently reported UFO phenomenon of the 1990s - and that is in keeping with UFO sightings in general as reported from across the world. In December 1994, a woman from Grangemouth, Terry Harrington, was astonished to be confronted by a ball of light hovering outside her lounge window. Though she got a fright Terry managed to snap several photos of the object. It was also reported that she had seen a shuttle-like craft heading towards her house which then shot off. This incident was reported to and published by the 'Daily Record' newspaper. I didn't have the opportunity to interview Terry Harrington myself, but the sighting was certainly in line with other reported encounters. Apparently, the intention was to forward the photographs to experts in the United States for analysis. There were at the time and certainly are now plenty of experts in Scotland not to mention the UK who could have examined the snaps so it's unclear why they would have to go to the USA. However, in any case, this seems to have been the last that was heard of these photographs, so unfortunately, as too often happens, it's difficult to be sure as to exactly what was seen.

On 21st November 1997 a witness was driving along a single-track road in the vicinity of Bonnybridge when he was almost blinded by a sudden flash of a light blueish coloured light. Though puzzled the witness carried on driving, but then a second intense flash exploded over the top of the car. This was too much for the witness who now quite alarmed put the car into reverse and headed back the way he had come. It's noteworthy that as each flash erupted instruments on the dashboard reacted jerking rapidly back and forth. UFOs interfering in car electrics is regularly reported though there's no mention in this report of any strange object having been observed. The incident certainly occurred, however, as there was a passenger in the vehicle at the time who confirmed the substance of the event.

As UFO researchers are well aware many sightings occur in the evening or at night making it difficult to determine just what has been seen. However, a sighting on Monday 16th November 1998 took place during the daytime. The witness, Martin, was located on a hill in Camelon, near to Falkirk High railway station at around 1.30pm. From his vantage point he was able to look down over Falkirk and Grangemouth. He watched the steam from the power station forming clouds - a common and interesting sight - as they billowed up into the sky. This was an important observation as the object he saw left a vapour trail as it came down and this matched the height of the clouds formed from the power station. The UFO descended west to east, Martin calculated, at an angle of 5 degrees. It came down at a very fast rate, and, in Martin's judgement, took no more than one second to cover roughly 5 miles. The UFO shone a silvery colour which suggests it could have been metallic and also appeared orb shaped. In many ways Martin's sighting might be described as a typical UFO, at least in popular conception though in truth UFOs come in all shapes and sizes. But what was it doing around Grangemouth? I have attempted to answer this question later on in the book.

Meanwhile, video footage of unexplained objects continued to emerge. On this occasion I was fortunate to be able to examine the tape and interview the woman involved. The 'Falkirk Herald' of 22nd April 1999 carried a report of the event which demonstrated that the sighting was considered unusual even among so many reported incidents in the Bonnybridge area. Carol Brown of Wardlaw Place, Carronshore was the witness involved in this strange incident. Carol aged 24 at the time having walked into her bedroom had then caught sight of two orange lights shining brightly in the sky near her home. They were sitting side by side close to, but high above, an area called the Braes. Carol had the presence of mind to grab her camcorder and film the objects. As she watched one of the UFOs appeared to fade and then disappear. The other moved from side to side for around five minutes then also vanished. A few minutes later two more lights appeared in the exact same place. Both these later objects hovered for several minutes before disappearing. Could it have been the lights of an aeroplane? The intensity of the beams seemed to rule it out and, in any case, there were no known flights in the vicinity at the time, as it turned out. However, nothing can be ruled out so we can't jump to a judgement that here was an alien craft. As with so many sightings of bright objects in the sky we can only label it 'unexplained'. The fate of many strange encounters. As UFO investigators are well aware witnesses to sightings come from all kinds of backgrounds. A university lecturer, who worked at Stirling University at the same time that I was employed there, reported a UFO he had spotted on 28th December 1996 as he was on the M9 motorway driving past the slip road which leads from the M80 to the Kincardine bridge and then crosses the Firth of Forth at a narrow point in the estuary. It was around 10pm and his attention was caught by a prominent light in the sky. He described it as 'like a laser beam moving from side to side' and added, 'My first reaction was that this must be the beam of on-coming cars reflecting off the clouds, which were very low-lying. I thought this was odd because I had never noticed this effect before and then realised there were not sufficient on-coming cars on the road for this to be the case. I then thought that it must be some laser beam coming from Stirling but thought it strange that it could travel such a long distance.' The witness continued along the motorway to Stirling but could find no obvious source for this strange light.

I did follow up our initial conversation with some specific written questions as below:

Ron Halliday: "I take it that the light was white"?

Witness: "That's my recollection".

Ron Halliday: "Was it clearly defined and circular? Or what shape was it"?

Witness: "The light was like a single (or perhaps multiple beam(s)) that was (were) moving across the sky in a to and fro fashion. There was no particular shape and certainly no circularity".

Ron Halliday: "How long do you think you observed it for"?

Witness: "The length of time it took to drive along the M80 from the Kincardine Bridge slip road to the Bannockburn roundabout, stop at the service station and then drive off. Between 10-15 minutes".

Ron Halliday: "Was it stationary during this period"?

Witness: "Difficult to say as I was moving".

Are some witnesses more believable than others? Do certain witnesses make better observers than others? There's a general view among ufologists that particular occupations produce more accurate witnesses. The obvious one being police officers who supposedly are trained to be good observers. This may be the case though I've found that individuals from all backgrounds from the well-educated to those less so can misidentify everyday objects so it's difficult to pick out the ideal witness so to speak. We can all make mistakes.

So, despite an avalanche of reports and some highly believable witnesses were we any nearer to discovering what was happening in the skies above Bonnybridge? Or had so many claimed sightings made an analysis more difficult? I spoke to a journalist discussing events at Bonnybridge and expressed my concern that with so much media coverage it was difficult to separate truth from exaggeration. I said something along the lines that it was 'turning into a bit of a circus.' The headline then appeared, 'Billy's Flying Circus'. I did not of course make that statement - it was a headline written by the paper to generate attention. It was unfortunate and obviously caused some upset, but didn't reflect my belief which was that strange events were definitely happening over Bonnybridge, though I stood by my opinion that it was becoming harder in view of all the publicity to clarify just what was going on. Meanwhile, sightings of UFOs in the 'Falkirk Triangle' were being picked up across the UK and the publication 'Northern UFO News' reported that a couple in Stenhousemuir, an area near Bonnybridge, saw ' a brightly coloured object hovering over some nearby fields and surrounded by lights'. Once again it was difficult to know if this referred to a sighting which had already been logged or one that had passed local investigators by. I freely admit that given the interest in the area and the widespread reporting it was almost impossible to keep track over what was taking place. All that could be said is that the phenomenon was genuine, real and undoubtedly happening.

In the beginning

So, to go back to the beginning. This is a different way of looking at the phenomenon, but, as I have indicated the general situation in Bonnybridge is well known. But how it all got underway is less well known and even now - decades on - is becoming shrouded in myth and speculation. Can we discover why and how it happened? What was it that had sparked this phenomenal interest in Bonnybridge UFOs? When, and more significantly why, did the wave begin and when did it end? It might be suggested that it has never stopped though the number of reports has declined dramatically in recent years. Or could it be that the media have lost interest in Bonnybridge? It has simply over-loaded itself out of the picture? There is simply nothing sensational left to report? I would suggest it's a more complicated situation than appears at first glance. As discussed, events surrounding the Sloggett family were the first to draw public attention to Bonnybridge. For the purpose of this discussion, I'll briefly recapitulate events. The encounter took place in March 1992 as the family including Isabella, Carole and Steven were walking from Hallglen to Bonnybridge. Sometime after 7pm Steven noticed a large ball of light which he drew to the attention of the other members of the family. As they continued walking, they next became aware of a blue light about the size of a football hovering just above or possibly bouncing along the road ahead of them. As they eyed this object they were distracted by a rattling sound and also a whirring noise, followed by what struck them as the echo of a door opening. A nerve tingling 'howl' erupted and a flash of light which convinced the family to leave the scene, understandably unsure as to what they had become involved in. It seems that, according to some reports, that the UFO they encountered might have followed them because when the family returned home, they saw the object hovering in the sky above their house. At the time I wasn't quite sure what to make of this incident. It sounded like something out of a 1950s science fiction 'B' movie. I've since changed my mind. And what made me rethink this episode was one of the aspects which might have seemed the most odd and out of place - the sighting of a bouncing *blue* ball. I was unaware in the early 1990s of the significance of the colour blue in reported cases of the supernatural. However, a few years after the Sloggett case I investigated an incident where a ten-year-old girl was confronted by small blue beings and then taken aboard a spacecraft. Following my investigation of this incident I was astonished to discover that in Scotland blue was a colour generally linked to the supernatural. So, there is the 'blue stane' or 'devil's stone' in the town of St Andrews and the 'Blue Men of the Minch', mermen in the waters near the island of Lewis, among many other connections. But I also discovered, to my surprise, that the link between blue and the supernatural also existed in England and, in fact, there is a worldwide tradition that the appearance of something blue heralds the opening of a portal into another dimension.

There's an incident, for example, which occurred in the Argentinian town of Villa Carlos Plaza on 13th June 1968. Nineteen-year-old Maria Elastia was confronted by a six-foot-tall man wearing a one-piece suit which she described as being made of blue scales. What struck me about this incident was that the 'man' had in his hand a *blue ball* which gyrated on his palm. You can only speculate about the purpose of such an object. A power source? A communication device of some kind? A type of 'beam me up Scotty' transportation mechanism? (This incident for anyone interested was reported in 'UFO Sightings', by Alan Baker, p91.)

So, in the case of the Sloggett family could we be talking about a possible UFO landing with an alien or strange creature of some kind on board? That, of course, has to be speculation though we may be dealing with the coincidental interplay of various phenomena. There's no doubt that odd balls of coloured lights have been reported many times across Scotland. They may indicate the presence of a portal into another dimension. So, it may well be that the Sloggett family encountered a possible supernatural phenomenon that evening which could have been connected to the appearance of a UFO. Given the significance of the colour blue I feel more confident that a strange encounter did take place that evening. But as the saying goes, 'one swallow doesn't make a summer'. So, what turns the UFO phenomenon into a 'wave' or 'hotspot'? Councillor Billy Buchanan the local elected representative was the man who was at the centre of it all. He reported that he was receiving calls from local constituents who had witnessed strange objects in the sky. He was quoted as saying that by December 1992 over 200 witnesses had come forward claiming to have seen an object they couldn't identify and had struck them as something out of the ordinary. Of course, this could mean that several people had witnessed the same UFO-there was no way of being sure, but even so it was clear that something odd was taking place over and around the Bonnybridge area. One of the effects of the Sloggett case was to galvanise people into practical action. Billy Buchanan organised a sky watch at a spot above Bonnybridge where several sightings of unidentified objects had been reported. It should be noted, however, that influential though the Sloggett case was in generating interest it was not the first UFO sighing in the area. In January 1992 James Walker witnessed a cross-shaped formation of stars hovering above the road he was driving along. He stopped the car to get a better view and noted that the lights had formed the shape of a triangle. He was sure that it wasn't due to an obvious source such as an aircraft.

On 3rd February 1994 the Falkirk Herald reported under the headline 'BBC in UFO Probe' the videoing of another UFO over Bonnybridge. At two minutes long the footage was of a reasonable length for an analysis to be made. I didn't have the opportunity to scrutinise this film, but it apparently had captured the image of a large white light travelling slowly over the Bonnybridge/Falkirk area. The video was passed to film experts at the BBC though what happened after that to the footage is as mysterious as a UFO sighting. Going on past experience of UFO reports it's possible that a slow-moving bright light could be, for example, an aircraft light. That, however, is no more than guesswork based on the generally accepted figure among ufologists that 95% of UFO reports can be explained by natural factors.

In September 1995 yet another mystery object was sighted over Bonnybridge A woman walking her dog close to Bonnybridge quarry at around 7pm on Sunday 3rd September spotted a hovering black triangular shape in the sky. The witness thought at first that the UFO could be a kite or glider but changed her mind when she realised it wasn't moving and seemed to gleam. It had an adverse reaction on her dog which went into the crouch position and refused to budge. The object suddenly moved towards Falkirk, hovered then just disappeared. However, before that happened the woman had managed to grab her camera from the car and quickly film the object. Yet more intriguing evidence, but another case of a disappearing video! Unfortunately, I've no idea what happened to this footage so we can only speculate as to the object that may have been filmed. The UFO being described as triangular in shape is in keeping with the numerous sightings of unidentified objects that took place in this period. There was speculation that these supposed UFOs were in fact sightings of the Stealth aircraft which was top secret at the time. In fact, there were several reports of black triangle shaped UFOs travelling down Scotland's west coast and I appeared on the programme 'Newsnight' to discuss these sightings with Jeremy Paxton and a representative from the Ministry of Defence. I made the point that the security services would be quite happy to label these sightings as 'Unidentified Flying Objects' or alien spacecraft rather than admit to testing advanced *human* technology across Scotland. Meanwhile around Bonnybridge there seemed to be no slow-down in the number of claimed UFO sightings. In February 1996 a couple driving on the B803 road in the direction of the village of Slamanaan between 8.30pm and 9pm were surprised to see two bright white objects coming down from the sky towards them. At first the UFOs drifted parallel to each other at a distance, the witnesses judged, about half a mile in front of them then suddenly moved away in the opposite direction. In response to this incident, Malcolm Robinson was quoted in the 'Falkirk Herald' as saying, 'Since 1992 Falkirk District has become a hot spot for UFO investigators and documentary film makers with many sightings in the so-called Bonnybridge triangle.' An early indication of how rapidly the village was becoming the focus of attention due to the alleged large volume of UFO reports. And on it went. More video footage of unidentified objects emerged to tantalise investigators. In 1996 Andrew McLeish filmed two brightly lit objects near the village of Maddiston as darkness was falling. The sequence opened with a definitely identifiable object, an aeroplane passing overhead, its headlights and strobe lighting could clearly be seen. For researchers this was a plus as it allowed comparison against anything else caught on the video. As the plane disappeared from view a bright circular light appeared roughly towards the south. This light slowly got brighter and then a second light appeared lower down and half a mile to the east. Mr. McLeish reported that there was no noise from either light which seems to rule out an aeroplane or helicopter as an explanation for the object. The second light then moved towards the first light before turning round and then disappearing. Inquiries with Air Traffic Control revealed no planes in the area at the time and no radar contacts though it has to be borne in mind that not all flights would necessarily be revealed to the public. However, there appeared to be no obvious explanation as to the objects which had been filmed by Mr McLeish so the footage was something of a mystery. Sky TV expressed an interest in the video and went to the trouble of sending a representative to view it for inclusion on the 'Earthscan' show on the SKY Sci-Fi channel. In addition, the footage itself was supposed to be going to a group of experts for analysis, but what the end result was does not appear to have been made public. On the evening of 9th November 1996 at 8pm a witness - a woman who wished to remain anonymous - sighted an object shaped like a pink star which appeared above a roundabout at the ReChem plant, a waste recycling centre, near Bonnybridge. Curiously, the date marked the anniversary of the famous Bob Taylor encounter at Dechmont Law in 1979. In this case the witness had first glimpsed the object through a clump of trees and guessed it was a star, but then it abruptly disappeared. However, as she came round a bend, she caught sight of the object again which had now grown considerably in size and was clearly too big to be a star. It was also, unlike a star, pink in colour. The 'star' moved to the right, moved back again then shot heavenwards and simply disappeared. One more unexplained encounter to add to the Bonnybridge mystery.

CHAPTER SIX
STRANGE STORIES AND CONTROVERSIES CLOUD THE CENTRAL UFO ISSUE

Bizarre and confusing aspects of the Bonnybridge phenomenon emerged through a series of strange incidents. As if the Bonnybridge story couldn't get any odder the 'Grangemouth Advertiser' of 15th October 1997 reported a proposal to develop a 'theme park' complete with an 'encounter centre, restaurants, and education centre' at a location to be determined, but around the Bonnybridge 'Hot Spot'. More specifically there was talk of a giant visitor centre made of glass and shaped like a mushroom which would be located under the flight path of passing UFOs. The media were certainly enjoying the idea which in truth did contain the germ of a possibility and definitely wasn't just a 'pie in the sky project'.

I can vouch for that as in 1999 I received a proposal for a 'UFO Centre' which would be based in Bonnybridge from Mr. Yan Tung Li. It listed an extensive series of constructions which I judged would have required significant financial input, but the idea was certainly exciting. Nothing came of it, unfortunately. However, the idea of a park of some type to celebrate the village's status didn't die and kept reappearing. In 2007 the 'Scotsman' newspaper reported that both Dutch and US companies were interested in a multi-million pound project based on the village's UFO status. It's hard to judge how definite the proposals were, but the idea of a UFO based theme park seemed to spark interest world-wide. In the same year NBC news in America reported that Roswell in New Mexico, site of the famous claimed crash of an alien spaceship in 1947, was hoping to set up a 'UFO-themed amusement park'. This project was costed at several hundred million dollars so anything constructed at Bonnybridge would not have come cheap! Roswell already boasted an 'International UFO Museum and Research Center' so there was - or is- no reason why

Bonnybridge shouldn't do the same though the money would of course have to be found to build it. There was also a suggestion that a song to celebrate Bonnybridge's special status might be recorded. Neither of these developments was 'out of the box'. A theme park might have worked. As to the song, again nothing utterly strange. A friend of mine Alan Forrester had written a song about the Bob Taylor encounter of 1979 titled 'Riddle of the sky at night 'which had been played on both BBC and STV. However, in the context of what was happening in Bonnybridge events seemed to be entering a surreal phase. Well might it be asked, and was at the time, what is real and what is not. Had fantasy intertwined with reality?

If it hadn't been for the 'Zalus', sometimes called 'Zal-us', affair it might all have been different. The incident surely didn't do much for the credibility of Bonnybridge as a world UFO centre it might be thought. However, the enormous publicity generated reinforced the image of the area in people's minds as synonymous with the UFO phenomenon. It even came to the attention of world-renowned UFO investigator, the late Stanton Friedman. He was the man in the USA who had done so much to reveal the story of the famous Roswell incident in New Mexico the alleged though much disputed alien spacecraft crash of 1947. He was also a nuclear physicist which gave his views on UFO matters an extra level of credibility. He had commented that, 'There are several hotspots for UFO sightings *like Bonnybridge* around the world.' (author's italics) This obscure village was certainly attracting attention. But not all of it was desired as in the Zalus event. But who was the mysterious Zalus? He, she or it was supposedly an alien entity who was going to appear at a meeting scheduled to take place at Falkirk Town Hall in October 1995. As can be imagined this claim met with derision in various newspapers with some calling it 'crackpot'. As the 'Daily Sport' put it, 'A public meeting in Britain's UFO capital may be called off...because the ALIEN due to address it has got cold feet!' But where this claim about Zalus came from seemed a complete mystery and was of course sheer nonsense.

Unfortunately, however it did detract from serious assessment of 'UFO Bonnybridge' and gave the impression that the phenomenon was descending into farce, but through no fault of those who had been investigating and dealing with Bonnybridge UFO reports. The unfortunate truth is that UFOs attract ridiculous headlines such as the 'Sun' newspaper of 26th September 1995: 'Beam me up Totty: Fellas are snatched by alien babes...all looking like Pammy': Pamela Anderson of 'Baywatch' fame. Definitely an attention-grabbing caption though playing to what might be seen as the 'little green men' aspect of Ufology.

Back on planet Earth, or just about! The 'Daily Mail' of August 12th, 1995, explicitly linked councillor Billy Buchanan to 'Zalus' stating, 'It may be hard to believe but councillor Billy Buchanan says a "weird" being called Zal-us [sic] plans to make a statement of world-wide significance in the town hall [Falkirk] on October 9th'. It explained that the two met when Zal-us turned up at councillor Billy Buchanan's town hall office. Understandably Buchanan was incensed by media misinterpretation of what had actually occurred. The so-called 'Zal-us' was not an alien but very much a human entity who was scheduled to speak at the October event in Falkirk town hall. Where the name 'Zal-us' or 'Zalus' originated from remains something of a mystery to this day though an explanation did surface in due course. The 'Daily Mail' followed this story up with another headline of 14th August 1995 which ran: 'Spaceman alienated by ridicule'. Perpetuating the 'Zalus' myth the short article suggested that 'Zal-us' who it implied claimed to be one of the 'Council of Nine' (of which more below) could be put off appearing at the conference because of the media ridicule his supposed attendance had attracted. You would have thought that an alien being would have sported a thicker skin having clearly originated from a more advanced civilisation than we Earthlings! It was another eye-catching, but for serious ufologists, unfortunate report which turned the Falkirk Town Hall event into something it most definitely was not intended to be.

But who, what or are the 'Council of Nine'? Apparently, it was and is a group of nine extraterrestrials who have been sent to guide the destiny of Mankind and to pass on knowledge to those 'Earthlings' who have the ability to make contact with them - by psychic means. Some claim that their contacts on Earth are chosen for no obvious reason or that those who can communicate with the 'Council' may have an alien background having been born of a union between an alien entity and an 'Earthling' without necessarily being aware of it. The Falkirk Town Hall meeting seemed primed to be an exciting event, but maybe not for the objectives the organisers had aimed for.

I still have a copy of the original press release in which it announced the Falkirk Town Hall event as a 'Cosmic Agenda Lecture'. Speakers listed were Councillor Billy Buchanan, Phyllis Schlemmer - an American author, Ken Macfarlane and Geri Rogers. Geri was described as being part of a British group in contact with the 'Council of Nine'. Zalus was not listed! And as I attended the event, I can confirm that he or she or 'it' definitely did not turn up. A blame game ensued over the Zalus issue though to all intents and purposes it had been a simple misunderstanding. At least that was my view at the time. But was I correct? In April 1999 Geri Rogers wrote to me disagreeing with what I'd written in my book 'UFO Scotland' which had been published the year before and in which I had blamed the machinations of the press for the Zalus affair.

But according to Geri, the 'Zalus' story had been created deliberately by a ufologist (whom he named) to sabotage the meeting as the individual in question had not been invited to take part. I have no evidence to back that up and I personally doubt it. I mention it to demonstrate the emotions that can be aroused on the UFO subject. A topic many of us take seriously. Serious or not various commentators saw the funny side. In 'Phenomenal News' (October 1995 edition), satirical commentator, Edward Talisman, pointed out the amusing aspect of the affair. He wrote:

'Sceptics of the Bonnybridge 'hotspot' were given added fuel by the unfortunate antics involving 'Zal-us' and the 'Council of Nine'. Zal-us, according to several newspaper reports, was an alien who had an important message to give to the world which was going to be revealed at a meeting in Falkirk Town Hall one evening in October. The hall had been booked for the event by Councillor Billy Buchanan, no less. So, Councillor Billy was at the centre of this enigma? The tabloids seemed to think so and one [...] labelled the unfortunate Buchanan, 'Bonnybridge's Crackpot Councillor'. Indeed, to be fair to the press someone somewhere seemed to have put words into Billy's mouth which appear to suggest that he had personally met an ET who claimed membership of some galactic body which was overseeing the development of the Earth .... All in all, it made a great read and, caught up in the excitement, I was devastated to learn it had all been a load of...nonsense. Billy Buchanan had never met an alien and the name Zal-us was alien (all right completely unknown) to him. Mr. Buchanan was, it transpires, utterly blameless and bemused and justifiably annoyed at his name being taken in vain. So where did 'Zal-us' come from? Without revealing all the twists and turns of a murky plot, it seems that another UFO group had somehow picked up the name. But where from I don't know [But] according to the 'Scotsman' the name originated with Ufologist Malcolm Robinson in his newsletter. However, claims Malcolm, 'I don't know how the name Zal-us crept into the article. I would never put in some false data ...just to jazz it up.' An enigma indeed!" In Spring 1996 with no sign of interest in the Zalus affair evaporating, Talisman returned to the topic under the headline, 'Farce over Bonnybridge: Update'. It ran:

'Off to Falkirk Town Hall ... to be greeted by Councillor Billy Buchanan ... On stage [he] introduced his list of speakers. First up Phyllis-of-the-unpronounceable name [Schlemmer] who, it turns out, has been abducted more times than any of the audience have had hot dinners. Perhaps ET was as bemused as the rest of us by the attractive lady's ramblings and needed all those meetings to make sense of what she was trying to say. I could have done with a few more myself! She was so DELIGHTED to be in Bonnybrook. WHERE? Had we all been transported to some Brigadoon in the sky even as we sat transfixed by this blonde beauty! Well, er, no. It seems she simply forgot that she was in the less delightfully named provenance of Bonnybridge, famous for its thousands upon thousands of UFO sightings, though not so well known, apparently, to ET's Ambassador on Earth (our own Phyllis). The audience I'm afraid were not on their best behaviour and booed the speakers to the gunnels. 'We want Zal-us' was the cry. But the alien, unfortunately, remained a figment of one ufologist's fervid imagination. Meanwhile the media were loving it. Don't UFOs and hilarity make exciting copy! 'The space brothers are watching over you, 'intoned Geri Rogers, to a dumbfounded audience. Didn't he realise he was in FALKIRK, for God's sake?'

There was more in the same vein. Of course, since that was published Phyllis Schlemmer has passed away. No disrespect intended for the UFO work Phyllis was involved in and was well known for, but the excerpt above is printed to give a flavour of the atmosphere surrounding the event at that time. One of the speakers that night, Geri Rogers, has his own view of how the name Zalus cropped up as I indicated earlier.

In an article in April 1997 issue of the publication the 'New Ufologist' Malcolm Robinson commented, ' I could go on at great length about the Bonnybridge issue, but as I am restricted for space, I'll close by saying that the ZAL-US affair that Ron mentions in his article was unfortunate, it was complete nonsense which the press loved and used greatly. There is a story behind that ZAL-US affair, and if the good-natured editor Paul Fuller lets me come back to this point in a future article, I'd be happy to inform the readers how all this came about. But honestly, it had "nothing" at all to do with [Billy] Buchanan.'

As I mentioned elsewhere the 'New Ufologist' lasted only a few issues, so Robinson's further explanation didn't appear. However, in 'UFO Case Files of Scotland', (published 2009, p83 et al) Robinson did admit, 'I had goofed' explaining, 'I had somehow transferred the name from [another] case study into the 'Mr. X' article about Billy and this 'strange' man.' A straightforward error which unfortunately for serious UFO investigators grew like Topsy into an enormous whirlpool of claim and counterclaim. The original story, it turned out, had appeared in Robinson's publication, 'Enigmas' (August/September 1995 issue) referring to an article in the 'Fortean Times' - a well-known magazine devoted to all things paranormal - which had described a mysterious 'Mr. X' who had turned up at Falkirk Town Hall to speak to Councillor Billy Buchanan. And from this throwaway remark a great and entertaining myth was born though not so funny for Councillor

Buchanan.

Back in the real world the 'Falkirk Herald' took a critical view of the town hall gathering. The headline ran 'Conference fails to solve mysteries of Bonnybridge. UFO buffs miss the target.' The article took the view that the general feeling from the audience had been that their questions about the UFO phenomenon in Bonnybridge had not been answered. In fact, given that an astonishing 900 people attended it seems understandable that not everyone might have been satisfied by the range of topics covered. The conference could in all honesty have been considered on the esoteric side with subjects covered including religion, ethics, government conspiracies, meditation and mythology. If people had been expecting a down-to-earth explanation as to why Bonnybridge had attracted 2,000 (according to the 'Falkirk Herald') UFO sightings that certainly didn't come over in actual fact as the focus of the conference and was only dealt with in a roundabout way. There was undoubtedly some heckling of speakers, and a number of the audience left well before the end, but the vast majority stuck it out.

They certainly heard some challenging claims. American Phyllis Schlemmer spoke of the many years she had been in communication with the 'Council of Nine' who, apparently, were the 'Principals of the Universe', that is the controlling force. However, even though this group was watching over the Earth, humanity, she said, had to take responsibility for their own actions, a not unreasonable view. At least Schlemmer had an answer of sorts for Bonnybridge's huge number of UFO sightings. Her explanation ran along the lines that it was the consequence of the positive energy being generated by the people of Bonnybridge. The aliens apparently respond to friendly feelings towards them. Ms Schlemmer told the audience that she had never experienced such kindness from people as she had felt in Scotland. She offered no explanation as to the means by which the aliens had been aware of the good vibes emanating from Bonnybridge though it could be guessed that they were conveyed knowingly or unknowingly via psychic channels. Ken McFarlane a Cheshire based UFO expert made the sensible point that with 40 million stars in our own galaxy -

never mind the millions of other galaxies in the universe it seems a reasonable assumption that a proportion of those stars would support planets which could produce intelligent life forms. A third speaker, Geri Rogers, suggested that historical events associated with the area might attract UFO interest. It's certainly true that the Falkirk district has experienced an interesting past with the Roman invasion and the building of the Antonine Wall, the battles arising from the Wars of Independence with England and the Jacobite risings in 1715 and then again in 1745 with Bonnie Prince Charlie at the helm.

However, many regions have experienced a dramatic past without having a UFO blitz in the twentieth century as a consequence. I would accept, though, that Mr Rogers had a valid point. Quite possibly there was a particular event or series of events which could have attracted alien curiosity. Nothing, in my view, can be ruled out. Overall, the conference even though it was not as directly focused on Bonnybridge UFOs as it might have been, was a general success, certainly in continuing media and public interest in the village. Councillor Buchanan was certainly satisfied with the general tenor of the event claiming that he had been contacted by a significant number of people to say how much they'd enjoyed it. In my view, as a member of the audience, the conference tended towards being "off beam" in terms of what could have been expected. The focus wasn't on explaining the Bonnybridge enigma except in a broad sense. That's not to say it wasn't interesting and talk of the 'Council of Nine' added an international if not to say other worldly aspect to the Bonnybridge story. However, it was a big jump for people who may have had little knowledge of UFO topics to be plunged into claims that an elite group of aliens was in control of the universe.

Understandably Billy Buchanan did not view the Zalus story as a big joke as he had been forced into the centre of it and had been the butt of derisory comments. The "Falkirk Herald announced his firm response with the headline, 'Councillor Plans Legal Action Over Alien Stories'. Buchanan was intending to take legal action against several newspaper which had published articles about the alleged alien, Zal-us. As I have explained there never was an alien of any sort that Buchanan had met or talked to. But the media accounts had led to many sarcastic comments, phone calls and letters directed at the councillor. The barrage of criticism directed against him was understandably difficult and annoying for him to have to deal with. Of course, there was a more serious side for Buchanan in the impact the Zalus affair had on his political credibility. As he explained to the 'Falkirk Herald', 'I've been held up to ridicule over this personal attack on my political credibility. My political opponents will try to take advantage of it. I wouldn't be surprised if people started demanding my resignation. They must think I'm off my head. All I've done is to try and keep the UFO in the public eye over the last three years. It would be easy to ignore it, but more than 2,000 people have come to me about it.' This response from Buchanan certainly summed up his predicament - trying to get to the bottom of the Bonnybridge phenomenon without being an object of ridicule.

However, it wasn't all bad news. In 1996 Buchanan wrote to the Falkirk Herald thanking the paper on behalf of the many UFO witnesses who had come forward with a report of their UFO sightings. In Buchanan's view the paper had taken a frank and open-minded attitude in its published articles on the subject unlike most of the tabloid media which had, he felt, ridiculed Bonnybridge in their coverage of the phenomenon. Contrary to popular belief, but understandably so given the Zalus debacle, the 1995 conference about Bonnybridge was not the only one to be held. On 6th January 1996 'UFO Magazine' got involved putting on an event in' Falkirk Town Hall', 'Scotland' helpfully added. You can't expect people especially from down south to know where the town is! According to the blurb circulated, ' Scotland has experienced one of the largest UFO "waves" seen in recent times, and events-in-and around Bonnybridge in particular have attracted. Much ado about nothing, or something tangible? Falkirk Town Hall is the venue for what promises to be an enthralling and informative professional presentation on the subject of UFOs which will not only examine the global nature of the phenomenon but will document its past history through a stunning montage of slides and incredible film footage. Sprinkled with some revealing case histories from home and abroad. UFO enthusiasts or just the plain curious will have much to see and hear as UFO magazine, Britain's only national newsstand [sic] UFO publication, launches the 1996 Conference season in Scotland'.

'UFO magazine' was certainly a key publication of the time and both those linked to it, Graham Birdsall and Tony Dodd, were seasoned UFO investigators so it was a measure of the widespread interest in Bonnybridge that they decided to hold a conference in Falkirk. It was also, unfortunately, true that at the time there was no regular UFO conferences taking place in Scotland. This had to wait till 2015 when I, Malcolm Robinson and Alyson Dunlop got together to set up the 'Scottish UFO and Paranormal Conference' which continues to this day as a regular annual event. Back in 1996 there were only three speakers at the 'UFO Magazine 'conference, Graham Birdsall, Tony Dodd and Malcolm Robinson. Billy Buchanan was limited to an opening address. Both Graham and Tony are now, unfortunately, deceased. Falkirk Town Hall has now been demolished although the 'UFO and Paranormal Conference' held its 2017 gathering there. How things change. For some reason I didn't attend the 1996 event, but by all accounts it went well though Bonnybridge was in reality only a lesser part of a presentation covering world-wide UFO events. But even so it was definite proof that Bonnybridge had established itself on the UFO map thanks to the efforts of Buchanan, Robinson, Halliday and the many UFO witnesses who came forward to give their various accounts.

The disappearing footage

Bonnybridge generated many odd incidents. One was a video, as reported in the 'Daily Record' of 24th February 1999, which caught on film several silver orb-shaped objects travelling across the sky. The film, taken by a witness identified as 'Brian', was labelled as a truly significant piece of evidence and was examined by a team from 'UFO' magazine. The tape lasted fifteen minutes so there was enough footage, you would think, to determine exactly what was being filmed. The witness had taken the video from a location in the town of Stirling rather than Bonnybridge itself. However, Stirling is less than ten miles from Bonnybridge so close enough to be a part of the UFO activity there and an object in the sky is notoriously difficult to pin down in relation to the ground. I have to admit that I have never viewed the tape so I can't comment on its significance as proof of alien visitation. But the image published in the 'Daily Record' certainly looks like the object caught on film by Stenhousemuir resident Margaret Ross three years earlier. So, it could well be the same UFO The current location of Brian's video is, unfortunately, a bit of a mystery. If it turns up modern techniques could allow us to give a better assessment of what was captured on film.

Mystery helicopter buzzes Larbert

With all the UFO activity taking place in the area, it was unsurprising that Larbert residents were intrigued by the appearance on the 12th of July 1996 of a Royal Airforce helicopter flying at rooftop level over the town which lies only a short distance from Bonnybridge. The immediate suspicion was that this was in some way connected with the UFO sightings that had been flooding in. Asked for an explanation the Ministry of Defence claimed that the helicopter, a twin-engined Chinook normally used for transporting men and machines, had flown at 1,000 feet above the town rather than at low level as witnesses had reported. In a further bizarre twist, it was claimed that the pilot involved, only known as 'Dave', had flown over Larbert to impress his parents. It seemed an unlikely though not impossible explanation except that resident reported sighting the Chinook on three consecutive days. It headed in the direction of the Westerglen masts where several unidentified flying objects had been reported. It is, of course, possible that it was no more than a coincidence, but there may well have been a more sinister explanation given the military's involvement in so many cover-ups, for example, denying for decades that they were not interested in UFO sightings when the opposite was the case.

Regarding the Ministry of Defence and UFOs it's interesting to note the article in the 'Sun' newspaper of Friday 24 November 1995 reporting that three tornado jets had been scrambled to intercept a UFO buzzing Edinburgh airport. It quoted a pilot who claimed he had spoken to a flight controller at RAF Kinloss who had told him that the jets had a UFO in their sights and were closing in on it when it suddenly shot straight up and left the fighters standing. Apparently, the UFO was seen by operatives in the control tower, and also by security personnel. The control tower had in addition followed the object on radar so there seems little doubt that whatever had been seen was real and not the figment of the imagination. I managed to speak to a member of airport staff who confirmed that there had been a real commotion around the incident. This suggests that a helicopter buzzing around the Bonnybridge and Larbert areas could be more than just a coincidence and reflected a response to the many UFOs being reported in the area.

Lotto Winners

Bonnybridge certainly attracted any number of strange stories. One of the weirdest was the claim that the Bonnybridge area was generating an unusually high number of lotto winners. As the 'People' newspaper reported it, 'It could be UFO! Aliens picked Lotto jackpot winners.' suggesting that there was a 'golden circle' of winners with eight punters having won more than a million pounds. Further into the article, however, it became clear that the jackpot winners were located in a wider area covering the strip of land between Edinburgh and Glasgow with Bonnybridge situated in the middle. This part of Scotland was described as 'Britain's major UFO hotspot' which the paper claimed could boast more than two-thirds of Britain's flying saucer sightings. How many winners actually came from the village of Bonnybridge itself is unclear. But just mentioning the village in this context shows just how much of an impact it had made. Unquestionably recognised as the UK's top UFO spot.

The lotto story should maybe go along with the claim that incidence of twins in the area had doubled, according to one survey and is twice the national average. This was reported in the 'Guardian' of 31st October 1999, one of the more serious newspapers. This was reminiscent of the 'Midwych Cuckoos' tale with the birth of alien children to normal human couples.

Could fiction be turning into reality? I'm sure that this statistic is pure chance and has no connection to the UFO phenomenon.

Synchronicity: The 'Joker' Universe

It has been suggested by researchers into the paranormal that we live in a 'joker universe'. That there's a cosmic intelligence that likes to trick or confuse us by creating strange events, including poltergeist activity and UFOs. Odd coincidences undoubtedly do occur. Here's one I came across, thanks to my brother Dr Neil Halliday. On the one hand we have the village of Bonnybridge in Scotland turning into a UFO hotspot. At the very same time, several hundred miles south, the similarly named village of Bonsall in Derbyshire - population 850 - was becoming a local centre for UFO reports with strange objects seen hovering above houses on at least nineteen occasions and a video taken of a disc shaped craft. Though as the local newspaper admitted, Bonsall had 'some stiff competition, as in Bonnybridge residents had claimed to have been visited by 500 UFOs since 1992'. Like so many aspects of the 'joker universe' there's just enough of a connection to arouse your interest if not enough to convince you of a connection!

However, even in Scotland there were other claimants to the title of 'UFO Hotspot Village'. Muchalls in Aberdeenshire with a population of only 360 could claim multiple UFO sightings over a twenty year period including a mysterious glowing figure floating above the road. Despite this competition there's no doubt that for sheer volume of UFO reports Bonnybridge was undoubtedly the gold star winner.

Alien Nests?

Such was the hype built up over Bonnybridge that anything out of the ordinary grasped the attention of the public. In 1996 a woman out walking spotted what she said had the appearance of giant nests lying in woods near an area known as Tamfourhill. Her curiosity was aroused because they hadn't been there the day before so must have been created overnight. Could these have some connection with the UFO phenomenon? Speculation was rife. Given that we can't be sure what alien beings would look like - many different types have been reported, or how they would behave was it possible that 'they' had built these nest like constructions as their place to live? Or could they be the home of an alien animal linked to the UFO phenomenon? Readers familiar with the controversial Fife case where, it was claimed, alien entities of various shapes and sizes were seen working in a field will recall that Gary Wood, of the A70 abduction case, who was investigating the events, came across several constructions made of branches while researching the area where witnesses claimed to have seen landed spacecraft. The tepee like structures Wood discovered, however, had apparently a straightforward explanation and the same was true of the 'nests' found in Bonnybridge. These latter, it was claimed, were the work of art school students engaged in a project. A witness reported that he had seen them working on them. Of course, not everyone was convinced, but in both this case and the Fife one there seemed no proven connection between the wooden structures and the appearance of UFOs. Commonsense would suggest that alien beings who travel to our planet from distant galaxies would use, and need, a more sophisticated residence, but where there are alien beings there may also be alien animals so these strange structures might still be linked to the UFO phenomenon speculative though that might seem.

Video Footage 'abducted'

In 1996 occurred one of the strangest episodes connected with Bonnybridge: the alleged 'abduction' of a key piece of video footage. An American ufologist, it was claimed, had flown out of Scotland having got hold of a piece, it was claimed, of amazing film which allegedly showed a solid triangular craft displaying three yellow lights forming the outline of a UFO. The video had been taken by, and shown to, the visiting ufologists by a Bonnybridge based couple. Several Scottish ufologists led by the late Andrew Hennessy protested against the removal of the video to the USA and commented adversely on the matter across the internet. Even though the world-wide web was in its infancy at that time word rapidly spread across the pond and beyond. So, what was it all about? It appeared to come down to a misunderstanding. As the indignant American ufologists pointed out the video had been loaned to them by agreement as no copy was available for them to take to carry out a requested analysis. But how good was it in any case as proof of the reality of the UFO phenomenon particularly in relation to Bonnybridge? By some it was described as the 'best evidence of a UFO' though others were less sure. I can't comment because to the best of my knowledge I have never viewed this piece of film and as far as I can gather it never seems to have been shown to a wider audience so it remains a tantalising bit of evidence that hasn't seen the light of day and may be buried in an American archive somewhere.

The late Andrew Hennessey at the time an active investigator of UFOs had, inadvertently, become entangled in the incident and on 18th October 1996 sent me an impassioned email with an explanation of the mix-up. Andrew wrote as below:

'Dear Ron,

I get this phone call from [a well-known UFO personality] - which to paraphrase the only copy of the best evidence ever has been flown out of Scotland by private interests in a private jet with no legal agreements. What am I to do [in these circumstances]? I trusted [name excised] because he has always come across as a reliable witness and if this was half as good as [name excised] thought it was it obviously shouldn't have gone anywhere except to the press and TV because it is so important. Please believe that I do not bear CSETI any grudge or ill feelings whatsoever. I had never heard of them and understandably they are angry because this lot of crap went round the global community. What a setback for our Transformation Studies Group in Edinburgh. We had hoped to Network with all these people not having them shouting at us. We are trying to do serious work - like yourself. Who can we trust? I am very angry with [name excised], but I understand why he over-reacted. He needs evidence like that to help him cope with his trauma and to see the only copy disappear must have wobbled him a bit. All I can do is apologise. I have written to [name excised] and umpteen other outraged serious researchers. From a local perspective there is absolutely no organisation, no networking, a whole lot of private interests and glory seekers and this has got to stop... Please feel free to pass this message by way of extra apology or information so that we can at least try to clarify matters.'

There's no question that the whole event was a simple misunderstanding, but it gives a good indication of the passion of those involved in the Bonnybridge saga at that time.

POP STAR?

One of the oddest stories connected with Bonnybridge was the opportunity for Billy Buchanan to record a pop song. The councillor reported that he had been phoned by a company based in Luton. The proposal involved Buchanan making a record with the unlikely title 'MY PAL ZAL'. Apparently, the company suggested that the deal could be worth thousands. And given the interest in Bonnybridge it's not too hard to imagine that a novelty record would attract considerable attention and be very saleable. There were precedents. In May 1987 a band called 'The Firm' issued the song 'Star Trekkin' on the theme as the title suggests of the 'Star Trek' television and film series. In addition, Scottish songwriter Alan Forrester in 1992 composed a song 'Riddle of the sky at night' on the Bob Taylor encounter which had been aired on both the BBC and STV. Understandably, however, Buchanan turned the opportunity down on the sound basis that given the hoo-ha over the Zalus stories getting involved in a jokey record would do nothing to restore his credibility. Probably a sensible decision.

CHAPTER SEVEN
BONNYBRIDGE IN ISOLATION?
The Falkirk Triangle Controversy

In an article in the 'Observer' newspaper of 23rd June 2002 I was quoted as saying about Bonnybridge, 'The area has become known as the "Falkirk Triangle." There have been various suggestions as to why it is such a magnet for UFOs. One theory is that the area near Bonnybridge is a window into another dimension. That is why certain people see a UFO and others don't because a UFO is some kind of paranormal phenomenon rather than a nuts-and-bolts spaceship'. But was there in reality a 'Falkirk Triangle' or was it the invention of the media. I know that my co-author Malcolm Robinson has no time for the 'Falkirk Triangle' claim. Is he right? As I touched on earlier which UFO cases should be included within the 'Bonnybridge' phenomenon given as previously indicated sightings connected to the village happened within an area which extended for several miles though Bonnybridge came to be the name linked to all this activity and can reasonably claim to be the focal point. So, was there in fact a 'Falkirk Triangle? Claims and counter claims on this issue have continued for years with ufologists espousing different views on the matter. A triangle suggests a defined area and it is difficult to see how it was possible to place all the reported sightings within a specific shape. Where would you locate the base? Where the top? And where the sides? It was an eye-catching headline, but difficult to fit with the variety of locations linked to such a diverse number of sightings. In a way though the designation isn't so way out. In a catchy sense it made the point that the Bonnybridge UFO phenomena covered an area for several miles extending outwards from the village. And maybe that craft from much further afield could be travelling over this area for reasons we can't even begin to understand.

But why Bonnybridge? The Sloggett case which sparked off the ensuing wave of interest in UFOs was linked to Bonnybridge. Billy Buchanan was a councillor representing the

Bonnybridge area who took up the UFO issue and so I'd suggest that these two facts came together to focus attention on the village from an early stage. However, fairly rapidly reports came in from sites a short distance away: from Grangemouth, Falkirk, Stenhousemuir and even into West Lothian. In fact, as the sightings extended into districts further apart, though adjacent to each other, it did suggest that a wider area was linked to the phenomenon and so an enterprising journalist coined the phrase 'Falkirk Triangle' - and it stuck. Some speculation went even further claiming the 'triangle' stretched into Fife - an area on the northern side of the body of water known as the Firth of Forth. There was undoubtedly a considerable number of UFO reports in the Fife region. But to most ufologists involved it seemed a stretch too far.

Bonnybridge: a sudden 'hotspot' or 'slowburner?

However, we have to be careful if we assume that the Bonnybridge phenomenon appeared out of nowhere. As far back as August 1908 a witness reported seeing what appeared to be some kind of signalling device in the skies over Larbert. Jump ahead several decades to 1968. In that year Wendy Forbes who was travelling by car with a boyfriend near the village of Polmont, around eight miles from Bonnybridge, saw an oval shaped object with coloured lights around the exterior descending at speed. It appeared to her that it was so low down that it might crash. Concerned about a possible impact the pair sped off so what happened to the UFO is unclear. If there was a crash, then I'm sure it would have come to public attention so the object may have simply flown away. Moving forward a decade to the December 1978, but still well before the famous Bonnybridge flap, a witness in nearby Denny reported seeing an oval shaped object flying over the rooftops of houses. Furthermore, there was a multi-witness case in July 1981 when six primary school children who were playing on the football field adjacent to the school said they had encountered a saucer shaped object hovering above them which frightened a herd of cows into a stampede. These events demonstrate that the area around Bonnybridge had experienced UFO incidents well before its rise to fame in the 1990s.

Alien autopsy

So why the sudden explosion of sightings in Bonnybridge and resulting world-wide interest? One aspect that has to be considered is whether, and to what extent, events in the wider world impacted on the developing Bonnybridge phenomenon. Could outside agencies have triggered in some way the Bonnybridge UFO flap? In 1995, for example, the UFO community and the wider world was hit by the extraordinary claim that alien beings had been filmed undergoing an autopsy on an air base in the USA. These entities were, it was alleged, the victims of the Roswell incident of 1947 where and when it was claimed an alien spacecraft had crash-landed.

The footage and ensuing discussion by the media caused a world-wide sensation. Ray Santilli a film producer claimed that he had obtained the film from a one-time military cameraman. The footage was shown London in May 1995 with a flotilla of the media in attendance. The stills released looked sufficiently life-like to at the very least capture the imagination and convince you for a moment that this really could have happened. For most ufologists reality kicked in and brought most of us quickly back down to earth. The film was, unfortunately, a hoax or at least not genuine footage of alien beings though there are some who are still convinced that the footage really is what it was claimed to be - a film of dead extraterrestrials. However, fact or fiction the key point is that the huge volume of publicity generated fed into UFO-icity and ramped up interest in extraterrestrial contact so indirectly helping to sustain Bonnybridge as a media phenomenon. But it certainly didn't cause it. Bonnybridge was well established as a UFO hot spot by 1995 when the alien autopsy footage appeared.

Ministry of Defence (MOD) and Nick Pope

Nick Pope became somewhat of a controversial figure arising from claims that he ran a 'UFO Office' at the Ministry of Defence (MOD) headquarters in London. It's unclear as to whether this was a product of media exaggeration or exactly where the story of the alleged existence of a UFO office in the MOD originated. It has to be noted that the MOD has categorically denied a 'UFO section' operated. Although the sceptical might say 'they would, wouldn't they'. However, there's no doubt in my mind that Pope was monitoring some UFO incidents because in the 1990s I wrote and asked Nick for locations of UFO sightings in Scotland, and he forwarded a map with appropriate sites marked. I will say that the number indicated was a fraction of sightings I was aware of. However, in my view the fact that Pope worked in the MOD (at whatever level - the subject of more debate!) or did or did not run a 'UFO section' is irrelevant in the wider UFO context. The mere suggestion that the MOD *might* be interested in unidentified flying objects was enough to add to the credibility of the UFO phenomenon: as was taking place in Bonnybridge, for example. Nick Pope claimed that there had been 8,000 sightings in Bonnybridge enough to excite the UFO imagination. But Pope's book 'Open Skies, closed minds' didn't appear till 1996 at a time when the Bonnybridge 'hot spot' may arguably have reached its peak. However, I would suggest that Pope's connection to the MOD, in whatever capacity, did give credibility to UFOs as a subject worth considering and so fed into media interest in events in Bonnybridge. Various ufologists have attempted to establish Pope's exact position in the MOD hierarchy. As far as I'm aware Mr. Pope was employed as an Executive Officer in 'Secretariat (Air Staff)2' holding the post designated as 'Sec(AS)2a.' The general duties he was assigned to deal with appear fairly routine though the MOD has admitted that he had responsibility for processing reports made by the public of sightings of UFOs. Note the 'from the public'. Not then reports, perhaps, from the military or other security or official bodies. The role of an Executive Officer, according to the Civil Service website is 'problem solving, business planning and policymaking, at the very highest level of government' *but* 'within a supportive team structure, under the direction of relevant team leaders'. In other words, involved in significant activities but not by any means directing policy or decision-making at the top. The current salary of between £29,500 to

£33,979 (2024) reflects the EO's position within the hierarchy of the Civil Service structure, that is at the lower end. I've laboured this point to clarify that Nick Pope was not in a position to possess significant knowledge of events in Bonnybridge. But, as noted above, this in the wider world was not relevant as the mere suggestion that the MOD was dealing with UFO reports and a person in a reasonable position of responsibility was allocated to deal with them was justification for the media to treat UFO reports if not seriously then at least with the confidence that there was official interest in the subject.

Having given the MOD the benefit of the doubt it's instructive to note that when Buchanan requested a meeting with the Ministry of Defence to discuss reported sightings in the area they simply refused claiming it wouldn't serve any useful purpose. Their stance was - and is -that as UFOs are of no significance to Britain's defences they have no interest in reported sightings. Or so the Ministry claims. But what if they are seen as a threat? We know that in both the UK and USA jet fighters have been dispatched to investigate unexplained objects in the sky. However, it's unlikely we'll ever know the truth behind these incidents' secrecy being in official circles a way of life. They adopt the mantra, 'don't let the public know unless absolutely necessary and unavoidable'. And in their view, it almost never is.

The 'X-Files'

But what about the power of television? In particular the 'X-Files' sci-fi series which first hit our screens in 1993. It was, of course, fiction, but it played on themes popular at the time - alien abduction, use of alien technology and secret alien bases among others. Whether it convinced people that there was some underlying truth to what was being portrayed or was seen as no more than entertaining fantasy, it certainly helped to boost interest in UFOs particularly with the suggestion that political leaders around the globe were concealing what they knew from the public including contact with extraterrestrials. The idea that governments in the UK and USA could be hiding the truth about UFOS chimed with increasing sceptisim over the integrity of politicians. Should our rulers be cajoled into admitting they had been lying to us? As to the 'X-Files' programmes although I believe it had a significant impact in boosting attention to and maybe belief in UFOs it can't have set off the interest in the Bonnybridge phenomenon which was well underway by the time the series first aired.

Role of the press

It's amazing when you look back to see the decline of the influence of newspapers over the last 25 years. By 2023 a once mighty Scottish paper the 'Daily Record was reduced to a daily sale of 60,000 down from 100,000 from three years previously and much lower than those of the mid-1990s. Most papers, in fact, in Scotland experienced a similar dramatic decline in sales. People these days just don't buy hard copies though they may subscribe to an on-line version. Back 'in the day' if you were on a bus or train you would see most commuters with their heads in a paper. These days people have their heads in their I-phones. Times have changed rapidly. But in the Bonnybridge era (1990s) the press had a huge impact in terms of encouraging interest in the UFO story. Most people unlike nowadays read a paper of some sort. The internet was only in its infancy so generally it was the press which brought the Bonnybridge phenomenon to the attention of the public on an almost daily basis.

At the time of Bonnybridge's rise to fame there was intense competition between several newspapers to maintain and even increase their circulation. The main local paper was (and still is) the 'Falkirk Herald' with its sister publication the 'Grangemouth Advertiser'. The nearby 'Stirling Observer' also covered events in Bonnybridge as did the 'Edinburgh Evening News' and the Glasgow based 'Evening Times'. The 'big beasts' engaged in a circulation war were the 'Daily Record' Scotland's biggest selling tabloid of the time, but under attack from Rupert Murdoch's 'Sun' which had adopted the title the 'Scottish Sun' and at one point even supported the campaign for Scottish independence and the SNP. The 'Daily Record' was well known as being in the Labour Party camp. To add to the competitive mix leading English tabloids particularly the 'Daily Mail' and the 'Daily Express' started running Scottish editions with increased coverage of events in Scotland which, of course, included Bonnybridge. Press agencies were particularly active during this period one based in Falkirk and one in Stirling. The innovative approach of local journalist Frank Gilbride had a significant impact in generating copy for the national press. Both press agencies, however, were making a determined effort in seeking out news stories and Bonnybridge provided a regular source of copy. Where the papers went the television (and radio) followed not as regularly perhaps but stories on both mediums featuring Bonnybridge reached a wide audience and so boosted interest in events in the village. However, any newsworthy story needs a catalyst particularly if it is going to continue to be reported most stories disappear quickly never to reappear. So, in the case of Bonnybridge without the involvement of Billy Buchanan councillor for the Bonnybridge area I doubt that coverage of UFOs there would have reached the heights that it achieved. The fact that an elected official put his backing to something as 'outlandish' as UFO reports gave these sightings a substance they might otherwise have lacked. For journalists it gave events a credibility and provided an intriguing aspect. The question could be asked 'If there's nothing to it why would a local councillor be willing to come out and testify to it.' But of course, one person could not have produced the torrent of interest Bonnybridge attracted. In reality, a whole range of issues seemed to coincide to bring about the long-standing fame the village achieved.

UFO Scotland?

In spite of the intense interest in Bonnybridge it should be noted that general UFO activity in Scotland was widespread and dated back to the start of the modern phenomenon in 1947 with Andrew Cherry's sighting in the Portobello district of Edinburgh of a typical round spacecraft, glass domed, containing an occupant. My book 'UFOs: the Scottish Dimension' appeared in 1997 and 'UFO Scotland' the following year. I devoted several pages to Bonnybridge, but I also covered hundreds of other incidents from the length and breadth of the land. Bonnybridge UFOS certainly did not exist in isolation even within Scotland. And this in fact adds to the puzzle - why the fascination with Bonnybridge? It could be argued that encounters as strange as anything happening in Bonnybridge were taking place elsewhere in Scotland. To give one example the 'Dundee Courier' of 21st February 1996 reported that three 'youngsters' had encountered a UFO which hovered above them in Orchard Park, a local play area, and shone a light at them. The witnesses described the craft as being shaped like a burger with a dome on top and a band of lights round the middle. The children, apparently, were terrified and ran off believing that, for some reason, the UFO was following them. A bizarre incident if reported accurately, but no matter what was occurring elsewhere it was the village of Bonnybridge which almost monopolised the attention of the media.

After the deluge

Whilst it's true that the number of UFO reports in the Bonnybridge area declined towards the end of 1990s they certainly didn't stop. Sightings continued to come in. In October 2017, for example, Ian Black reported seeing a strange formation of lights moving towards the Falkirk High Station area. Mr. Black was based in Camelon, an area in Falkirk. These lights appeared in the shape of a kite and sometimes changed direction moving towards Bonnybridge from the Grangemouth locality. The lights usually appeared between 9pm and 12am. They pulsated, or appeared to do, growing brighter then diminishing. At one point it seemed as if it was being followed by what looked like a slightly elongated saucer shape 'almost as if a UFO was following the bright light'. Interestingly, on 28th September 2017 one of these kite shapes had been seen hovering in midair above the wooded area of Bantaskin estate which lies within Falkirk district. - it did this in complete silence. So, the UFO mystery remained active even if at a reduced level.

Puzzling aspects: Absence of ET contact and Abductions

One aspect of the Bonnybridge 'wave' which puzzled me at the time and continues to puzzle me is the lack of ET contact cases or alleged abductions. We know that several such cases were reported at sites to the east of Bonnybridge in the West Lothian area, but it's almost as if there was a line drawn which separated Bonnybridge from these alien encounter areas. Was this deliberate? An extraterrestrial ploy of some kind? One of Scotland's most famous cases the Bob Taylor encounter at Dechmont Law (or hill) at Livingston took place no more than sixteen miles (25.75 kilometres) from Bonnybridge. And then in 1990 came the A70 abduction incident at a time when the Bonnybridge phenomenon was just getting underway. In this encounter Gary Wood and Colin Wright were, it is reported, lifted from the car in which they were travelling and taken to a craft of some kind where they underwent a medical examination by alien beings. And then in October 1999 a man taking his dog for a walk near Deans High School close to the location of the Bob Taylor sighting of 1979 - was confronted by a figure seven feet tall (2.13 meters) with a glowing head, hands and feet. The witness approached to within ten feet of the figure and called out, 'hello, can I help you?'. The entity did not reply but turned in the direction of the witness who took fright and left the area.

Though the A70 event took place at a distance of a no more than a few miles from the centre of Bonnybridge there was nothing similar taking place within the Bonnybridge core area of activity. Why was that? It's possible that any such events were not drawn to my attention at the time. However, there was one case of an alien presence that allegedly occurred. Unfortunately, I did not have the opportunity to investigate this incident and only became aware of it sometime later and so can't vouch for the details. I've no doubt though that those who did follow it up reported the events accurately having interviewed those involved.

The events took place in the town of Grangemouth just a few miles north of Bonnybridge on the flat area of land beside the Firth of Forth. The reported encounter involved two young girls aged four and two who lived with their parents in a block of flats. The incidents started with the appearance of odd-looking lights hovering in the sky. The lights could not be identified, apparently. Was there a connection with what happened next? Or was it just coincidence? Events took a dramatic turn when the four-year-old was frightened by the appearance of a strange being in her bedroom. These encounters continued for several days. The girl's mother wasn't sure if these events were real or imagined, but she herself got a shock when a light hovering in the distance moved rapidly towards the block of flats and actually entered her bedroom. Those interested in the UFO phenomenon will be aware that a strange light entering a room apparently travelling through brick or stone walls or glass has been reported in a number of cases. It's always difficult to know what to make of a report involving a young child. Is it, as the mother wondered, real or imagined? On the other hand, it seems to be the case that children often see and take for granted the appearance of entities - ghostly figures are often reported by toddlers - so the appearance of alien like beings might fall into this category. As children grow older this almost psychic like ability to see beyond everyday reality seems to fade away. So, I certainly don't dismiss this particular encounter simply because it involved a child. Overall, however, the absence of significant alien contact and abduction cases linked to Bonnybridge is rather strange. I investigated at least two other detailed abduction cases in West Lothian which borders the Falkirk area. As I suggested I'm inclined to link these incidents to the Bonnybridge phenomenon. Little distance separates these two cases from the village, but I remain puzzled as to why there were no similar incidents not only in Bonnybridge itself, but even in places close by such as Grangemouth or Stenhousemuir both areas where several UFOs had been seen. Maybe any abduction incidents or alien entity sightings simply, for whatever reason, have not been reported to investigators.

Mutilations?

What other events generally associated with the UFO phenomenon are absent? One that struck me is the controversial subject of animal mutilation. It's certainly true that the mutilation of animals occurs quite separately from any obvious link to UFO encounters and, for example, are sometimes connected - unfairly and with no evidence - to contemporary witchcraft activity. In the USA Linda Moulton Howe caused controversy by claiming that a wave of apparent cattle mutilation in the 1960s was linked to UFO activity, particularly in the state of Colorado. It was reported that cow parts, for example udders, had been surgically removed and could not have been done in a random manner by, for example, predators or by a process of natural decay. (for a more detailed discussion see Moulton Howe's book, 'An Alien Harvest').

Linda's claims were contested with some suggesting that the ranchers were inventing stories of UFO sightings and consequent cattle mutilation to support claims for government compensation. But in 1973 police forces in Kansas and Nebraska investigated more cases of cattle mutilation with sexual organs apparently surgically removed. Then in 1975 senator Frank Haskell claimed that there were over 100 cases of mutilation in his state of Colorado and demanded an FBI investigation. Cases were reported in Colorado as recently as 2021 with similar reports coming in from Australia. So there appears little doubt that going by incidents not only in Scotland, but world-wide that inexplicable attacks, often on farm animals, do occur. Non-farm animals have also been reported to have suffered mutilation, pet cats in particular and perhaps other animals which because they live in the wild just don't get noticed. That being said there is no evidence that the phenomenon of animal mutilation occurred around the village of Bonnybridge. There is a claim of a mutilated sheep in West Lothian in the vicinity of Edinburgh airport dating from 1998 - a video was made of the scene which I did view, but whether or not it fitted the description of 'mutilation' it was difficult to determine without having the opportunity to examine the carcass.

A bit closer to home, however, was an incident at Whitehill Farm, Denny. As noted in the 'Falkirk Herald' under the headline, 'Sheep Farmer Horrified by Dog attack' the paper reported that dogs had carried out a frenzied attack on several sheep grazing in a farmer's field. The sheep suffered horrific injuries with their stomachs having been ripped open and their legs badly mutilated. What was odd was that the subject of these attacks had been pedigree rams and rams are perfectly capable of defending themselves. In 2015, for example, the 'Journal of Forensic Science' reported the case of an 83-year-old man killed by a four-year-old ram weighing 120 kilograms (nearly 19 stone). In fact, a ram's headbutt can exert almost 800 pounds of force. They are no pushover by any means. So, it seems odd that they had suffered in this way and to such an extent. The farmer Mr. Harry Bennie, however, was convinced that dogs were the culprits on the quite reasonable grounds that it was hard to believe what else could have been responsible. It has been speculated that this incident didn't resemble a typical dog attack as it was of a peculiarly savage nature. But if not carried out by dogs - and it must have involved more than one dog - then could it be as some have speculated carried out by a puma or even some unknown animal like the chupacabra? This beast is a legendary creature recorded in folklore in the Americas and is linked to vampirism - sucking the blood of farm animals which it generally finds an easy target. However, before delving into the darker possibilities it has to be noted that a dog attacking sheep in the Bonnybridge area had led to a court case and a conviction, but not in the above incident.

Looking across the whole of Scotland there appears to be little evidence of animal mutilation being linked to alien activity in the sense that we can connect UFO sightings to those mutilation cases that have definitely occurred. But in fact, Bonnybridge is no different then from Scotland, or the world, as a whole. Might we expect animal mutilation cases? It's difficult to be definite but given that across the globe the incidence of mutilation is comparatively rare by comparison to the number of reported UFO encounters then in that sense Bonnybridge is not the anomaly rather it's animal mutilation that stands out as being different.

CHAPTER EIGHT
CAN WE EXPLAIN EVENTS IN BONNYBRIDGE?

Where do UFOS come from?

The central mystery of the Bonnybridge phenomenon, of course, lies in the origin of the unidentified flying objects apparently sighted with such regularity. I suggest that to answer this question we have to look beyond the immediate Bonnybridge area to surrounding parts. In Scotland we tend to think of forty miles as a long way whereas in other countries people would drive that distance just to pick up a newspaper. So, in my view the distance between Bonnybridge and say the town of Livingston at 30 odd miles as the crow flies is not so far off. Furthermore, if we are considering nuts-and-bolts spacecraft it's hardly the blink of an eye to travel across that gap. On the other hand, if we think out of the box it could be the case of a multi-dimensional explanation and that alien beings could, in fact, be living right beside us. There are so many possible answers to the UFO enigma that nothing can be taken for granted. That is why I certainly don't dismiss the suggestion that the Bonnybridge UFOs might have come from an underground base located just a few miles from the village. It's a possibility worthy of serious consideration. Gary Wood who was allegedly abducted by alien entities on the A70 road, having contemplated the origin of the beings he encountered, took the view that he might have been taken to a site below the ground rather than to a craft in the sky.

Another abductee from West Lothian, living not far from the site of the A70 incident, also thought that he had been transported to a location that struck him as being below the earth's surface. He came to this conclusion because the layout of the environment he found himself in appeared to him, as an engineer, to be of a building of some type rather than a spaceship. Of course, that's not to rule out a craft of some kind being involved in an initial abduction, but it does provide a possible explanation as to where some of the UFOs might be coming from and why they manage to appear then disappear so frequently and quickly.

UFOs - the answers?

I don't intend to simply run through all potential answers to the UFO enigma. My aim is to relate explanations - put forward by various researchers - to events in Bonnybridge. Does what happened in the village either confirm or cast doubt on those theories which try to answer the perplexing questions - what are UFOs and where do they come from? And can we apply general, all encompassing 'solutions' to the UFO phenomena in Bonnybridge? Given the volume of evidence that we appear to have in this concentrated area do particular theories about UFOs make more sense than others? When it comes to a general explanation of the UFO phenomenon you can take your pick from multiple ideas. Are *we* in fact the 'aliens'? A race from a distant galaxy that was stranded on Earth millennia ago? If not, have aliens from distant planets been visiting the Earth for generations? Did they in fact build the pyramids, structures which seem beyond the capabilities of past civilisations, as we know them, to erect? But it might be asked, supposing that this was the case what was the point of our alien visitors in doing this? And why just the Egyptian pyramids?

The case for an alien race building the pyramids of ancient Egypt though well-argued by a number of writers, does seem hard to believe. However, even some scientists have put forward theories that stretch the imagination suggesting, for example, that our universe is one among multiple universes or that we are part of a multi-dimensional universe which interacts with itself in bizarre ways allowing time travel to the past and future. I remember a popular theory from the early 2000s that a passing comet had deposited bacteria which drifted to the Earth and from which life then developed. As the 'Daily Mail' of 22nd November 2000 put it, 'Did an alien bacteria trigger life on Earth?'. The truth is that we have no idea of how the universe was formed, if it ever ends or how life developed - unless you swallow the theory (and it is a theory not proven fact) of evolution and natural selection. And you don't have to believe that God created the world to be sceptical of Neo-Darwinist claims or 'explanations' from scientists as to how the 'universe' was born. We have to face up to the fact that we just don't know.

Nuts-and-bolts spacecraft

There are many involved in Ufology who would ask, 'What's the problem? It's quite clear that we *are* being visited by alien entities travelling here in their spacecraft and observing us, and for reasons which aren't clear, abducting some people although on the other hand, if some ufologists are to be believed, protecting we Earthlings from self-destruction. So maybe there are both good aliens and bad aliens? And if not how can we account for those incidents in which some individuals are taken away without their consent yet at the same time cosmic groups like the 'Council of Nine' are supposed to be looking after us. It's puzzling and contradictory. So, at the risk of upsetting those who take this view I'd pose some questions on the nuts-and-bolts theory.

On the surface it appears a straightforward and reasonable solution to UFO sightings. But there are, of course, some obvious practical problems. In the first place the sheer mind-boggling distance that any spacecraft would have to travel has to be borne in mind. The nearest star is three million light years away. So, travelling at the speed of light, that is 186,000 miles per second, it would take an impossible time for we Earthlings to travel to any nearest habitable planet even if we could identify one that it was possible to land on. There are other issues which have been raised in connection with the moon landings, an object a mere 240,000 miles away. There is endless talk by vested interests, for example, NASA of a trip to Mars, 34 million miles away at its nearest point. With our present propulsion systems, a three year round trip has been suggested - presupposing the astronauts survive the journey and manage a lift off back from Mars.

In general, the assumption is that alien spacecraft would employ a propulsion system which would allow them to travel incredible distances in rapid time. The difficulty with this is the belief that it is not possible to travel faster than the speed of light. So even a journey from whatever habitable planets are out there would appear impractical. So, if these nuts-and-bolts craft are from distant planets there must be other ways we can only guess at to get here. Is it via worm holes or some other strange cosmic aberration? It should be noted that in respect of the propulsion systems and UFO sightings there are what appear to be anomalies. Tom Coventry for example when he experienced his encounter in Glasgow described a craft spouting flames and this is by no means unique - other witnesses have reported cases where a UFO has emitted what appears to be blasts of a fuel exhaust. Alien spacecraft seemingly driven by some form of jet propulsion? It makes absolutely no sense, but this is a part of the continuing puzzle of the UFO phenomenon. Bonnybridge can shed no particular light on this issue. As in many hot-spots the sightings are too diverse or too distant to come to any conclusion. UFOs - whatever they are - must move as in most cases by a system we can only guess at.

Role of Councillor Billy Buchanan

In his book 'Zones of Strangeness' writer Peter McCue suggests that Buchanan was the key factor in developing the Bonnybridge UFO phenomenon. Buchanan has been described both as an eccentric and a publicity seeker. I don't believe this to be the case - particularly if reports in the 'Falkirk Herald' are anything to go by. But how did Buchanan emerge on to the UFO scene? It's clear that he was a well-known figure in Bonnybridge area by the early 1990s.

On 20th February 1992, for example, he appeared in an article headed, 'Bats will prevent church demolition', reporting Buchanan's opposition to the demolition of historic Dennyloanhead church. In May 1992 Buchanan stood for Falkirk District Council in the Antonine ward which covered Bonnybridge, saying as quoted in the 'Falkirk Herald', 'Decline must be reversed. I've been involved in the community since I came back from abroad after many years playing football in Hong Kong, Australia and South Arabia. It appeared to me that there seemed an inability by our elected councillors to stem the decline of living standards in this area[...]We could have a thriving tourist trade with our natural heritage.' Other issues Buchanan was involved in included advocating the organising of an event for teenagers, arguing for a police station to be located in Bonnybridge, and criticising a court decision to allow a woman to keep a dog which had savaged sheep.

I mention these to correct any impression that Buchanan was obsessed with UFO sightings. Furthermore, there's little doubt that Buchanan was a popular local figure. As an independent candidate in the council elections, he romped home beating Labour and SNP candidates and securing a majority of over 800. Was there any need, therefore, for Buchanan to get involved in a topic as 'way out' as UFOs? On the face of it, it seems, given his local support and his later election to the regional council, that far from boosting his popularity, an interest in 'flying saucers' ran the risk of denting his credibility. According to Malcolm Robinson Buchanan was understandably concerned about this possible effect. However, he did put his name to the UFO subject which according to his account was forced on him by concerns expressed by his local constituents. If Buchanan was a publicity seeker and was using UFOs as a vehicle there's evidence to counter this view. The first article covering UFOs in the area appeared in the 'Falkirk Herald' of 12th November 1992. It covers the Sloggett and Stocks cases. There's no mention of Councillor Buchanan though Malcolm Robinson who had by this time teamed up with Buchanan was name-checked. The same is true of the next UFO story covered by the paper in which Buchanan's name was notable by its absence though once again Robinson is mentioned.

If Buchanan was such a publicity seeker it's hard to believe that if he'd chosen to, he could have inserted himself into these articles. He may, of course, have been reticent about appearing in the local press but if the national press were interested, coverage in the locals would not have made much difference to his standing. However, there's little doubt that once the UFO story took wings Buchanan became fully involved appearing in various TV programmes and quoted in many newspaper articles. Having once had his name linked to the phenomenon it was difficult to escape media interest. It would have taken a real effort to step back from it and there was certainly speculation that Buchanan felt that outside interest would be of benefit to Bonnybridge if only on the tourist front. He had a fair point. It's hard to escape the fact that because Buchanan was a local councillor it was enough to fuel the Bonnybridge phenomenon, in the sense that it almost gave it official status. How many councillors in Scotland would have been willing to risk their credibility by becoming involved in the UFO phenomenon? In that sense Buchanan stood out as someone willing to put his reputation on the line.

Earthlights

One explanation put forward for UFO sightings is that they are the product of the phenomenon known as 'earthlights' - balls of energy emitted from the ground due to tectonic pressure. Balls of light have certainly been observed in areas around Bonnybridge. At a location known as 'High Camillity' just a few miles from the village spheres of glowing light were regularly reported by residents living in a property located there. The glowing orbs came right up to the house on several occasions and even penetrated the building. Earthlights resemble another phenomenon called 'ball lightening': this is certainly an event recognised by science but remains controversial. It is possible that ball lightening could explain a few UFO incidents in Bonnybridge, but it is an unusual occurrence not often reported. However, there have been far too many UFO sightings for this phenomenon to provide an answer to the diverse range of witness reports that have been recorded across the world over the last seventy years.

But if we rule out ball lightening does the same apply to earthlights? These are associated with areas of earthquake activity and Scotland does regularly experience earthquakes. I've taken 1996 as an example of seismic activity as this was a time of continued UFO activity in Bonnybridge. In that year, according to the 'Bulletin of British Earthquakes' there were an amazing 100 earthquakes recorded in Scotland. However, most of these were at the bottom of the seismic scale at level 1 (it goes up to the highest:10) which is classified as 'not felt'. The most violent earthquake that year was at Loch Fyne hundreds of miles from Bonnybridge, an event registered as just under level 3. But even at that level this incident was still classified as 'weak': the vibration is felt indoors by a few people and people at rest feel a swaying or light trembling. It seems unlikely that these minor tremors would bring about the appearance of earthlights.

However, the key aspect from our perspective is that no seismic tremors were recorded in 1996 within the Bonnybridge area. It is true though that tremors between level 1 and 2 were recorded in Clackmannanshire several times - a few miles across the Firth of Forth from Bonnybridge. However, I would suggest these minor 'quakes' were far too insignificant to impact on Bonnybridge and cause light effects that would produce UFO sightings. So, in spite of suggestions that this phenomenon could account for Bonnybridge UFOs I would argue that there is no evidence to support this theory.

But to be sure I contacted the 'British Geological Survey' (BGS). In response the BGS confirmed the existence of 'earthquake lights 'and gave the example of the 'luminous night sky which was reported north of Fruili in Italy before and after the 6 May 1976 earthquake' [magnitude 6.5 incidentally] adding, 'other examples of similar lights or flashes close to the time of earthquake occurrences have been reported.' The reply continued, 'There has been speculation that quartz crystals in the rock respond to rapidly changing stresses by emitting electro-magnetic radiation which give rise to the "lights" seen.' The reply concludes, significantly in my view, 'the West Lothian area is not seismically a particularly active area even by UK standards'. It's fairly conclusive then that 'Earthlights' even if they exist can't explain events in Bonnybridge. Interestingly, in January 1998 a group did investigate possible earthquake activity in East Kilbridge which can certainly boast a significant number of UFO incidents. In this instance the organisation involved was one from the Netherlands titled 'UFO and Space Research Investigations'. The group were collecting witness reports of strange objects in the sky and relating them to possible quake activity. There had been claims of weird booming sounds which could have resulted from earth tremors though according to British Geological Survey scientists they were unsure of origin of the noise which they described as neither sonic nor from below ground. A double mystery.

However, there's a suggestion that at least some of the sightings could be attributed to ball lightning. Given that UFO witnesses on a number of occasions have commented on seeing a bright glowing object then it's possible we are dealing with the phenomenon of ball lighting or something of a similar nature. An interesting twist on this came in a letter to the 'Falkirk Herald' from Alan Smith of Melton Mowbray, Leicestershire. Mr Smith speculated that balls of light could be the product of the motorway system. He suggested that the continual flow of traffic could electrostatically charge the atmosphere in the vicinity. I haven't heard this theory propounded elsewhere and I don't have the technical knowledge to evaluate it. The nearest motorway to Bonnybridge is the M80 which runs from Stirling to Glasgow and lies only a few miles away. My only query would be on the basis that the vast majority of UFO sightings occur miles distant from motorways and even if this could be an answer it can only explain an insignificant number of incidents.

Misidentification

Those involved in investigating UFO reports are well aware that many are simply misidentification of everyday objects such as planes and even night-time stars. In fact, sceptics ask, 'Are there really any UFOs?' Can't it all be explained by simple mistakes on the part of witnesses? In his book, 'The Loch Ness Monster: the Evidence' (1991) author and investigator Steuart Campbell argues that simply because there have been many alleged sightings of the Loch Ness 'monster' doesn't automatically prove that there's an unknown flesh-and-blood beast living there. In other words, a large number of claimed reports, including video and photographs, proves nothing if each sighting is based on a misidentification of an everyday object, boats or tree trunks floating in the loch for example.

It's a valid point. So, can the same apply to UFO reports? Estimates of how many sightings are simply misidentification vary according to the ufologist in question, but a figure of 95% is bandied about. It's unclear as to how this figure is arrived at. I can't confirm or deny it. There's no doubt though that a high proportion of sightings can be explained. I mentioned the supposed UFO video which turned out to be the planet, Venus. A phone call I received one evening reported a strange red object in the sky. 'Is it moving', I asked. Answer, 'no'. I explained that it was probably the planet Mars prominent in the sky at that time of year. I'd seen it myself not long before the call came. The caller seemed rather taken aback by my explanation. If you're not particularly interested in the night sky it's understandable that you might be unaware that at certain times of the year planets can be relatively easily seen and, for example, that stars can give the appearance of moving. In general night-time sightings of odd objects can be difficult to pin down. But the same can be true of reports of daytime objects. Planes can look a strange shape when viewed from an odd angle even appearing circular. There are a large number of flight paths over Scotland and not every flight can be monitored. The military for example isn't going to reveal RAF flights readily or without good reason. Plus, there are an extensive number of 'over flights' by planes from other countries particularly military aircraft and these are unlikely to be revealed to an inquisitive ufologist.

If we consider the location of Bonnybridge which lies within the central belt of Scotland, then its proximity to Scotland's main airports of Edinburgh and Glasgow with another (though minor one) at nearby Cumbernauld suggests that these can't be ruled out as a possible factor in generating UFO reports. According to the published figures in 2023, for example, there were over 300 flights to and from Edinburgh airport per day. Glasgow slightly less but still significant. It's true that in the 1990s there were fewer flights, but still a substantial number. Cumbernauld is of a different order, but light aircraft and helicopters operate from it on a daily basis. I'd be very surprised if some of these flights didn't generate a number of UFO sightings in the Bonnybridge area, but I'm convinced it can't explain them all or even a majority though it is difficult to quantify how many are simply mistakes and how many genuine

UFOS. Local witnesses insist they can tell the difference between a plane -as they see them so often- and an object in the sky they can't recognise.

The Millenium: The prospect of the year 2000

The Bonnybridge phenomenon occurred during the 1990s in the run up to the millennium, 2000 years since the birth of Jesus Christ - that's the historic reason for the celebration even if you are sceptical of the Christian narrative. Other religions have their own dating systems of course, for example 2023 in the Muslim countries was 1445 AH. The arrival of a new millennium can generate a range of emotions in humanity. The excitement produced in the British Isles as the year 1000 approached is well documented though on that occasion it was the second coming of Christ which generated the emotional frenzy recorded with individuals claiming to have seen all kinds of signs that heralded the arrival of the saviour back on Earth.

One thousand years on the prospect of Jesus returning to his people in the year 2000 was believed in by only a tiny minority. But if we were not going to have the wonderment of a return of the man who, in Christian belief, died to save us, the veritable 'son of God', perhaps a different revelation might be a substitute. The arrival of alien creatures from distant planets might be the new equivalent. Strange signs in the skies, but this time of Unidentified Flying Objects. Whether or not a new millennium does bring drastic change is debatable, but I'd suggest the atmosphere created, that we were on the verge of some kind of a great transposition, could be a factor in leading people to be more susceptible to the possibility of spacecraft from far away locations travelling vast distances to visit us.

Ley Lines

An explanation for the presence of UFOs which has been put forward to account for a number of incidents in Bonnybridge is what are known as 'ley lines'. The idea of ley lines was first put forward by Alfred Watkins in his book 'The Old Straight Track' published as far back as 1925. Watkins believed that ancient monuments such as stone circles had been sited in a series of straight lines so that they aligned with each other and were connected by a 'straight track' as in the title of the book. Investigators into this phenomenon then wondered why this should be the case - why would our ancestors have sought to build these monuments so that they aligned with each other? It was suggested that in a sense it was accidental. The Earth it is argued is criss-crossed by a series of 'energy lines' - lines of some kind of unknown force. Our ancestors, either unknowingly or by some shamanistic method tapped into the energy emitted by these lines and built the stone monuments we see today to tap into this mysterious force.

Modern dowsers, for example David Cowan based in Crieff, can detect the route of these lines through dowsing. I can confirm their existence as I have dowsed in various parts of Scotland and discovered that wherever you go these lines of energy will be found. But what is the connection to UFOs? It was suggested that alien craft follow these lines to extract energy to run their propulsion systems. This was proposed as far back as 1961 by Tony Wedd in his book 'Skyways and Landmarks' though he saw it as a path of some type alien spacecraft made use of to navigate. Wedd and researcher John Michell developed this idea proposing that ley lines possessed some kind of paranormal force which had been used for directional purposes. This does strike me as unlikely. You would think that UFOs would be advanced enough to travel vast distances without relying on mysterious energy lines beneath the Earth. And in any case this theory can't explain the intensity around Bonnybridge as ley lines can be found everywhere so there would be no reason to focus on one area. But as with everything in ufology anything seems possible.

A multiverse Universe?

Puzzling over the UFO problem ideas pop up which may seem 'out of the box'. Or quite simply so fantastic as to be unbelievable. But should we dismiss possible solutions out of hand because they are difficult to get our collective heads around? In the case of Bonnybridge we have many witnesses to sightings of all kinds. There's no doubt that 'something' is being seen, but it's reasonable to ask, why don't we have 100% proof that what is taking place is an alien visitation - for whatever reason. Where are the nuts-and-bolts spacecraft landing in the centre of Bonnybridge? It appears that on numerous occasions the object seen appears real and solid so where has it come from and where does it go?

One possible answer could be from another 'dimension' which I would interpret as from a different universe, one which exists in conjunction with our own and on occasions interacts with it. The inhabitants of this alternative universe would not necessarily be aware of our existence and could be as mystified as we are by the appearance of Earth produced objects - planes, rockets and even humanity itself. The multiverse theory would explain why witnesses to UFOs remark on their ability to seemingly defy the laws of gravity and disappear in a split second. *But*, and it's a big *but*, the multiverse is only a theory though there are claims that it has been proved mathematically. If this theory holds water a witness standing on Bonnybridge High Street and seeing a UFO could in fact be literally gazing into another world. Not one located a billion light years away, but to all intents and purposes rubbing shoulders with our own. Furthermore, it wouldn't necessarily be a world in our time-frame. It could be from times past or in the future. I'm aware that the more you consider this idea the more fantastic and unreal it strikes you. Yet unless UFOs are simply misinterpreted natural phenomena which I don't believe, there must be an answer, and it may be as mind-boggling as the multi-universe theory. One thing is certain. Our view of the cosmos is constantly changing, and discoveries made which challenge, and even radically alter, the currently accepted structure of the universe. In January 2023, for example, Pallab Ghosh a BBC science correspondent penned an article headed, 'Huge ring of galaxies challenges thinking on the cosmos'. Scientists at the University of Central Lancashire had announced the discovery of an enormous structure shaped like a ring out in the vastness of space. Astronomers had labelled it the 'Big Ring' and it consisted of galaxies and galaxy clusters. But for those of us interested in the UFO question the interesting aspect is that according to scientists this collection of gigantic objects should not exist if our current knowledge of the universe is accurate. In fact, the 'Big Ring' is so huge it challenges the existence of the cosmos as we understand its present form. What can we take from this? We don't have to be scientists or astronomers to ask the question - can we be sure that everything we have been taught about what the universe is and how it acts is correct? Is the cosmos so strange that even seemingly impossible things could in fact be possible. And could this include time-travel? One of the explanations for UFO sightings is that these are spacecraft from the future. 'Time' may be a man-made construction, but it reflects what appears obvious that 'things' - including humanity - undergo changes, as the universe in its entirety appears to do. However, time-travel suggests that events that happened hundreds, even thousands of years in the past or in the future exist at this very moment. So that the Battle of Bannockburn (AD 1314) is somehow, and somewhere, still taking place and that if we by some means made a return visit from today it would still be underway.

On the face of it it seems unlikely. But if the multiverse is a reality, then by some means a planet 'Earth' exists in another universe and so, in theory, we could actually visit past and future events. And this could be with or without time-travel if another world operates on the same plane as our own. To say there are a number of 'buts' to this idea is an understatement. By what method would we get to the past and future? How do UFOs travel to our world from other universes? Is there some kind of 'window' which opens to allow us to see into these various worlds as some ufologists have speculated? Even if we apply this idea to Bonnybridge sightings it still brings us back to the question 'why Bonnybridge?' UFOs are reported from every part of Scotland, and of course the world, so can we put all this down to the 'window into another dimension' theory? We have to be honest and admit that multiverses and time-travel are at the level of speculation even fantasy. They may provide an answer but also raise a host of questions which at the moment simply can't be answered. UFOs from other universes rather than distant planets? It's a solution, but more evidence is required to back it up. And maybe that will not be too far in the distance. In an article in the publication 'New Scientist' writer Miriam Frankel reported that experiments were underway at the University of Cambridge to test whether the multi universe was a possible reality.

Illness generating UFO reports

One factor rarely considered is the role which might be played by a person's illness in generating UFO sightings. In his book 'The UFO Mystery Solved' writer Steuart Campbell raised this in connection with the Bob Taylor sighting of a hovering spacecraft on Dechmont Law in November 1979. Campbell suggested that Taylor could have suffered an epileptic fit and so imagined the UFO encounter, that is the events were generated within his brain and had no existence in reality. This explanation has not been generally accepted but remains a theory worthy of serious consideration.

In my years of investigating the phenomenon I've only come across one case where the witness had an illness which could have affected the UFO encounter experienced. For the obvious reason of anonymity, I won't reveal either the individual or details of the sighting. In this case the person had a brain tumour a condition which can of course have a significant impact on various functions of the mind. But not withstanding the tumour the individual was still going to work and perfectly lucid when I conducted an interview. The sighting itself lasted several minutes which the witness related in detail. I believe the ability to recall the event so minutely suggests that what was seen was not the product of an unwell brain. It is true that in this case the event took place in an urban setting, but even so no one else reported seeing the UFO. However, that is a regular occurrence. A witness sights a seemingly prominent object - a spacecraft - and no one else appears to see it. However, I would refer to the cases involving witnesses Angela Humphreys and Pat Macleod where UFOs which it seemed impossible to miss were seen by no one other than the sole witness in each incident. In Angela's encounter which occurred on the busy bridge which crosses the river Tay in the city of Perth she observed a translucent object between thirty to forty feet long hovering in front of her. Through a window she could make out several small entities. However, in spite of continuous passing traffic and pedestrians no one else seemed to be aware of it.

In Edinburgh Pat Macleod was driving along Duddingston Park at 9.50am when she became aware of a bright light in the sky which moved closer with the light becoming ever more intense. Pat described the object as Saturn like as it had a prominent flange round it. It hovered about thirty feet from the road then appeared to land on a piece of ground nearby. However, when Pat went to investigate there was no sign of it. This incident which I investigated at the time generated significant publicity but not a single additional person came forward to report having seen this UFO. Yet one more mysterious aspect of the UFO phenomenon.

There are cases - again I know of at least one important incident in Scotland - where the witness felt unwell after the encounter and had to take to bed for a few days. However, was this caused by the UFO experience or was the witness 'going down' with something before the event occurred? Had the witness been suffering from a virus or infection of some kind which distorted the senses and somehow generated the encounter? It goes without saying that viruses can affect people's perception so that they 'see' people who aren't there, the condition known as 'delirium' is a case in point. But those affected are usually quite obviously unwell so don't simply hallucinate without other symptoms. With so many UFO sightings by individuals clearly not suffering from any illness it's reasonable to assume that being unwell can -if at all- only explain a tiny fraction of UFO reports.

A hollow earth?

Admittedly a strange theory but does it have any relevance to events in Bonnybridge? Though it may be hard to believe this concept has had many followers. Essentially the argument runs that below the surface, underground, there are other civilisations in existence. And that these could have an alien origin. It is claimed that there are specific entry points to these underground complexes - ones at the North and South poles are cited, for example, but in theory there are access tunnels spaced out across the world and even below the seas and oceans. In fact, they might be only a few miles from where you or any of us are living.

Robert Lei a Norwegian who came to Scotland during the war to escape the Nazi invasion of his country was convinced that UFOs which passed over his house in the village of Kinbuck in Perthshire were emerging from hills he could see from a rise behind his house. I spent many hours with Mr Lei watching the area he indicated and there did seem to be shining objects which appeared and disappeared. But was this just the effect of the sun and changing light patterns? The hills were several miles distant, and you had to view the area in question via binoculars. The site where the UFOs were seen was only accessible by foot over incredibly rough ground and though we attempted to walk there one day the terrain defeated us which was deeply disappointing. Robert never mentioned the 'hollow earth' theory to me and as far as I was aware hadn't heard of it. On top of this it's worth noting that Gary Wood of the A70 case suspected that rather than being transported to a spacecraft he had actually been taken underground. This was also the view of another witness from a nearby location who believed he had been at a base below the earth though taken aboard a disc shaped UFO first.

UFOs have also been reported below or emerging from under the water. In 1997 to take one incident in Loch Nevis in Scotland a micro light pilot, Hamish Smith, spotted an unidentified object lying below the surface of the loch. Hamish claimed that he had 'never seen anything like it. It was not a shoal of fish and the entrance to the loch is only eight meters deep so it couldn't be a submarine'. The coastguard and police were alerted but they took several days to investigate so found nothing though echo sounding equipment apparently registered an 'anomaly'. Given the size of the object if the photo taken was accurate then entry via the sea seems unlikely and perhaps it did enter the loch through an underwater hole of some kind and belonged to a civilisation inside the Earth.

But admittedly it's all speculation. So, is there really any solid evidence in support of the 'hollow earth' theory? Even in remote spots such as the Arctic, Antarctic or Amazon forest there's a lack of solid information to provide significant support for this idea. In relation to Bonnybridge we're in the same ballpark: speculation and possibilities rather than any definite evidence. For example, I'm not aware of any reports of eyewitness seeing a UFO emerge from the ground in or around the general Falkirk area. Even a single report would be interesting though not conclusive. Most Bonnybridge UFO sightings are 'in the sky' occasionally near or on the ground but not coming out of it. I find it an attractive theory, but nothing more than a theory, unfortunately.

Zodiac Signs?

Heading into the mystical may be nothing out of the ordinary for those interested in ufology but could there conceivably be any connection to the zodiac symbols under which we, according to astrologers, are all born. My 'star sign' is Leo as my birth date is 16th August. But does that make me more or less susceptible to having a UFO encounter? The astrology signs are split into sun, water, earth and fire. Is there any evidence that people born under one zodiac division, say earth signs, rather than another, say fire signs, are more likely to experience a mystical experience of some kind? Looking at the UFO phenomenon in general there simply isn't adequate data to determine it one way or another. My 'guesstimate' is that there is no evidence to suggest that one star sign produces more UFO witnesses than another. And applying this to Bonnybridge there's nothing to convince me that the position is any different from the general, that is, that all star signs produce similar levels of UFO witnesses. But I'm willing to be convinced otherwise if the proof is out there.

However, we're not just considering individual witnesses, but times when UFO sightings take place. Is there any obvious links between star signs and the months of the year when incidents are reported? The star sign Leo to take one runs from July 23rd to August 22. Is there any evidence that UFO reports occur more frequently during this period or occur less frequently? According to the data I analysed up to the late

1990s (to cover the Bonnybridge period) UFO reports did vary from month to month and from season to season, but there are a variety of possible explanations for this variation. The months with the highest proportion of reported sightings were November, December January, February while the months March to July were lowest. It's possible that odd lights in the sky were more noticeable in the darker winter months and less evident during the period when nights were lighter. Following up the zodiac connection the star signs most closely linked to the months when UFO reports were higher are Sagittarius, Capricorn, Aquarius and Pisces. I'm unclear if there is any significance to this, but as far as I can see there's no evidence that UFO sightings are linked to a witnesses' star sign fascinating though this would be, but if anyone has a contrary view, I'd be interested to hear about it.

Role of Investigators

As one of the investigators into the Bonnybridge UFO phenomenon I've asked myself if those of us involved played a part in establishing the Bonnybridge hotspot reputation? The fact that we were looking into events there undoubtedly gave it from the start a certain credibility. Journalists could justify writing articles about the village on the basis that if UFO researchers were interested something significant must have encouraged them to investigate. Malcolm Robinson, for example, was well known to the media and his arrival on the scene gave the press a hook on which to hang UFO reports with comments from an 'expert' on the phenomenon. It's noticeable that in the late 1990s media interest in the area declined around the time in 1998 that Robinson moved to England, but that may well have been coincidence as Billy Buchanan was still in place and UFO stories continued to appear though the frenetic pace of earlier years had moved down a couple of gears. Overall, though, it's hard to escape the conclusion that the involvement of individuals who researched and were knowledgeable on the UFO topic fed into and boosted media interest in Bonnybridge.

Grangemouth Complex

Turning to a more practical explanation there have been observers to the UFO scene who argue that UFOs have a particular interest in certain types of establishments - military bases, nuclear power plants and large industrial complexes among others. There could be a case for arguing that aliens could have an interest in sites where nuclear weapons are located, for example, but would this extend to manufacturing plants? At Grangemouth a few miles north of Bonnybridge lies one of the biggest crude oil refineries in Europe covering an area of 1,700 acres and the only one of its kind in Scotland. In the 1990s it employed between 1,500 to 2,000 people processing over ten million tonnes of crude oil per year. Given its vast scale could this industrial giant have attracted the interest of alien spacecraft? For whatever reason that might be?

In November 1991, for example, two witnesses watched a UFO moving over the Grangemouth area and managed to photograph the object. Certainly, during this period various UFOs were witnessed close to the complex, but as there were multiple sightings of unidentified objects at many locations in the general area it's hard to make out a case for Grangemouth being a site of special interest to beings from another world. What would spacecraft from advanced civilisations gain from observing or gathering information on the refinery? I'm inclined to believe that UFO activity around here was simply coincidence, but without further evidence it's hard to come to any definite conclusion.

Illuminati

Where UFOs are concerned nothing seems beyond consideration as an explanation. Supposedly the Illuminati are a secret, or semi-secret society which has been operating behind the scenes for centuries, possibly even millennia. It is made up of powerful individuals who run or attempt to run the world hiding in plain sight. In this scenario we - the vast majority of the human race - are mere puppets even slaves in a gigantic deception perpetrated on us by the Illuminati.

But what possible connection could there be between this ancient secretive organisation and UFOs. Various suggestion have been made. The Illuminati is run by shapeshifting aliens who arrived on Earth many epochs in the past and have been ruling us ever since. Alternatively, the Illuminati are conspiring with alien reptilians to take over the world by stealth. The appearance of UFOs could be part of a plot to distract us from the real conspiracy or genuine transport vehicles from distant planets which are supporting in some way the Illuminati/alien plan to dominate our world. However, the evidence for this in respect of events in Bonnybridge appears non-existent as there is no obvious Illuminati contact who could act as source for any planned invasion. On the other hand as part of a plan to distract the world from an alien takeover or prepare us for it then Bonnybridge could fit that scenario. However, it's fair to say that to date there have been no great revelation arising from 'UFO Bonnybridge' and the Illuminati and Bonnybridge seem a world apart.

Aliens are our friends. Or are we the aliens?

Various organisations, and individuals, claim or have claimed to be part of an intergalactic federation receiving and passing on messages from 'extraterrestrials'. The implication of this is that 'aliens' don't in reality exist as we on Earth are not unique, but simply one component of all that there is that makes up the cosmos - if only we would realise it. In this scenario the UFOs people see are not alien visitors monitoring us, on the contrary they are spreading the message that in this vast universe we are all one. Some ufologists take this one step further and argue that aliens are actually here among us cooperating with various governments. In fact, some proponents of this idea suggest that as we are all part of a huge interplanetary alliance and that as the Earth itself was populated by beings from distant solar systems in millennia past we, therefore, are in a sense the 'aliens'.

Certainly, there are those who hold the belief we are all part of groups such as the 'Planetary Liberation Organisation' which itself contains other 'departments' such as the 'United Stellar

Army Corps of Engineers' or the 'Royal Celestial Air Force'. Much of this has to be taken on trust as it is relayed by individuals who claim to be in touch with these galactic individuals, usually it has to be said without providing any solid evidence to back it up. What would be convincing? The obvious proof would be for one of the 'guardians of the Earth' to put in an appearance to a wider audience. But maybe these entities have their own reason for not doing this. I should say that I didn't deal with anyone in the Bonnybridge area who claimed to be in contact with or receive messages from these 'higher' - in a spiritual - sense individuals. I would add that in general alien contact in Scotland has been more of an unpleasant than pleasant experience. One individual claimed to have been persecuted by aliens masquerading as - or looking identical to - human beings. But this didn't happen around Bonnybridge and was an unusual case. In a general sense if UFOs are spreading a message that there are alien worlds 'out there' the activity around Bonnybridge certainly for many people achieved that aim.

Was the UFO presence in Bonnybridge evil?

We have to consider this crunch issue: are UFOs evil? Are they a manifestation of a demonic realm which is trying to distract or confuse us for some reason not obvious to us the inhabitants of Earth? Are we being naive and too trusting? Does the UFO phenomenon have evil intentions? By this I don't mean an alien invasion by entities who are to all intents and purposes alive and breathing beings, journeying from distant planets. But spirit beings the opposing force to the angelic world, entities who are under the control of satanic forces whose aim is not our physical selves but our spiritual aspect - our very souls. There are people who view UFOs in this light and see them as the vehicle of the anti-Christ.

At first glance it does appear far-fetched, it has to be admitted. And yet can we be so sure? In my book *'Alien Spirits?'* I described my experiences with the Edinburgh psychic Ray Tod. Through his mediumship I witnessed – among other things - a variety of alien beings. They differed in appearance.

They did not come across as threatening, but neither did they appear friendly - 'watchful' is the word that I would associate with them. At first glance they did seem alive - quite different from humanity, but even so breathing, intelligent beings. Or were they on the other hand the spirits of dead aliens? As they made no attempt to communicate, I could never be quite sure, but at the same time faces of human beings who were quite clearly from the past and so no longer alive would appear. This experience with Ray Tod could definitely be interpreted in different ways.

My own feeling is that it was a message that humanity is absolutely not alone, and we should take account of this in our daily lives. But at no time with Ray did I experience any attack on my inner self. So, whatever was going on it wasn't demonic forces at work. But I'm not ruling it out at as one aspect of the appearance of UFOs. Spiritual experiences do sometimes appear intertwined with the UFO phenomenon. In Glasgow a witness believed a spacecraft of some kind had landed on the roof of her house and then a being who she described as looking like the European depiction of Jesus Christ appeared in her house. What has this got to do with Bonnybridge? The main point is that a psychic medium on a level as Ray Tod can bring through alien entities so could prove a link between the supernatural realm and our own world. So are UFOs, in fact, a manifestation of this 'other world'? A connection of which we should be wary? On the other hand, as far as I'm aware there was no one in the Bonnybridge area who felt persistently threatened by UFOs. Either in the physical sense or as a phenomenon attempting to take over their souls.

Abduction is clearly an aspect of the UFO phenomenon which is disturbing and can be considered as evil. The medical examination of individuals against their will is an event we on Earth would consider a straightforward crime. If alien beings are taking people without their consent, then that can only be considered as an unfriendly act which doesn't say much for our cosmic 'friends'. The closest abduction cases were a few miles distant, for example the A70 Gary Wood case, but as I would argue near enough to fall into the wider remit of the Bonnybridge phenomenon. These incidents appeared to involve physical entities rather than being a supernatural threat. But again, the separation between the supernatural and the physical world sometimes falls down. John Adams in Glasgow experienced poltergeist activity alongside UFO incidents and came to the conclusion that there were both 'good' and 'bad' spirits - could both also be active in the appearance of UFOS? There are, therefore, examples of the supernatural and the UFO phenomenon inter-acting, but incidents of that seem less obvious In Bonnybridge. But it could be that we are misinterpreting events and ruling out the paranormal by focusing on UFOs as a physical reality. Perhaps we should look at events in Bonnybridge in a more nuanced light.

Was Bonnybridge a unique phenomenon?

It was certainly so in Scotland, and I would argue unique well beyond the borders of this country. There are other areas which at various times have earned the description 'UFO hot spot': Dumfriesshire in the 1970s, East Kilbride in the 1990s, and as far back as Aberdeen in the 1950s. But in terms of a continued period of UFO reports and media interest, Bonnybridge was by far the hottest of the hot spots in Scotland. And could we say the UK? There is at least one competitor for the title and that is the village of Warminster in the county of Wiltshire with a population of 18,000 - over twice that of Bonnybridge. For a period in the 1960s, like Bonnybridge in the 1990s, it swarmed with UFO sightings. Several books, numerous articles and even television and radio programmes have covered the Warminster phenomenon, and much was publicised about its involvement with UFOs at the time. The mystery even earned a title - 'The Warminster thing'. In 2015 a mural was unveiled to mark 50 years since the appearance of UFOs over the town.

However, we should bear in mind that though interest in Warminster ran from around the 1960s to mid-70s in other words almost a ten year period there was no internet, a limited number of TV channels, no Netflix, Prime or Facebook! Given these limitations the alleged UFO sighting nonetheless generated wide interest. But what is particularly interesting is that - as in Bonnybridge - the events were very much linked to one individual, a journalist called Arthur Shuttlewood. He appears to have been somewhat of a local personality and apparently served on the council for a time. It was Shuttlewood through his report of UFO sightings who spread the notion of a Warminster hot spot - he worked on the local paper the 'Warminster Journal' so was in a prime position to encourage interest in the phenomenon. It's not my intention to delve further into the Warminster UFO story except to make the point that an individual with a strong connection to a local area can act as a conduit which intentionally or unintentionally encourages media interest. On the world scene there are various areas which seem to be a focus for UFO sightings. The town of Pensacola in Florida was one such for a time. The community of Roswell in New Mexico is well known as a UFO spot. But this is not because of the number of reported sightings, but because of its association with the alleged crash of an alien spacecraft in the vicinity as far back as 1947. Bonnybridge can't claim the same dramatic event, but its fame lies in the sheer number of UFOs seen and in this sense, it may well be unique even on the global scene. However, it has to be admitted that it is difficult to make a comparison which in any event may be a pointless exercise.

Commonality of UFO Reports in Bonnybridge

In common with UFO reports from around the world the objects reported in Bonnybridge came in all shapes, sizes and colours. There is no 'typical' UFO I would suggest. Witnesses in the Bonnybridge area report circular UFOs, oval ones, box shapes, objects looking like cones and, even a Toblerone shape. Various coloured balls of light have been recorded - red, yellow, white and a combination of these. There is no defining Bonnybridge object which in my view adds to the mystery. Why so many different types of UFO appearing in the area? But this is no different from UFOs reported from across the world. Many types have been witnessed and recorded. Once more it's a mystery piled on another mystery. Can an analysis shed any light on events in Bonnybridge to allow us to get to the heart of the mystery?

I have attempted to do just that. Following the excitement that Bonnybridge generated I made an investigation of the reports that I had compiled from across Scotland to ascertain how the Bonnybridge phenomenon fitted into the overall UFO situation in Scotland. Of course, I must make clear that I have no idea as what proportion of UFO sightings did not come to my attention. And this, of course, refers to reports collected from every area in Scotland including Bonnybridge. However, I do believe that my research gives an indication of general trends and where Bonnybridge fits into the overall picture. I'm more than happy to receive different opinions, or observations, from anyone who has conducted an investigation into UFOs in Scotland in terms of numbers, areas of activity, types of reports, times/periods of sightings, and objects reported.

To dig into this a bit further I would have to agree that statistics are a bit of a minefield. I am not an expert on the subject, but I believe that this shouldn't deter us from considering the data though again it has to be agreed that numbers can be interpreted in various ways. I've no axe to grind, in particular, on the Bonnybridge phenomenon, but I had and still have an interest in assessing how Bonnybridge stands and stood in relation to the UFO scene in general. Does it deserve the attention it has received? Do events in Bonnybridge display a different pattern from the UFO scene elsewhere?

So how did I go about gathering data on this particular topic? Thanks, has to go to dedicated researcher Ken Higgins who was the first investigator to compile a database of UFO sightings. I should mention that researcher John Morrison also brought together an extensive list of UFO incidents. More recently Steve Hammond in the 'Scottish UFO Casebook', has listed a comprehensive number of UFO reports. In the late 1990s I put together an amalgamation of UFO reports based on Ken Higgins's database and my own extensive collection of sightings. I'll come back to the cases listed in Steve Hammond's book once I have considered my earlier database. It goes without saying that not every case listed was one I personally investigated. Many were but a significant number of reports were of events which stretched back to the 1950s and could only be looked at via the newspapers and magazines of the time. This, I would agree, is not ideal, but as we are looking at the overall reports of incidents rather than attempting to prove the validity of a particular UFO sighting, I believe it is acceptable to include these reports in a database. To take an example, you might not have interviewed Bob Taylor (I did) of the well-known 1979 Livingston UFO event but given the newspaper coverage it would be perfectly reasonable to consider it for inclusion as a *'reported'* UFO incident and so add it to a list of UFO encounters. Of course, not all UFO cases reported in the media are as well covered as the Taylor event, but not all cases were as dramatic, and many consisted simply of odd lights seen in the sky and similar incidents.

My own database consists of material gained from a variety of sources. Incidents I personally investigated, reports sent in by individuals who did not wish to be involved in any follow-up (unfortunately!) and historical cases compiled from magazines and newspapers or sent to me by individuals years after the event they witnessed and so difficult to analyse. There were also contemporary cases which for various reasons could not be followed up because, for example, other groups or individuals were dealing with them. After eliminating several cases simply because of lack of detail I ended up with 395 cases dating from 1947 to 1998 at which point the Bonnybridge phenomenon though not ended had certainly declined. So, what can we state from these 395 cases? I've no doubt observers will comment, 'only 395 cases'? A claim has been made that there were 8,000 cases alone in Bonnybridge! I will come back to this, but first of all I would like to detail findings from the 395 cases considered.

It will come as no surprise to have confirmed that the majority of sightings are by a single individual. Solo sightings make up 59% of the cases included in the survey. Cases involving two witnesses comprise 20%, three witnesses 4% and for four witnesses we are down to 2% of the total. In 6% of the cases there were more than a single witness, but the exact number is unknown. And in 9% we simply have a report without the number of witnesses indicated. Although a single witness made up the majority of cases in 32% of reports there was more than one witness. But does that make a report more believable or significant? Probably not as, for example, in the 1979 Livingstone case Bob Taylor was the only witness to the encounter, but it remains one of the most significant Scottish cases. There is general agreement that something out of the ordinary happened to Taylor though sharp differences of view as to exactly what. By comparison the A70 alleged abduction event involved two witnesses - Gary Wood and Colin Wright - but the involvement of regression hypnosis caused significant controversy and doubt about the validity of their narrative even though there is ample evidence that they experienced an 'otherwordly' event. So, the number of witnesses doesn't necessarily have a bearing on what is believed or not believed. And single witness encounters - for example the Pat Macleod case in Edinburgh as mentioned previously - stand up well against multi-witness incidents. I also looked at events in Bonnybridge against the overall geographic distribution of UFO reports:

Table 1 below gives the geographical distribution of the 395 reports used by percentage:

Edinburgh and Lothian 32%
West Lothian 21%
Aberdeen/ North of Scotland 8%
Glasgow 9%
East Lothian 5%
Stirling/ Clackmannanshire 5%
Ayr/West coast 4%
Falkirk/Bonnybridge 4%
Fife 3%
Borders 2%
Dumfriesshire 2%
Outer Glasgow conurbation 2%
Perth/Blairgowrie 2%
Dundee 1%

I understand that after scrutinising the above figures it might be said that in spite of the claims about Bonnybridge the village in fact accounts for only 4% of the sightings so why the fuss over it as a UFO phenomenon. However, this would be a mistake. In fact, given the extensive time period of the reports - over 50 years - and the small size of the Bonnybridge area and population compared for example with Edinburgh, Glasgow or Dumfriesshire 4% is an astonishingly high percentage. Furthermore, if you include areas in close proximity as West Lothian which I have argued should be, for example, the total comes to an astonishing 25% of the survey!

Of course, simply because there are a significant number of reports it doesn't necessarily prove the significance of one area compared with another. Referring again to the Bob Taylor case (1979) this would mark West Lothian as a significant UFO spot on its own and one could add to that the A70 case. But in my view the significant aspect to Bonnybridge when compared to other 'hotspots' is the volume of video evidence produced. We have the Margaret Ross videos, Barry McDonald's, and the Craig family collection among others. This, of course, reflects the arrival of affordable camcorders, but does provide visual evidence that can be analysed to add to the reports of eyewitnesses.

The modern era of UFO reports is dated to 1947 with the Kenneth Arnold 'flying saucer' sighting in the USA. The earliest Scottish sighting also dates from 1947 in Edinburgh though details were only confirmed in the 1990s. However, taking the fifty year period from 1947 to 1997 UFOs have been regularly reported in Scotland with a peak around the Livingston UFO incident in 1979. After that sightings came in at a regular pace until 1986 at which point a significant rise began. After this (1987 being an exception for some reason) UFO reports remained well above previous levels into the late 1990s. In my book 'UFO Scotland' (1998) I designated the 1990s 'the decade of the UFO' and nothing since then has changed my mind. In fact, some ufologists have asked 'where have all the UFOs gone?'. They are still there of course with reports continuing to come in, but perhaps there have been no cases as significant as those from earlier decades. But who knows what might turn up.

During the 1990s however one curiosity was that the largest group of UFO reports came not during 1991/94 when Bonnybridge was according to media interest at its 'hottest', but during 1995/96 when it seemed on the surface that Bonnybridge though still very active was maybe past its peak. However, that period produced the Margaret Ross and Barry McDonald videos so it may be more accurate to speak of peaks and troughs rather than a straight upwards trajectory and a subsequent straight decline. Below is a table indicating the proportion of reports by percentage in the 1990s:

Table 2: Scotland's UFO reports in the 1990s by year and percentage:

1990 (5%)
1991 (14%)
1992 (24%)
1993 (1%)
1994 (5%)
1995 (19%)
1996 (26%)
1997 (6%)
Total: 100%

Table 3 below gives the percentage of all UFO sightings in Scotland by decade:

Table 3: Reports by decade
1990s   75%
1980s   13%
1970s   7%
1960s   2%
1950s   2%
1940s   1%

The dominating position of the 1990s is unmistakably clear and I've no doubt that this was due to the Bonnybridge phenomenon. Of course, other factors need to be taken into account. Increasing media interest, as I have previously discussed, plus the arrival from the 1970s onwards of organisations, and individuals, dedicated to investigating UFO reports and to whom UFO sightings could be reported. However, whichever way you look at it the 1990s remains the

UFO decade which appears to dwarf any other in terms of UFO incidents.

But these figures were based on my own calculations as at that time there was no other collection of Scottish UFO reports to compare the figures with. That changed when in 2022 Steve Hammond published 'The Scottish UFO Casebook'. Mr. Hammond's book was a compendium of Scottish UFO sightings gathered from various sources. The individual reports comprised all types of encounters - lights in the sky to events like the A70 abduction case though not every case known to me was included, for example the Andrew Cherry case of 1947, but it is nonetheless an impressive achievement. I've excluded cases Hammond reported pre 1950 in compiling a total and taken my analysis up to 1997 to correspond roughly to the period I covered for comparison.

Steve Hammond lists 718 cases for this period significantly more than the database I drew on for my calculations. He lists 50 from the 1950s, 76 from the 1960s, 190 from the 1970s, 168 from the 1980s and 177 for the 1990s. So, we have a discrepancy in that according to Hammond's evidence the 1970s come out top in terms of UFO reports. And the 1980s is not far behind with 168. It's curious and demonstrates the difficulty in compiling meaningful data on the UFO topic when a sighting may be reported in a less widely read newspaper and pass UFO investigators by. However, I come back to the fact that the quality of the report is a crucial factor in determining where the 'hotspots' occur, and a list can't really quantify that aspect, and I would say it's not meant to. A list is simply a valuable starting point and no more.

Of the reports listed by Hammond around sixteen (I write around because in a number of cases the exact location isn't easy to determine) are linked to Bonnybridge. Again, that appears to contradict the focus on the village as a Scottish, let alone global, leading hotspot but nonetheless is a significant number of sightings. However, since I compiled my initial data as appeared in 'UFO Scotland' (1998) another significant book appeared. This was Malcolm Robinson's 'UFO Case Files of Scotland' published in 2009. In his book Robinson devotes 99 pages out of a total of 365 to the Bonnybridge phenomenon roughly one third of the book. As a key investigator and surveyor of the Bonnybridge scene Robinson cites (in varied detail) significantly more cases linked to the village than included in 'The Scottish UFO Casebook'. In fact, the 'UFO Case Files of Scotland' provides us with a total of 37 cases. This is a significantly higher number than indicated in Hammond's book and I believe is nearer the true total of cases of significance reported. However, it goes without saying that as many sightings as came to the notice of investigators may have not been reported and so not logged. It's to be doubted in all honesty that we will ever learn the true number of incidents that occurred. Robinson, I know, did not include every case he was aware of in the Bonnybridge hotspot.

But note again that even if Robinson's figure is doubled or trebled or even quadrupled, we are nowhere near the 8,000 sightings stated by ex-MOD employee Nick Pope. I should add that in 'UFO Scotland' published by B&W I covered only eight cases directly linked to the Bonnybridge phenomenon. However, by way of explanation, the book covered the whole period from 1947 to 1998 and UFO reports from every part of Scotland so I could only focus on what at the time appeared to be key Scottish cases. Incidentally, I agree with Malcolm Robinson's statement in 'UFO Case Files' that the number of UFO cases in the Bonnybridge area dropped after 1997. Overall, a key question by which to compare the volume of UFO reports in Bonnybridge with other locations is how many UFO reports should we expect per head of the population? Unfortunately, there doesn't seem to be an obvious answer, not one at least which we could arrive at without a vast research effort and, one could guess, might not in any case shed any further light on the phenomenon. Some areas appear to report more UFO sightings per head - Bonnybridge is the obvious one - but is that coincidence or...what? I think that all we can usefully note at the moment is that there just isn't enough data to quantify. All we can say unscientifically is that some areas - the famous 'hotspots' - seem to attract more UFO reports than others and for the moment leave it at that.

Is it no more than a mirage?

So, is the Bonnybridge phenomenon a mirage? On what is its fame based? Is it all no more than a blast of publicity arising from a limited number of cases? Are writers on the village relying on the same data? I decided to analyse the four main books published to date that have covered events in Bonnybridge. These are Steven Hammond's 'Scottish UFO Casebook', Malcolm Robinson's 'UFO case files of Scotland', Peter McCue's 'Zones of Strangeness' and Ron Halliday's 'UFO Scotland.' In doing this analysis I was fascinated to see what would emerge by surveying the data. In the appendix I have listed the cases covered in each of the aforementioned books, but for this comparison I have used those discussed in Robinson's book as he provides the most comprehensive list.

Following on from this compilation of cases recorded in each book I did the following comparison. I have listed the name and date of each incident as the identifier and have based this analysis on the reports covered by Robinson's book as he gives the most comprehensive list of cases linked to Bonnybridge with additions from the other books reviewed.

[key: Hal=Halliday; Hamm=Hammond: Mc=McCue: Rob=Robinson]

Case
Wendy Fobes: 1968: Rob/Mc
Wendy Forbes: 1970:Rob/Mc
Wendy Forbes: 1974:Rob/Mc
Linda Taylor: 1980:Rob/Mc
Alison Clarke: 1982:Rob/Mc
Elsie Beveridge:1982:Rob
James Anderson:1982: Rob./Mc/Hal
Janet Middleton:1983:Rob/Mc
Robert Muir: 1989: Rob/Mc
Phil Trevis: 1991: Rob/Mc
Jim Walker: 1991: Rob/Mc
Sloggett family:1992: Rob./Hamm/Mc/Hal
April Welsh: 1992 : Rob/Mc

Steven Wilson: 1992: Rob/Mc
Patrick Forsyth: 1992: Rob/Hamm/Mc

James Thompson:1992:Rob/Mc
Marion Napier: 1992:Rob/Mc
Mary Young: 1993:Rob/Mc
Ray Procek: 1993:Rob/Hamm/ Mc/Hal
(and Cathy Procek)
Colin Robertson: 1993: Rob
Neil Malcolm: 1994:Rob
Mary Higgins: 1994:Rob
William Bestall: 1994:Rob
May Macleod: 1994:Rob
John Morrison: 1994:Rob
Jane Shaw: 1994:Rob
Beatrice Campbell et al:1994: Rob/Hal
Mark Wilson: 1994:Rob
Craig Black: 1994:Rob
David Rowston: 1995:Rob/Mc
Mary Crozier: 1995: Rob
Paula Jack: 1995:Rob
Barbara Stocks: 1995:Rob
Mark Wilson: 1995:Rob
Mary Roy: 1995:Rob
Cameron Murphy:1995:Rob
'A couple': 1995:Rob
Craig Malcolm: 1995:Rob/Hal
Vera Prosser: 1995:Rob/Mc
James Westfield: 1995: Rob
Amanda: 1995: Rob/Mc
Margaret Ross: 1996: Rob/Hal
Barry McDonald: 1996: Rob/Mc/Hal
Andrew McLeish:1996: Rob/Mc
Terry Harrington: N.D.:Rob
Craig Morrison: N.D.:Rob

Conclusion:

To summarise from the above analysis: in the case of Steven Hammond's 'Scottish UFO Casebook' there are incidents listed which are quite clearly covered in Robinson's 'Scottish Case Files'. Of the others from the dates and descriptions it seems clear that of the several other cases that can be linked to Bonnybridge these are covered in Robinson's book. This suggests that there is nothing in Hammond's book which adds to the core incidents described by Robinson.

Of the 24 cases considered by McCue in 'Zones of Strangeness' all but one are covered by Robinson. In the case of Halliday's 'UFO Scotland' of the eleven incidents covered nine were written about in Robinson's book and two were absent. My book of course predated the others by several years having been published in 1998.

Overall, it is clear that Robinson's is the most extensive list and outside the cases he covered there is little additional material - at least material that has been published. So, if these cases are the core of the Bonnybridge phenomenon it again begs the question of why the village reached such giddy heights of global fame. I have attempted some suggestions as to how it came about. It undoubtedly was a phenomenon - maybe a phenomenon of its time which is unlikely to be repeated anywhere in Scotland if not the world.

APPENDIX

The UFO cases dealt with by the following authors:
The 'Scottish UFO Casebook' (Hammond)
The UFO cases Hammond mentions are as follows (in chronological order):
(Unidentified witness) 6th December 1990: Falkirk
Sloggett Family March 1992: Bonnybridge
Patrick Forsyth 27th October 1992: Denny
(Unidentified witness) 3rd November 1992: Bonnybridge
Ray and Cathy Proceck 16th January 1993: Bonnybridge
(Unidentified witness) October 1994: Falkirk
(Unidentified witness) December 1994: Grangemouth
(Unidentified witness) 18th March 1995: Falkirk
(Unidentified witness) 7th January 1996 Grangemouth
(Unidentified witness) 2nd February 1998: Grangemouth
(Unidentified witness) 'End of 1998': Stirling
Brian McPhee 6th January 1999: Stirling

Note that I added the last two entries as sightings in the Stirling district can by a stretch be included in the general Bonnybridge area. Furthermore, Hammond cites other UFO incidents from the West Lothian area which could potentially be included.

'Scottish UFO Case Files' (Robinson)

The cases covered by Robinson are as follows in chronological order:
Wendy Forbes 1968: Polmont
Wendy Forbes 1974: Laurieston
Wendy Forbes 'late 1970s': Bathgate
Linda Taylor October 1980: Denny
Mrs Alison Clarke and Mr John Clarke 26th April 1982: Shieldhill
Mrs Elsie Beveridge 1982: Denny
James Anderson 1982: Denny
Mrs Janet Middleton September 1983: Lauriston
Robert Muir 1989: Shieldhill
Phil Trevis November 12th, 1991: Polmont Reservoir (Fife)

Jim Walker January 1992: Dennyloanhead/Denny
Sloggett family March 1992: Hallglen/Bonnybridge
April Welsh May 1992: Carronshore/Larbert
Steven Wilson and David Gillespie 20 September 1992: Whitecross/Maddiston
Patrick Forsyth 27th September 1992: Dunipace/Denny
James Thompson 11 November 1992: Greenhill, Bonnybridge
Miss Marion Napier and William Napier 15th November 1992: Standburn (Falkirk)
Mary Young January 1993: Bannockburn (Stirling)
Ray and Cathy Procek: 15th January 1993: Castlecary Viaduct (A80)
Colin Robertson 12th December 1993: Falkirk
Neil Malcolm 19th January 1994: Larbert/Falkirk
Mary Higgins 8th August 1994: Westquarter (Falkirk)
William and Mary Bestall 8th August 1994: Falkirk?
Mrs May Macleod August 1994: Falkirk
John Morrison 14th September 1994: Grangemouth
Jane Shaw September 1994: Falkirk
Beatrice Campbell et al 28th October 1994: Carronshore
Mark Wilson 26th December 1994: Grangemouth
Craig Black and Karen Clark 1st January 1995: Grangemouth
David Rowston 29th January 1995: Castlecary Railway Viaduct (M9)
Mary Crozier January 1995: Bainsford
Paula Jack 24th January 1995: Falkirk
Barbara Stocks February 1st, 1995: Bonnybridge: [Malcolm mentions this as from the magazine 'Eva' but it first appeared in the 'Falkirk Herald']
Mark Wilson 5th February 1995: Grangemouth
Mary Roy 11th March 1995: Falkirk?
Cameron Murphy 18th March 1995: Denny
'A couple' end of March 1995
Craig Malcolm 14th June 1995: Larbert/Stenhousemuir?
Vera Prosser October 1995: Falkirk
James Westfield 3rd February 1995: Grangemouth
Amanda and family 1995: Grangemouth
Margaret Ross October 1996: Larbert/Stenhousemuir
Barry McDonald 15th October 1996: Hallglen/Falkirk

Andrew McLeish 27th November 1996: Muiravonside.
Mrs Terry Harrington (no date): Grangemouth
Craig Morrison (no date): Larbert

'Zones of Strangeness' (McCue)

The following are the cases considered by McCue in chronological order:
Wendy Forbes 1968: Polmont
Wendy Forbes 'summer 1974': Laurieston
Linda Taylor October 1980: Denny
Alison Clarke 26th April 1982: Shieldhill (Falkirk)
James Anderson Winter 1982: Denny
Janet Middleton September 1983: Laurieston
Robert Muir 1989: Shieldhill
Philip Trevis 12th November 1991: witness located at Polmont reservoir
Jim Walker January 1992: Denny/Dennyloanhead
Sloggett family: March 1992: Hallglen/Bonnybridge
April Welsh May 1992: Kincardine/Carronshore
Steven Wilson 20th September 1992: Whitecross/Maddiston
Patrick Forsyth 27th September 1992: Dunipace/Denny
James Thompson 11th November 1992: Greenhill (Bonnybridge)
William Napier 15th November 1992: Standburn (Falkirk)
Ray and Cathy Procek 15th January 1993: Castlecary (A80) near Bonnybridge
Mary Young January 1993: Bannockburn (Stirling)
Craig Black 1st January 1995: Dennyloanhead
David Rowston 29th January 1995: Castlecary
Vera Prosser October 1995: Bonnybridge
Amanda/Sarah 1995: Grangemouth
Barry McDonald 15th October 1996: Hallglen/Falkirk
Andrew McLeish 27th November 1996: Muiravonside country park

'UFO Scotland' (Halliday)

Catherine Penman early 1990s: Hallglen
James Walker January 1992: no location given
Sloggett family March 1992: Bonnybridge
Mr Anderson November 1992: no location given
Roy and Cathy Proceck 1993: driving to Cumbernauld
Beatrice Campbell (and others) October 1994: Grangemouth
Diane Keating October 1994: Grangemouth
Margaret Ross May1996: Stenhousemuir
Barry McDonald October1996: Camelon (Falkirk)
'University Lecturer' 28th December 1996: M80 (near Larbert/Stenhousemuir)
Craig Malcolm 21st October 1997

Bibliography

The Bonnybridge phenomenon was widely covered in the media at the time. The material I have listed can only be selective and I have not included television and radio sources which were extensive, but more difficult to pin down and harder to consult.

Books

Ron Halliday, 'UFOs: the Scottish Dimension' (1997)
Ron Halliday, 'McX: Scotland's X-Files' (1997)
Ron Halliday, 'UFO Scotland' (1998)
Ron Halliday, 'Alien Spirits?' (2022)
Steve Hammond, 'The Scottish UFO Casebook' (2022)
Philip Mantle, 'UFO Landings UK' (2022)
Peter McCue, 'Zones of Strangeness' (2012)
Jenny Randles, 'The Paranormal Year' (1993)
Jenny Randles, 'Strange But True' (1995)
Malcolm Robinson, 'UFO Case Files of Scotland' Volume 1 (2009)
Malcolm Robinson, 'UFO Case Files of Scotland' Volume 2 (2017)
Malcolm Robinson, 'The Dechmont Woods UFO Incident'

(2019)
Malcolm Robinson, 'The A70 UFO Incident' (2022)

Magazines
'Enigmas' (publication of the 'Strange Phenomenon Investigations' group)
'Northern UFO News'
'Phenomenal News' (publication of the 'Scottish Earth Mysteries Research' group)

Newspapers
'Daily Record'
'Dundee Courier'
'Falkirk Herald'
'Grangemouth Advertiser'
'Guardian'
'Scottish Sun'
'Stirling Observer'
'Sunday Post'
'Sunday Times'
'The Herald'

Miscellaneous
Parliamentary Debates (Hansard): House of Lords (1978/1979)

END

www.ingramcontent.com/pod-product-compliance
Lightning Source LLC
Chambersburg PA
CBHW070456120526
44590CB00013B/666